Walter Benjamin

For Thomas and Roisín

Walter Benjamin

Critical Constellations

Graeme Gilloch

Polity

First published in 2002 by Polity Press in association with Blackwell Publishers Ltd

Editorial office:
Polity Press
65 Bridge Street
Cambridge CB2 1UR, UK

Marketing and production:
Blackwell Publishers Ltd
108 Cowley Road
Oxford OX4 1JF, UK

Published in the USA by
Blackwell Publishers Inc.
350 Main Street
Malden, MA 02148, USA

Library of Congress Cataloging-in-Publication Data
Gilloch, Graeme.
    Walter Benjamin—critical constellations / Graeme Gilloch.
       p.   cm. — (Key contemporary thinkers)
    Includes bibliographical references and index.
    ISBN 0-7456-1007-2 (HB)—ISBN 0-7456-1008-0
    1. Benjamin, Walter, 1892–1940—Philosophy.   I. Title.   II. Key
contemporary thinkers (Cambridge, England)
PT2603.E455 Z6743   2001
838'.91209—dc21

                                        2001002110

Typeset in $10\frac{1}{2}$ on 12 pt Palatino
by Best-set Typesetter Ltd., Hong Kong

Printed in Great Britain by TJ International, Padstow, Cornwall
This book is printed on acid-free paper.

Key Contemporary Thinkers

Published

Jeremy Ahearne, *Michel de Certeau: Interpretation and its Other*
Peter Burke, *The French Historical Revolution: The* Annales *School 1929–1989*
M. J. Cain, *Fodor: Language, Mind and Philosophy*
Michael Caesar, *Umberto Eco: Philosophy, Semiotics and the Work of Fiction*
Colin Davis, *Levinas: An Introduction*
Simon Evnine, *Donald Davidson*
Edward Fullbrook and Kate Fullbrook, *Simone de Beauvoir: A Critical Introduction*
Andrew Gamble, *Hayek: The Iron Cage of Liberty*
Graeme Gilloch, *Walter Benjamin: Critical Constellations*
Karen Green, *Dummett: Philosophy of Language*
Espen Hammer, *Stanley Cavell: Skepticism, Subjectivity, and the Ordinary*
Phillip Hansen, *Hannah Arendt: Politics, History and Citizenship*
Sean Homer, *Fredric Jameson: Marxism, Hermeneutics, Postmodernism*
Christopher Hookway, *Quine: Language, Experience and Reality*
Christina Howells, *Derrida: Deconstruction from Phenomenology to Ethics*
Fred Inglis, *Clifford Geertz: Culture, Custom and Ethics*
Simon Jarvis, *Adorno: A Critical Introduction*
Douglas Kellner, *Jean Baudrillard: From Marxism to Post-Modernism and Beyond*
Valerie Kennedy, *Edward Said: A Critical Introduction*
Chandran Kukathas and Philip Pettit, *Rawls: A Theory of Justice and its Critics*
James McGilvray, *Chomsky: Language, Mind, and Politics*
Lois McNay, *Foucault: A Critical Introduction*
Philip Manning, *Erving Goffman and Modern Sociology*
Michael Moriarty, *Roland Barthes*
Harold W. Noonan, *Frege: A Critical Introduction*
William Outhwaite, *Habermas: A Critical Introduction*
John Preston, *Feyerabend: Philosophy, Science and Society*
Susan Sellers, *Hélène Cixous: Authorship, Autobiography and Love*
David Silverman, *Harvey Sacks: Social Science and Conversation Analysis*

Dennis Smith, *Zygmunt Bauman: Prophet of Postmodernity*
Nicholas H. Smith, *Charles Taylor: Meaning, Morals and Modernity*
Geoffrey Stokes, *Popper: Philosophy, Politics and Scientific Method*
Georgia Warnke, *Gadamer: Hermeneutics, Tradition and Reason*
James Williams, *Lyotard: Towards a Postmodern Philosophy*
Jonathan Wolff, *Robert Nozick: Property, Justice and the Minimal State*

Forthcoming

Maria Baghramian, *Hilary Putnam*
Sara Beardsworth, *Kristeva*
James Carey, *Innis and McLuhan*
Rosemary Cowan, *Cornell West: The Politics of Redemption*
George Crowder, *Isaiah Berlin: Liberty, Pluralism and Liberalism*
Thomas D'Andrea, *Alasdair MacIntyre*
Eric Dunning, *Norbert Elias*
Jocelyn Dunphy, *Paul Ricoeur*
Matthew Elton, *Daniel Dennett*
Nigel Gibson, *Frantz Fanon*
Keith Hart, *C.L.R. James*
Sarah Kay, *Žižek: A Critical Introduction*
Paul Kelly, *Ronald Dworkin*
Carl Levy, *Antonio Gramsci*
Moya Lloyd, *Judith Butler*
Dermot Moran, *Edmund Husserl*
Kari Palonen, *Quentin Skinner*
Steve Redhead, *Paul Virilio: Theorist for an Accelerated Culture*
Chris Rojek, *Stuart Hall and Cultural Studies*
Wes Sharrock and Rupert Read, *Kuhn*
Nicholas Walker, *Heidegger*

Contents

Acknowledgements

I am grateful to many people for their help, guidance and support during the writing of this book. I would especially like to thank John Thompson, who suggested the project initially, and Tim Dant, David Frisby and Neil Leach for their support throughout. My work has benefited greatly from conversations with many people, to whom I would like to extend my thanks: Paul Aylward, Jon Fletcher, Hans-Joachim Hahn, Jaeho Kang, Esther Leslie, Brian Longhurst, Scott McCracken, Tim May, Ulrich Oevermann, Deborah Parsons, Thomas Reghely, Barry Sandiwell, Greg Smith, Gordon Tait, Paul Taylor, Charles Turner, and Cas Wouters. I would also like to thank Troels Degn Johanssen, Claus Krogholm Kristiansen, Erik Steinskøg and the Aesthetic Theory seminar of the Nordic Summer University for their ideas and encouragement.

The section on photography in chapter 6 draws upon a paper jointly written with Tim Dant and presented at the International Walter Benjamin Association conference in Amsterdam in July 1997. I am grateful to Tim for permission to develop these ideas here.

Parts of the present Introduction and Conclusion appear in an earlier version in *Profiles in Contemporary Social Theory*, edited by Bryan Turner and Anthony Elliott (Sage Publications, London, 2001).

I am very grateful to the Leverhulme Trust, whose generous funding supported the initial work on this book.

I would also like to thank the sociology secretarial staff at the University of Salford (Linda Jones and Beryl Pluples) and the staff at Polity for their practical help and support. Special thanks are due to Jean van Altena for her superb editorial work and to Gill Motley for her patience and help throughout.

Most of all, I wish to thank Bernadette Boyle for all her patience, understanding and encouragement, and Thomas and Roisín, who provided the most delightful distractions possible and to whom this book is dedicated.

The author and publishers would like to thank the following for permission to use copyrighted material:

Harvard University Press and Suhrkamp Verlag for permission to quote from *Walter Benjamin: Selected Writings, Volume I 1913–1926*, edited by Marcus Bullock and Michael W. Jennings, copyright 1996 by the President and Fellows of Harvard College; and *Volume II 1927–1934*, translated by Rodney Livingstone, edited by Michael W. Jennings, Howard Eiland and Gary Smith, copyright 1999 by the President and Fellows of Harvard College; and *The Arcades Project* translated by Howard Eiland and Kevin McLaughlin, copyright 1999 by the President and Fellows of Harvard College, Cambridge Mass.: The Belknap Press of Harvard University Press.

Harvard University Press and Suhrkamp Verlag for permission to quote from *Gesammelte Schriften*, edited by Rolf Tiedemann and Hermann Schweppenhäuser, Frankfurt am Main, 1974/1991.

HarperCollins Publishers for permission to quote from *Illuminations* by Walter Benjamin.

The University of Chicago Press for permission to quote from *The Correspondence of Walter Benjamin*, edited Gershom Scholem and Theodor W. Adorno, translated by Manfred Jacobson and Evelyn Jacobson, Chicago and London, 1994.

Verso for permission to quote from *One Way Streets and Other Writings* translated by Edmund Jephcott and Kingsley Shorter, London 1985; *The Origin of German Drama* translated by John Osbourne, London 1985; *Understanding Brecht* translated by Anna Bostock, London 1983; and *Charles Baudelaire: A Lyric Poet in the Era of High Capitalism*, translated by Harry Zohn, London 1983.

Every effort has been made to trace the copyright holders, but if any have been inadvertently overlooked, the publishers will be pleased to make the necessary arrangements at the first opportunity.

Abbreviations

Where possible, existing English translations have been used. Otherwise, translations are my own. References to the 'Arcades Project' are given by Convolute number and page.

GS *Gesammelte Schriften*, vols I–VII, eds. Rolf Tiedemann and Hermann Schweppenhäuser, with the collaboration of Theodor Adorno and Gershom Scholem. Frankfurt am Main: Suhrkamp Verlag, 1974. Taschenbuch Ausgabe, 1991.

SW1/SW2 *Selected Writings*, vols 1 and 2, ed. Marcus Bullock, Michael Jennings et al. Cambridge, MA: Harvard University Press, 1996, 1999.

ABC *Theodor W. Adorno – Walter Benjamin: The Complete Correspondence 1928–1940*. Cambridge: Polity, 1999.

AP *Aesthetics and Politics: Debates between Bloch, Lukács, Brecht, Benjamin, Adorno*, trans. and ed. Ronald Taylor, 'Afterword' by Fredric Jameson. London: Verso, 1980.

ARC *The Arcades Project*, trans. Howard Eiland and Kevin McLaughlin. Cambridge, MA: Belknap Press of Harvard University Press, 1999.

CB *Charles Baudelaire: A Lyric Poet in the Era of High Capitalism*, trans. Harry Zohn. London: Verso, 1983.

COR *The Correspondence of Walter Benjamin*, ed. and annotated by Gershom Scholem and Theodor Adorno, trans. Manfred Jacobson and Evelyn Jacobson, 'Fore-

	word' by Gershom Scholem. Chicago and London: University of Chicago Press, 1994.
CP	'Central Park', trans. Lloyd Spencer, *New German Critique*, 34 (Winter 1985), pp. 28–58.
GER	*The Correspondence of Walter Benjamin and Gershom Scholem 1932–1940*, ed. Gershom Scholem, trans. Gary Smith and Andre Lefevre, 'Introduction' by Anson Rabinbach. Cambridge, MA: Harvard University Press, 1992.
ILL	*Illuminations*, ed. and with an 'Introduction' by Hannah Arendt, trans. Harry Zohn. London: Fontana, 1973.
MD	*Moscow Diary*, ed. Gary Smith, trans. Richard Sieburth, Preface by Gershom Scholem. Cambridge, MA: Harvard University Press, 1986.
OGTD	*The Origin of German Tragic Drama*, trans. John Osbourne, 'Introduction' by George Steiner. London: Verso, 1985.
OWS	*One-Way Street and Other Writings*, trans. Edmund Jephcott and Kingsley Shorter, 'Introduction' by Susan Sontag. London: Verso, 1985.
UB	*Understanding Brecht*, trans. Anna Bostock, 'Introduction' by Stanley Mitchell. London: Verso, 1983.

Introduction: Benjamin as a Key Contemporary Thinker

Origins

Writing from Paris to his closest friend, the Judaic scholar Gershom Scholem, on 20 January 1930, the German-Jewish philosopher, literary and cultural theorist Walter Benjamin (1892–1940) makes his intellectual ambition plain:

> The goal I had set for myself has not yet been totally realized, but I am finally getting close. The goal is that I be considered the foremost critic of German literature. The problem is that literary criticism is no longer considered a serious genre in Germany and has not been for more than fifty years. If you want to carve out a reputation in the area of criticism, this ultimately means that you must recreate criticism as a genre. (*COR*, p. 359)

This is a particularly ironic and peculiarly appropriate statement. It is ironic because of Benjamin's own precarious, marginal situation at the time of writing: the enforced withdrawal of his *Habilitationsschrift*[1] a few years earlier had ended any hope of an academic career, and he was now limited to eking out an indigent living as a freelance writer, reviewer and translator, and even as the author and narrator of radio broadcasts for children. Indeed, Benjamin was to return to Paris only a couple of years later in the even more impoverished guise of a refugee fleeing Nazi tyranny. If Benjamin was to become the 'foremost critic of German literature', it was to be an expertise in exile.

It is an ironic statement, moreover, because Benjamin's attempt to 'recreate criticism as a genre' led him not only far beyond the confines of literary criticism as such, but also to its dissolution as a distinct sphere of endeavour. For Benjamin, traditional bourgeois aesthetic categories and practices were to be imploded, and new modes of representation pioneered, modes inspired by and appropriate to the possibilities created by new forms of media amid the transformed social, political and cultural patterns of the inter-war period. Film, photography, magazines, newspapers, advertising, radio – the importance of these for literature and drama was to be captured not by the conventional literary critic, but by another figure: the experimental, polytechnical aesthetic 'engineer'. It is in this role that Benjamin undertakes a fragmentary but politically charged critique of modern culture, metropolitan experience, technological innovation and historical change. To 'recreate criticism as a genre' means to transform it into a panoramic critique of modernity itself.

It is ironic first and foremost, however, because, after a substantial period of neglect, Benjamin *is* now widely recognized as the most important German literary theorist of his generation and, indeed, as one of the most original and insightful thinkers of the twentieth century. Benjamin has achieved his lofty ambition and more, but only fifty years after his death.

The statement is appropriate because, in Benjamin's view, it was only the critical outcast who could, freed from the moribund mediocrity of bourgeois (pseudo-)scholarship, develop innovative forms of literary, cultural and social critique. His own radically politicized understanding of art and aesthetics emerges not from the confines of the academy, but in the form of practices and strategies necessitated by the economic exigencies which beset the intellectual as outsider and 'trailblazer'.

It is appropriate, above all, because central to Benjamin's work is the insight that texts, objects and images have a particular existence, or 'life', of their own which goes beyond, and cannot be reduced to, the intentions and purposes of those who created them. This is not an act of fetishization, the ascription of human capacities and qualities to inanimate things. Rather, it is the contention that the meaning and significance of a text are not determined by the author at the moment of writing, but are contested and conceptualized anew as it enters subsequent contexts, as it is subject to reading and criticism through time. This continuing existence of the text as an object open to reconfiguration and re-evaluation is termed its 'after-history' (*Nachgeschichte*) or 'afterlife' (*Nachleben*). This notion of the afterlife of an object as a period of critical appreciation and political appropriation aptly anticipates the posthumous fate of Benjamin's own texts, for, as recent commentators have noted,[2] these formerly overlooked, now revered writings are the clearest examples imaginable of the critical contingencies and fluctuating fortunes experienced by a corpus of texts.

In the immediate post-war period, Walter Benjamin was in danger of becoming a forgotten figure. In the 1950s, the publication of a two-volume edition of a selection of his writings under the joint auspices of Theodor Adorno and Gershom Scholem brought a modicum of recognition. By the late 1960s, Benjamin's more explicitly Marxist cultural writings from the 1930s had begun to attract attention in both West and East Germany: in the West, Benjamin the hashish-experimenter, the brilliant maverick, the melancholy outcast, could not fail to appeal to the rebellious sentiments of the student movement; in the East, he was but one among many heroes of the anti-Fascist struggle, a revolutionary thinker who bridged the gap between German and Soviet cultures. In both cases, though, he was overshadowed by the accomplishments of friends and colleagues: in the West, by Herbert Marcuse, whose writings proved inspirational for the counterculture, and in the East, by revered figures like Bertolt Brecht and Ernst Bloch, who had chosen to settle in the newly established DDR in preference to the Bundesrepublik. That Benjamin should be envisioned, given his view of the 'author as producer', as a melancholy genius, or, given his mystical and Messianic motifs, as some kind of orthodox Marxist, is a double irony.

The gradual publication of the *Gesammelte Schriften* since 1974 under the editorship of Rolf Tiedemann and Hermann Schweppenhäuser, the more recent appearance of Benjamin's *Gesammelte Briefe*, and the proliferation of translations of his texts, have been instrumental in the recovery and reception of Benjamin's work over the last twenty years. Although traces of the earlier sentimentalism[3] and political 'crude thinking' remain, Benjamin's work is now subject to rather more sophisticated readings and sensitive appraisals. His *Habilitationsschrift*, *The Origin of German Tragic Drama* (*Ursprung des deutschen Trauerspiels*),[4] a text dismissed as utterly arcane and incomprehensible by its examiners, is now esteemed and honoured as his critical masterpiece. Some studies never intended for publication, such as the 1916 fragment on language and the 1940 'Theses on the Concept of History', are now considered among his most

brilliant and suggestive works. Benjamin's radio scripts for children, which he himself belittled as a mere journalistic sideline,
have become the focus of sustained and psychoanalytic study.
And his unfinished, and perhaps unfinishable, *magnum opus* the
'Arcades Project' with its attendant, equally incomplete study of
Charles Baudelaire, writings hidden away in the Bibliothèque
nationale in Paris during the Nazi occupation, are now celebrated
as being among the most intriguing and dazzling of modern
cultural analyses.

Main themes

Two concepts, the notion of the afterlife of the object, and in particular of the work of art, and the figure of the 'polytechnical engineer', are the leitmotifs of this book. They capture two moments of
Benjamin's dialectical thinking: destruction and (re)construction.
Afterlife refers to the patient process of disintegration and ruination in which the object emerges from earlier contexts, shorn of
some of its original features but with new accretions upon it.[5] Afterlife is the period in which the pure but deceptive surfaces of the
object are eroded, in which hidden meanings are unfolded and
truth is ultimately disclosed. It is the time in which the object is
subject to transformations and interventions which re-cognize its
significance and 'actualize' its potential: translation, transcrip-
tion, imitation, criticism, appropriation, (re)construction, reproduction, remembrance, redemption. These are precisely the tasks of
Benjamin's 'aesthetic engineer'. Objects, edifices, texts and images
are fragmented, broken and blasted from their usual contexts so
that they may be painstakingly recomposed in critical contemporary constellations. The eclectic engineer juxtaposes disparate and
despised artefacts, forms and media, so as to generate an electrifying tension, an explosive illumination of elements in the present.

  Further, engineer and afterlife are concepts which help us see
why Benjamin should be viewed as, and what it means to be, a 'key
contemporary thinker'. First, Benjamin was preoccupied with the
contemporary. Although much of his work explored obscure, forgotten historical forms and fragments, his purpose was always a
present (and political) one. Dismal dramas, no longer read or performed; obsolete objects and absurdly outmoded fashions; unfre-
quented places and buildings; and the faces of now-forgotten,

long-dead people captured in photographs – Benjamin's abiding concern with all such dusty, derelict things arose not from an anti-quarian interest in the esoteric and arcane. Rather, it derived from the critical imperative to perceive the secret significance of such untimely things in the present, to 'actualize' them by identifying and igniting their explosive, incandescent potential. In addition, Benjamin focused the same scrupulously attentive, sublimely appreciative gaze on the marginalia and minutiae of his own time and place: the modern metropolis. In the inconspicuous, incidental details of everyday life lay the most profound insights into, and profane illuminations of, the contemporary condition. Children's books and toys, postage stamps, automata in Berlin shop windows and Italian fairgrounds, unfashionable yet seemingly indestructible domestic furnishings – through such curios and collectibles, Benjamin sought to reveal and redeem the innermost tendencies and possibilities of contemporary cultural forms and practices.

Benjamin recognized and addressed, albeit in a distinctly unsys-tematic, often ambiguous, and sometimes thoroughly contradictory manner, a number of social, political and cultural transformations and tendencies which preoccupied his own generation of critical thinkers, avant-garde artists and radical intellectuals. They form a set of key themes in his writings.

Cultural fragmentation

Benjamin's writings are marked, like those of so many of his con-temporaries in Germany, not least the first generation of Frankfurt School Critical Theorists, by the catastrophic historical events and experiences of the early twentieth century: the First World War, eco-nomic chaos and inflation in the Weimar years, the Russian Revo-lution and its descent into Stalinist totalitarianism, the rise of Fascism and National Socialism, enforced emigration and exile. In a cultural environment characterized by disintegration and disori-entation as a result of these upheavals, by rapid and unprecedented technological change and by the collapse of traditional values, hier-archies and boundaries, Benjamin recognized the urgent imperative to rethink the tasks and tactics of the writer as author, critic, histo-rian and refugee. How to interpret, and then give critical form to, the modern? This question, which lies at the heart of Charles

Baudelaire's critical prose, also occupied Benjamin. It led to an unequivocal scepticism and scorn for totalizing, systematizing 'scholarly' approaches, and a privileging instead of more immediate, more ephemeral, more explosive textual practices. Attentive and attuned to the contemporary technical innovations and transformations within the sphere of cultural production, Benjamin pioneered modes of critical reading and textual representation which were in keeping with the fragmentation, eclecticism and dynamism of modernity – the monad, the treatise, the constellation, the aphorism, the ephemeral 'thought', 'dream' and 'dialectical' image, the textual 'snapshot', cinematic montage.[6] For Benjamin, the era of long-winded 'weighty tomes' was long past, and a new, urgent language was essential. To this end, he was inspired by the artistic avant-garde of his time (the writings of the Surrealists and the theatre of Bertolt Brecht, in particular), by the contemporary techniques of journalism and advertising, radio, photography and film, and especially by the fragmentary writings of the early German Romantics, radical critical and textual pioneers in their own turbulent times.

Consumption and commodification

The historical development and contemporary pre-eminence of consumer capitalism with its emphasis on and manifestation in the acquisition, conspicuous display and advertising of fashionable commodities; the very proliferation and fate of the commodity form itself; and the accompanying commodification of time, space, human experience and sexuality – these became central themes in Benjamin's work and, in particular, in his ever-expanding study of the Parisian shopping arcades begun in the mid-1920s. In seeking to develop a sophisticated and subtle historical materialist critique of the mystifications attending consumption practices, Benjamin drew upon a number of key notions: Georg Lukács's key insight in *History and Class Consciousness* (1974 [1924]) that the commodity and, above all, commodity fetishism must be recognized as the fundamental category of historical materialist critique; the Freudian and psychoanalytic understanding of the fetishized object as the result of a misdirected genuine sexual impulse; Georg Simmel's insights into the cyclical character of fashion as a form of social differentiation and integration; and the Surrealist preoccupation with the critical energies and, in particular, the comical condition of the now obsolete artefact in the derelict display window. He pioneered dialectical techniques with which to implode the dazzling, dizzying 'dreamworld' of consumerist fantasies formed by spectacular shopping complexes, exclusive department stores, extravagant World Exhibitions and saturation advertising, and thereby to bring the intoxicated consuming masses to their sober senses.

Metropolitanism

Benjamin recognized the rapidly expanding and ever-changing metropolitan environment as the principal site of capitalist domination, and saw the interrogation of the city's architectural forms, spatial configurations and experiential modes as the key to unravelling the fantastical, 'mythological' features of modernity. The construction, development and eventual decline of the nineteenth-century Parisian arcades, with their magical inversion of street and interior and use of mirrors to achieve perspectival illusions, formed the specific foci of his reading of the urban phantasmagoria of the recent past. Moreover, as I have argued elsewhere,[7] Benjamin's life-long fascination with the big city leads to a plethora of writings which articulate the distinctive experiences and central tendencies of modern urban life: 'shock', acceleration and overstimulation, a sense of fragmentation, disorientation and amnesia, anonymity and depersonalization, and spatial rationalization, interiorization and privatization.

Benjamin here drew explicitly on Simmel's famous vision of the indifferent, neurasthenic urbanite in the 1903 essay 'The Metropolis and Mental Life' (in Simmel, 1971). But, for Benjamin, the big city is not only a site of alienation and the diminution of experience. In envisioning the metropolis as a setting of cultural innovation and intellectual excitement, of electrifying encounters and erotic adventures, of intoxication and sophistication, Benjamin offers a differentiated perspective on the city that is sensitive to its delights and distractions. He was well aware that urban life, however traumatic, was also absolutely indispensable for the modern critic as internationalist and cosmopolitan. Benjamin's writings on the metropolis thus clearly reject the simple-minded, reactionary anti-urbanism espoused by critics like Ferdinand Tönnies in *Community and Association* (*Gemeinschaft und Gesellschaft*) (1988 [1888]) and Oswald Spengler in *The Decline of the West* (*Der Untergang des Abendlandes*) (1991 [1918]), authors whose sentimental privileging of small-scale communities and peasant life is imbued with parochialism, anti-intellectualism and latent anti-Semitism.

Benjamin not only offers a series of provocative insights into metropolitan culture and experience, but also discerns and argues for a number of important affinities between the urban and particular forms of representation, most notably between the city and the cinematic. Film becomes the privileged medium for the exploration and depiction of the metropolitan environment – a key consideration for the urban 'engineer' who wishes not merely to decipher but also to 'cut' his or her way through the urban labyrinth.

Mass mediation and reproduction

Benjamin's critique of the modern metropolis goes hand in hand with his analysis (and utilization) of new mass media: radio, photography, film, sound recordings and newspapers. He was not the first, of course, to write on the experiential and perceptual consequences and possibilities of these technologies, but his understanding of the inherent reproducibility of photographs, films and sound recordings is distinctive and important. For Benjamin, the key question raised by film, photography and radio is not whether they are worthy of being classed as art forms but, rather, how these media transform the entire realm and role of art, the categories of aesthetics, and the fundamental relationships between artist/ performer and audience. The artist as producer, as engineer – such a materialist view 'disenchants' art, and leads the discussion of the new media away from the ethereal domain of aesthetic concerns and into that of everyday political practice. During the mid-1930s, in particular, he developed a highly suggestive conceptual vocabulary so as to reconfigure our understanding of 'the work of art in the age of its technological reproducibility' – the 'optical unconscious', the 'spark of contingency', 'schooling', 'habit', 'aura' and 'distraction'. In so doing, Benjamin offered an equivocal, differentiated analysis of contemporary popular media and cultural forms, which, in endorsing their radical political *potential* at least, served as a significant counterpoint and corrective to the all too one-dimensional denunciation of the 'culture industry' which emerged in the writings of Horkheimer and Adorno, a critique which, in the lamentable absence of contemporary discussions of other Critical Theorists concerned with popular culture like Siegfried Kracauer and Leo Löwenthal, is, alas, only too often misunderstood as *the* Frankfurt School view of mass/popular culture.

Technological change and historical 'progress'

The promise of the new media is the production and proliferation of cultural forms not just accessible to the masses, but in which the masses recognize their own (class) situation and interests and are prompted thereby to interrogate and transform their circumstances. This revolutionary pedagogic aspiration is thwarted, however, by the incorporation of the new media into the ideological services of capitalism as illusory spectacle, sentimental compensation and 'harmless entertainment'. This misdirection of a potentially critical, liberating technology into one driven by the interests of profit and domination is but one instance of the fate of modern technological innovation in general. In his programmatic writings on history and elsewhere, Benjamin outlines an uncompromising, albeit fragmentary, critique of the notions of scientific and technological 'progress' as the ever more sophisticated exploitation of nature by humankind. 'Progress' is the great myth of modernity. The Enlightenment has betrayed itself. Under capitalism, the Enlightenment has sacrificed its original emancipatory promise of a just, humane society freed from superstition and fear, and has instead aligned itself with vested interests to become the enemy of critique and truth. It is not reason that has flourished in modernity, but a cold, calculating instrumentalism geared to the maximization of profit. As the hireling of capitalist industry, science contents itself with the technical question of 'how?', and all too rarely addresses the real moral-practical and political question of 'why?' (and 'for whom?'). Benjamin was neither the first of the Frankfurt School Critical Theorists to develop such a critique (Kracauer had pioneered these themes in his notion of the '*Ratio*' in his 1927 essay 'The Mass Ornament'[8]), nor, of course, the last (the 'dialectic of enlightenment' thesis became axiomatic for Theodor Adorno, Max Horkheimer and Herbert Marcuse). Nevertheless, Benjamin's critique of progress and his related vision of history as perpetual catastrophe lead to a distinctive critique of orthodox Marxism and to a provocative call to redeem the hopes and struggles of those who have been oppressed and silenced in the past, to remember the forgotten dead. Roused from our complacent slumbers, reminded of the sufferings of the past and the present, deprived of the illusion of Communist revolution as historical *telos*, our task becomes clear: to halt the triumphal procession of technological barbarism, to interrupt the course of history.

'Alienation' and the intellectual

In a world shattered by catastrophic events, marked by the depersonalization of everyday life in metropolitan environments and under bureaucratic apparatuses, and shorn of any higher meaning or sense of spiritual/religious consolation, Benjamin, like many other writers of his time, was acutely aware of the impoverished, isolated existence of the modern individual and, above all, of that most marginal and maligned of figures, the contemporary 'intellectual'. The pessimistic vision of an acute inner loneliness and longing and of a profound spiritual 'homelessness' pervading modern culture find frequent expression. In Lukács's *Theory of the Novel* (1971 [1920]), the contemporary world is marked by a condition of 'transcendental homelessness', one which lies at the heart of the bourgeois novel. Simmel (1903, in Simmel, 1971) argued that the metropolitan individual shuns the overstimulation of the external world ('objective culture') and retreats into indifference, neurasthenia and eccentricity. For Kracauer, the new white-collar workers, who increasingly come to predominate in the contemporary metropolitan centres, are characterized by a condition of 'spiritual homelessness' (Kracauer, 1998, p. 88) and lack both the class consciousness of the traditional working class and the economic rewards and cultural consolations of the middle classes, the *Bildungsbürgertum*, to which they aspire. Moreover, the intellectual is the ultimate metropolitan figure condemned to 'isolation from the absolute . . . isolation and individuation' (Kracauer, 1995, p. 131); unconvinced by pseudo-theological speculation and unmoved by naive revolutionary zeal, he or she must join the ranks of 'those who wait' ('Die Wartenden', 1922, in Kracauer, 1995) in existential uncertainty. And, as for so many German intellectuals, such disquiet, such 'spiritual homelessness', was for Kracauer and Benjamin exacerbated by the 'real' homelessness of enforced emigration and exile.

In Benjamin's work the crisis of the modern thinker is characteristically understood in both theological and materialist terms. On the one hand, it is but an element of the sorrowful world-historical condition attendant upon fallen humanity, an all-pervasive melancholy which finds its most precise expression in the allegorical poetics of the baroque and, much later and in profane form, of Baudelaire. On the other hand, the precarious position of the critic results from a failure to perceive his or her true socio-economic and class position as 'producer', an intellectual labourer with a clear task: to foster the revolutionary consciousness of the class of which he or she is unambiguously a member. Melancholy and mobilization, *acedia* and aesthetic 'engineering' – these are the two poles of Benjamin's attempt to articulate the distinctive character of, and the practices incumbent upon, the radical writer under the calamitous, chaotic conditions of his time. The brooding polytechnician – this figure is the very model of the key contemporary thinker for Benjamin then, and even (perhaps, especially) for us now.

Benjamin *was* a thinker of the contemporary, and *is* a key contemporary thinker. The evidence for this is overwhelming. There is now a vast literature on Benjamin, encompassing collected editions, translations, scholarly monographs and articles, special issues of journals, student-friendly and cartoon-strip-style introductions, and at least one novel.[9] It is a literary mountain, a baroque pile of fragments upon fragments, which has accumulated at an ever more rapid rate over the last twenty years and to which this book inevitably adds yet another piece.[10] There are, in addition, web pages, videos, conferences and an international organization dedicated to Benjamin,[11] and, most recently, a literary prize for translation has been named after him by the city of Frankfurt am Main. He is required reading for students in a plethora of academic disciplines and interdisciplines – German, French, English, and comparative literature, philosophy, sociology, history, cultural studies, film studies, urban studies and architecture. He is a star in the current academic firmament.

This acclaim is not simply a matter of intellectual whim or fashion. Rather, it reflects the complex and manifold ways in which his ideas, themes and insights are increasingly recognized as having special significance for, and resonance with, current (post-)modern social and cultural analysis. Rapacious consumption and all-pervasive commodification, the tumult of urban experience, the proliferation of new media technologies and our supersaturation by images, the destructive capacities and dominating consequences of 'progress' and scientific knowledge, the preservation of the precious counter-histories of oppressed groups and the importance of collective memory and individual testimony – such concerns have not diminished in importance, but are, on the contrary, even more acute today than when Benjamin was writing. His work lays bare with incomparable clarity and critical power *his* modernity as the 'prehistory' of our own 'post' or 'late' or '(dis)organized' or 'second' modernity. In a Europe wherein war, economic ruin, totalitarianism, genocide and concentration camps are far from distant memories, Benjamin's work has a vital presence in our present.

Biographical sketch

In contrast to the impecunious and imperilled condition of his later life, Benjamin's childhood was a time of material comfort and tedious tranquillity. Born on 15 July 1892, the son of an auctioneer and eldest of three children, Walter Benedix Schönflies Benjamin grew up in the desirable West End of Berlin in an affluent, assimilated German-Jewish family. As has been commonly observed, his semi-autobiographical reflections on his formative years, 'A Berlin Childhood around 1900' and 'Berlin Chronicle' (both written in 1932), are more treatises on the promises and prohibitions attending a middle-class, urban childhood in general than an intimate account of Benjamin's boyhood. He recalls a solitary, sickly childhood cloistered in the insufferably 'cosy', cluttered bourgeois interior of the time, the dull and dutiful round of visits to ageing, gossiping relations, and the petty strictures of school life. His reminiscences speak eloquently and poetically of a child whose main consolations for this dry existence consisted in the daydreams stimulated by reading, in the visits to the enchanting Tiergarten and Berlin zoo, in the annual hunt for Easter eggs, the occasional illicit nocturnal pilferings of confectionery, and, on one memorable occasion, an unintended, unsanctioned foray into a seductive, seedy district of the city.

In the belief that he would benefit from the country air, Benjamin was sent away from Berlin to spend two years (1905–6) at a relatively progressive boarding school at Haubinda in Thuringia. There he met and studied under Gustav Wyneken (1875–1964), a key advocate of educational reform and a luminary of the radical wing of the Youth Movement (*Jugendbewegung*). Originally formed in 1901 as a boys' hiking organization, the Youth Movement in Imperial Germany expanded and diversified to cover a wide political and social spectrum, from proto-Fascist, anti-Semitic elements such as the Wandervogel with their *Volkish* ideologies, eulogizing of German nature, sense of martial brotherhood, and privileging of leadership, to the Jewish section of the movement, the Blau-Weiss.[12] The radical wing of the Youth Movement to which Benjamin was attracted advocated a complete break with the traditional school system to ensure the free development of youth unencumbered by the dogmas and disciplines of conventional pedagogy. The renewal of German culture and intellectual life could be achieved only through the liberation of youthful creativity and energy. Under the influence of Wyneken, Benjamin became intensely preoccupied with the cultural and educational condition of youth, though not in any practical or instrumental sense. Benjamin's vision of the mission of students, unsullied by material or political considerations, was couched in the rarefied and abstract terms of the idealistic renaissance of *Geist* (spirit), the solitary, individual life of the mind.[13]

Although Benjamin returned to complete his school studies in Berlin and then enrolled to study philosophy at Freiburg University in 1912, he remained in regular contact with Wyneken. The year 1913 saw the publication of a number of poetic and idealistic polemics in Wyneken's journal *Der Anfang* (*The Beginning*) as Benjamin returned to Berlin once more to pursue his university studies. Back in his native city, Benjamin was elected to the committee and then to the chair of the 'Free Students' (*Freie Studentenschaft*), an association instigated to oppose the various conservative and martial university fraternities and clubs. This official position notwithstanding, Benjamin's days of involvement with the idealism of the Youth Movement and the naive student politics of the 'spirit' were numbered. August 1914 was to transform everything.

The outbreak of the Great War split the Youth Movement into its numerous factions. Some militants relished the outpourings of patriotic sentiment and the opportunity for imperial adventure and military glory. Some viewed the conflict as the necessary defence and revitalization of German *Kultur*, in opposition to the decadent foreign (especially French) values of *Zivilisation*.[14] Some saw the war from the very outset as an appalling, futile sacrifice of a betrayed generation, and there were others who changed their minds. In 1913 Wyneken had criticized the warmongering and national fervour of the time – youth must resist the simplistic appeal of sabre-rattling sloganeering.[15] In November 1914, however, his speech on 'War and

Youth' in Munich was a rallying call to youth to defend the besieged and beleaguered 'fatherland'. Expecting to be called up anyway, Benjamin initially, and without any enthusiasm, volunteered to join the cavalry, but, fortunately for him, was deemed unfit for military service.[16] Then, on 8 August 1914, two of Benjamin's closest friends, Fritz Heinle and Rika Seligson, committed suicide as a despairing protest against the hostilities. Deeply moved by these deaths and feeling utterly betrayed by his mentor, Benjamin broke completely with Wyneken in March 1915.[17]

Three months later Benjamin met an 18-year-old student of mathematics, Gershom Scholem, an acquaintance who would prove a lifelong friend and profoundly influence Benjamin's work in the direction of Judaic thought, mysticism and the Kabbalah. Benjamin's concern with the critical, spiritually redemptive task of youth gave way to a preoccupation with redirecting philosophical enquiry away from the impoverished Enlightenment conception of experience, cognition and knowledge, towards an understanding of the linguistic grounding of truth in Revelation. In his enigmatic fragments from 1916–17, Benjamin identifies the task of philosophy, to call things by their proper names, as the recovery of the perfect language with which Adam named Creation at God's behest. Benjamin thus sought a new avenue for his concern with the purity of a language and an intellectual realm uncontaminated by immediate interests and instrumentalism. Both those who advocated Jewish assimilation within the German state, like Hermann Cohen, and those who later came to advocate Jewish political mobilization and emigration, like Martin Buber, were tainted by their initial enthusiasm for the war.[18] Indeed, the politics of Jewish militancy and Zionism were far too pragmatic and partisan to appeal to Benjamin at this time, and his political thinking eventually took a rather different direction. He never learned Hebrew, though he promised Scholem on numerous occasions that he would do so; and he never even visited Palestine when Scholem emigrated there in 1923, let alone emigrate himself.[19]

Benjamin had been profoundly disappointed by his studies at the University of Freiburg, especially the lectures of the pre-eminent neo-Kantian philosopher Heinrich Rickert, which he found particularly boring. Subsequently, he showed considerably more enthusiasm for the classes and ideas of the sociologist Georg Simmel at the Royal Friedrich Wilhelm University in Berlin. But in the aftermath of the break with Wyneken, Benjamin was keen to leave the Imperial capital. In the autumn of 1915 he moved to Munich, ironically the city where Wyneken had recently delivered his fateful 'War and Youth' address. Benjamin managed to avoid subsequent call-ups by feigning sciatica, and in 1917 relocated to neutral Switzerland and Berne University with Dora Kellner, whom he had married in April 1917. Benjamin spent the remaining war years in self-imposed Swiss exile, and completed his doctorate on 'The Concept of Art Criticism in German Romanticism' in 1919, a study in which he sought to develop a notion of immanent criticism as the unfolding of the inherent tendencies of a work of art, its 'truth content', through critical reflection. Back in Germany, he subsequently provided an exemplary instance of such an approach in an extended essay on Goethe's peculiar novel *Elective Affinities*. Eschewing conventional readings of the story as a cautionary moral tale of tragic, illicit love, Benjamin foregrounded the opposition between human subjection to fate and characterful, decisive action, a contrast which serves as an instructive lesson in the need to contest mythic forces. In particular, Benjamin contended, the protracted death of one of the miscreant lovers, Ottilie, presents the demise of beauty for a higher purpose, truth, and thus serves as an allegory of the task of criticism itself.

In the early 1920s Benjamin hoped to make his mark in literary criticism by editing his own journal, *Angelus Novus*, the *New Angel*. Suspecting, however, that the erudite and arcane material would prove commercially unviable, the prospective publisher pulled out before the first issue was finalized. This bitter disappointment prompted Benjamin's return to the academic sphere. He embarked upon his *Habilitationsschrift* at the University of Frankfurt, taking as his theme the seventeenth-century German play of mourning, the *Trauerspiel*. Dismissed as bastardized tragedies, these baroque dramas with their preposterous plots and bombastic language had long been consigned to the dusty attic of literary failures. Benjamin's immanent critique of these scorned and neglected works distinguished them from the classical tragic form, and reinterpreted and redeemed them as the quintessential expression of the frailties and vanities of God-forsaken human existence and the 'natural history' of the human *physis* as decay. In so doing, Benjamin argued for the importance of allegory as a trope which renders and represents the world precisely as fragmentation, ruination and mortification. Benjamin's *Ursprung des deutschen Trauerspiels*, with its obscure subject matter and impenetrable methodological preamble, baffled and bemused its inept examiners, and he was advised to withdraw it, rather than face the ultimate humiliation of outright rejection. By late summer 1925, his ambitions for an academic career lay in ruins.

Benjamin was to remain an intellectual outsider for the rest of his life, free to lambaste and lampoon scholarly conventions, but at the same time utterly dependent on the good offices of publishers, the press, commissioning editors and others who, like Ernst Schoen at Südwestdeutscher Rundfunk and Siegfried Kracauer at the *Frankfurter Zeitung*, offered what work they could. Benjamin's growing friendship with Theodor Adorno, whom he met in 1923, led to an associate membership of the Frankfurt Institute for Social Research and a small stipend; yet, his life was dogged by financial anxieties. The fragmentation and astonishing diversity of Benjamin's *oeuvre* is a clear consequence of economic exigencies. Benjamin translated and wrote on Marcel Proust; he produced eloquent essays on such key literary figures as Franz Kafka, Bertolt Brecht, Karl Kraus, the Surrealists and Charles Baudelaire; he also penned a radio piece entitled 'True Stories of Dogs', a set of reflections on Russian peasant toys, and a review of Charlie Chaplin. Only this can be said of such enforced eclecticism: the least likely and most maligned of things always attracted his attention, and always provided his most telling insights.

Benjamin was never to write another book in the, for him, compromised, 'scholarly' style of his *Trauerspiel* study, which was eventually published in 1928. Instead, the aphorism, the illuminating aside, the quotation, the imagistic fragment, became his preferred – indeed, essential – mode of expression. In presenting and representing the everyday in a new light, observing it from an unexpected angle, such miniatures were intended to catch the reader off guard (like a series of blows decisively dealt, Benjamin once observed, left-handed[20]). Starting with pen portraits of cities he visited ('Naples', 'Marseilles', 'Moscow') and his 1926 montage of urban images, *One-Way Street*, Benjamin's writings began to take on a more pronounced contemporary inflection and radical political colouring. While working on the *Trauerspiel* study on Capri in the summer of 1924, Benjamin had read Georg Lukács's *History and Class Consciousness*, and had been introduced to a Latvian theatre director, Asja Lacis. His enthusiasm for the former and troubled love affair with the latter drew Benjamin to Marxist ideas. In the winter of 1926–7 he visited Moscow to see the new Soviet system for himself. His initial enthusiasm waned in response to the indifference of the Soviet authorities, the impossibility of the language and, especially, the artistic impoverishment and intellectual compromises already discernible. Benjamin returned to Berlin, where, through Lacis, he met and became friends with the playwright Bertolt Brecht. To the dismay of Adorno and Scholem, who saw Benjamin's always unorthodox, unconvincing espousal of Marxist ideas as a foolhardy flirtation, he became an advocate of Brecht's 'epic theatre' with its blunt political didacticism. While Benjamin himself refrained from 'crude thinking', its traces and imperatives are evident in many of his writings during the 1930s on the situation and task of the contemporary artist ('The Author as Producer', 1934) and the character and consequences of new media forms for the work of art and aesthetics ('The Work of Art in the Age of Mechanical Reproduction', 1935).

Benjamin's concern with the fate of art within capitalist modernity, with the Marxist critique of commodity culture, and with the character and experience of the urban environment were to combine in a project which was to occupy him from 1927 until his untimely death in 1940. Inspired by the Parisian perambulations of the Surrealist writer Louis Aragon (1987 [1926]), Benjamin embarked upon a study of the then derelict Parisian shopping arcades built in the first half of the nineteenth century. Initially modest in scope, Benjamin's *Passagenarbeit*, or *Passagen-Werk* ('Arcades Project') was eventually to comprise more than 1,000 pages of notes, quotations, sketches and drafts, and today remains as an unfinished – indeed, never written – 'prehistory' of nineteenth-century Paris as the original site of modern consumer capitalism, a plethora of fragments providing a panoramic and kaleidoscopic exploration of the city's fashions and phantasmagoria, architecture and boulevards, literature and politics.

Significantly, it was to Paris, rather than to Moscow or Palestine, that Benjamin fled in 1933 to escape the Nazi terror. There he pursued his researches for the 'Arcades Project' in the Bibliothèque nationale, work which led to a proposed book on Baudelaire and a series of historiographical principles intended as a methodological introduction. Like the wider *Passagenarbeit*, these too were never completed. Despite the advice and efforts of Adorno and Horkheimer, then in exile in New York, Benjamin lingered too long in Paris, and was trapped in 1940 by the German invasion. He fled to the south of the country, was temporarily interned, and, once released, desperately sought an escape route. It was not to be. Benjamin attempted to cross into the relative safety of Spain, but was turned back at the border. Wearied by his exertions, facing certain arrest on his return to France, Benjamin committed suicide on 26 September 1940. He is buried at Port Bou.

Overview

Benjamin's fragmentary *oeuvre* presents a highly eclectic and provocative combination of concepts, themes and motifs drawn from a distinctive and diverse set of sources: Judaic mysticism and Messianism; early German Romanticism; modernism and, in particular, Surrealism; and an extremely unorthodox Marxism. His writings form a complex constellation with those of a number of friends and associates whose competing influences contribute to the highly paradoxical, ambiguous and elusive character of Benjamin's principal concepts and arguments. His early ideas on language, translation and mourning were deeply indebted to his close and long-standing friendship with Scholem, who continually urged him to learn Hebrew and to devote himself to his 'true' calling: the esoteric domain of Jewish theology. Surprisingly, given the convolutions and intricacies of his own writing, Benjamin was drawn less to the enigmas and subtleties of the Kabbalah, and more to its very antithesis: the Marxist 'crude thinking' of Brecht, a writer to whom every hint of mysticism was an anathema. The gravitation of Benjamin's thinking towards Brechtian didacticism in the 1930s was lamented not only by Scholem, but also by Horkheimer and Adorno, as the most needless self-betrayal. Horkheimer and Adorno wished to claim Benjamin for their own camp – a Critical Theorist and dialectician of the highest order – and tried to persuade him to eliminate from his work not only Brechtian elements, but also concepts drawn from other writers who did not meet with their approval: the supposedly 'behaviourist' aspects of Simmel's urban social psychology, for example. As a result, their treatment of Benjamin's writings was not always benign, as exemplified by their editorial intransigence and interference *vis-à-vis* the Baudelaire studies of the late 1930s.[21]

Benjamin's work exists in a complex interplay with the Critical Theory of the Frankfurt School. Of all the writers associated with the Institute, it is Kracauer who in many ways demonstrates the closest thematic and conceptual connections: a fascination with the city, urban architecture and flânerie; an appreciation of film and popular culture; a privileging of fragments and surfaces; and a pre-occupation with Parisian culture during the Second Empire – to say nothing of Kracauer's later historiographical interests. Benjamin and Kracauer saw much of each other – they were in the same places at the same time (Frankfurt in the mid-1920s, Berlin in the early 1930s, Paris from 1933) – and they reviewed each other's work with some enthusiasm.[22] Their association was a tense, difficult one, however. Kracauer was sceptical of Benjamin's theological vocabulary,[23] and regarded the notion of immanent criticism as an open invitation to highly subjective (mis)readings.[24] For his part, Benjamin, doubtless mortified by the appearance of print of so many of his 'Arcades' themes (arcades as phantasmagoria, Paris as dream-world, flânerie and boredom) albeit in watered-down form, dismissed Kracauer's 1937 study of the composer Jacques Offenbach: 'the book itself only makes one angry' (*ABC*, p. 238).

Benjamin's evaluation of cultural phenomena was highly distinctive. Kracauer's 1926 notion of the 'cult of distraction' as involving a breakdown in class distinctions among the audience, but one which offers only stupefaction as compensation for the emptiness of daily life,[25] is radically recast in Benjamin's later privileging of 'distraction' as a form of reception which crystallizes class consciousness and promotes proletarian critical expertise. Similarly, Benjamin's critique of the cultic origins of the 'authentic' work of art and his advocacy instead of film and photography as critical and popular media ran directly counter to Adorno's insistence upon the critical role of 'autonomous art' and the 'infantilization' of mass media audiences. Given such tensions and fundamental disagreements, it is a pity that Adorno's plan to publish in one volume Benjamin's 'Work of Art' essay, his own 1938 polemic against jazz ('On the Fetish Character in Music and the Regression of Listening') and a specially commissioned piece by Kracauer on the detective story (on which he had already written a philosophical treatise in the early 1920s) did not come to fruition – for the tension between these pieces would have been electrifying.[26] Nevertheless, it is perhaps instructive that, given the range of possible collaborators among the writers of the Frankfurt School, Benjamin chose to work with none of them, and indeed, only ever collaborated with one person – the writer and journalist Franz Hessel – and then only on translations of Proust and a one-page fragment of the 'Arcades Project'. For all his concern with the 'author as producer' and class comrade, the role of the polytechnical aesthetic engineer and the task of recreating criticism as a genre proved to be solitary ones for Benjamin.

How can one do justice to such an intriguing figure and such a rich body of work within the necessary limits of a book like this? Benjamin's own playful attempts to map out his life and work on paper produced only that ultimate figure of complexity and confusion: the labyrinth.[27] Attempts to categorize Benjamin's work by distinguishing between his early and late writings, dividing his texts into an initial messianic phase influenced by Judaic motifs and themes and a subsequent materialist period characterized by Brechtian elements and Marxist orientations, have been rightly criticized for their failure to perceive the complex continuity of his thought. From mysticism to Marxism – such a simplification obscures more than it illuminates, and suggests a linearity of development which is thoroughly alien to Benjamin. I wish to suggest another way of mapping Benjamin's work, one which draws on another of his key metaphors: not the labyrinth, but the constellation – a figure constituted by a plethora of points which together compose an intelligible, legible, though contingent and transient, pattern. Benjamin's work might usefully be viewed in terms of two textual constellations: first, that of the *Trauerspiel* study, comprising his early reflections on language and translation (1916 and 1921), his doctoral dissertation (1919) and the essay on Goethe's *Wahlverwandschaften* (1921–2), his plans for *Angelus Novus*, and various fragments on fate, history, tragedy, *Trauerspiel* and allegory; and, second, that of the 'Arcades Project', including his urban *Denkbilder, One-Way Street*, the essays on Proust (1929), Surrealism (1929) and Baudelaire (1937–8 and 1939), the texts on Brecht (1930 and 1931), photography (1931) and film (1935), his childhood reminiscences (1932) and his historiographical theses (1940). Inevitably, and regrettably, this book is a highly selective study. It necessarily focuses – in an un-Benjaminian way, alas – on his major texts, and even then there are significant omissions: 'On the Programme of the Coming Philosophy' (1917–18), 'Critique of Violence' (1921), the essays on Karl Kraus (1931) and Franz Kafka (1934), and 'The Storyteller' (1936). Hence, it does not pretend to provide an all-encompassing, exhaustive introduction to Benjamin's work, but offers instead what I hope will be an engaging, illuminating examination of a selection of his major writings, themes and concepts. It is an investigation which serves, above all, as an invitation to read and explore both the texts discussed here and Benjamin's wider *oeuvre*.

Chapter 1 begins with a discussion of Benjamin's first major attempt to 'recreate criticism': his 1919 doctoral dissertation on early

Romantic thought. In it Benjamin draws upon the writings of Friedrich Schlegel and Novalis to articulate a notion of 'immanent critique', a method which, with its emphasis upon unfolding truth from within the work of art itself, becomes a fundamental critical imperative for Benjamin. In the Romantics' conception of 'immanent critique', Fichte's idea of the human individual coming to self-consciousness and self-understanding through a never-ending process of self-reflection is transposed to the work of art. For the Romantics, criticism provides the successive mirrors in which the artwork comes to reflect upon itself and thereby disclose its meaning and truth. Truth does not reside in the intentions of the author, but is continually constituted anew through the work of critique until, recognizing its relationship with other works of art, the artwork takes its rightful place within the pantheon of art, dissolving itself into the Idea of Art. The self-disclosure of the truth of the work of art occurs during its 'afterlife', conceived as ongoing criticism and final dissolution.

Like the essay on *Elective Affinities*, Benjamin's *Trauerspiel* study (discussed in chapter 2) sought to provide an exemplary instance of immanent critique, in which the work of art was subjected to a process not so much of reflection, as of ruination or mortification for the sake of its truth content. Benjamin's intention was to correct two fundamental misunderstandings of the *Trauerspiel* form: that the *Trauerspiel* was merely a feeble imitation of tragedy, and that its key literary device, allegory, is inferior to the symbol. For Benjamin, the baroque play of mourning was to be distinguished from classical tragedy because of its completely different grounding and purpose: rather than being concerned with myth and the fate of the tragic hero, the *Trauerspiel* presented the dismal events of history as they conspired to ruin the sovereign. It is not ennobling heroic action, but human indecision, which leads to catastrophe and melancholy. The *Trauerspiel* articulates a mournful, utterly profane realm of creaturely compulsion and human misery in a God-forsaken world. Benjamin's notion of melancholy here draws not on Lutheran theology, but on the Judaic mystical tradition, with which he had toyed in a series of earlier fragments: 'On Language as Such and on Human Language' (1916), 'The Task of the Translator' (1921) and the 'Theologico-Political Fragment on Human' (1920–1). According to Hebrew scripture, language in the form of the divine word of God is the origin of things. Adam is called by God to name Creation, to give things their proper names – that is, to translate the divine, creative word of God into human language. The blissful,

paradisiacal language of Adamic naming comes to an end with the
Fall, and shatters into the multiplicity of historical human languages. Unlike Adam's perfect language, these languages are arbitrary in terms of the relation between word and thing, and, in their
plethora of terms for the same phenomenon, overname nature.
Human history is this continuing life amidst a Babel of languages
which reduce nature to a state of mournful silence.

Benjamin contends that it is precisely this overnaming of nature
by fallen humanity which finds expression in baroque allegory.
Arguing against both the neoclassical tradition and the Romantic
aesthetic legacy, Benjamin rejects what he sees as the conventional privileging of the symbol as the aesthetic figure *par excellence*,
arguing instead for the importance of the much-derided allegorical form. Drawing on medieval emblematics, the dramatists of the
baroque employed allegory to imbue objects with multiple significance. In this overdetermination of meaning, objects and words lose
any precise sense. Allegory hollows out meaning, and reduces
language to verbose prattle. Allegory, like criticism, thus becomes
a form of mortification which discloses a truth: the post-lapsarian
condition of language as arbitrary overnaming.

Chapter 3 explores Benjamin's growing interest in the character
and critical representation of the urban environment during the
mid- to late 1920s. First, it examines some of the main features of
Benjamin's *Denkbilder*, his plethora of urban pen portraits. Then it
discusses the fragments composing *One-Way Street*, and introduces
the notion of the politically engaged writer as an exponent of, and
expert in, polytechnical, urban engineering. As elaborated in chapters 5 and 6, this figure is not just a literary critic, but rather a
writer/artist who engages with the manifold cultural forms and
media of modernity to illuminate and explode the present. The
notion of 'profane illumination' pioneered by Surrealism seemed to
promise a model of this, but Benjamin's response to the writings of
Louis Aragon and André Breton was guarded: on the one hand,
these authors enthused and inspired his work on the Parisian
shopping arcades; on the other, he saw their preoccupation with
intoxication and the occult as negating the radical potential of
Surrealism.

Although the change in thematic focus and textual style between
the *Passagenarbeit* and the *Trauerspiel* study seems immense, the
continuities in Benjamin's writings must be stressed. Accordingly,
chapter 4 initially highlights some of the parallels between these
undertakings. The arcade and the play of mourning were both

monadological, ruinous entities from which to unfold fragmentary insights into the past and its relationship with the present: of the nineteenth century as the prehistory of modernity, and the seventeenth century as the origin of the baroque imagination. If the *Trauerspiel* study brought together immanent critique, ruinous history and mournful, mute nature, the 'Arcades Project' and its constellation of texts combined 'strategic critique' (Caygill, 1998, p. 61), redemptive history and the melancholy, mnemonic cityscape. The chapter then analyses some of the key themes and concepts of the *Passagenarbeit*. Arcades, fashions, commodities – these phantasmagorical and fetishized forms are indices not of historical progress, but of continuing mythic domination and human subservience. Benjamin's gaze focused on the afterlife of these fantastical 'dream' forms – the ruined arcade, the obsolete object, outmoded fashions – with the goal of disenchanting them and redeeming their utopian promise. As they are ruined, ridiculed and demolished, the enslaving forms of yesteryear yield their critical potential, their revolutionary energy, their truth.

Chapters 5 and 6 consider Benjamin's attempt during the 1930s to develop a political understanding of the writer within the capitalist production process and the 'meltdown' of conventional bourgeois aesthetic forms and categories. Benjamin argues that the progressive critic/artist must pioneer and embrace new cultural forms (epic theatre), practices (interruption, montage, distraction) and media (radio, photography, film) to explode the boundaries between different art forms and implode the traditional work of art itself. 'Aura' is the fundamental concept here. In his 'Small History of Photography' (1931) and his 'Work of Art in the Age of Mechanical Reproduction' (1935), Benjamin famously argues that 'aura' – the sense of awe, reverence and distance experienced in the presence and contemplation of the work of art, a function of its cultic origins, authenticity and embeddedness in tradition – is dissolved by the advent of the new media. Film and photography replace the unique painting with the multiplicity of the negative and the print, where there is no distinction between original and copy. In these media, Benjamin controversially claims, distance gives ways to proximity, concentrated contemplation to distracted appropriation, cultic worship to political engagement and pedagogical practice.

Chapter 7 takes as its point of departure Charles Baudelaire's sonnet 'To a Passer-by' (*À une passante*), and explores Benjamin's understanding of metropolitan experience, the character of modern memory and the imperatives of redemptive historiography. The 'Arcades Project' was to draw on the practices of polytechnical aesthetic engineering, and develop methodological principles which radically contested what Benjamin saw as bourgeois 'historicist' understandings of the past and of the duty of the historian. The *Passagenarbeit* was to be imagistic in character, juxtaposing fragmentary insights in a mosaic, or, in Benjamin's new terminology, a montage of elements. It was conceived not as a simple narration of the past, but as a political intervention in its afterlife. For Benjamin, history is not to be a banal recounting of events, but a political intervention in, and actualization of, the past. The past is not something given, but is continually reconfigured according to the interests of the present. This intersection and interplay of the 'then' and 'now' was conceptualized by Benjamin within a visual register: as the 'dialectical image', the key methodological category of the *Passagenarbeit*.

The 'dialectical image' was inspired both by the instantaneousness of the photographic snapshot (Konersmann, 1991) and by the transformation of experience and memory in the modern metropolis. For Benjamin, the cityscape is a site of shock, amnesia and remembrance. Baudelaire's allegorical poetics constitutes a melancholy language with which to give expression to the hollowed-out commodity form and the collapse of coherent, communicable experience (*Erfahrung*) amid the swarming metropolitan crowd. The figures of the flâneur, the gambler, the prostitute and the ragpicker serve as allegories of the modern poet, who endures the shocks, collisions and fleeting encounters of the cityscape. Forgetfulness might seem the obvious corollary of such trauma, but the city is also the setting and stimulus for a particular mode of remembering: Proust's *mémoire involontaire*. Memories are not recoverable at will, but return unexpectedly and unbidden. An occurrence or accident in the present fleetingly recalls former, forgotten impressions and experiences. Past and present momentarily intersect, and mutually illuminate one another. The dialectical image is the transposition of the *mémoire involontaire* into a historiographic method which recalls those whom conventional history has consigned to the oblivion of forgetting.

Intentionless knowing and the fleeting, fragmentary disclosure of truth, melancholy silence and the sorrowful condition of human existence, history as ruination and redemption, criticism as mortification and (re)construction: these themes underpin the *Passagenarbeit*, the *Trauerspiel* study and, indeed, Benjamin's work as a whole. Hence – and this is absolutely fundamental – the conceptualization of Benjamin's *oeuvre* as two constellations does *not* reproduce the facile dichotomy of Messianism versus materialism. These constellations are *not* to be envisaged as distinct chronological phases; rather, they must be imagined as superimposed, one upon the other, so that now this one, now the other, takes precedence and appears closest to us. The notion of the constellation captures both the potential deceptiveness of any scheme – points which seem nearest to one another may prove to be those furthest apart – and their contingency. Each constellation must be recognized as only one permutation among an infinite number of possible configurations, conjunctions and correspondences. Such is the intricacy, such the interplay, such the ingenuity of Benjamin's writings.

The recent, continuing ascent of Benjamin's star means that the contemporary (would-be) student of Benjamin's work has the enviable task of choosing between many and varied English-language introductions, each with its own thematic and conceptual emphases and inflections: the experience of modernity and redemption (Wolin, 1982); the liquidation and conservation of cultural tradition (McCole, 1993); the dialectics of melancholy (Pensky, 1993); visual culture and perception (Caygill, 1998), and the politics of technological change (Leslie, 2000). Some provide detailed contextualization (Roberts, 1982), some focus on biographical material (Brodersen, 1997), while others offer more impressionistic overviews (Bolz and van Reijen, 1996). Some are distinguished by the lucidity of their discussion (Wolin, 1982, and McCole, 1993), some by the subtlety and elegance of their writing (Pensky, 1993), and others by their verve and style (Leslie, 2000).

This book also has its own distinctive features. It seeks to unfold Benjamin's critical engagement with the cultural phenomena and experiences of modernity by foregrounding three key notions: afterlife (as a moment of disintegration), engineering (as a moment of reconstruction) and the constellation (as a mode of actualization and representation). My intention is to provide something approaching an 'immanent criticism' of Benjamin work – a critique which privileges the activity of close, careful interpretation, rather than the pronouncement of final judgements. Like Benjamin's own immanent critique, it too is directed against would-be misappropriations of his work – appropriations by those who insist upon establishing a definitive Benjamin, a single reading of the 'true' authorial intention behind his works. This book is written against those who fail to recognize the contingency of their own reading,

and who find pleasure only in determinations, ultimate specifica-
tions, final delineations – in short, in conclusions. Hence, my own
Conclusion is written in a different spirit: as an initial, tentative
gesture towards some of the contemporary constellations in which
Benjamin's themes now seem to, or might, appear. It points not to
answers, but to questions which themselves lead back into Benjamin's work. It is designed to be suggestive, indicative and contingent. After all, anything else would be truly un-Benjaminian.

1

Immanent Criticism and Exemplary Critique

Introduction

Benjamin's concern with rethinking and reconfiguring the activity of literary and cultural criticism underpins his doctoral dissertation, 'Der Begriff der Kunstkritik in der deutschen Romantik' ('The Concept of Art Criticism in German Romanticism'), written between June 1917 and June 1919.[1] Acutely aware of the intellectual compromises required in this work and their injurious consequences,[2] Benjamin nevertheless did not regard his dissertation as some arcane academic undertaking. Rather, he understood it as a timely, pointed attack upon prevailing interpretations of German Romanticism and the movement's intellectual legacy, a legacy with significant ramifications in the present. In a letter to Ernst Schoen dated 8 November 1918, Benjamin states clearly:

> The work treats the romantic concept of criticism (art criticism). The modern concept of criticism has been developed from the romantic concept; but 'criticism' was an esoteric concept[3] for the romantics . . . which was based on mystical assumptions about cognition. In terms of art, it encapsulates the best insights of contemporary and later poets, a new concept of art that, in many respects is our concept of art. (*COR*, pp. 135–6)[4]

Benjamin's study was to insist on the modernity and actuality of Romanticism, and stress the profoundly mystical character of its critical practice.

For Benjamin, it was in the early writings of Friedrich Schlegel (1772–1829), which appeared in the Romantics' own *Athenaeum* publication (between 1798 and 1800),[5] and of Novalis (Friedrich von Hardenberg, 1772–1801), whose earliest philosophical fragments date from 1795, that the modern notion of literary criticism begins to take shape. These texts thus form the logical and necessary starting point for any serious attempt to 'recreate criticism as a genre'. Breaking with the prevailing artistic orthodoxies of neoclassicism, the early Romantics explored and developed new modes of aesthetic appreciation and a conceptual vocabulary appropriate to the modern spirit of intellectual critique and revolutionary transformation. Their ideas appeared against the backdrop of, and were attuned to, the unprecedented socio-historical, political, cultural and intellectual changes of the age: the French Revolution, incipient industrialization, nationalist fervour, European war. Such radical ambitions amid turbulent times clearly had a particular resonance for Benjamin, given his own youthful rejection of what he saw as the rigid hierarchies and obsolete values of bourgeois culture and the imminent collapse of Imperial Germany.

This forward-looking, pioneering sensibility of the Romantics was not that of Enlightenment thought, with its emphasis on the disenchantment of nature, scientific rationality and calculation. Rather – and for Benjamin this was of the utmost significance – early Romanticism retained a deeply mystical understanding of art and criticism as emanations and/or reminders of a pure, poetic original language (*Ursprache*). In the work of Novalis, for example, nature constitutes a universe of signs and hieroglyphs,[6] a hidden language which finds expression in the medium of art, such that 'the most perfect poetry will be that which, like a "musical fantasy" or like the "harmonies from an aeolian harp" makes us so forget the artistic medium that "nature itself" appears to speak' (Frank, 1989, p. 281). Similarly, Schlegel suggests, in fragments from 1804–5, that in the medium of art humanity could come to perceive the traces or intimations of divine Revelation.[7] Such mystical ideas may seem obscure to the contemporary reader, and the very opposite of rational modern thinking, but for Benjamin the 'esoteric' aspects of Romanticism had a particular fascination and relevance. Influenced by Judaic mysticism and the Kabbalah,[8] and by such marginal thinkers as the eighteenth-century anti-rationalist Johann Georg Hamann,[9] some of Benjamin's own earliest texts – most notably his impenetrable 1916 fragment, 'On Language as Such and on Human

Language' – speculate on the intricate connections between the act of divine creation and various orders of language: the creative word of God, which brings into being and suffuses the world; the original language of Adam, which names things according to divine intention; and the proliferation and confusion of human languages after the Fall.[10] For Benjamin, as for the Romantics, the view that external nature is inert material existing solely for human manipulation and exploitation is symptomatic of an impoverished human condition and inner nature, and of the failure to understand the genuine imperative for modern technology, which is, as Benjamin later insists in *Einbahnstrasse*, not the human control of nature, but control of humanity's *relationship* with nature.

Far from diminishing the critical potency of Romantic thought, such mystical tendencies formed its critical core. This is because – and it is absolutely crucial for Benjamin – early Romantic thought did not, unlike its later decadent manifestations, espouse and privilege forms of reactionary and irrationalist thinking: the cult of artistic genius, the mythical idolatry of nature, quasi- and pseudo-religious dogmas. Instead, early Romanticism combined an emphasis upon forms of mystical illumination and intuitive insight which were anathema to Enlightenment thought with an insistence upon critical rigour and sobriety that distinguished it from the irrationalism of more recent movements – in particular, the circle around the poet Stefan George (1868–1933), the so-called Georgekreis, a group with its own plan to recreate German criticism and culture. For Benjamin, the cool precision and lucidity which lent early Romantic writing such critical power stand in stark contrast to later, and even our own popular contemporary, understanding of 'Romanticism' as effusive emotionalism, sentimental pastoralism or self-indulgent nostalgia. Here the main purpose of Benjamin's doctoral dissertation becomes apparent: in recognizing early Romanticism as the ancestor of modern criticism, his study unmasked its many bastard offspring, and established a true heir in its rightful place: a new German criticism which captures the original iconoclastic impulses, critical energy and mystical insights of early Romanticism; a revitalized criticism which possesses 'infinite profundity and beauty in comparison to *all* late romanticism' (*COR*, p. 88); an immanent criticism which, concerned with unfolding the innermost tendencies of the work of art, is appropriate both to the artwork itself and to the changing circumstances in which it now exists.

This chapter provides an exposition of the main themes of Benjamin's doctoral dissertation. It takes as its point of departure Fichte's notion of reflection as an endless coming to consciousness of the self, and proceeds to indicate how the Romantics transposed this idea on to the domain of art. Criticism is to be conceived not as the recovery of some original authorial intention, but as an interpretative intervention in the afterlife of the artwork. Meaning is transformed and reconfigured as the artwork is read and understood in new contexts and historical constellations. As will become evident in this book, this notion of 'immanent criticism' lies at the very heart of Benjamin's work: not just his literary criticism, but also his studies of modern commodities, urban architectural forms and mass media. Benjamin's understanding of a number of key concepts in early Romanticism is then sketched – 'criticizability', ironic destruction, the *Gesamtkunstwerk*, allegory and monadology, and, above all, the sober, prosaic character of criticism – and their significance outlined.

After a brief consideration of Benjamin's proposed, but never published, journal *Angelus Novus*, the remainder of the chapter focuses on Benjamin's most notable attempt to utilize the critical tools developed in the dissertation and illustrate how they might facilitate a new, critical appreciation of literary texts. Provocatively, Benjamin selects a text by the greatest figure of German literary *Kultur* and of the traditional *Bildungsbürgertum*: Johann Wolfgang Goethe's *Wahlverwandschaften* (*Elective Affinities*). In this exemplary critique, Benjamin castigates the misappropriation of Goethe's work by the Georgekreis, and demonstrates how an immanent reading of the dialectical tensions in the narrative lead to a completely different – indeed antithetical – interpretation of the text. Far from celebrating the power of fate and mythical forces, Goethe's story extols resolute human action to overcome them. Benjamin goes on to argue that, in the death of one of the novel's central characters, Ottilie, Goethe's tale itself provides an allegorical figure of the process of immanent criticism – the demise of superficial appearances for the sake of an emerging truth. *Elective Affinities* thus anticipates its own immanent critique. In short, Benjamin not only wrests Goethe from the clutches of the Georgekreis and its irrationalist world-view, he also appropriates him for his own vision of criticism. Hence, it is not only in the writings of the early Romantics that Benjamin perceives the intimations of his own critical practice, but also in those of Goethe. One could claim no more illustrious forebear than this.

Reflection in Fichte and early Romanticism

Concerned with establishing the 'epistemological presuppositions' (*SW*1, p. 116) of the Romantic concept of criticism, Benjamin's dissertation identifies the fundamental German idealist category of 'reflection' as 'Schlegel's basic epistemological conception' (*SW*1, p. 120).[11] This is 'the most frequent "type" in the thought of the early Romantics' (*SW*1, p. 121) and 'the style of thinking in which . . . the romantics expressed their deepest insights' (*SW*1, p. 121). More precisely, Schlegel's concept of criticism involved a particular interpretation and reformulation of Fichte's insights, expounded in his 1794 *Über den Begriff der Wissenschaftslehre oder der sogenannten Philosophie*, as the subject's coming to self-consciousness through reflection.[12] For Fichte, it is through the process or medium of reflection that the 'subject', the 'I' or 'ego', is constituted and reconstituted through time. The individual subject thinks about and reflects upon itself, comes to know itself, and through this new awareness of self is changed. The subject is in a perpetual process of coming to know itself and of modification. For Fichte, the subject is not a fixed or static entity, but is formed and transformed through the act of the 'I' reflecting upon the 'I', and in so doing, moving to an ever higher state of self-consciousness.

This vision of the constitution of the self through reflection has a number of consequences. First, the 'self' is not something which exists independently of the reflecting 'I'; it is not a pre-formed 'thing' patiently awaiting exploration, but, as the product of the activity of reflection, is itself an activity. The self is a product of reflection, rather than reflection being a consequence of self; in short, 'reflection is logically the first and primary' (*SW*1, p. 134). Secondly, in reflection the distinction between the subject and object of knowledge is dissolved. The 'I' is both subject and object of knowledge. It is the subject/object of knowledge. Finally, this reflection is 'an infinite process' (*SW*1, p. 125), an endless becoming of the self, an endless becoming of knowledge of the self, the processual and incremental elevation of the self-consciousness of the subject. Benjamin cites Fichte thus: ' "Thus we shall continue, *ad infinitum*, to require a new consciousness for every consciousness, a new consciousness whose object is the earlier consciousness, and thus we shall never reach the point of being able to assume an actual consciousness" ' (*SW*1, p. 125). He then comments: 'Fichte makes this argument no less than three times here in order to come to the conclusion on each occasion that, on the basis of this limitlessness of reflection, "consciousness remains inconceivable to us"' (*SW1*, p. 125). Self-consciousness is both immediate knowledge, mediated by reflection, and ever elusive. For Benjamin, this paradox of reflection forms the epistemological basis of Romantic thought.[13]

Fichte sought to circumvent the problem of 'an endless and empty process' (*SW1*, p. 126) of reflection by positing the immediacy of knowledge through the terminus of an 'absolute I'. By contrast, the Romantics had no wish to eliminate the infinity of reflection, but made it the basis of their understanding.[14] Reflection for them was not to be understood as the activity of an individual subject, or located within an individual consciousness, a cognitive 'I' engaged in an endless and futile pursuit of a definitive self-consciousness. Rather, reflection is the critical medium in which art recognizes and (re)constitutes itself. The individual work of art unfolds itself and comes to reveal its innermost tendencies *in*, rather than *through*, reflection; for the medium of reflection is art itself.[15] Just as the 'I' was both subject and object of reflection for Fichte, so art is both subject and object of reflection for the Romantics. In reflection, the meaning of the work of art yields its meaning and significance with ever-greater clarity. Whereas for Fichte, reflection brings with it ever increasing self-consciousness in the subject, for the Romantics, the work of art realizes itself ever more fully through reflection in the medium of art. The work of art, like Fichte's subject, is in an endless state of becoming. Schlegel writes: 'the romantic type of poetry is still in a state of becoming; indeed, that is its true essence – forever to become, never to be complete' (cited in McCole, 1993, p. 103). Infinite incompletion is not a problem to be overcome by arbitrary foreclosure, but is rather the essence of art itself.

Through reflection, the individual work of art neither seeks nor attains completion, but rather fulfils itself in dissolving itself. As the work of art is unfolded through reflection, it comes to point beyond itself, to suggest and disclose its relationship with all other artworks. Reflection in the medium of art ultimately reveals the contiguity and interconnectedness of all works of art, a continuum composed of all individual examples, genres and forms: namely, the Idea of Art. In reflection, the individual work of art reveals itself as nothing other than a fragment of the Idea of Art. The individual artwork is like a knot, which, once it has been carefully untied, appears as part of a continuum. Reflection unravels the borders of a work of art, dissolving it into the 'Absolute'. The 'Absolute' is nothing other than the processual dissolution of all works of art into the Idea of Art.

Immanent criticism

In Benjamin's view, the early Romantics' understanding of reflection has a number of important consequences for their concept of art criticism. First, it means the centrality of immanent critique: the work of criticism must be in closest accord with the work of art which is its object. Secondly, it envisages the work of art as a monadological fragment of the Idea of Art, as a minute part of a greater whole into which it is ultimately to be dissolved. Thirdly, it requires the objective 'positivity' of criticism, as opposed to the subjectivity of judgement. The task of criticism is the elevation of the genuine work of art, not the determination of, and distinction between, 'good' and 'bad' art. For the Romantics, 'bad art' is simply impervious or insensitive to criticism, and therefore does not take its place in the Idea of Art. 'Bad art' is not art: it is to be subjected to ironic destruction rather than critical dissolution. Lastly, it means an insistence upon the sobriety of prose as the constitutive principle of the Idea of Art.

For Benjamin, the early Romantics' concept of criticism is nothing other than the moment of 'reflection in the medium of art' (*SW1*, p. 134) in which knowledge of the artwork is extended.[16] Immanent criticism seeks to awaken the tendencies and potentialities which lie dormant within the work of art. It involves an 'intensification of consciousness' (*SW1*, p. 152), an ever-greater realization of the actual meaning of a work of art. It is not the task of the critic to second-guess the purposes and motives of the author, poet or artist; the latter do not possess privileged insight into the significance of their works, and it would be folly simply to accept their own self-appraisals and estimations. Rather, the critic seeks to bring to light the secret of the artwork, its inherent but hidden possibilities, which elude the author because they manifest themselves only later under different circumstances. Meanings emerge (and disappear again) posthumously, during the 'stage of continued life' (*ILL*, p. 70) of the artwork, its 'afterlife'. Criticism is the immanent illumination and actualization of the artwork in the present moment of reading.

Benjamin's later work on the poet Charles Baudelaire (see chapter 7) provides a useful example of this rejection of authorial intention. For Benjamin, Baudelaire is the allegorical lyricist *par excellence* of Parisian life in the 'era of high capitalism'. His poetry and prose express a series of contradictions: the intense pleasure and melancholy longing of the modern metropolitan environment, the alluring yet ruinous character of the commodity form, the frisson and fears generated by the urban crowd, and the attempt to give enduring form to the most ephemeral phenomena. Baudelaire's writings give *expression* to these things because he was himself immersed in the phantasmagoria of Paris, the grand illusions and self-deceptions of the Second Empire. This is not necessarily to say that Baudelaire consciously and directly engages with such themes as his principal subject matter (Benjamin admits that the crowd, for instance, rarely figures in Baudelaire's poetry); and it certainly does not mean that Baudelaire offered any particularly insightful socio-historical analysis of his own into such things. In short, Benjamin is not interested in establishing exactly what Baudelaire thought he was doing when he penned his texts, but is concerned instead with the significance of these writings, their 'truth content', when viewed from the perspective of his own time: as documents which give voice to the dreamworld of nineteenth-century capitalist modernity and the transformation of metropolitan culture and experience. Immanent critique thus opens up the possibility of – indeed becomes the imperative for – reading literary texts and other cultural phenomena against, rather than with, the authorial 'grain'. Such texts present themselves for ever-new interrogations, ever-new interpolations. Moreover, this kind of criticism begins to situate both text and reader historically. Such is Benjamin's interpretation of Baudelaire then; but we will have another now, dependent upon our interests, concerns and understandings. Our reading of Baudelaire will be different from Benjamin's if for no other reason than the fact that we must take Benjamin's interpretation into account. Hence, criticism is the continuing, productive and processual revelation and actualization not only of the truths inherent in a work of art, but also of the historical reception of the artwork which filters and colours it for the current reader as well.

For Benjamin, immanent criticism is a 'philological' (*SW1*, p. 151) or 'historical experiment' (*SW1*, p. 178) on the work of art, which 'exposes its inner nature' (*COR*, p. 84) so that 'it is brought to consciousness and to knowledge of itself' (*SW1*, p. 151). This notion of the 'self-knowledge' and 'self-judgement' (*SW1*, p. 151) of the artwork is fundamental. A central feature of the Romantic concept of criticism, for Benjamin, was its rejection of the subject–object relation.[17] The critic does not scrutinize the artwork in order to pass arbitrary judgement upon it. Rather he or she is an observer who shares in the self-knowledge of the work of art released through the critical experiment, like a scientist monitoring and recording a chemical reaction.[18] Benjamin writes:

> Experiment consists in the evocation of self-consciousness and self-knowledge in the things observed. To observe a thing means only to arouse it to self-recognition. Whether an experiment succeeds depends on the extent to which the experimenter is capable, through the heightening of his own consciousness, through magical observation . . . of getting nearer to the object and of finally drawing it into himself. (*SW1*, p. 148)[19]

In the genuine experiment, 'there is in fact no knowledge of an object by a subject' (*SW1*, p. 146), because in the process of reflection subject and object are, as we have seen, one and the same. Indeed, preservation of the subject–object distinction comes to designate precisely the failure of the critic to participate in the self-knowledge of the work of art, the inability to assimilate this self-knowledge to his or her own.

For immanent criticism to call forth the self-knowledge of the work of art successfully, it must be continuously in accord with it, corresponding and responding to its changing nuances.[20] Criticism must be as fluid as the ever-changing work of art itself.[21] Moreover, as the work of art is unfolded only through the medium of art, criticism itself must partake of the sphere of art, must itself be a work of art. Benjamin writes: 'the Romantics called for poetic criticism, suspending the difference between criticism and poetry and declaring: "Poetry can be criticised only through poetry. An aesthetic judgement that is not itself a work of art . . . has no rights of citizenship in the realm of art".' (*SW1*, p. 154). Criticism is an infinite process of supplementation so as to '"present the representation anew . . . form what is already formed . . . complement,[22] rejuvenate, newly fashion the work"' (*SW1*, p. 154). Novalis expresses this succinctly: '"The true reader must be the extended author"' (*SW1*, p. 153). Criticism as a perpetual reconfiguration, as a mode of ceaseless becoming, constitutes the basis of the afterlife of the work of art.

Such 'extended authorship' leads not so much to the 'completion' of the work of art but, paradoxically, to its dissolution. In its continual self-realization through critical reflection, the artwork comes to transgress its own limitations as a solitary, isolated entity. The work comes to point beyond itself, to recognize its relationships with, and proximity to, other works, genres and forms. As the artwork increases in self-knowledge, in criticism its boundaries are gently eroded and rendered permeable. It merges into the continuum of the Idea of Art, of which it is but one particular instance. There are two important concepts here: the Idea of Art as *Gesamtkunstwerk*, and the individual work of art as monad.

The Romantics see art as a unity or totality of all works of art, as the Absolute, or the Idea of Art. Schlegel hence describes the purpose of Romantic poetics and criticism as:

> 'to reunite all the separate genres of poetry . . . It embraces everything so long as it is poetic, from the greatest systems of art that contain in themselves still other systems, to the sigh, the kiss that the musing child breathes out in artless song. . . . The Romantic genus of poetry is the only one that is more than genus and is, so to speak, poetry itself.' (*SW1*, p. 166)

Schlegel develops this view further in the mystical thesis that all artworks 'conjoin' to compose a single, all-encompassing organic whole, that 'art itself is one work' (*SW1*, p. 167).[23] The Idea of Art here becomes the total work of art, the *Gesamtkunstwerk*, which is both constituted by and constitutes individual works of art.[24] The individual work of art is simply a particular moment, a concrete manifestation, an indicative fragment of the *Gesamtkunstwerk*.[25] Each individual work of art is thus nothing other than a monad in which the Idea of Art is encapsulated and from which it may be distilled. Criticism simultaneously recognizes the Idea of Art as it is refracted in the monadological fragments of the *Gesamtkunstwerk*, and 'completes' them by assimilation in this totality. In 'completing'/dissolving the individual work of art, criticism adds to, and further 'completes', the *Gesamtkunstwerk*. It is thus in the medium of criticism that both the endless process of 'completion' of the individual work of art and the ceaseless becoming of the *Gesamtkunstwerk* occur.

For the Romantics, criticism does not judge the work of art – indeed, it is the very deferral of judgement, its infinite postponement. Whereas judgement seeks to establish and impose external measures and evaluations according to supposedly immutable and eternal aesthetic criteria, the Romantics recognized 'the impossibility of a positive scale of values', and insisted upon 'the principle of the uncriticizablity of inferior work' (*SW1*, p. 159). Romantic criticism distinguishes itself by its 'complete positivity' (*SW1*, p. 152). There was to be no criticism of the bad, for the bad is simply that which is uncriticizable, that which cannot be unfolded because it simply does not partake of the Idea of Art. Thus, for the Romantics there are no bad works of art. Either an artefact is a work of art, in which case it lends itself to criticism, or it is not, in which case it does not. For the Romantics, 'the value of a work depends solely on whether it makes its immanent critique possible or not' (*SW1*, p. 159). The artwork's openness to criticism, its very criticizability, thus 'demonstrates on its own the positive value judgement made concerning it' (*SW1*, p. 160). By contrast, the bad, the phoney or pseudo work of art does not lend itself to critical unfolding, but can only be destroyed through irony, through the withering howl of scornful laughter.[26]

Whether the elevation of works of art through immanent unfolding, or the 'annihilation of the nugatory' (*SW1*, p. 178) through corrosive satire, it is ultimately the prose of the critic that is at the core of Romantic thought.[27] It is only in critical prose that the poetic work of art is reflected, brought to self-consciousness and dissolved into the Idea of Art, that the *Gesamtkunstwerk* is infinitely reconstituted. Hence, though it may appear paradoxical, the Romantics came to see prose rather than 'poetic' writing itself as the fundamental basis or 'creative ground' (*SW1*, p. 174) of the 'idea of the poetry' (*SW1*, p. 174), the Idea of Art. For Benjamin, 'The conception of the idea of poetry as that of prose determines the whole Romantic philosophy of art' (*SW1*, p. 175) and points unequivocally to the critical sobriety and austerity of the Romantics' thinking.[28] He is critical of the misappropriation of the term 'Romanticism' and its degeneration at the hands of subsequent writers. Romantic thought is not to be equated with the ecstatic raptures of the poetic genius,[29] or with the mythological idolatry of nature, or with 'the depraved and directionless practice of contemporary art criticism' (*GS* I, p. 708).[30] Romanticism is firmly anchored in the crystal clarity of prose: 'In ordinary usage, the prosaic . . . is, to be sure, a familiar metaphorical designation of the sober. As a thoughtful and collected posture, reflection is the antithesis of ecstasy' (*SW1*, p. 175).

Benjamin's study is an intervention in the reception of Romanticism, an attempt to disturb its own hitherto treacherous afterlife by unfolding what he sees as its true, radical character. Immanent critique, not irrational bombast, is the early Romantics' 'decisive methodological innovation' (McCole, 1993, p. 89) and their fundamental critical legacy. His study thus constitutes an exemplary immanent critique of early Romanticism, and of immanent criticism itself. For Benjamin, 'to get to the heart of romanticism' (*COR*, p. 139) meant to redeem its endangered radical and mystical impulses for the present.

Benjamin and Romanticism

Benjamin's engagement with the work of the early Romantics was his 'decisive intellectual encounter during the war years' (McCole, 1993, p. 81) and had a profound and enduring impact upon his subsequent writings. In purging Romanticism of its later decadent manifestations and modern misconceptions, Benjamin appropriates and critically reworks some of its key insights and motifs:

Meaning as a contemporary construct   The Romantics' view that the 'object' of inquiry is not 'discovered' but constituted in the moment of perception or reflection has a particular resonance in Benjamin's later thought. Novalis observes:

> 'Only now is antiquity starting to arise. . . . It is the same with classical literature as with antiquity. It is not actually given to us – it is not already there; rather, it must first be produced by us. A classical literature arises for us only through diligent and spirited study of the ancients – a classical literature such as the ancients themselves did not possess.' (*SW1*, p. 182)

'Antiquity' and 'classical literature' are historical constructs, generated by the interpretations and interpolations of the present. The image of the past is formed only in the moment of present recognition,[31] through the interaction of what was and what is. In short, we are never concerned with the past *per se*, but with how the past appears in the present, with its contemporary significance. Indefinite and indeterminate, the past is ever open to (re)construction, (re)appropriation and contestation. Such an understanding becomes the key to the historiographical and epistemological principles pioneered in Convolute N of Benjamin's *Passagenarbeit* and elaborated in the 'Theses on the Concept of History'.

'Silent' criticism   Immanent critique seeks to unfold the innermost tendencies and truths of the artwork from within, to allow it to

know and speak for itself. The critic abstains from overarching commentary, so as to 'become the medium for the work's unfolding' (McCole, 1993, p. 93). This erasure of the critic's voice becomes an essential principle for Benjamin, and explains his later emphasis upon the use of quotation and his concern to achieve the greatest 'facticity' and 'concreteness'. Most significantly, it accounts in part for Benjamin's subsequent fascination with imagistic forms of representation – in the mosaic, the constellation and montage, meaning is generated in the juxtaposing of individual fragments, rather than in theoretical overlay. The 'silent' critic 'shows' in the skilful act of construction.

The contingency and transience of truth   Truth is not pursued and grasped by an intentional subject, but unfolded from within under the patient critical gaze. This notion of the observer as a recipient of that which is disclosed becomes an important motif for Benjamin, particularly in his later fascination with the Proustian *mémoire involontaire*. Truth appears only, like a memory, unbidden. Moreover, the moment of such recognition is always transient. Given its endless and perpetual transformation, the past, or the artwork, is perceptible and legible only fleetingly.[32] Truth is encountered *en passant*; critical insight is possible only in the instant in which this motion is momentarily frozen.[33] Criticism thus both facilitates and interrupts the becoming of the work of art, catching it in flight. Truth is only ever an ephemeral apparition – a motif that is of profound significance for Benjamin's later writings (see chapter 7).

This moment of passing recognition is that in which the work of art comes to reveal itself as a fragment of the Idea of Art: namely, at the instant of its final dissolution and absorption. Truth appears at the *last* moment, as the object or work of art is about to disintegrate. The demise of the object is the precondition for the liberation of its inherent truth content. The 'completion' of the work of art paradoxically occurs at the moment of its extinction. Immanent criticism here becomes the ruination, or 'mortification', of the artwork – a fundamental insight which came to underpin both the *Trauerspiel* study and the *Passagenarbeit*.

It is here that an important paradox appears, both in the Romantic notion of immanent criticism and in Benjamin's appropriation and reworking of it. The object of criticism is a construction, the product of a purposive act of critical engagement between, or dialectical interplay of, present interests and past phenomena, critic and artwork. This construction, however, is intended precisely to permit the supposedly *intentionless* (self-)disclosure of the truth of the object. In other words, the truth of the work of art is both constructed and discovered by the critic. Immanent criticism, then, privileges neither the object (the artwork) nor the subject (the critic); or rather, it privileges both. For the Romantics and for Benjamin, this 'problem' is pre-empted or circumvented by dissolving the subject–object distinction altogether – the critic simply facilitates and partakes of the *self-knowledge* of the artwork. Nevertheless, it is a tension which is unresolved – indeed, one which, articulated in terms of the figure of the 'engineer' (the principle of construction) and the notion of 'afterlife' (the principle of decomposition and disclosure) lies at the heart of Benjamin's work, and indeed of this book.

The monadological fragment   The fragment, the individual work, is a monad,[34] one which points beyond itself, comes to stand for, or stand in for, the totality of which it is a part. What is present is incomplete, apparently trivial; what is complete is absent, unrepresentable except through the trivial. This paradox frames the ambiguous status of the monadological fragment: it is derided and prized in the same moment. Above all, the fragment serves as a sign for or, more precisely, becomes an allegorical representation of, the infinite. Schlegel writes: ' "in short, allegory is the tendency towards the absolute in the finite itself. As allegory the individual element exceeds itself in the direction of the infinite" ' (cited in Frank, 1989, p. 291). Allegory is thus an ' "intimation of the infinite . . . the outlook upon the same" ' (cited in Frank, 1989, p. 294). As an allegory, the finite, empirical moment or work is the only possible access to, and representation of, the infinite and hence unrepresentable idea.[35] Hence, for the Romantics, allegory is not to be understood as a crude or mechanical literary device, inferior to the majestic and mystical symbol, but is rather to be prized above all.[36] For Benjamin, it is thus not only their understanding of immanent criticism that distinguishes the early Romantics, but also their appreciation of the allegorical, monadological fragment as the most humble, yet most important intimation of the elusive divine.[37]

From *Angelus Novus* to *Elective Affinities*

Benjamin's subsequent attempts to elaborate and exemplify the critical principles developed in his doctoral dissertation experienced mixed fortunes. His hopes of becoming the editor of his own literary journal, the perfect forum in which to publish and encourage such work, were thwarted. His essay on Goethe's *Wahlverwandtschaften* (*Elective Affinities*) met a kinder fate, receiving fulsome critical praise, and eventually appearing in what Benjamin described as 'the most exclusive of our journals' (*COR*, p. 237). This boost to his academic reputation was to be short-lived, however. In 1925 he was obliged to withdraw his *Habilitationsschrift* after his examiners at Frankfurt University greeted it with incomprehension and threatened him with the humiliation of rejection.

In a letter to Scholem from Heidelberg of 4 August 1921 Benjamin wrote: 'I have my own journal. Starting the first of January next year I will be publishing it through Weissbach. . . . [I]t will have a very narrow, closed circle of contributors. I want to discuss everything with you in person, and will now tell you only its name, *Angelus Novus*' (*COR*, p. 186).[38] He further noted his hope 'to arrive in Berlin at the beginning of October with the materials on the basis of which I can put most of the journal together for an entire year (four issues, one hundred and twenty pages each)' (*COR*, p. 186). On 4 October 1921 Benjamin informed Scholem that 'The first issue is slowly taking shape' (*COR*, p. 189), and a month later (8 November 1921) was able to specify its principal contents.[39]

Benjamin envisaged *Angelus Novus* as a critical, timely engagement with the prevailing condition of German letters and thought. It was to have both positive and negative moments. On the one hand, it was to be a forum for fostering writings which exemplified and accorded with the literary principles he had developed through his engagement with Romanticism. Benjamin emphasizes the importance of immanent critique for the journal: 'the function of great criticism is not, as is often thought, to instruct by means of historical descriptions or to educate through comparisons, but to cognize by immersing itself in the object. Criticism must account for the truth of works' (*SW1*, p. 293). On the other hand, the journal would provide an opportunity for the destruction of the bad through irony: 'spiritualist occultism, political obscurantism, and Catholic expressionism will be encountered in these pages only as the targets of unsparing criticism' (*SW1*, p. 295). Through presentation of exemplary criticism and denunciation of the spurious, the journal would 'restore criticism to its former strength' and 'proclaim the spirit of its age' (*SW1*, p. 293).[40] Moreover, it would register the true character of the contemporary, by 'distilling what is truly relevant from the sterile pageant of fashionable events, the exploitation of which can be left to the newspapers' (*SW*1, p. 293). This concern with identifying the truth amid the transient provided Benjamin with his title:

> according to a legend in the Talmud, the angels – who are born anew every instant in countless numbers – are created only to perish and to vanish into the void, once they have sung their hymn in the presence of God. It is to be hoped that the name of the journal will guarantee its contemporary relevance, which is the only true sort. (*SW*1, p. 296)

Sadly, *Angelus Novus* was never to make even this brief appearance. On 1 October 1922 Benjamin informed Scholem that Weissbach had decided to 'suspend temporarily the setting up of the *Angelus*' because he had been asked to pay a large advance for it. Benjamin was under no illusion as to the meaning of this. The journal was not to be, and he sadly confesses that 'the editor's throne of honor in my heart is empty' (*COR*, p. 200).[41]

Benjamin's critical exploration of Goethe's *Wahlverwandtschaften* was written against the background of this debacle, between the summer of 1921 and February 1922. His study drew together themes from a number of earlier fragments, most notably a five-page sketch dated 1917 of a critical review of Friedrich Gundolf's 1916 book *Goethe*.[42] Gundolf was a member of the Georgekreis,[43] a group whose vision of the cultic elevation and adoration of the poet as inspired genius was an exemplary instance of the artistic self-indulgence and narcissism from which Benjamin sought to redeem the true critical spirit of early Romanticism. Although Gundolf is the target specified in the essay, Benjamin uses him primarily as an exemplary figure for the ideas of Georgekreis and, in particular, Roberts (1982, pp. 104–5) claims, as a substitute for Ludwig Klages (1872–1956), the group's leading thinker, whom Benjamin regarded too highly to attack directly. The 'symbolism' expounded by the Georgekreis envisaged the world of nature as a daemonic realm of mythic symbols and fateful correspondences whose meaning, eluding the rational mind, may be apprehended only in intuition, mystical insight or poetic rapture. The Georgekreis scorned what they saw as the anaemic language and enfeebling consequences of modern civilization and reason,[44] and sought instead the spiritual renewal of German culture through the development of a pure poetic language which would celebrate the vitality and vigour of natural life, the potency of drives and compulsions, and the power of mythic forces. As McCole points out, 'George and his circle stood for a revival of myth and a frankly pagan poetic ideal' (1993, p. 79), embracing aestheticism and the fervent worship of the heroic poetic genius by a martial brotherhood grandly conceived in the image of the Templars.[45] Such views were anathema to Benjamin, given his understanding of both the sobriety of Romantic criticism and the purity and orderliness of Adamic language. In his view, Gundolf's attempt to appropriate and locate Goethe as poetic genius within the mythic world-view of the Georgekreis resulted in 'a formulation that is distinguished from the mentality of a fortune-cookie motto only by the bloodthirsty mysticism of its wording' (*SW1*, p. 326). Benjamin's study of *Elective Affinities* had a threefold purpose: to expose the erroneous thinking of the Georgekreis; to demonstrate the power and lucidity of his own critical practice; and to reclaim Goethe's work from, on the one hand, the excesses of the irrationalists, and, on the other, the tedious mediocrity of conservative, bourgeois scholarship. It was thus to be a model of the withering annihilation of the shoddy (Gundolf's criticism) through irony, of the unfolding of the innermost tendencies of the genuine artwork (Goethe's novel) through immanent critique, and of the radical (re)appropriation and actualization of cultural texts.

Benjamin's *Wahlverwandtschaften* study was planned as an 'exemplary piece of criticism' (*COR*, p. 194) for inclusion in the *Angelus Novus*. Hence the journal's failure left it homeless. Through the intercession of his friend Florens Christian Rang, however, the essay came to the attention of the writer Hugo von Hofmannsthal, who, while ironically an associate of the Georgekreis and a contributor to its journal, the *Blätter für die Kunst* (published 1892–1919), expressed his 'boundless admiration'[46] and enthusiasm for it in a letter to Rang of 21 November 1923.[47] Much to Benjamin's delight, the study appeared in two instalments (April 1924 and January 1925) in Hofmannsthal's own journal, the *Neue deutsche Beiträge*. In a letter of 5 March 1924, Benjamin expressed his satisfaction with these arrangements and how they might add to the essay's impact:

> From an author's point of view, this mode of publication in the most exclusive of our journals by far is absolutely invaluable. . . . [T]his is just the right outlet for my attack on the ideology of George and his disciples. If they should find it difficult to ignore this invective,[48] it may well be due to the uniqueness of this outlet. (*COR*, p. 237)

The 'New Angel' had vanished, but Benjamin's intellectual ambitions had not disappeared with it. Rather, they had found the firmer footing provided by Hofmannsthal's prestigious journal: an exemplary publication for Benjamin's own 'exemplary piece of criticism' (*COR*, p. 194).

Exemplary criticism

Written in 1808–9, Goethe's novel derives its strange nomenclature from a term then used in chemistry to refer to the readiness (or reluctance) of chemical elements to interact with one another and form compounds. As one of the central characters helpfully explains, ' "Those natures which, when they meet, quickly lay hold on and mutually affect one another we call affined" ' (Goethe, 1971, p. 52). Whereas some substances appear to avoid contact, others ' "most decidedly seek and embrace one another, modify one another, and together form a new substance" ' (Goethe, 1971, pp. 52–3). Goethe's story dramatizes this chemical theory of attraction with respect to human relationships. It is concerned with the complications and misfortunes which occur when Charlotte and Eduard, a seemingly happily married couple residing in comfortable idleness on their extensive rural estate, decide to invite, first, Eduard's friend (the Captain) and then Charlotte's niece (Ottilie) to stay with them. As human 'elective affinities' take hold, companionships give way to ill-omened romantic entanglements between Charlotte and the Captain, and between Eduard and Ottilie. Recognizing the danger of these attachments, Charlotte and the Captain renounce their love, and he promptly leaves the estate. Charlotte, now pregnant by Eduard, insists on a similar act of sacrifice from her reluctant husband; but this results instead in *his* departure from the house, on the understanding that Ottilie be allowed to remain in Charlotte's care. Charlotte gives birth to a baby boy, and Eduard finally returns, having distinguished himself in military service. With their love untempered, and a divorce inevitable, all seems set for Eduard and Ottilie's union until a boating accident occurs in which the infant drowns while in Ottilie's care. This misfortune is taken by Ottilie as a sign of the sinfulness of her romance with Eduard. Renouncing her love for him, she withdraws into silent isolation and eventually dies. Her place of burial becomes a shrine for the local villagers, who are astonished by the miraculous healing powers afforded by touching Ottilie's body and funeral dress. Eduard dies soon afterwards and is buried, at Charlotte's behest, next to Ottilie. The story concludes with the dead lovers lying side by side awaiting the day of resurrection: 'what a happy moment it will be when one day they awaken again together' (Goethe, 1971, p. 300).

Written in three parts, each subdivided into three sections, Benjamin's critical essay is constructed as an exemplary model of dialectical thought.[49] 'Part One, The Mythic as Thesis,' outlines his critical concepts, and rejects the obvious interpretation of the novel as a critical – and, for its time, scandalous – disquisition on morality and the institution of marriage. Benjamin insists, however, that 'Marriage can in no sense be the center of the novel' (*SW1*, p. 346). Nor should it be understood within some simplistic biographical or pseudo-psychological perspective as the mere thematization and dramatization of Goethe's own marital problems and romantic complications of the time.

'Part Two, Redemption as Antithesis' considers the reception of Goethe's novel, and focuses upon what Benjamin regards as Gundolf's erroneous interpretation of the story. Far from being, as the Georgekreis would have it, a celebration of the violence of mythic forces and the triumph of tragic fate, Benjamin contends that the story extols and exhorts decisive, courageous human action in the face of danger as the *overcoming* of mythic powers. Appropriately, his argument hinges on what initially seems a rather insignificant part of the story: namely a tale (or novella) within the novel recounted by one of the minor characters, 'The Wayward Young Neighbours'.[50] The reckless daring and successful love of the characters in this tale serve as a counterpoint to the inaction and fatalistic resignation which distinguish the figures in the main narrative.

'Part Three, Hope as Synthesis' explores the significance of Ottilie's death. Her passing, Benjamin suggests, represents the death of beauty, the demise of beautiful appearance, which is the precondition for both the recognition of truth and reconciliation in God. The *Wahlverwandtschaften* is only superficially a story about the conflict between love and marital conventions, which, to borrow Benjamin's language, constitutes only a veil through which, in time, one can discern the genuine significance of the story. It is a disquisition upon, and representation of, the relationships between beauty and truth, and death and the hope of salvation. Hence, Benjamin argues, *Elective Affinities* possesses a distinctive reflexive quality: it is an artwork which reflects upon the domain of aesthetics, an Idea of which it is but one monadological fragment.

Benjamin's study exemplified the concept of criticism which he had elaborated in his doctoral dissertation. Criticism is to move beyond conventional interpretations of the work of art, which deal merely with its subject matter (its 'material content') in order to unfold its hidden meaning (its 'truth content'). According to Benjamin, this distinction between 'material' and 'truth content' corresponds to different levels of analysis: commentary and criticism:

> Critique seeks the truth content of a work of art; commentary its material content. The relation between the two is determined by that basic law of literature according to which the more significant the work, the more inconspicuously and intimately its truth content is bound up with material content. (*SW1*, p. 297)

The material content perceived by the commentator should not obscure the truth content which discloses itself only to the persistent, perceptive critic. The genuine critic of Goethe's novel, for instance, recognizes that 'The subject of *Elective Affinities* is not marriage' (*SW1*, p. 302). Such an insight into the individual work of art may not be available to its contemporary critics,[51] however, and may certainly elude the actual author him or herself.[52] The thoughts of the author and of contemporary critics are significant only as stations of reflection in the unfolding of the artwork's truth content. It is only in the course of time, and through this ongoing process of critical reflection, that the truth content is coaxed, as it were, from its hiding place into the light of recognition. Truth content is visible only under certain circumstances, and at particular historical moments.[53] Benjamin writes:

> The concrete realities rise up before the eyes of the beholder all the more distinctly the more they die out in the world. With this, however, to judge by appearances, the material content and the truth content, united at the beginning of a work's history, set themselves apart from each other in the course of its duration, because the truth content always remains to the same extent hidden as the material content comes to the fore. (*SW1*, p. 297)

This is an important passage in two respects. First, the distinction between material and truth content is connected with the notion of a palimpsest, the mystical conception of a text or series of texts hidden beneath or within another. Benjamin writes of the critic: 'One may compare him to a paleographer in front of a parchment whose faded text is covered by the lineaments of a more powerful script which refers to that text. As the paleographer would have to begin by reading the latter script, the critic would have to begin with commentary' (*SW*1, pp. 297–8). Layers of earlier criticism and interpretation adhere to the work of art itself, partially revealing it, partially obscuring it. The contemporary critic must work backwards from the most recent of these textual layers. Criticism is a contemporary moment of reflection not only of the work of art, but also of the series of critical reflections to which it has already been subject, its entire afterlife.

Secondly, although material content and truth content may initially appear irrevocably coupled, this bond disintegrates through time and through criticism. The historical process of decomposition fractures surface layers to disclose the truth beneath them. Criticism is the 'mortification', as Benjamin later terms it, of the work of art so as to permit the redemption of its truth content. Critical destruction of the artwork is simultaneously and paradoxically the moment of its completion, of its assimilation into the Idea of Art.[54] Appropriately, Benjamin formulates this with respect to the metaphor of a chemical experiment:

> If, to use a simile, one views the growing work as a burning funeral pyre, then the commentator stands before it like a chemist, the critic like an alchemist. Whereas, for the former, wood and ash remain the sole objects of his analysis, for the latter only the flame itself preserves an enigma: that of what is alive. Thus, the critic inquires into the truth, whose living flame continues to burn over the heavy logs of what is past and the light ashes of what has been experienced. (*SW*1, p. 298)

The afterlife of the work of art culminates in a fleeting, incendiary moment of illumination and transcendence.

In revealing the truth content of *Elective Affinities*, Benjamin sought both to save Goethe from the muddled thinking of Gundolf and to demonstrate the power and precision of sober Romantic criticism. His interrogation of Gundolf's text was to be scrupulous and merciless,[55] with the verdict clear from the outset: 'The legally binding condemnation and execution of Friedrich Gundolf will take place in this essay' (*COR*, p. 196).[56] Gundolf was guilty on two main counts: misreading the book and misappropriating its author.[57] Gundolf envisaged Goethe as a heroic, creative genius, and interpreted the *Elective Affinities* as a celebration of the omnipotence of mythic forces. Writer and text were thereby transformed by Gundolf into exemplary instances of the 'vitalist' George creed.

First, for Gundolf, in accordance with the precepts of the Georgekreis, the work of art is to be regarded as the outpourings of a poetic genius. The poet is one who possesses extraordinary artistic gifts, rare talents and insights which set him or her apart from ordinary mortals. The artist as hero is fated to wrestle with these immense, yet uncontrollable, 'creative' powers throughout his or her tortured life, and to bring forth from deep within him or herself the inspired and sublime artworks of divine genius. For Benjamin, however, the poet is no 'creator' (*Schöpfer*); nor are his or her works 'creations'.[58] As Benjamin makes clear in his earlier 'On Language' fragment, Creation and the creative Word are exclusive to God. Creator and Creation, poet and artwork, correspond to different orders: divine and human. Creation, the divine inception of the cosmos and life *ex nihilo*, is complete, perfect and lasting truth. The work of art, fashioned by the poet from the Babel of fallen human language, is imperfect, ephemeral and subject to (mis)interpretation and (mis)appropriation. The poet does not create, but rather gives 'form' or 'structure' to language, and thereby produces meaning.[59] This work of giving form also distinguishes the poet from the 'hero' of myth. Whereas the latter is resolute in his clear-sighted confrontation with fate, the poet has no such clarity in his struggle to render the work of art.[60] Benjamin's later description of Charles Baudelaire is apt: 'Baudelaire battled the crowd – with the impotent rage of someone fighting the rain or the wind' (*CB*, p. 154).

Envisioning the poet as a heroic creative genius has important ramifications for understanding the task of the contemporary critic; for then the meaning of the artwork is to be found solely in the artistic intention. It can therefore only be explained with respect to the life of the poet, the supreme source of inspiration and only ground of critical understanding. Indeed, Gundolf seeks to collapse the life and works of the poet into each other, such that 'the life itself is seen as a work' (*SW1*, p. 325).[61] For Benjamin, to conflate the meaning of a text with its author's intention is to abandon criticism altogether. Gundolf's preoccupation with the biographical details of Goethe's life exemplifies his failure to recognize and pursue both the specific task of 'authentic biographism, as the archive containing the documents (by themselves undecodable) of this existence' (*SW1*, p. 324), and the essential labour of the genuine critic – unfolding truth content. In confusing life and work, Gundolf provides clear insight into neither.[62] Benjamin concludes:

So triumphs the dogma which, having enchanted the work into life, now through no less a seductive error allows it, as life, to petrify back into work; and which purposes to grasp the much-vaunted 'form' of the poet as a hybrid of hero and creator, in whom nothing further can be distinguished yet about whom, with a show of profundity, anything can be affirmed. (*SW1*, p. 324)

Fate and character: novel and novella

The key to the 'vitalist' mythical cosmology was an idolatrous[63] vision of human abasement before the blind, omnipotent forces of compulsion, repetition and fate. Nature constituted a realm of portents and omens warning of calamitous future events. As Benjamin recognizes, the *Elective Affinities* is pervaded by uncanny coincidences and inauspicious signs which foretell the disaster which will befall the unwitting characters. The novel is suffused by what he terms a 'death symbolism' (*Todessymbolik*) rooted in the 'daemonic' character of nature.[64] Since all aspects of nature, all events and all circumstances can become possible omens of good or ill fortune, one becomes hopelessly lost in the infinite and impenetrable proliferation of ambiguous signs. The 'daemonic' refers to this illegible, inscrutable world of superstition and fear. The daemonic is the chaotic, anomalous condition of nature, a realm which eludes clear specification and defies human reason and understanding. As Benjamin points out, a troubling intimation of the daemonic accompanied Goethe from his childhood days onwards. He cites Goethe's autobiographical reflections thus:

'He [the young Goethe] believed that he perceived something in nature (whether living or lifeless, animate or inanimate) that manifested itself only in contradictions and therefore could not be expressed in any concept, much less in any word. It was not divine, for it seemed irrational; not human, for it had no intelligence; not diabolical, for it was beneficent; and not angelic because it often betrayed malice. . . . This essence, which appeared to infiltrate all the others . . . I called "daemonic".' (*SW1*, p. 316)

In the *Walhverwandtschaften*, the principal element of this sinister ambiguity, of death symbolism, is water. Cleansing, purifying, life-giving, water is also mysterious, unfathomable and murderously engulfing to the unwary. Beneath the inscrutable 'mirroring surface' of the still waters of the lake on which Ottilie sets out, lie the silent depths in which the baby will drown. Benjamin comments:

> Water as the chaotic element of life does not threaten here in desolate waves that sink a man; rather, it threatens in the enigmatic calm that lets him go to his ruin. To the extent that fate governs, the lovers go to their ruin. Where they spurn the blessing of firm ground, they succumb to the unfathomable. (*SW1*, p. 303)

This passage points both to Benjamin's rejection of Gundolf's interpretation and to his own argument regarding the *Wahlverwandtschaften*.

The image of the absence of solid ground, of the abyss, comes to define mythological thought for Benjamin. The mythic not only lacks ground, it also avoids grounding. He provides the following striking image of Gundolf's text (and the mythic) as 'a jungle where words swing themselves, like chattering monkeys, from branch to branch, from bombast to bombast, in order not to have to touch the ground which betrays the fact that they cannot stand: that is, the ground of logos, where they ought to stand and give an account of themselves' (*SW1*, pp. 326–7).

Moreover, the novel is crucially not a paean to the awesome and uncontrollable powers of nature and myth. Still waters, not turbulent waves, are to prove most deadly. Goethe's novel does not celebrate omnipotent natural powers, but rather explores the struggle between human self-determination and mythical compulsion, between resolute action in the face of danger and meek resignation before the forces of fate.[65] Such powers hold sway only when they remain unheeded, uncontested by human beings lulled into apathetic acquiescence or frozen in fearful indecision. The failure to act leads to catastrophe. Far from celebrating blind natural forces, Goethe exhorts humans to struggle against the daemonic.

Benjamin's argument here draws on the contrasting fortunes enjoyed by the characters of *Elective Affinities* and those in the tale of 'The Wayward Young Neighbours' (*wunderlichen Nachbarskindern*), a story told by the companion of a visiting English nobleman to entertain Charlotte and Ottilie one evening.[66] The tale concerns a boy and a girl who, despite the hopes of their parents, display nothing but animosity towards each other. When they grow up, the young man leaves for military service, and the young woman makes plans to marry another suitor. The young man returns and hosts a party for the betrothed on board a riverboat. The young woman, realizing that she has been in love with this young man all along, despairingly throws herself into the river. She is rescued by the prompt action of her beloved, who plunges in after her. The young man seeks help at the house of a newly-wed couple, where he revives the young woman, and the two change into the only spare dry clothes to hand, the wedding apparel of their astonished hosts. When they are finally discovered there by their parents and the other party guests, they fall on their knees and beg the forgiveness and blessing of the assembled congregation.

The *Wahlverwandschaften*, which itself constitutes a hybrid of novel and novella forms,[67] contains within it a second novella, which, for Benjamin, is the key to understanding it. This novella serves as a counterpoint to, or negation of, the novel within which it stands. This involves a number of elements: myth and freedom, inclination and love, appearance and reconciliation, silence and language, fate and character.

The marvellous events recounted in the novella point to the human contestation of, and triumph over, the very mythic powers that hold sway in the novel itself.[68] In the novella, decisive human action and love are rewarded with joyful reconciliation; whereas in the novel, the indecision and apathy of the characters lead only to chaos and death. The 'elective affinities' of the four figures in the novel, apparently freely chosen yet ultimately predetermined, constitute a surrender to the inexplicable forces of attraction. These characters do not so much fall in and out of love as give way to passion, the mere appearance of love.[69] Their fateful and fatal romantic entanglements are too strong to resist, yet at the same time too feeble to allow them to rupture and transgress social proprieties.[70] These characters seek to reconcile and accommodate their troublesome inclinations within prevailing social norms.[71]

Genuine love (*wahre Liebe*), love which spurns convention, appears only in the novella. It is this real love of the 'Wayward Young Neighbours',[72] discovered with astonished joy at the end of the story, which prompts and guides their bold actions and makes their final plea for forgiveness irresistible. Whereas illusory love, timid and compromised, can win only the illusion of reconciliation, appeasement, genuine love risks all and wins over everyone.[73] The 'Wayward Young Neighbours' readily confront death, and in so doing place all their trust in the mercy of God. Their unhesitating dive into the turbulent waters of the river constitutes a literal leap of faith. Benjamin writes:

> True reconciliation with God is achieved by no one who does not thereby destroy everything – or as much as he possesses – in order only then, before God's reconciled countenance, to find it resurrected. It follows that a death-defying leap marks that moment when – each one wholly alone for himself before God – they make every effort for the sake of reconciliation. (*SW1*, pp. 342–3)

Genuine love brings genuine reconciliation: reconciliation, that is, not with social norms but with God.[74] Thus, for Benjamin, the novella ultimately constitutes an allegory of the triumph and redeeming power of courageous human action and selfless love.

The figures in the novel itself are not only bereft of such love, they are also marked by the absence of language. Language is surrendered by the characters in the novel as events reduce them to silence. The figure of Ottilie is of special significance here. Like the still waters of the lake, Ottilie herself becomes inexpressive, blankly returning the gaze cast upon her, mirror-like. Her death remains obscure, not only to the other characters, but even to herself.[75] Her speechless demise is not the consequence of any definite moral resolve,[76] but stems rather from an urge to retreat into the tranquillity of nothingness, 'the longing for rest' (*SW1*, p. 336). It is a sorrowful, not a tragic, end. Hence Gundolf's view that ' "the pathos of this work" ' is ' "no less tragically sublime and shattering than that from which Sophocles' *Oedipus* arises" ' constitutes for Benjamin 'the falsest of judgements' (*SW1*, p. 337). The tragic hero challenges fate and the gods, an act of hubris which reconfigures the moral order of the community. Ottilie merely retreats from the world. Her silence is not to be confused with the speechlessness of the tragic hero who is struck dumb at the instant when he 'becomes aware that he is better than his god' (*OWS*, p. 127). Ottilie is not a tragic figure, because, in her fatalistic resignation, she lacks 'character'. Benjamin's verdict on Ottilie's passive, 'plant-like' (*SW1*, p. 336) withering is clear: 'Nothing more untragic can be conceived than this mournful end' (*SW1*, p. 337).

In Benjamin's view, Gundolf's errors were both manifold and crass: Goethe's tale is in no sense a eulogy to vital mythic powers; the figures in the novel are in no sense heroic characters; Ottilie's sorrowful death must not be confused with the tragic demise of the mythic hero; consequently, the *Wahlverwandtschaften* must on no account be understood as a tragedy. Nor should notions of myth and heroism be transposed on to the life of the poet, thereby casting him in the spurious role of creator. Such a misunderstanding amounts to an injustice to the true skill and value of the artist as a form-giver. Gundolf's work constituted nothing less than 'a veritable falsification of knowledge' (*GS* I, p. 828).

Reconciliation, hope and the death of beauty

Unfolding the antithetical moments of the novel and the novella reveals the truth content of Goethe's tale: *Elective Affinities* is a representation of the sorrowful consequences of human fallibility and submission to mythic forces, and a forceful reminder that one must confront fate 'with cunning and with high spirits' (*ILL*, p. 102). Furthermore, through the structural device of the novella, a 'fairy tale for dialecticians', the *Wahlverwandtschaften* explores the interplay between love and the hope of reconciliation. It is in the third and final, synthetic phase of Benjamin's study, however, that the full significance of the novel is elaborated: it is a disquisition on the death of beauty and the revelation of truth, a treatise on the relationship between art and philosophy.

Benjamin's argument becomes complex and convoluted here. Although beauty is intimately related to appearance, it should not be simply equated with it. Beauty is not mere appearance: superficial, deceptive, a mask or 'veil' (*Hülle*) which disguises something else. Rather, beauty is precisely this 'something else': truth, not concealed behind, but discerned within, its 'veil'.[77] The work of art, the beautiful, is truth (truth content) within its veil (material content). The task of the genuine critic is not to lift or tear away this veil, for truth always eludes those grasping hands which all too eagerly seek to strip it bare. Rather, the critic must appreciate both the veil and the beauty of truth within it.[78] Criticism aspires to the clearest possible perception of the true (the philosophical truth) within the beautiful (the work of art), the enduring within the ephemeral, the immortal within the mortal.

Benjamin's theological motifs return once more in this context. Just as the work of the poet is not to be confused with the act of Creation, so the labour of the critic does not bring Revelation. Both Creation and Revelation are divine acts, limited to God. Even to the most scrupulous critic, truth always remains a secret.[79] Beauty is part of the divine order of Creation, in which truth, awaiting divine Revelation, can be apprehended by the critic only more or less obscurely, as an intimation.[80] The truth discerned by the critic can only ever be partial, provisional, contestable. Revelation, the eventual and actual stripping away of the veil can occur only in that final reconciliation with God, prefigured in genuine love[81] and found in death. All that is mortal will one day have its truth unveiled.[82] Truth is ultimately manifest on the Day of Judgement, the moment of redemption.

The figure of Ottilie is crucial here. She is the very incarnation of beauty and, as such, is an allegory of the beautiful work of art. And just as Ottilie dies, so the artwork is also apt to 'die out in the world' (*SW1*, p. 297). In the artwork's perishing, its truth content and material content become more readily distinguishable. Truth is unfolded as the artwork withers. Here Ottilie's silent, 'intentionless' demise serves as an allegory of the mortification of the beautiful work of art for the sake of its truth content. Moreover, just as the individual work of art comes to point beyond itself to the Idea of Art, of which it is an exemplary instance and within which it is finally dissolved, so Ottilie's death anticipates that moment of reconciliation with the absolute, with God, denied her in life. Her death indicates the hope of redemption. Benjamin writes: 'the certainty of blessing that, in the novella, the lovers take home with them corresponds to the hope of redemption that we nourish for all the dead' (*SW1*, p. 355). The hope of redemption is for those who can themselves hope no longer, the dead.[83] Hence Benjamin's essay concludes with this 'mystery' (*SW1*, p. 355), this paradox of hope: 'Only for the sake of the hopeless ones have we been given hope' (*SW1*, p. 356).

Goethe's *Elective Affinities*, his tale of doomed, illicit love, is a philosophical enquiry into the very character of art and the relationship between beauty, truth and redemption. Indeed, it is precisely this philosophical-theological truth content that distinguishes it as a genuine work of art. For Benjamin, the novel is an allegorical presentation of the mortification of beauty – that is, of the work of art itself – for the sake of truth and for the hope of reconciliation in God. In this way, as Roberts (1982, p. 132) astutely points out, the novel contains within it, as its truth content to be unfolded, as its secret, the very key to the disclosure of this secret, which is at the same time the secret of the work of art *per se*. It is the discernment of this 'secret as a secret' (Roberts, 1982, p. 132), that constitutes the ultimate achievement of Benjamin's critical unfolding, his exemplary criticism of Goethe's exemplary work of art.

Conclusion

In this chapter I have tried to show how Benjamin's concern to 'recreate criticism as a genre' led him to engage with the writings of the early Romantics, the first *modern* critics. Drawing on their works, Benjamin develops a complex, intricate notion of immanent criticism. Conceived as an intervention in, and reconfiguration of, the afterlife of the artwork, immanent critique involves the processual disclosure of the truth content of the work of art as it is subject to gradual disintegration and ruination. Truth is made manifest only at the moment of extinction. Such a vision of critical practice has a number of important consequences for Benjamin:

1   The decentring of the author. Criticism does not involve the empathetic recovery of some original artistic intention.
2   The artwork as monad. The work of art is but a fragment composing and expressing in abbreviated form a greater totality (be it the Idea of Art or the sociocultural matrix in which it appears) which otherwise eludes analysis.
3   The imperative of construction. Unfolding the artwork as a monadological fragment requires forms of textual construction and representation which abstain from theoretical intrusion.
4   The historical situatedness of artwork and critic. Works may be legible only in certain ways, if at all, at certain historical junctures and moments of construction.
5   The actuality of meaning. The significance of an artwork is contingent upon, and enters into, a particular constellation with current circumstances and interests.
6   The contestability of interpretation. The cultural and political significance of a work of art is not specified in advance, but is subject to (mis)appropriation according to political and other struggles in the present.
7   The absence of judgement. Opinions as to the supposed aesthetic merit of an artwork (as in the critical reception of the *Trauerspiel*) say more about the prejudices of the critic than the artwork itself, and have no place in genuine criticism.
8   The disenchantment of art. The task of the sober critic is to dispel the mystifications and illusions which surround the artwork and artist, not to perpetuate or proliferate them.

These consequences had a profound and enduring impact not only on Benjamin's subsequent literary criticism, but also on his wider cultural criticism and historiographical writings. Immanent criticism provides a method for the critical analysis not only of Goethe, the *Trauerspiel*, Surrealism, Proust and Baudelaire, but also of a plethora of cultural phenomena – the commodities and fashions of the recent past, the crumbling metropolitan architecture of the 'prehistory of modernity'. In Benjamin's later writings, these are all subject to mortification, presenting their afterlife for critical scrutiny. Moreover, in his appropriation of immanent critique, Benjamin begins to discern and articulate the character and role of the modern intellectual as critic and writer, and thereby to locate and orient himself within the sociocultural milieu of which he was a part – the writer as sober producer, as compiler and composer of fragments, as partisan in the political conflicts of the present, as redeemer of the forgotten dead.

2

Allegory and Melancholy

Introduction

On 14 October 1922, two weeks after the collapse of the *Angelus Novus* enterprise, Benjamin wrote to Rang, expressing both the significance for him of this failure and his new resolve:

> this unwritten journal could not be more important or dear to me if it existed. But today – even if Weissbach were to come to me with a printing press ready to use – I would not do it again. For the time is past when I would make sacrifices for it. And it would all too easily demand the sacrifice of my habilitation dissertation. Maybe I will be able to see the Angelus flying toward the earth at some future time. (*COR*, p. 203)

Benjamin's hopes of completing a *Habilitationsschrift* had already foundered once, when, following the completion of his doctoral thesis, his professor at the University of Berne, Richard Herbertz, offered him the opportunity to write it in philosophy there.[1] Further study in Switzerland proved unfeasible, however, in the wake of post-war German inflation.[2] But, in the aftermath of the *Angelus Novus* fiasco, Benjamin's ambitions were rekindled, and after exploring the possibility of studying at Heidelberg,[3] he finally decided on the University of Frankfurt in 1923, taking as his subject matter the long-forgotten seventeenth-century German baroque play of mourning, the *Trauerspiel*.

At first sight, such unfashionable and undistinguished dramatic productions certainly seem an unpromising theme for someone who wished to carve out a reputation as a prominent literary critic. But it was precisely their obscurity and low critical esteem that were attractive to Benjamin. For to reconfigure, and thereby rehabilitate, a whole theatrical and literary form (or idea) as neglected and derided as the *Trauerspiel* would require that established aesthetic categories and conventional literary judgements be disputed and radically overturned. As an intervention in the afterlife of the *Trauerspiel*, his study was intended to contest the misconceptions and erroneous evaluations of its previous critics, such as there were.[4] By unfolding the inherent tendencies and linguistic tensions of the *Trauerspiel*, Benjamin was to expose the muddles and mis-understandings of those who dismissed the play of mourning as a failed imitation of Greek tragedy, and to foster an immanent appreciation of its own peculiar merits and significance. *The Origin of German Tragic Drama* was thus written as an exemplary immanent critique, one which elaborated and refined the critical principles pioneered in his doctoral dissertation. Although it may not be readily apparent, Benjamin's highly erudite and seemingly arcane study of the *Trauerspiel* was conceived as a challenge (for his own critical practice) and a provocation (to the literary establishment).

Moreover, as we will see, Benjamin's *Trauerspiel* study brings together, and provides a further opportunity for reflection upon, mystical themes and motifs which had long fascinated him: nature as sorrowful, history as messianic catastrophe, and human language as post-lapsarian 'prattle'.[5] It involves an intricate interleaving of the Lutheran understanding of the God-forsaken world which informed the baroque dramatist and the mystical Judaic vision of fallen Creation which suffuses Benjamin's own writings. For him, the play of mourning is a ruin about ruination. It represents human life as the futile search for meaning in an abandoned world, as the relentless accumulation of broken fragments, as the inevitable decomposition of the wretched creaturely body. The melancholy human condition and the misery of overnamed nature are the bases of the pitiful lamentation expressed in its language. In their emphasis upon allegory, that linguistic trope wherein one image or object comes to stand for another or for a plethora of others, the authors of the *Trauerspiel* foregrounded the arbitrary character of the linguistic sign and its imposition upon a mute, sad nature. In *Trauerspiel*, the meaning of language is hollowed out in the uncontrollable proliferation of allegorical figures and emblems.

Such ideas had a particular pertinence for Benjamin. The bleak desolation of a world convulsed and torn apart by the carnage of war, political intrigue and instability, the fear of impending collapse and chaos, the sense of cultural degeneration and decadence marked by hyperbole and bombast – the historical context and content of the *Trauerspiel* were of painful relevance to a generation which had just experienced the horrors of the Great War and its subsequent crises. Benjamin notes that 'In this state of disruption the present age reflects certain aspects of the spiritual constitution of the baroque, even down to the details of its artistic practice' (*OGTD*, p. 55). For Benjamin, the baroque's 'desire for a vigorous style of language, which would make it seem equal to the violence of world events' (*OGTD*, p. 55) had its contemporary stylistic echo in expressionism:

> The analogy between the endeavours of the baroque and those of the present and recent past is most apparent in the use of language. Exaggeration is characteristic of both . . . like expressionism, the baroque is not so much an age of genuine artistic achievement as an age possessed of an unremitting artistic will. This is true of all so-called periods of decadence. (*OGTD*, pp. 54–5)

Excessive, ostentatious, verbose – such characteristics of early modern drama were not without significance for the artistic sensibility and practice of contemporary modernism. This 'actuality' of apparently extinct forms was also central to Benjamin's redemptive project.

This chapter sketches the background to, and ultimate failure of, Benjamin's *Habilitationsschrift* before providing a detailed reading of the *Trauerspiel* study. Attention is initially focused on unravelling the dense and intimidating 'Epistemo-Critical Prologue', in which Benjamin introduces and reconfigures a number of mystical, philosophical and Romantic literary concepts: the Idea and the monad, criticism as mortification, the treatise and digression, the mosaic and the constellation, and afterlife and 'origin'. The chapter then presents Benjamin's two key arguments. The first is that the *Trauerspiel* must be understood and evaluated on its own terms, and not as a second-rate version of tragedy. Indeed, *Trauerspiel* is, like 'tragedy' and 'comedy', a distinctive, legitimate dramatic form or 'idea' possessing its own distinguishing features: a grounding in historical events and temporality, the foregrounding of such non- and anti-heroic figures as the tyrant or martyr and the intriguer, world-weary *acedia* rather than defiant action, bombast and a propensity to comic laughter rather than silent agonistics. The second is that allegory, as the decisive linguistic trope of the *Trauerspiel*, must be re-evaluated. Benjamin argues against the conventional privileging of the symbol by demonstrating how, far from being an inferior poetic device, allegory accords with, and gives expression to, the ruinous world and creaturely human condition envisaged by the baroque dramatist. Benjamin's *Habilitationsschrift* sought not only to rehabilitate the *Trauerspiel* through an exemplary immanent critique, but also to unfold a number of methodological and conceptual ideas that were to be of enduring significance for him: the fragment as monad and as tessera, criticism as destruction and reconstruction, melancholy and allegory, and history as catastrophe and redemption.

Background

Benjamin was under no illusions regarding the significance of the *Trauerspiel* study. 'Conceived 1916. Written 1925' (*OGTD*, p. 25), it constituted the culmination of his work of the previous ten years. He was acquainted with the *Trauerspiel* long before embarking on the *Habilitationsschrift*, having sketched two fragments in 1916 entitled '*Trauerspiel* and Tragedy' and 'The Meaning of Language in *Trauerspiel* and Tragedy'.[6] In these miniatures Benjamin had begun to articulate 'the fundamental antithesis of mourning and tragedy', and to challenge the widely perceived inferiority of the former.[7] He sought to distinguish the (usually conflated) notions of *Trauerspiel* and tragedy with respect to their very different relationships to time and history. Graced by the majestic presence of the heroic figure, elevated by the grandeur of his actions and sacrifices in the face of uncompromising fate, the mythic (or 'individually fulfilled') time of tragedy stands beyond the flow of historical time.[8] By contrast, the *Trauerspiel* is defined by the mechanical procession and repetition of events rooted in the bleak emptiness of 'unfulfilled' (profane, historical) time. The play of mourning portrays only the futile gestures and schemes of the brutal tyrant and the treacherous courtier, ignoble actions which culminate only in ruin and death. In this bleak context, the bombastic language characteristic of the *Trauerspiel* takes on a particular significance: not as evidence of the limited poetic talents of baroque dramatists, but as the clearest indication of their understanding of the desolation of humankind. The ornate, clumsy language of the *Trauerspiel* is overladen with, and hollows out, meaning. It translates the sorrow and lamentation of fallen Creation into a distinctive acoustic register – not meaningful human speech, but rather, evocative music.[9] The 'meaning of language' in the *Trauerspiel* is thus, paradoxically, the very absence of meaning – language as pure sound or 'prattle'.

This theological vision of a melancholy human life in a world bereft of significance and grace is fundamental for the *Trauerspiel*, and for Benjamin's early mystical speculations regarding language and history. Responding to an essay by Scholem on lamentation within the Judaic tradition, 'Über Klage und Klaglied', Benjamin notes that his own 1916 texts were written 'Without reference to Hebrew literature, which as I now know, is the proper subject of such an analysis' (*COR*, p. 120). The reflections contained in his 'On Language as Such and on Human Language' (1916) were precisely intended as this corrective. A brief consideration of some of the key ideas of this enigmatic text provides some essential background themes for the *Trauerspiel*.[10] The 'On Language' fragment develops a mystical-philosophical understanding of language, in opposition to the supposed poverty of prevailing rationalistic thought and the so-called bourgeois scientific (positivistic) world-view. Benjamin rejects the view of language as a mere instrument of communication and arbitrary sign system, on the grounds that it is predicated on an inadequate and impoverished conception of human experience. At the same time, in arguing for a theory of language grounded in a theological understanding of truth, he also engages in an implicit critique of Martin Buber's theological conception of the fundamental inexpressibility of the most profound and privileged forms of human experience: namely, communion with God.[11]

According to Scripture, the act of divine Creation is understood as a linguistic one in which God's Word called things into being. Genesis tells us that 'God spoke – and there was' (*OWS*, p. 114). For the mystical tradition of the Kabbalah, Creation is at the same time the Revelation of God's Word. Adam is called by God to name Creation, to give things their proper name according to the sign that he had placed upon them – that is to say, to translate[12] the divine and creative word of God into human language. Language as naming is not a mere medium or instrument for the conveyance of conventional signs. In the paradisiacal human language of naming, the relationship between object (signified) and name (signifier) is not arbitrary, but fundamentally guaranteed by God. Benjamin cites Hamann thus: 'everything that man heard in the beginning, saw with his eyes, and felt with his hands was the living Word; for God it was the Word. With this Word in his mouth and in his heart, the origin of language was as natural, as close, and as easy as a child's game' (*OWS*, p. 118). In translating Creation directly into name, human beings have immediate, blissful access to the revealed Word of God.

The Fall is the catastrophic end to this paradisiacal state of naming. Adam eats of the apple from the Tree of the Knowledge of Good and Evil and is expelled into the historical world. The Fall is a descent from the purity of Adamic naming into 'the empty word, into the abyss of prattle' (*OWS*, p. 120). Things no longer have one name guaranteed by God, but many, based on convention.[13] With the Fall, the descent into Kierkegaardian 'prattle' (*OWS*, p. 119) and the multiplicity of human languages begins, the profusion and confusion of signs: Babel.

Benjamin writes of post-Fall – that is historical – nature: 'now begins its other muteness, which we mean by the deep sadness of nature. It is a metaphysical truth that all nature would begin to lament if it were endowed with language' (*OWS*, p. 121). The source of this sadness is fallen human language. In the post-Fall epoch, human beings continue to name things, but they do so arbitrarily, without reference to the Word. Silent nature is subject to, and designated by, the 'prattle' of human beings. The plethora of human languages results in a multitude of 'names' with things being misnamed and 'overnamed' (*OWS*, p. 122). This is the source of their sorrow, for Benjamin sees 'overnaming as the deepest linguistic reason for all melancholy and (from the point of view of the thing) of all deliberate muteness' (*OWS*, p. 122). The cacophony of human languages and the mute misery of nature are indices of the pitiful condition of the profane world. According to Benjamin, blithely transposing Judaic and Lutheran notions, it is this lamentable and lamenting world – God-forsaken, creaturely, sorrowful, meaningless, verbose – which finds expression in the *Trauerspiel*.

The purpose of Benjamin's *Trauerspiel* study emerges most clearly in this context. If the task of criticism and philosophy itself is to disclose 'truth', then what is this 'truth' if not the proper naming of Creation in the paradisiacal language of Adam, wherein name and thing correspond perfectly? Indeed, in his felicitous and truthful naming of God's Creation, Adam is not only 'the father of the human race', but also, Benjamin wryly observes, 'the father of philosophy' (*OGTD*, p. 37) as well. Philosophical enquiry is the search to call things by their proper names, to recall the original names imparted by nature and bestowed by Adam.[14] As such, it is an act of receptivity, 'renewal',[15] and remembrance.[16]

In his letter to Rang of 10 January 1924, Benjamin voices his anxieties regarding his *Habilitationsschrift* and his determination to complete it. Buried in the dusty volumes of plays long unread and the obscure complexities of baroque emblems, Benjamin notes the results of his labours with dissatisfaction:

> What has been piling up during months of reading and repeated reflection is now ready, not so much as a mass of building blocks, than as a gigantic heap of kindling to which I am supposed to carry the first spark of inspiration from some other place ... My foundation is remarkably – indeed awfully – narrow: a knowledge of some few dramas, by no means all the relevant ones. (*COR*, p. 227)[17]

In early March 1924, Benjamin noted that the 'eccentric meticulousness' (*COR*, p. 236) of his research and preparation had brought the project to the point where 'I have at my disposal about six hundred quotations and, in addition, they are so well organized that you can get an overview at a glance' (*COR*, p. 236). The structure of the study was apparent:

> The beginning and conclusion ... will contain methodological observations on the systematic study of literature, in which I want to introduce myself with a romantic concept of philology to the best of my ability. Then the three chapters: On History as the Content of *Trauerspiel*; On the Occult Concept of Melancholy in the Sixteenth and Seventeenth Centuries; On the Nature of Allegory and Allegorical Art Forms. (*COR*, p. 237)

Although the thematic outlines were clear, and the materials collected were ready for combustion, the 'spark of first inspiration' was still wanting. Benjamin notes that 'The elan that brings about the transition to actual writing simply does not seem to want to make an appearance, and I am planning to complete most of the work abroad' (*COR*, p. 236).

'Abroad' meant Italy. Benjamin spent the summer of 1924 on the island of Capri. This stay was to have a profound effect upon his personal and intellectual life. It was on Capri that he met his future lover, Asja Lacis. Here too he read Georg Lukács's seminal *History and Class Consciousness*. Despite, or because of, such distractions, the 'elan' finally appeared, and the *Trauerspiel* text with it. By the middle of September, Benjamin had completed the introduction, first chapter (now renamed 'The King in the *Trauerspiel*') and most of the second.[18] A month later he informed Scholem that 'Part Three and the conclusion of the book are still not done, but they are ready to go' (*COR*, p. 252).[19] This letter also contained sad tidings: Rang had died. Benjamin notes: 'I was indebted to this man not only for his support and validation, but also for whatever essential elements of German culture I have internalised' (*COR*, p. 252). Furthermore, as he later observed, the *Trauerspiel* study had 'lost the reader for whom it was intended. For who will be able to participate fully in these esoteric and forgotten issues?' (*COR*, p. 262).[20]

Back in Berlin in December 1924, with only the methodological introduction and conclusion to write, Benjamin reflected:

> I have gradually lost my perspective on what I have done. I would have to be mistaken, however, if the organic power of the allegorical realm were not to emerge vividly as the fundamental source of the baroque. Yet what surprises me most of all at this time is that what I have written consists, as it were, almost entirely of quotations. It is the craziest mosaic technique you can imagine. (*COR*, p. 256)

Despite this loss of overview, not only was the 'primary concern' clear – namely, allegory – but Benjamin had also settled on the title and final structure of the book: 'The book will look something like this (excluding the introduction and conclusion): The Origin of German Tragic Drama [*Der Ursprung des deutschen Trauerspiels*] as the title. 1. "*Trauerspiel* and Tragedy." 2. "Allegory and *Trauerspiel*." Both parts are divided into 3 sections, headed by six mottoes' (*COR*, p. 256).

Early 1925 saw Benjamin in Frankfurt, with the introduction drafted to his evident satisfaction: 'This introduction is unmitigated *chutzpah* – that is to say, neither more nor less than the prolegomena to epistemology, a kind of second stage of my early work on language . . . dressed up as a theory of ideas. To this end I also plan to read through my work on language once more' (*COR*, p. 261).[21] Refusing the 'demands of symmetry', Benjamin chose to drop his proposed methodological conclusion, since 'The climax reached in the conclusion of the main part could not be surpassed' (*COR*, p. 264) – at least, not given the time constraints within which he was operating. Accordingly, by 6 April 1925, the text was ready for the printers, but things were starting to go awry. The dean at Frankfurt, Schultz, having decided that the work was inappropriate to Germanistik, 'is pushing me to get my habilitation in aesthetics', Benjamin reports (*COR*, p. 263). Benjamin formally submitted his study on 12 May, and wrote resignedly: 'My chances are so slim that I put off my application until the last possible moment. Since it was finally and irrevocably deemed impossible for me to be granted the *habilitation* in German literary history due to my "preparation", I was forced into "aesthetics"' (*COR*, p. 266).[22]

Benjamin's text, as he feared, met with bewilderment. His examiners ('two old crocks', Hans Cornelius and Rudolf Kautzsch) 'claimed not to understand anything of my dissertation' (*COR*, p. 275), and advised him to withdraw it from consideration rather than face the ignominy of an official rejection. On 21 July 1925 Benjamin notified Scholem of 'the wreckage of my Frankfurt plans' (*COR*, p. 275). His hopes of the *Habilitation* and of a university post as a *Privatdozent* were gone for ever. He would remain an intellectual outsider, scornful of an academy[23] which had passed such a blinkered judgement on perhaps his most profound text, a work which, notwithstanding its eventual publication in January 1928, was destined to become in his own lifetime, as Steiner aptly puts it, 'an extinct work' (*OGTD*, p. 7).

'Unmitigated chutzpah'

As Steiner points out, Benjamin's 'Epistemo-Critical Prologue' to the *Trauerspiel* study forms 'one of the more impenetrable pieces of prose in German or, for that matter, in any modern language' (*OGTD*, p. 13), supposedly comprehensible only to a reader well versed in the intricacies of the Kabbalah (*OGTD*, pp. 13–14). Nevertheless, some familiarity with the 'On Language' study, Benjamin's doctoral dissertation and the *Elective Affinities* essay provides some basis for understanding, given that the Prologue reiterates and reconfigures a number of motifs and principles pioneered in these texts:[24] the (fragmentary) representation of truth (as ideas) as the task of philosophy, the relationship between truth and beauty, the relationship between the individual work of art and the idea, the notions of the constellation and the monad, and the concepts of origin (*Ursprung*) and afterlife.

In his doctoral dissertation, we recall, Benjamin presents the early Romantic understanding of the task of criticism as the dissolution of the individual work of art into the pantheon or Idea of Art. Benjamin's Prologue articulates important modifications of this critical vision. He is less concerned with the Idea of Art as some all-embracing *Gesamtkunstwerk*, and more with the aesthetic sphere as a plethora of ideas – 'Idea' understood here very much in Platonic terms as a kind of essence (the 'tragic', the 'comic', the 'lyric' and the 'epic'). Benjamin's concern is to represent the *Trauerspiel* as itself a particular aesthetic idea,[25] through the critical exploration and articulation of its various individual manifestations. For him, the task of philosophy, and of criticism, accordingly lies in 'the representation of an idea' (*COR*, p. 224).[26] And it is in the configuration and interplay of the manifold of ideas, in, as Benjamin puts it, 'the dance of represented ideas' (*OGTD*, p. 29), rather than in the absorption of works into a unified totality, that truth emerges. Truth – calling things by their proper names – is 'an intentionless state of being, made up of ideas' (*OGTD*, p. 36).

This concern with the constitution and representation of the 'idea' raises the question of the relationship between the individual work of art and the idea of which it is merely one particular instance. What is the relationship between a specific baroque 'play of mourning' and the idea of the *Trauerspiel* itself, between phenomenon and idea? It is this question which stands at the heart of Benjamin's Prologue. And since it is precisely the task of the critic to discern and give expression to this relationship as the 'truth content' of the individual artwork, one might say that this question is really the one that dominates much of Benjamin's work: what is the purpose of criticism?

Romantic criticism as the gradual and immanent unfolding of the truth content of the work of art through reflection provides a starting point, but he moves beyond it in the *Trauerspiel* Prologue. Truth is not just 'intentionless'; it is 'the death of intention' (*OGTD*, p. 36). The genuine critic must abandon 'intention and knowledge' – knowledge as the illegitimate pursuit and seizure of the object, knowledge as 'possession' (*OGTD*, p. 29), knowledge which, misappropriating and misnaming things according to arbitrary schemes and classifications, stands in the same relation to truth as the 'prattle' of post-Fall language does to Adamic naming. Recalling the notion of criticism as an experiment on the artwork, Benjamin notes that 'truth content' 'does not appear by being exposed; rather it is revealed in a process which might be described metaphorically as the burning up of the husk as it enters the realm of ideas, that is to say a destruction of the work in which its external form achieves its most brilliant degree of illumination' (*OGTD*, pp. 31–2). Criticism brings about the illumination of truth through a process of self-immolation. Truth becomes manifest not so much in a process of successive reflection, as in the moment of destruction. He remarks: 'Criticism means the mortification of the works . . . Mortification of the works: not then – as the romantics have it – awakening of consciousness in living works, but the settlement of knowledge in dead ones' (*OGTD*, p. 182).[27] Appearance (material content) is set aflame for the sake of the truth content of the work of art which endures as a ruin.[28]

If the moment of critical illumination is a sudden one, the preparation for it may prove a laborious task requiring patience and persistence – the careful bringing together and proper arrangement of the combustible materials needed[29] may involve much fruitless searching and many return trips. Here Benjamin advocates one particular form of writing as the proper mode of critical and philosophical representation – the treatise (*Traktat*). He observes:

> Its method is essentially representation. Method is a digression. Representation as digression – such is the methodological nature of the treatise. The absence of an uninterrupted purposeful structure is its primary characteristic. Tirelessly the process of thinking makes new beginnings, returning in a roundabout way to its original object. This continual pausing for breath is the mode [*Daseinform*] most proper to the process of contemplation. (*OGTD*, p. 28)

The 'irregular rhythm' of the treatise corresponds to the protracted processes of thinking, writing and reading. 'Philosophical style' involves 'the art of interruption in contrast to the chain of deduction' (*OGTD*, p. 32). Benjamin notes that

> the writer must stop and restart with every new sentence. And this applies to the contemplative mode of representation more than any other, for its aim is not to carry the reader away and inspire him with enthusiasm. This form can be counted successful only when it forces the reader to pause and reflect. (*OGTD*, p. 29)

The treatise is sober in tone, and discontinuous in composition. The representation of ideas occurs in the most careful organization of these fragments so as to recognize their patterning. It is the power of their combination and arrangement, not of their 'encyclopaedic accumulation' (*OGTD*, p. 33), which is important. The mosaic, a form of representation constituted by a multitude of crafted tesserae, becomes his essential model: 'In their supreme, western, form the mosaic and the treatise are products of the middle ages; it is their very real affinity which makes comparison possible' (*OGTD*, p. 29). Genuine criticism, philosophical writing, involves the production of textual mosaics.

In this analogy of the mosaic, Benjamin articulates several key methodological insights which underpin all his subsequent writings. First, he stresses the importance of the smallest fragment, each individual instance, for the success and comprehension of the totality. In the philosophical treatise as mosaic, 'The relationship between the minute precision of the work and the proportions of the sculptural or intellectual whole demonstrates that truth-content is only to be grasped through the immersion in the most minute details of subject-matter' (*OGTD*, p. 29). Nothing is too arcane, nothing too marginal, to be ignored or excluded. Fragments which seem inconsequential may be the most precious for the purpose of oblique representation.[30]

Secondly, for Benjamin, the truth of the artwork finds representation in the use of the textual fragment, the quotation: 'In the canonic form of the treatise the only element of an intention . . . is the authoritative quotation' (*OGTD*, p. 28).[31] The treatise as a composite of quotations becomes the basis of a method which is intended to allow the object to speak for itself and in its own words. The use of quotations facilitates the self-presentation of the truth of the artwork. For Benjamin, the *Trauerspiel* study was to be an experiment in such an approach.[32] Composed according to 'the craziest mosaic technique you can imagine' (*COR*, p. 256), *The Origin of German Tragic Drama* was to be an exemplary treatise, a philosophical jigsaw puzzle of quotations.

Finally, immersion in the fragment is essential, but precludes any overview during the process of construction. Like the pattern or picture formed by the mosaic, the representation of the idea occurs only in the moment of completion. Here treatise as mosaic and as digression combine:

> Only by approaching the subject from some distance and, initially, foregoing any view of the whole, can the mind be led through a more or less ascetic apprenticeship, to the position of strength from which it is possible to take in the whole panorama and yet remain in control

of oneself. The course of this apprenticeship is what had to be described here. (*OGTD*, p. 56)

The totality, the representation of truth, on which one labours so patiently, is available to the gaze only in the final instance, 'at last sight'.

The notion of the mosaic provides insight into the interplay between the individual work of art and the idea of which it is one specific instance. Benjamin seeks to move beyond what he terms 'inductive' and 'deductive' approaches to focus on the mediating role of the concept. The 'inductive method' starts with the identification and collection of individual manifestations and examples of the idea – that is, of what is commonly termed comic, tragic or sorrowful. These diverse phenomena are then examined with a view to discovering common characteristics and shared traits. On the basis of these similarities, a set of underlying principles and rules is posited, which constitute the tragic, the comic and so forth. Ideas are initially distilled from individual works. This method, Benjamin notes, 'is clearly futile' (*OGTD*, p. 44), and 'can lead nowhere' (*OGTD*, p. 39).

'Deduction' supposedly reverses this logic, but fares no better. According to this method, the idea is defined in advance as a complex of rules and precepts for a particular genre. Subsequently, the search begins for actual examples which measure up to these specified criteria. Deduction is, in short, 'based on a combination of induction and abstraction' (*OGTD*, p. 42). As such, it fails to attend to the historical significance and specificity of meaning. Benjamin rejects the misconceptions and misapplications arising from the utilization of trans-historical aesthetic categories. His study is directed precisely against the misrecognition of the *Trauerspiel* as an inferior or decayed form of tragedy. Further, Benjamin's central aesthetic principle remains the Romantic insight that the meaning of an object unfolds only in and as a historical process. The meaning of a work of art cannot be fixed once and for all by mere assimilation to a pre-given model. Indeed, in Benjamin's view, works of art are more interesting and provocative the more imperfect their fit into any supposed genre.[33]

In reducing individual works of art and ideas to one another, inductive and deductive approaches do justice to neither. The facile compilation of examples and the arrogant postulation of rules should not be confused with the representation of ideas, the true task of criticism. For Benjamin, the uniqueness of the work of art and its relationships with others appear only through the use of concepts. It is in the identification and analysis of concepts (mourning, fate, melancholy, *acedia*, allegory, historical time, ruination) that superficial relations are contested and disturbed, and the true affinities between apparently disparate phenomena are established and structured. For example, whereas Shakespeare's *Hamlet* is commonly read as a 'tragedy', for Benjamin it is one of the 'great *Trauerspiele*' (*OGTD*, p. 136). Hamlet is no tragic hero. He is instead the quintessential melancholy prince, paralysed by indecision, tormented by the consequences of his folly, and slain in a final royal bloodbath. Benjamin notes that 'the death of Hamlet ... has no more in common with tragic death than the Prince himself has with Ajax' (*OGTD*, p. 136). *Hamlet* as *Trauerspiel* – the play is uprooted from its conventional context, and repositioned and illuminated afresh as a fragment of a different idea.

The idea is neither a pile of instances nor a mere complex of precepts. Rather, it is a pattern of finely crafted, carefully positioned fragments composed by concepts: a mosaic. Benjamin observes that 'The set of concepts which assist in the representation of the idea lends it actuality as such a configuration. For phenomena are not incorporated in ideas. They are not contained in them. Ideas are, rather, their objective, virtual arrangement, their objective interpretation' (*OGTD*, p. 34). Like each individual tessera of the mosaic, the work of art is a constitutive fragment of the idea, and simultaneously derives its significance from its location within it. The idea is constituted in the particular formation or pattern adopted by a set of fragments, and manifests itself only within them. Phenomena (individual works of art) contain as their truth content the idea they compose. Composition and containment, not distillation and abstraction, are the key to the relationship between ideas and individual artworks. This in turn points to two of Benjamin's key figures in his understanding of the character and significance of the idea: the constellation and the monad.

As their 'objective, virtual arrangement', Benjamin writes, 'Ideas are to objects as constellations are to stars' (*OGTD*, p. 34). However, the notion of the idea as a constellation is used by Benjamin not only to articulate the importance of the patterning of phenomena by concepts, but also to point to the characteristics of this process. In a constellation of stars, the most remote objects are conjoined to form a unique, legible figure, which cannot easily be undone. Similarly, in the idea, a sudden yet enduring connection between extreme phenomena is brought into being. Pensky describes this process well:

the constellation emerges – discloses itself – only insofar as the concept divests the particulars of their status as *merely* particular, refers them to their hidden arrangement, but also preserves their material existence. At that point, a meaningful image jumps forward from the previously disparate elements, which from that point onward can never be seen as merely disparate again. In this way the phenomena are rescued from their status as phenomenal or fragmentary, without simultaneously sacrificing the phenomena in the name of an abstract concept. (Pensky, 1993, p. 70)

The constellation involves a fleeting but irrevocable shift in the perception of phenomena which preserves both their individual integrity and their mutuality. Hence, for Benjamin, 'Ideas are timeless constellations, and by virtue of the elements being seen as points in such constellations, phenomena are subdivided and redeemed' (*OGTD*, p. 34).

Here again, Benjamin moves beyond Romantic criticism. The individual work is not dissolved in the realm of ideas, but, subject to immolation, remains ablaze as a point of illumination within the constellation. Moreover, this constellation is only one of a manifold of other constellations. Benjamin writes, mixing his astronomical metaphors, 'Every idea is a sun and is related to other ideas just as suns are related to each other. The harmonious relationship between such essences is what constitutes truth' (*OGTD*, p. 37). The individual artwork is a tiny point of light, one of many forming the idea (the tragic, the comic, the sorrowful), which in turn is just one element of the wider realm of ideas (the Idea of Art), which is itself part of the universal, divine Creation: truth.

This movement from the individual instance to the totality is matched by a corresponding tendency in the opposite direction. For Benjamin, the idea is not just a constellation, it is also a monad. Derived from Leibniz, the notion of the monad is based upon a pantheistic conception of nature. According to this view, every fragment of Creation, however insignificant, contains and indicates its divine origin, intimates God. Each element possesses, in miniature yet legible form, the totality of which it is a part. Benjamin transposes this conceit on to the realm of ideas:

The idea is a monad. The being that enters into it, with its past and subsequent history, brings – concealed in its own form – an indistinct abbreviation of the rest of the world of ideas, just as, according to Leibniz's *Discourse on Metaphysics* (1686), every single monad contains in an indistinct way, all the others. (*OGTD*, p. 47)

As a monad, every idea intimates the realm of ideas of which it forms a part, and in this way too, every phenomenon partakes of this realm, since phenomena contain the ideas they represent. Every work of art is a microcosm of the greater realm of ideas. Not only this: Benjamin writes that 'The idea is a monad – that means briefly, every idea contains the image of the world. The purpose of the representation of ideas is nothing less than an abbreviated outline of this image of the world' (*OGTD*, p. 48). Hence, in unfolding the long-forgotten dramas of the seventeenth century, Benjamin seeks to discern the 'image of the world' of the baroque.

The *Trauerspiel* as an idea, and each individual *Trauerspiel* as a work of art, contains in 'abbreviated outline', and serves as an expression of, the baroque age, its literary-cultural sensibility, its theological understanding, its historical condition. In this sense, one might argue, following Steiner, that herein lies the 'origin' of these dramas. For Benjamin, however, the notion of origin (*Ursprung*) has a particular significance. He writes, in one of the most puzzling passages of his impenetrable Prologue:

> Origin, although an entirely historical category, has, nevertheless, nothing to do with genesis [*Entstehung*]. The term origin is not intended to describe the process by which the existent came into being, but rather to describe that which emerges from the process of becoming and disappearance. Origin is an eddy in the stream of becoming. (*OGTD*, p. 45)

What does this mean? For Benjamin, origin does not refer to literary antecedents, precursors, influences or textual models. The notion of origin is more complex than this. After all, at what moment does *Trauerspiel* as an idea come into being? In the production of a particular play by a particular author? In the retrospective determination and specification of a set of rules and genres by literary historians? Such a dilemma arises from, and defeats, inductive and deductive approaches. For Benjamin, 'origin' refers to the moment when the constellation of phenomena comes into being, when it is suddenly recognized *as* a constellation, when the idea is perceived by the critic. This is fundamental. Individual works which compose the idea are always in flux, always becoming something other than what they were, through the corrosive, ruinous action of criticism. Although individual works of art come into existence at a particular moment, their meaning is not thereby fixed by the author, but instead is continuously reconstituted in their afterlife. Origin as the recognition of the meaning of, and truth within, the phenomenon is not so much an occurrence *prior to* the afterlife of the work of art as, paradoxically, *its final moment of mortification*. Origin is a temporal disturbance, an 'eddy in the stream of becoming' as time is folded back upon itself. Thus, origin is a historical moment in which the idea is represented and recognized and the phenomena which compose it are redeemed. Origin becomes the *goal* of study, not its starting point.

This instant of recognition, which is later conceived as the 'dialectical image', is precisely Benjamin's concern. The *Ursprung des deutschen Trauerspiels* was not written as an arcane examination of obscure dramas. It is an intervention in the afterlife of these works of art, a moment of re-cognition, of rethinking, in which the misunderstandings of previous scholars are exposed and contested in such a way that the true meaning and significance of these texts is disclosed. For Benjamin, the origin of the idea of the *Trauerspiel* is to be found not so much in the baroque imagination as in the critical contemporary redemption of its truth, in its actuality.

Trauerspiel and tragedy

For Benjamin, a genuine critical understanding of the *Trauerspiel* can develop only by uncovering its truth content and acknowledging its distinctiveness – in short, in recognizing the *Trauerspiel* as an idea. Such an appreciation has been hampered by the erroneous conflation of *Trauerspiel* and tragedy, based upon certain superficial resemblances. The *Trauerspiel* did not conform to the Aristotelian poetics and dramatic conventions of ancient Greek tragedy,[34] but, nevertheless, was examined and evaluated in such terms.[35]

> The *Trauerspiel* of the German baroque appeared to be a caricature of classical tragedy. There was no difficulty in reconciling with this scheme of things everything about these works which was offensive or even barbaric to refined taste. The theme of the *Haupt- und Staatsaktionen* was seen as a distortion of the ancient royal drama, the bombast as a distortion of the dignified pathos of the Greeks, and the bloody finale as a distortion of the tragic catastrophe. The *Trauerspiel* thus took on the appearance of an incompetent renaissance of tragedy. (*OGTD*, p. 50)

Benjamin's study is directed against such spurious equations and judgements, based as they are upon the presupposition and elevation of certain 'timeless' aesthetic categories.[36] Why privilege classical tragedy? One could equally well regard Greek tragedy as (rather unsuccessful) experiments in the writing of *Trauerspiele*. The baroque claimed the superiority of the *Trauerspiel*. As Benjamin observed, it 'regarded its own forms as "natural", not so much the antithesis, as the conquest and elevation of its rival. Ancient tragedy is the fettered slave on the triumphal car of the baroque *Trauerspiel*' (*OGTD*, p. 100).

Benjamin rejected such futile debates, and abstained from judgements regarding not only the purported relative merits of tragedy and *Trauerspiel*, but also those of different *Trauerspiele* themselves. Supposedly mediocre examples of the mourning play are no less worthy of attention than the more celebrated works.[37] Indeed, these 'inferior' texts, in which tendencies may manifest themselves in extreme form, may be more valuable to the genuine critic, since

> It is one thing to incarnate a form; it is quite a different thing to give it its characteristic expression. Whereas the former is the business of the poet elect, the latter is often done incomparably more distinctly in the laborious efforts of minor writers . . . [T]he form itself becomes evident precisely in the lean body of the inferior work, as its skeleton so to speak. (*OGTD*, p. 58)

And it is, of course, in this mortified form, as a 'skeleton', that the truth of the *Trauerspiel* is to be discerned.

Benjamin specifies a number of fundamental differences between *Trauerspiel* and tragedy, with respect to the dramatic plot (in terms of its relationship with history and myth), the central heroic character (as regards decisiveness and action), and the inevitable 'heroic' death (as melancholy and as comedy). The *Trauerspiel* is not to be understood as failed tragedy, but is rather to be restored in its own terms as the glory of the allegorical imagination – that is, as a vision of a God-forsaken world and its representation through the sorrowful musicality of the language of lament.

Benjamin's key insight into the content of the *Trauerspiel* is the recognition that it is concerned with the portrayal, however outlandish, absurd or grotesque, of fallen, human history. The catastrophic downfall of princes and kings, the sinister machinations of the court, the bloody butchery and ignominious ends of tyrants, the pitiful sufferings of martyrs – such were its principal subject matter.[38] Benjamin writes:

Historical life, as it was conceived at that time, is its content, its true object. In this it is different from tragedy. For the object of the latter is not history but myth, and the tragic stature of the *dramatis personae* does not derive from rank – the absolute monarchy – but from the prehistoric epoch of their existence – the past age of heroes. (*OGTD*, p. 62)

Whereas Greek tragedy presents the intercourse of mortals, gods and fantastical beings, locating them in an epoch outside ordinary historical life, it was precisely the inescapable, abject condition of profane human existence that concerned the baroque playwright. Indeed, just as history was the source of the *Trauerspiel*, so too did the play of mourning become a metaphor for the unfolding of historical events themselves.[39] 'The *Trauerspiel*, it was believed, could be directly grasped in the events of history itself; it was only a question of finding the right words' (*OGTD*, p. 63). The *Trauerspiel* gave voice to sorrowful history, translating its lament into dramatic speech.

The *Trauerspiel* expressed ruinous historical events principally in the central figure of the absolute sovereign. In the *Trauerspiel*, 'The sovereign is the representative of history. He holds the course of history in his hands like a sceptre' (*OGTD*, p. 65). Or rather, historical forces hold the king in their grasp, like a plaything; for the sovereign does not control happenings, but becomes their abject victim. Hence, although 'again and again, it is the single fact of the royal hero which prompted the critics to relate the new *Trauerspiel* to the ancient tragedy of the Greeks' (*OGTD*, p. 61), the sovereign of the mourning play is no tragic hero. In classical drama the hero disturbs divine law through transgression and hubris, and confronts fate with bold defiance. By contrast, the sovereign in the *Trauerspiel* represents feeble humankind enslaved by passion, folly and caprice. Goaded into hasty, murderous actions by ephemeral desires, rash jealousies and foolish pride, the sovereign as tyrant perpetrates unspeakable horrors upon his hapless victims, before all-consuming vengeance for these crimes is unleashed upon him.[40] The sovereign as martyr stoically undergoes mental and, above all, physical torments in his own terrible demise.[41] Indeed, whether tyrant or martyr or both, it is the gulf between the seeming omnipotence of the sovereign and his eventual pathetic powerlessness, so violently inscribed upon his ruined body, which is the key to the *Trauerspiel*.[42] Benjamin notes that 'The enduring fascination of the downfall of the tyrant is rooted in the impotence and depravity of his person, on the one hand, and, on the other, the extent to which the age was convinced of the sacrosanct power of his role' (*OGTD*, p. 72). The sovereign, the noblest human, cannot escape the weaknesses and wretchedness of the creaturely condition.[43] He or she is only ever 'the supreme creature' (*OGTD*, p. 86). In the *Trauerspiel*, the sovereign embodies history as catastrophe precisely through the history of the doomed creaturely body. History thus appears in a particular manner, as 'natural history' (*Naturgeschichte*), as the inevitable ruination of the *physis* and its transformation into the corpse. The *Trauerspiel* presents the lavish spectacle of earthly power, wealth and honour, only to reveal these as mere vanities, the trifling decorations upon a world emptied of substance and significance.

The final death of the sovereign does not point to the prospect of everlasting life in the hereafter. This is an important, distinctive feature of the baroque drama. Unlike its medieval predecessors,[44] the drama of the baroque did not culminate in the redemption and resurrection of the Day of Judgement, but rather, insisting on the absolute separation between divine and profane realms, envisaged only apocalyptic destruction. Benjamin writes:

> The baroque knows no eschatology; and for that very reason it possesses no mechanism by which all earthly things are gathered in together and exalted before being consigned to their end. The hereafter is emptied of everything which contains the slightest breath of this world . . . in order to clear an ultimate heaven, enabling it, as a vacuum, one day to destroy the world with catastrophic violence. (*OGTD*, p. 66)

The violent end met by the sovereign, his or her court and the various other characters of the *Trauerspiel* is an anticipatory representation of the common fate of humanity.

The death of the sovereign is neither heroic nor tragic. Benjamin contends that in classical tragedy the hero perishes in the form of a sacrifice which marks a rupture in the life of the community and ushers in a new moral order.[45] Tragedy is comparable to legal trial,[46] in which, in the final judgement and execution of the guilty hero, a new precedent is set, a new heaven and a new earth created.[47] Drawing on the work of Franz Rosenzweig, he suggests that this fatal moment is one of silence. The tragic hero is reduced to 'dumb anguish' (*OGTD*, p. 107) by the final recognition that, though mortal, he is superior to the gods who have connived in imposing a terrible, unjust fate upon him.[48] Here, judge and accused are reversed:

> what appears before the public is not the guilt of the accused but the evidence of speechless suffering, and the tragedy which appeared to be devoted to the judgement of the hero is transformed into a hearing about the Olympians in which the latter appears as a witness and, against the will of the gods, displays the honour of the demi-god. (*OGTD*, p. 109)

Speechlessness becomes both a fundamental indictment of the gods and the 'manifestation of the agonal in the tragic sphere' (*OGTD*, p. 108). For Benjamin, silence is thus the very foundation of tragedy.[49]

Silent sacrifice has no place in the drama of the baroque. In the *Trauerspiel*, death occasions pandemonium and a cacophony of dirges and lamentations. The sovereign as tyrant dies not as a consequence of tragic fate, but rather because he is heedless of, and undone by, the maddening impulses and irresistible temptations which enthral the creature.[50] Death is the final triumph of the creaturely over the human being, not the elevation of the mortal before tarnished deities. It is this which provokes the ceaseless outpourings of grief; it is this which defines *Trauerspiel* as unmistakably as silence defines tragedy.

The sovereign's demise is not ordained by questionable gods, but 'choreographed'[51] by the other key figure of the *Trauerspiel*, the duplicitous courtier, the intriguer. Quick-witted and cunning, the intriguer is the unscrupulous schemer who, as a perpetual source of lies and rumour, lures the gullible sovereign into those foolhardy actions which ensure his ruin. The intriguer 'corresponds to an ideal which was first outlined by Machiavelli' (*OGTD*, p. 95), a figure in whom knowledge of the workings of government and of human nature are combined in the ruthless pursuit of power. Above all, the intriguer is intimately acquainted with the prejudices and passions of the creature, weaknesses which he provokes and channels for his own malevolent purposes. The intriguer is the puppet-master pulling the strings of the hapless sovereign. The metaphor here is not accidental. In the continual wordplays and ironies which distinguish his speeches, the intriguer is a figure not only of evil, inspiring terror, but also of morbid humour, provoking laughter. The *Trauerspiel* oscillates between sorrow and daemonic merriment. In the anti-heroic character of the arch-villain, the *Trauerspiel* displays close affinities with, and frequently descends into, comedy

(*Lustspiel*),[52] pantomime[53] and puppet-play.[54] Indeed, Benjamin claims that 'The finest exemplifications of *Trauerspiel* are not those which adhere strictly to the rules, but those in which there are playful modulations of the *Lustspiel*' (*OGTD*, p. 127). For him, nothing distinguishes *Trauerspiel* and tragedy more clearly than this comic tendency.

Benjamin writes that 'Comedy – or more precisely the pure joke – is the essential inner side of mourning which from time to time, like the lining of a dress at the hem or lapel, makes its presence felt' (*OGTD*, pp. 125–6). This duality and reversibility is incarnated in the figures of the grinning intriguer and the sorrowful sovereign.[55] The despondency and despair of the sovereign are fundamental,[56] for his downfall is not simply a product of the machinations of the wicked courtier, but, first and foremost, a consequence of his failure to act decisively under the oppressive burden of sadness. He is doomed not by heroic action, but by melancholy, creaturely inaction, *acedia*. Sorrow does not arise from catastrophe; it precedes it, finding solace in its grim contemplation. For Benjamin, this is the very heart of *Trauerspiel*: 'these are not so much plays which cause mourning, as plays through which mournfulness finds satisfaction: plays for the mournful' (*OGTD*, p. 119). The *Trauerspiel* as the dramatic exploration and representation of the melancholy mind and the saturnine temperament here leads Benjamin into an *excursus* on the arcane intricacies of medieval and baroque pathological and astrological systems.

For Benjamin, melancholy is to be understood conceptually not as 'the emotional condition of the poet or his public' (*OGTD*, p. 139), but rather as a historical sensibility or cultural condition, a particular 'way of seeing' (Pensky, 1993, p. 15), or *Weltanschauung*. As such, melancholy involved a complex of attributes, associations and astrological connections which fascinated the baroque. Benjamin's point of departure here is the classical theory of the temperaments and humours as elaborated by medieval scholars. Following Hippocrates,[57] physicians of the Middle Ages diagnosed melancholia as a pathological condition brought about by an excess of black bile, the cold, dry humour associated with the spleen, slowness, lethargy, earthliness and the planet Saturn.[58] Such theories had a particular resonance in the baroque, which endlessly multiplied and codified them in emblematic schemes. Melancholy is the ' "least noble complexion" ' (*OGTD*, p. 145), rendering its sufferer ' "envious, mournful, greedy, avaricious, disloyal, timorous, and sallow" ' (*OGTD*, p. 145). This uninspiring list of attributes suggests affinities with the intriguer, rather than the sovereign.[59] However, there are antithetical moments which give the saturnine individual a particular quality and propensity. Selfish and self-absorbed, the melancholic is also pensive and reflective, not a cunning schemer, but a gloomy thinker, a brooder.[60]

Melancholy involves a renunciation of action and engagement in the world in favour of a retreat into the inner life of the mind, meditation and contemplation. The melancholy individual recognizes the God-forsaken condition of the world and the futility of human struggle within it. Melancholy is the basest, 'the most genuinely creaturely of the contemplative impulses' (*OGTD*, p. 146), precisely because it involves the recognition of oneself *as creaturely*. The wisdom of the melancholy figure 'is secured by immersion in the life of creaturely things, and it hears nothing of the voice of revelation. Everything saturnine points down into the depths of the earth' (*OGTD*, p. 152). Lacking 'the lightening flash of intuition' (*OGTD*, p. 153), the brooder 'bores into the ground with his eyes' (*OGTD*, p. 152), and gazes steadily into the abysmal depths of the profane world. Slow but unrelenting, the melancholy figure is the 'tireless investigator and thinker' (*OGTD*, p. 152) who fixes himself upon, and intensely scrutinizes, the domain of objects. Hence, while melancholy pensiveness appears to abandon profane existence for a loftier realm, it is in fact 'born of a loyalty to the world of things' (*OGTD*, p. 157). Benjamin notes that 'Melancholy betrays the world for the sake of knowledge. But in its tenacious self-absorption it embraces dead objects in its contemplation, in order to redeem them' (*OGTD*, p. 157).

Patience, digression,[61] absorption, redemption – these are the hallmarks of melancholy thought and, of course, of Benjamin's own methods of criticism. The genuine critic, the philosopher, is a figure of melancholy *par excellence*, and one for whom the profane world becomes a book, a script to be contemplated and deciphered. In one of his most memorable phrases, Benjamin writes: 'The Renaissance explores the universe; the baroque explores libraries. Its meditations are devoted to books. "The world knows no greater book than itself"' (*OGTD*, p. 140).[62] The world is a text, a series of signs and hieroglyphs to be interpreted by the brooding gaze of the sorrowful thinker. Here, the melancholy world of Lutheran doctrine portrayed in the *Trauerspiel*, the Judaic post-lapsarian world of Babel discussed in the 'On Language' essay, and Benjamin's own understanding of the redemptive task of philosophy combine. As the name-giver of Creation, Adam is not only the first philosopher, but also the first melancholy man, the first to possess, according to Paracelsus, 'creaturely mournfulness' (*OGTD*, pp. 146–7). *Trauerspiel* seeks to give voice to this world-historical sorrow, to express the sadness of Creation and its creatures. It does so in 'the only pleasure the melancholic permits himself' (*OGTD*, p. 185): allegory.

Allegory redeemed

The negative judgement passed on the *Trauerspiel* stemmed not only from its misrecognition as tragedy, but also from the devaluation of its central poetic element: allegory. For Benjamin, the critical recovery of the *Trauerspiel* is possible, therefore, only through a 'philosophical understanding' (*OGTD*, p. 189) and appreciation of the richness of allegory as a mode of expression. Thus it is to this that the third and final section of his *Trauerspiel* study is devoted.

At its simplest, allegory may be understood as a figure of speech in which an element or object comes to signify or stand for something else. Gold as an object or a colour, for example, might be used by the dramatist to represent wealth. An element from one register (metallurgy) points to one from another (economic), based upon some perceived similarity or correspondence. This process of signification may be subject to proliferation, and it is here that allegory as a complex trope becomes apparent. Depending upon context, gold might also, or instead, signify nobility, purity, beauty, pomp and splendour, ostentation, gaudy show, artifice, decadence, greed, or the vanity of earthly riches. Allegory is conventional, extensive (moving from one term to another) and diachronic (this movement occurring through time). Moreover, as the example demonstrates, allegory may, as referents multiply, suddenly reverse direction to act as the negation of its other possible meanings.

For Benjamin, the neoclassical prejudices and preferences of nineteenth-century commentators resulted, on the one hand, in the elevation and privileging of the supposed merits of the symbol and, on the other, in 'the denunciation of a form of expression, such as allegory, as a mere mode of designation' (*OGTD*, p. 162).[63] Whereas the meaning of allegory depends upon an oscillation between two discrete terms, the power of a symbol resides in the unity and immediacy with which it expresses an idea. The meaning of a symbol is not dispersed across a plethora of disparate referents, but is concentrated intensively in a single image as a '"momentary totality"' (*OGTD*, p. 165). Full, complete, self-contained, the symbol encapsulates the virtues of '"clarity . . . brevity . . . grace . . . and beauty"' (*OGTD*, p. 163). Moreover, its success relies not upon the recognition of conventional associations, but precisely upon its inspired originality. In a phrase which anticipates his own notion of the dialectical image, Benjamin quotes Friedrich Creuzer's eulogy to the symbol thus: '"It is like the sudden appearance of a ghost, or a flash of lightning which illuminates the dark night. It is a force which seizes hold of our entire being"' (*OGTD*, p. 163). The symbol is astonishing in its economy, captivating in its brilliance, breath-taking in its power.

Just as *Trauerspiel* was seen to constitute failed, bastardized tragedy, so allegory appeared to be a feeble imitation of the symbol.[64] Instead of brevity and beauty, allegory offered only the long-winded elaboration and excessive ornamentation of strained, commonplace associations. Allegory was derided as clumsy, con-voluted and crude, the mechanical construction of an impoverished poetic imagination. But for Benjamin, such prejudices obscure the true significance of allegory, which is disclosed only in immanent critique: allegory conforms to, and potently conveys, the baroque world-view within the framework of the *Trauerspiel*. It is the mode in which the baroque represented itself to itself. Benjamin saw allegory as capturing the world, not in its fullness and perfection, but in its ruination and fragmentation.[65] Allegory aspires neither to clarity nor grace, but lays itself bare as meaningless verbosity, as the broken, arbitrary language of fallen humanity and mournful nature.[66] Allegory is not failed symbol; it is the divine symbol's creaturely counterpart.

The symbol presents the eternal in the lightning flash of the mys-tical instant, the *Nu*. Allegory portrays the transient and ephemeral in the duration of sorrowful contemplation.[67] For Benjamin, allegory presents life subject to time: natural history as decay and ruina-tion.[68] In the absence of eschatology, the allegorical gaze is fixed upon 'the form in which man's subjection to nature is most obvious' (*OGTD*, p. 166), that is, creaturely death. Benjamin writes:

> in allegory the observer is confronted with the *facies hippocritica* of history as a petrified, primordial landscape. Everything about history that, from the very beginning, has been untimely, sorrowful, unsuc-cessful, is expressed in a face – or rather in a death's head . . . This is the heart of the allegorical way of seeing, of the baroque, secular

explanation of history as the Passion of the world; its importance resides solely in the stations of its decline. (*OGTD*, p. 166)

It was over this desolate, profane world that the allegorical imagination brooded.

Ruin and resurrection

The pre-eminent figure for the demise of the creaturely as natural history is the ruin, an object which fascinated the baroque.[69] The ruin presents the vanity and transience of human labour as a process of gradual yet relentless collapse and final extinction. Benjamin writes:

> In the ruin history has merged into the setting. And in this guise history does not assume the form of the process of an eternal life so much as that of irresistible decay. Allegory thereby declares itself to be beyond beauty. Allegories are, in the realm of thoughts, what ruins are in the realm of things. (*OGTD*, pp. 177–8)

The allegory and the ruin have a particular affinity. As allegory unfolds its wealth of potential referents, the specific meaning of the allegorical object is lost in a profusion of possible interpretations such that 'Any person, any object, any relationship can mean absolutely anything else. With this possibility a destructive, but just verdict is passed on the profane world: it is characterised as a world in which detail is of no importance' (*OGTD*, p. 175). The downcast gaze of the allegorist is focused on the object world, and recognizes the capacity of things to point beyond themselves in the act of signification (and hence their ultimate interconnection), but, in the last instance, can discern no particular sense within them. Hence the brooder (*Grübler*) endlessly accumulates and patiently ponders over fragments whose meaning eludes him. Benjamin writes:

> That which lies here in ruins, the highly significant fragment, the remnant, is, in fact, the finest material in baroque creation. For it is common practice in the literature of the baroque to pile up fragments ceaselessly, without any strict idea of a goal . . . in the unremitting expectation of a miracle. . . . The baroque writers must have regarded the work of art as just such a miracle. (*OGTD*, p. 178)

On the one hand, the *Trauerspiel* is 'just such a miracle' of meaningfulness. On the other, it has allegory as its principal linguistic figure – that is to say, at its core is the evaporation or disintegration of meaning. 'In the spirit of allegory', Benjamin notes, the *Trauerspiel*, 'is conceived from the outset as a ruin, a fragment' (*OGTD*, p. 235) hollowed out like a worm-eaten corpse by the allegorical poetics within it.

Allegory is a mode of ruination for the sake of truth. The corpse is 'emblematic' here (*OGTD*, p. 218). The human being reduced to a corpse is the ultimate representation of the natural history of the body. In martyrdom, the living body of the sovereign is subject to the agony of dismemberment at the hand of the torturer. In allegory, the corpse of the creature is dissected by the dramatist so that the fragments of the *physis* can be imbued with meanings and associations.[70] The allegorical mutilation of the corpse is not for the purpose of salvation, but in order to disclose in the ruined body the truth and hopelessness of the creaturely condition.[71] Benjamin writes: 'the human body could be no exception to the commandment which ordered the destruction of the organic so that the true meaning as it was written and ordained, might be picked up from its fragments' (*OGTD*, p. 216).

In allegory, the meaning of the object is torn apart, subject to a process of mortification, scattered to 'the manifold regions of meaning' (*OGTD*, p. 217). The action of allegory here parallels that of criticism. In the search for truth, both allegory and criticism are concerned with the ruination of (beautiful) appearance and the illusion of totality which characterize the work of art and, in particular, the symbol. Allegory itself becomes an allegory for criticism. The very methods of genuine philosophical criticism which Benjamin proposes in the Prologue correspond precisely to the processes already at work within baroque drama. Benjamin writes of the *Trauerspiele* that 'from the very beginning they are set up for that erosion by criticism which befell them in the course of time' (*OGTD*, p. 182). In this recognition, immanent critique displays its full power and significance. Criticism is the continuation of the baroque work of art by other means.

Allegorical poetics partake not of divine beauty, but of creaturely anguish. Benjamin bluntly states that 'Its language was heavy with material display. Never has poetry been less winged' (*OGTD*, p. 200). This is not a judgement but an insight. The language of the *Trauerspiel* involves a seemingly unstoppable outpouring of the most concrete images[72] and tropes.[73] Benjamin notes that 'Occasionally the imagery seems almost to get out of control and the poetry to degenerate into flights of ideas' (*OGTD*, p. 199). Language gilds itself until it is burdened down with ornament. The ever more obscure meanings of allegorical figures are elaborated and developed. Convoluted metaphors are extended to the point of incoherence. Arcane emblems, signs and hieroglyphs proliferate and accumulate for their own sake. Baroque poetics exhausts itself in verbosity and bombast, in a superabundance, an overdetermination of meaning – that is to say, in meaninglessness.[74] The language of the *Trauerspiel* rebels against the communication of meaning: sound and music come to confront and supplant meaning.[75] The musicality of the mourning play consists in the lamentation of the creature. Nor is it only human misery that was to be given voice, but also the sufferings of fallen nature. In his 1916 essay on language, Benjamin contends that, were mute nature to be given voice, it would begin to lament. Baroque drama is preoccupied with translating and presenting this sound. The conventional character of allegory and its ceaseless hollowing-out of meaning are not signs of aesthetic failure. Rather, they correspond to the arbitrariness of the over-naming of nature and the proliferation of post-lapsarian human language. The *Trauerspiel* conforms to 'the stylistic law of bombast' (*OGTD*, p. 210), not due to the clumsiness of the baroque poet, but rather because it was through such a cacophony of meaningless sound that the prattle of languages in the profane world could find dramatic representation. The language of *Trauerspiel* expresses the melancholy of all Creation.

Benjamin is at pains to stress that 'a critical understanding of the *Trauerspiel*, in its extreme, allegorical form, is possible only from the higher domain of theology' (*OGTD*, p. 216). This theological interpretation depends in the final instance upon recognition of the dialectical, reversible character of allegorical thinking. In its concern with expressing the God-forsaken world, allegory tumbles from one image to another in its descent into the abyss of meaninglessness. Yet:

> As those who lose their footing turn somersaults in their fall, so would the allegorical intention fall from emblem to emblem down into the dizziness of its bottomless depths, were it not that, even in the most extreme of them, it had so to turn about that all its darkness, vainglory, and godlessness seem to be nothing but self-delusion. (*OGTD*, p. 232)

Just as gold, in the earlier example, can become an allegory not only for sovereign splendour, but also for earthly vanity, so the allegories of decay and ruination finally reverse direction and transform themselves into those of salvation and redemption. Benjamin writes:

> Allegory goes away empty-handed. Evil as such, which it cherished as enduring profundity, exists only in allegory, is nothing other than allegory, and means something different from what it is. It means precisely the non-existence of what it presents. The absolute vices, as exemplified by tyrants and intriguers are allegories. They are not real. (*OGTD*, p. 233)

In the dialectical play of allegory, the profane world is cast down only for it to be raised up once more. In allegory, the pre-eminent image of creaturely existence, the mortified flesh of the corpse, suddenly becomes 'the allegory of resurrection' (*OGTD*, p. 232).[76] The grinning skull, the '"death's head"' becomes an '"angel's countenance"' (*OGTD*, p. 232). All that is profane is made holy once more.

Benjamin notes that 'an appreciation of the transience of things, and the concern to rescue them for eternity, is one of the strongest impulses in allegory' (*OGTD*, p. 223). Allegory does not merely express the creaturely condition, it redeems it. Allegory, 'left entirely to its own devices, re-discovers itself, not playfully in the earthly world of things, but seriously under the eyes of heaven' (*OGTD*, p. 232). But in the final instance, it cannot be left alone. Allegory itself is in need of salvation, and this is the achievement of the *Ursprung des deutschen Trauerspiel*. Benjamin's study recognizes and redeems the profundity of the allegorical imagination as a form of melancholy redemption, as a moment of creaturely hope in the contemplation of hopelessness.

Conclusion

Far from being an esoteric study of obscure 'cobwebbed texts', Benjamin's work on the *Trauerspiel* continues his engagement with, and transformation of, contemporary literary and cultural criticism. He develops and extends the notion of immanent critique derived from Schlegel and Novalis, not just to recover and restore a neglected theatrical form for its own sake, but to demonstrate its resonance in the present, its contemporary affinities, its actuality. In his Prologue

Benjamin delineates and elaborates a number of key critical principles and concepts:

1 The domain of truth, the perfection of Adamic naming, as a manifold or universe of 'ideas' or essences, among them aesthetic 'ideas'.
2 The representation of the aesthetic 'idea' as the task of criticism. The 'idea' is conceived as a 'constellation' of artworks, of disparate phenomena which combine to form a legible pattern.
3 The monadological fragment. The 'idea' is the truth content of the individual work of art, which in turn encapsulates and expresses the 'idea' in miniature.
4 Criticism as 'mortification'. Truth content is perceptible only in the ruinous afterlife – indeed at the final moment of extinction – of the artwork or object.
5 The notion of 'origin'. This refers to the instant in which, distinct from material content and appearance, truth content takes its place in the constellation, and the 'idea' is recognized as such.

Benjamin envisages and presents criticism as a process of destruction and (re)construction. The disintegration of the artwork and its liberation from traditional interpretations and contexts (afterlife) permit its relocation, reconfiguration and redemption as part of a wider pattern (as mosaic, as constellation). Mortification and (re-)engineering – these critical activities not only 'recreate' the work of art (illuminate it in a new way) but also 'recreate' criticism as a genre (reconceptualize and reorient it as a practice). Criticism is directed to the moment in which the truth of the artwork suddenly manifests itself as the idea comes into being as a constellation – in other words, to the moment of origin.

Benjamin's attempt to disclose the origins of the *Trauerspiel* then offers a powerful and persuasive rereading and rehabilitation of this arcane dramatic form and its allegorical poetics. Freed from the misperceptions and misappropriations of past critics, the 'idea' of *Trauerspiel* is represented by Benjamin as a derelict ruin, as the most profound and least 'poetic' expression of profane history as catastrophe, human existence as creaturely compulsion, and language itself as senseless babble. And it is in allegory, that trope wherein meaning is endlessly multiplied and mortified, that the baroque dramatist found a fitting linguistic figure for the profusion and confusion of post-lapsarian prattle and the lament of overnamed nature, and that Benjamin, in turn, found a counterpart to his own conception of criticism as ruination and redemption.

Monad and constellation, illumination and redemption, history and ruination, melancholy and allegory – in interweaving and elaborating these themes, the *Trauerspiel* study constituted a moment of closure for Benjamin. Even before its failure he confided to Scholem in a letter of 19 February 1925: 'this project marks an end for me – I would not have it be a beginning for any money in the world. . . . I want to work in a polar climate. This would be very different from what has become for me the all too temperate climate of my baroque project' (*COR*, p. 261). Although Benjamin was indeed to toil in more extreme, perilous circumstances following the *Trauerspiel* study's completion, that completion should not be viewed as a *caesura*. The conceptual repertoire it developed was to inform all Benjamin's subsequent writings: the origin and contested afterlife of the monadological object/artwork, fragmentary representation as constellation and montage, remembrance and redemption as critical imperative, discontinuity and ruination rather than historical 'progress', the allegorical imagination of the brooder. Hence, the *Trauerspiel* study does not mark a moment of rupture, but rather one of *inter*ruption, an 'eddy in the stream of becoming' of Benjamin's ideas, a point of origin itself. Benjamin was to return to these themes again and again, but from shifted viewpoints and with different objects of analysis: Surrealism and cityscapes; the arcades, fashions and commodities of Paris; film and photography; Brecht's plays and Baudelaire's poetry. The *Trauerspiel* study concludes Benjamin's early writings just as it looks forward to his later ones: it is Janus-faced.

3

From Cityscape to Dreamworld

Introduction

In a letter of 30 January 1928 to Scholem, Benjamin wrote:

> Once I have, one way or another, completed the project on which I am currently working, carefully and provisionally – the highly remarkable and extremely precarious essay 'Paris Arcades: A Dialectical Fairy Play [*Pariser Passagen: Eine Dialektische Feerie*] – one cycle of production, that of *One-Way Street*, will have come to a close for me in much the same way in which the *Trauerspiel* book concluded the German cycle. The profane motifs of *One-Way Street* will march past in the project, hellishly intensified . . . [I]t is a project that will just take a few weeks. (*COR*, p. 322)

This is a revealing passage. First, it reiterates Benjamin's conviction that the *Trauerspiel* study marks the culmination of a particular phase of his work. It is evident, however, as almost all commentators emphasize, that Benjamin's *oeuvre* is not to be understood in terms of a division into 'early' and 'late' works. Rather, the continuities between his 'production cycles' must be stressed: Benjamin's Parisian writings exhibit numerous, surprising thematic, conceptual and methodological affinities with the *Trauerspiel* study.

Secondly, the letter makes clear Benjamin's understanding of his 1925–6 collection of aphorisms, *One-Way Street* (*Einbahnstrasse*), and its connection to his subsequent study of the shopping arcades of nineteenth-century Paris as part of a new complex, one which gives voice to his abiding fascination with the French capital as the pre-eminent site of avant-garde culture, and indeed of modernity itself.[1] It also reveals how modest Benjamin's initial intentions were for this 'Arcades' study. The *Passagenarbeit* was to prove far more extensive than a 'highly remarkable and extremely precarious essay' and came to occupy him for considerably longer than 'just a few weeks'. It eventually grew to encompass more than 1,000 pages of notes, drafts and sketches, the project remaining unfinished – indeed, unwritten – at the time of his suicide more than twelve years later, in 1940.

The 'Arcades' study may have begun within a 'cycle of production, that of *One-Way Street*', but, in retrospect, *Einbahnstrasse* forms a transitional rather than a 'pivotal' text,[2] part of the earliest phases of the 'cycle of production' of the *Passagenarbeit*. Indeed, the 'Arcades Project' became, if not their actual point of inception, then certainly the sun around which virtually all Benjamin's major writings from the late 1920s onwards revolved: his critical 1929 text on Surrealism; his essays on the transformation of art and perception brought about by new media technologies ('A Small History of Photography' of 1931 and the famous 1935 text 'The Work of Art in the Age of Mechanical Reproduction'); his explorations of memory, flânerie and the cityscape of his native Berlin ('The Image of Proust' of 1929, the reviews of books by Franz Hessel, the reminiscences contained in his 1932 'Berlin Chronicle' and 'Berlin Childhood around 1900'); his studies of the Parisian poet Charles Baudelaire written in the late 1930s; and, finally, the 1940 'Theses on the Concept of History', fragmentary reflections intended to form the historiographic principles underpinning the Paris study. The *One-Way Street* 'cycle' was never brought to a conclusion, but rather, through continual reorientation and reconfiguration, was trans-formed into the 'Arcades' 'cycle', a 'charmed circle of fragments',[3] a constellation of texts on which he was to work for the rest of his life. Ultimately, then, Benjamin's letter is noteworthy in that what it says is wrong in both cases: neither the *Trauerspiel* study nor the 'Dialectical Fairy Play' ever really formed moments of closure.

This chapter examines some of the key early texts in the *Passagenarbeit* constellation: his urban *Denkbilder* from the mid-1920s, his intriguing and provocative *Einbahnstrasse* collection, and his essay on Surrealism. Together these texts begin to articulate a biting, albeit fragmentary, critique of modern urban experience and cultural politics. In *Einbahnstrasse*, Benjamin's literary meta-critique intensifies, and widens into a vociferous attack upon bourgeois culture, morals and scholarship. Here one encounters an unequivocal demand for a new, vital critical practice informed by the techniques of modern media – film, journalism and advertising – and by the experience of the contemporary metropolitan environment. Velocity, tactility, proximity – these were to be the principles of a radical new criticism. *One-Way Street* not only advocated, but also exemplified this enterprise in its own distinctly metropolitan literary architectonics. It involved the interpenetration of urban architecture and writing.

Benjamin's 'thought-images' of Naples and Moscow are of special significance in this context. For him, the highly eclectic, impressionistic *Denkbild* form is a mode of representation appropriate to the dynamism and disorientation of the cityscape. Explicitly renouncing the claims of theory, Benjamin seeks to discern the cityscape through immersion in its 'concrete' particulars, and to illuminate it through the juxtaposition of images. Moreover, 'Naples' and 'Moscow' focus upon forms of urban life and culture that are the very antithesis of the bourgeois individualism, the private isolation and impersonality, the 'restrained cosmopolitanism' of modern European capitals. Naples is 'oriental', feudal and anarchic; whereas Moscow is 'Asiatic', proletarian and revolutionary. Such vital cities, impossibly chaotic, utterly exhausting and seductively labyrinthine, offer Benjamin the opportunity to reflect scornfully upon the stupidity and sterility of life in the Weimar Republic (and Berlin in particular). Fragmentary construction and devastating critique: these two imperatives transform the genuine radical writer into a textual technician – indeed, into an 'engineer' of the aesthetic, the urban and the erotic.

In its montage of wordplays and dream-images *Einbahnstrasse* displays a number of affinities with Surrealist writing. Accordingly, the chapter concludes with a discussion of Benjamin's engagement with Surrealism and, in particular, his critical reception of the writings of Louis Aragon and André Breton. Benjamin's 1929 essay is conceived as an intervention in the immediate afterlife of the Surrealist movement for the purpose of identifying and recovering its radical energies and illuminations. In their recognition of the contemporary city as a 'dreamscape' of erotic adventures, chance finds and mythological forms; their preoccupation with marginal phenomena and outmoded objects; and their privileging of the image and the fragment, the Surrealists provide Benjamin with important insights into the reading and representation of modern culture, insights which were to prove valuable not only for *One-Way Street* but also for the initial conception of the 'Arcades Project'. Moreover, the Surrealist critique of traditional art and aesthetics, and insistence upon proximity, shock and estrangement, also suggested categories and techniques which Benjamin developed later in his writings on film and photography. All this would seem to recommend Aragon and Breton as exemplary 'engineers'. But Benjamin was not convinced. The Surrealists were too immersed in, too intoxicated by, the fantastical forms and uncanny experiences they discovered to provide the necessary clear-sighted, sober criticism. Obscure premonitions of the supernatural, occultism and superstition – such Surrealist predilections had no place in a radical critique of capitalist modernity. For Benjamin, the Surrealists linger in the realm of dreams, whereas what is needed is to awaken from it. Profane illumination is not enough: engineering demands an *explosive* moment.

Urban 'thought-images'

Susan Buck-Morss perceptively writes of the origins of the *Passagenarbeit*: 'the moment is arguably the summer of 1924, and the place is not Paris, but Italy' (1989, p. 8). It was then, and there, that Benjamin's highly idiosyncratic, always unorthodox interrogation and appropriation of Marxist thought began. During his summer sojourn on Capri, Benjamin, busy writing his *Habilitationsschrift*, was introduced by Ernst Bloch to Lukács's recently published *History and Class Consciousness*. Benjamin's avid reading of this key work, which was to become a fundamental text in the historical materialist analysis of the commodity form and the processes of fetishization and reification, constituted his first serious engagement with the Marxist tradition. For Benjamin, it was to suggest a new thematic framework and conceptual vocabulary for his abiding, radical critique of modern bourgeois culture. For Lukács, the commodity form must be recognized as 'the central, structural problem of capitalist society in all its aspects', since 'Only in this case can the structure of commodity relations be made to yield a model of all the objective forms of bourgeois society together with all the subjective forms corresponding to them' (Lukács, 1974, p. 83). For Benjamin, the commodity, as fetish, as fashion, as fossil, was to become the privileged monodological form for the 'Arcades Project'.

Further impetus was given to this new orientation in Benjamin's thinking by another fascinating encounter on Capri that summer. Benjamin embarked on an ill-fated affair with a Latvian actress and theatre director, Asja Lacis, whose own political commitments to Communism and contacts, most notably with the playwright Bertolt Brecht, were to prove highly influential. The significance of Lacis for Benjamin's thinking at this time is indicated by his numerous references in, and final dedication of, *One-Way Street* to her: 'This street is named Asja Lacis after her who as an engineer cut it through the author' (*OWS*, p. 45),[4] an image which, as Cohen notes (1993, p. 184), is suggestive of the creation of the Parisian boulevards and the radical reconstruction of the city under Baron Haussmann during the Second Empire, and indeed of the contemporary 'urban surgery' advocated by Le Corbusier.

Lacis and Lukács were not the only distractions from the *Trauerspiel* study. The cities of Italy also proved seductive. Benjamin writes:

> my inductive way of getting to know the topography of different places and seeking out every great structure in its own labyrinthine environment of banal, beautiful or wretched houses, takes up too much time. . . . But I do come away with an excellent image of the topography of these places. The first and most important thing you have to do is feel your way through a city so that you can return to it with complete assurance. (*COR*, p. 254)

It was neither Rome nor Florence which seized his imagination, however, but rather the chaos of Naples. He notes:

> as soon as I have finished a fair copy, 'Naples' [*Neapel*] will be published in Latvian and German. I still have not bid farewell to this city, even with my stay in Rome. The restrained cosmopolitan atmosphere of Rome left me cold, especially after the highly temperamental way of life in Naples. Only now can I really judge how oriental a city Naples is. (*COR*, p. 253)

Composed in conjunction with Lacis in September/October 1924 'Naples' was the first of Benjamin's numerous, impressionistic city portraits, fragments which he termed *Denkbilder* ('thought-images'). Others were to follow, indicating a growing fascination with cityscapes and forms of urban experience: 'Moscow' (December/January 1926–7), 'Weimar' (June 1928), 'Marseilles' and 'Hashish in Marseilles' (October 1928–January 1929), 'Paris, the City in the Mirror' (January 1929), 'San Gimignano' (published August 1929) and 'North Sea' (15 August 1930).

These *Denkbilder* are imagistic miniatures which seek to capture the fluid and fleeting character of metropolitan existence. The cityscape is not naively perused by the 'banal tourist' (*OWS*, p. 168), but rather is dissected by the keen, critical eye of the physiognomist *en passant*, so that it may subsequently be represented with the precision and plenitude of an urban photograph. Dispensing with the superficial overview offered by guidebooks, bypassing conventional tourist attractions, Benjamin seeks a special relationship with the urban setting, an immersion within its spaces and quotidian experiences, a tactile proximity which enables him to 'feel' his way through. His city portraits are concerned with identifying and articulating the structuring principles of the cityscape as they manifest themselves in their particularity and concreteness within everyday urban life. The city is to be read and represented through the scrupulous rendering of its apparent minutiae and trivia: the momentary, the accidental and the neglected.

This attention to the smallest manifestations and traces of the everyday is fundamental. Abstraction is to be avoided at all costs. In a letter to Buber concerning 'Moscow', Benjamin announces:

> My presentation will be devoid of all theory. In this fashion I hope to allow the 'creatural' to speak for itself . . . I want to write a description of Moscow at the present moment in which 'all factuality is already theory' and which would thereby refrain from any deductive abstraction, from any prognostication, and even within certain limits, from any judgement. (*MD*, p. 132)

The theoretical grounding of the *Denkbilder* is paradoxically the absence of theory, or a wilful dissolution of theory. Interpretation and analysis, commentary and critique – these are to be eschewed in favour of an approach which 'can grasp the concrete' (*OWS*, p. 177) and enable it to speak for itself. The task of the writer is, through selection and arrangement, to show, to demonstrate without comment. Composed of a plethora of carefully gathered, juxtaposed particulars, the *Denkbilder* are not so much single 'snapshots' as kaleidoscopic representations, miniature mosaics, or, in the new language of the 'Arcades' production cycle, cinematic 'montages'.

The *Denkbilder* exhibit many of the methodological innovations and textual strategies of *One-Way Street* and the 'Arcades Project': tactile intimacy, concreteness, immediacy, and imagistic and fragmentary construction. Further, the thematic contents of the city miniatures prefigure these more extensive studies. The *Denkbilder*

take as their principal focus the energetic, ephemeral spectacle of
the urban street: its architecture, objects and spaces; its milling
crowds and deafening traffic; its teeming markets and bazaars;
the various theatrical performances of street vendors, swindlers,
beggars and other eccentric characters; its encounters, contingencies and seductions. These constitute a series of monadological fragments which reveal the true character of the city.

In 'Naples', Benjamin opens with an anecdote concerning the
public humiliation of a miscreant priest (*OWS*, p. 167), an episode
which points not only to the enduring power and authority of
Catholicism, but also to the carnivalesque, reversible character of
all social arrangements in Naples. 'Porosity' is the 'inexhaustible
law' (*OWS*, p. 171) of Neapolitan life and the key to understanding
its 'rich barbarism' (*OWS*, p. 167), its 'oriental' character. In the
design of its architecture and the practices of its inhabitants, Naples
retains a 'passion for improvisation' (*OWS*, p. 170), one which
demands and ensures that 'the stamp of the definite is avoided' so
that the city can 'become a theatre of new, unforeseen constellations'
(*OWS*, p. 169). It is in Naples, above all, that urban orientation and
navigation are a sensuous, tactile experience, where one must 'feel'
one's way through 'the tightly packed multiplicity' (*OWS*, p. 174)
and the 'anarchical, embroiled, village-like' centre, into which, in a
phrase anticipating Benjamin's *Einbahnstrasse* dedication, 'large net-
works of streets were hacked only forty years ago' (*OWS*, p. 170).

If in 'Naples' the abiding metaphor is the 'theatre of the new',
then in 'Moscow', composed during a visit to the new Soviet capital
in the winter of 1926–7, it is the revolutionary 'experiment'.[5]
Although Benjamin notes unsuspected similarities between
Moscow and Naples (its labyrinthine character,[6] the chaotic vitality
of the street markets,[7] the persistence of beggars,[8] the dazzling sun-
light and whirl of colour[9]), and traces the interaction between
archaic and modern forms,[10] the signature of Muscovite urban experience is not so much the 'porosity' or interpenetration of traditional
and contemporary elements, but rather their radical incongruity[11]
and unpredictable transformation. In 'Moscow', Benjamin juxtaposes an 'Asiatic' sensibility and the spatial and temporal demands
of the incipient Bolshevik system, ones which have 'accelerated the
process of Europeanization' (*OWS*, p. 197).

Moscow is a city in a state of constant mobilization, perpetual
flux. Accordingly, it is the pace and rhythm of motion in the city
which are decisive for Benjamin's *Denkbild*. 'Moscow' registers
the distinctive challenges and experiences – technical, tactical and

tactile – encountered by the visitor who wishes to explore the cityscape. The newcomer to Moscow must abandon all lofty pretensions. To make progress along the overcrowded, narrow pavements, the pedestrian must devise a 'strategy of shoving and weaving', a distinctive 'serpentine gait'. Simultaneously, one must master again 'the technique of achieving locomotion' in that on the 'thick sheet ice of the streets walking has to be relearned' (*OWS*, pp. 178–9). One becomes like a child again. Similarly, in the sleigh, the city's principal mode of transport, 'You feel like a child gliding through the house on its little chair' (*OWS*, p. 191). This involves a particular sense of intimacy:

> The passenger is not enthroned high up; he looks out on the same level as everyone else and brushes the passers-by with his sleeve. Even this is an incomparable experience for the sense of touch. Where Europeans, on their rapid journeys, enjoy superiority, dominance over the masses, the Moscovite in the little sleigh is closely mingled with people and things. (*OWS*, p. 191)

Benjamin sees the child as having a privileged proximity to, and special tactile appreciation of, the urban environment. The child sees the city 'at first sight', with a gaze unencumbered by the tedium of familiarity and habit, with a receptivity and acuity the recovery of which occupies Benjamin in *One-Way Street* and in his later reflections on Berlin. In Moscow, 'The instant one arrives, the childhood stage begins' (*OWS*, p. 179). Nothing could be more precarious, nothing more precious.[12]

It is, however, neither the unsteady pedestrian nor the gliding sleigh, but rather the streetcar which provides Benjamin with the definitive monadological fragment in 'Moscow'.[13] This, too, is 'a tactical experience' for the newcomer. Boarding involves 'A tenacious barging and shoving', until the vehicle is 'overloaded to the point of bursting' (*OWS*, p. 190). It is an unpredictable journey. Unable to see through the windows of the tram, and unable to get out in any event because of the 'human wedge' barring the exit, one awaits a suitable moment to alight with the mass of fellow passengers, wherever that happens to be. The streetcar ride is a 'mass phenomenon' in which one is even more 'closely mingled with people and things' (*OWS*, p. 191).

To 'feel' one's way through a city, be it Naples or Moscow requires and privileges a familiarity and reciprocity with its jostling crowds, a proximity to its profusion of objects, an expectancy and excitement in its encounters. This receptivity to, and appreciation of, public urban experiences may be seen as the antithesis of the attitude of the haughty, insular bourgeois subject, who, maintaining distance and shunning contact, hurries joylessly past to seek refuge in exclusive cultural spaces or private interiors. Hence 'Moscow' foregrounds a series of pointed, ironic asides on the modern bourgeois urban sensibility as manifested in Benjamin's native Berlin. Indeed, Moscow becomes the lens through which the German metropolis is rendered comprehensible, the 'touchstone' (*OWS*, p. 177) of contemporary experience and politics.[14] Hence, 'Moscow' opens with the bold assertion: 'More quickly than Moscow, one gets to know Berlin through Moscow' (*OWS*, p. 177). Berlin seems like 'a deserted city' by comparison, a setting of 'Princely solitude, princely desolation' awash with 'unspeakable' luxury, a cityscape wherein the streets 'are like a freshly swept, empty racecourse on which a field of six-day cyclists hastens comfortlessly on' (*OWS*, p. 178).

This critical link with Berlin is important, because Benjamin's vehement rejection of bourgeois culture and intellectuals, of the bourgeois subject and private space, finds its fullest and most bitter articulation in a text prompted by another journey he undertook, one which did not result in a city portrait as such, but in a text which, given its form and themes, appears as a series of urban thought-images: his 'Imperial Panorama: A Tour of German Inflation', Benjamin's *Denkbilder* of the Weimar Republic.

The 'charmed circle'

Benjamin confessed to Rang on 24 February 1923: 'these last few days of travelling through Germany have again led me to the brink of despair and let me peer into the abyss' (*COR*, p. 207). The reflections prompted by this journey were to become, under the title 'Imperial Panorama: A Tour of German Inflation',[15] the longest and most vitriolic section of *Einbahnstrasse*. This critique is pitched at a high level of abstraction, however. The material deprivation of his crisis-ridden homeland features little in 'Kaiserpanorama'. His target is 'the amalgam of stupidity and cowardice constituting the mode of life of the German bourgeoisie' (*OWS*, p. 54). The collapse of the German economy becomes a metaphor for the bankrupt German intellect. The contrast with 'Naples' is striking and illuminating. The Neapolitans, who also tend to appear in the guises of 'starveling or . . . racketeer' (*OWS*, pp. 59–60), live a precarious economic existence based upon speculation and chance. Yet, in this city, 'Poverty has brought about a stretching of frontiers that mirrors the most radiant freedom of thought' (*OWS*, p. 175), such that 'Even the most wretched pauper is sovereign in the dim, dual awareness of participating, in all his destitution, in one of the pictures of Neapolitan street life that will never return, and of enjoying in all his poverty the leisure to follow the great panorama' (*OWS*, p. 170). The 'great panorama' of Weimar Germany presents a very different spectacle. Here, the most selfish, 'narrowest private interests' combine with the dullest 'instincts of the mass' (*OWS*, p. 55), such that 'The people cooped up in this country no longer discern the contour of human personality. Every free man appears to them as an eccentric' (*OWS*, p. 58). If in Moscow the intellectual energies and creative powers of the collectivity are directed towards the transformations and possibilities of an uncertain future, in Germany 'everyone is committed to the optical illusions of his isolated standpoint' (*OWS*, p. 58), ensuring that the banal mind clings with forlorn fervour, with hopeless hopefulness, to the remnants of a thoroughly redundant mode of existence. Incomprehension and inaction reign supreme. Benjamin writes:

> society's attachment to its familiar and long-since-forfeited life is so rigid as to nullify the genuinely human application of intellect, forethought, even in dire peril. So that in this society the picture of imbecility is complete: uncertainty, indeed perversion of vital instincts, and impotence, indeed, decay of the intellect. This is the condition of the entire German bourgeoisie. (*OWS*, p. 55)

Although he remained in Berlin until 1932, it is not surprising that, in this uninspiring intellectual scene, Benjamin came to see his own 'German cycle' as finished. Indeed, it is an ironic moment, for the German bourgeoisie, mired in pettiness, stupefied and paralysed by indecision at the onset of crisis, resigned to the catastrophe remorselessly engulfing it, comes to resemble both the doomed figures in Goethe's *Elective Affinities*, who fall under the power of daemonic forces, and the irresolute tyrant of the *Trauerspiel*, transfixed by the melancholy spectacle of his own inevitable destruction. Herein lies further evidence both of the acute actuality of Benjamin's engagement with these texts, and of the pressing need to 'recreate' German criticism.

In a letter of 5 June 1927 to Hofmannsthal, Benjamin reflects upon his predicament and upon alternative sources of intellectual stimulation:

Given my activities and interests, I am completely isolated among
those of my generation. . . . In France individual phenomena are
engaged in something that also engages me – among authors
Giraudoux and especially Aragon; among movements, surrealism.
In Paris I discovered the format for the notebook. I sent you some
excerpts from it a long time ago, very prematurely. (*COR*, p. 315)[16]

This 'notebook', *Einbahnstrasse*, was first mentioned in a letter to
Scholem some two and a half years earlier (22 December 1924):

I am preparing . . . 'Plaquette für Freunde' ['Plaques for Friends']. (In
France, a *plaquette* is a narrow, brochurelike, short, special issue containing poems or something similar – a bookdealer's *terminus techni-
cus*). I intend to collect my aphorisms, witticisms and dreams in
several chapters, each of which will carry the name of someone close
to me as its only heading. (*COR*, p. 257)

Benjamin's visit to Paris in the spring of 1926 was to prove decisive
in recasting this collection. Writing to Jula Radt, 30 April 1926,
Benjamin muses: 'I am very patiently wanting to test the efficacy of
a persistent courtship of this city. Such a courtship will turn time
into its ally' (*COR*, p. 298). This is significant because it was to be
precisely this combination of the metropolitan and the erotic that
was to inform his fragments for friends. A month later the transformation is evident in a letter to Scholem (29 May 1926): 'I am
working only on the notebook that I am reluctant to call a book of
aphorisms . . . The latest title – it has already had quite a few – is
"Street Closed" [*Strasse Gesperrt*!]' (*COR*, p. 302). On 18 September
1926, Benjamin informed Scholem that the text – now complete and
retitled *One-Way Street* (*Einbahnstrasse*) – 'has turned out to be a
remarkable arrangement or construction of some of my "aphorisms"' (*COR*, p. 306), a 'street' of textual fragments. The kaleidoscopic, surrealistic city of Paris was to provide Benjamin with the
architecture, the 'format' for *One-Way Street*, his exploration and
expression of an urban eroticism dedicated in the final instance not
to his various friends, but to his own metropolitan muse, the 'engineer' of the city who 'cut it through the author'.

Under headings derived from the 'linguistic cosmos' (P3,5, *ARC*,
p. 522) of the metropolis (street and traffic signs, the names of places
and edifices, billboards and advertisements), *One-Way Street* collects
an eclectic and eccentric assortment of aphorisms, dream-images,
jokes and other fragments, 'nothing but bitter, bitter herbs' (*COR*,

p. 298) which together offer a stinging critique of the sterility of contemporary bourgeois life and culture. *One-Way Street* is a constellation, or montage, of insights, whose power lies not so much within the individual elements, but rather in the sparks occasioned by their juxtaposition and incongruity. It incorporated and relied upon exactly that sense of extremity, of polarity,[17] which Benjamin sought in the wake of his *Trauerspiel* study. The book constitutes a provocation, both a timely and an untimely critique: untimely, because *Einbahnstrasse* was to be out of step with prevailing conventions and fashions, and heap scorn upon the affected ' "scholarly" stance' (*COR*, p. 281) of current German academic 'style', the ' "tenor of the age" ' (*COR*, p. 325); timely, because of its formal and thematic modernity, its resonance and preoccupation with the fleeting and momentary. Benjamin endeavours to discern and trace 'topicality' (*Aktualität*)[18] in its multitudinous and most concrete manifestations: dismal bourgeois interiors choked with monstrous, outdated furniture; children's games and play; curios, souvenirs and postage stamps; fairground attractions; the activities of beggars and prostitutes. In attending to such disparate phenomena, there is an enduring attempt – often insightful, sometimes baffling, occasionally banal – to articulate innovative modes of intellectual engagement, imaginative encounter and tactile experience which privilege proximity, immediacy, playfulness and eroticism. These are to be understood not as points of departure from which to escape moribund German bourgeois culture, but rather as tactics and techniques with which to accomplish the urgent task of its ultimate abolition.[19]

In 'Closed for Alterations' Benjamin writes: 'In a dream I took my life with a gun. When it went off I did not wake up but saw myself for a while lying. Only then did I wake' (*OWS*, p. 91). One may understand this suggestive dream as an allegory of the afterlife of German bourgeois culture. Unable to endure its thoroughly useless existence any more, this culture belatedly implodes. Incapable of recognizing its own death, it momentarily contemplates itself lying lifeless. Only then, after this terrible moment of final confirmation, is the nightmare at an end and the dreamer restored to his or her senses. *One-Way Street* articulates this moment of delayed reaction in which the old stares in blinking disbelief at its own corpse and the new remains dormant. In this instant of intellectual rupture, when cultural activity is fleetingly 'closed for alterations', Benjamin's study writes the epitaph for what was, and pioneers the programme for what already is and must be. Such radical intentions are evident from the outset. *One-Way Street* both announces and embodies a profound transformation in the character and purpose of intellectual activity, literary production and criticism:

> true literary activity cannot aspire to take place within a literary framework – this is, rather, the habitual expression of its sterility. Significant literary works can only come into being in a strict alternation between action and writing; it must nurture the inconspicuous forms that better fit its influence in active communities than does the pretentious universal gesture of the book – in leaflets, brochures, articles, and placards. Only this prompt language shows itself actively equal to the moment. (*OWS*, p. 45)

Lean times require 'slender' (*COR*, p. 284) texts rather than 'Fat Books' (*OWS*, p. 63). The 'Weighty Tome' is being displaced by more pertinent and potent forms of writing, which correspond to the demands for immediacy and concreteness, precision and concision. Benjamin is under no illusion that the book has already long renounced any claim to genuine intellectual insight, and 'in this traditional form is nearing its end' (*OWS*, p. 61). Only those befuddled by bourgeois sentimentality and nostalgia lament this demise and hanker for the book's comforting certainties and completeness. The true writer has other, more demanding ambitions:

> To great writers, finished works weigh lighter than those fragments on which they work throughout their lives. For only the more feeble and distracted take an inimitable pleasure in conclusions, feeling themselves thereby given back to life. For the genius each caesura, and the heavy blows of fate, fall like gentle sleep itself into his workshop labour. And about it he draws a charmed circle of fragments. 'Genius is application.' (*OWS*, pp. 47–8)

Similarly, the true reader, the critic, is transformed. He or she does not approach the text with reverential awe, but confronts it with a destructive capability[20] and a ravenous appetite.[21] Criticism must become a tactical act in a compressed space wherein, like the Muscovite street, there is precious little room for manoeuvre. Benjamin notes that 'Fools lament the decay of criticism. For its day is long past. Criticism is a matter of correct distancing. It was at home in a world where perspectives and prospects counted and where it was still possible to take a standpoint. Now things press too closely on human society' (*OWS*, p. 89). Too closely for traditional forms of criticism perhaps. But this new proximity suggests other modes of perception and representation: in particular, the 'insistent, jerky nearness' (*OWS*, p. 89) of film and the immediacy of advertising.[22] But it is neither advertising nor the cinematic which are most significant, but rather their location within and affinity with the city.[23]

Immediacy, brevity, proximity, tactility, strategy[24] – these are urban imperatives. What *One-Way Street* articulates first and foremost is an 'urbanization' of the text. Benjamin's ambivalence is apparent here. On the one hand, with the demise of the book, the text is rudely hauled from between the covers, 'pitilessly dragged out onto the street by advertisements and subjected to the brutal heteronomies of economic chaos. This is the hard schooling of its new form' (*OWS*, p. 62). Here, in the sober light of day, the book is revealed as an intellectual impostor and an already utterly prostituted form.[25] On the other hand, the proliferation of texts and images may obscure more than it illuminates. Benjamin writes:

> before a child of our time finds his way clear to opening a book, his eyes have been exposed to such a blizzard of changing, colourful, conflicting letters that the chances of his penetrating the archaic stillness of the book are slight. Locust swarms of print, which already eclipse the sun of what is taken for intellect for city dwellers, will grow thicker with each surrounding year. (*OWS*, p. 62)

Most important for Benjamin, however, is that the metropolitan environment itself comes to offer a model of innovative textual practices, a radical, vital literary architectonics. With its abrupt, often bewildering captions pilfered from the semiological cityscape, its profusion of startling signs and distracting images, *One-Way Street* mimics urban forms and experiences. It is imbued with that sense of disorientation, transience and shock which Benjamin identifies in the *Denkbilder* and his subsequent Paris studies as the hallmarks of metropolitan life. The text becomes 'city-like' just as the city becomes a 'linguistic cosmos', a text.

The urban 'engineer'

In *One-Way Street*, the urban environment becomes the terrain of erotic encounters and assignations.[26] For Benjamin, as for Baudelaire, the metropolis promises sexual intrigue. For the poet, it is the prospect of 'love at last sight', the fleeting, unexpected encounter with the stranger in the crowd, which provides for passionate excitement and melancholy longing. For Benjamin, it is a first sight-ing of the beloved, the exhilarating possibility of an unplanned *ren-dezvous* with Lacis, which generates an erotic charge electrifying the cityscape. In 'Ordinance', he recalls:

> I had arrived in Riga to visit a woman friend. Her house, the town, the language were unfamiliar to me. Nobody was expecting me, no-one knew me. For two hours I walked the streets in solitude. Never again have I seen them so. From every gate a flame darted, each cornerstone sprayed sparks, and every streetcar came towards me like a fire-engine. For she might have stepped out of the gateway, around the corner, been sitting in the streetcar. But of the two of us I had to be, at any price, the first to see the other. For had she touched me with the match of her eyes, I should have gone up like a magazine. (*OWS*, pp. 68–9)

In such games of urban hide-and-seek, the mundane cityscape is transformed by the beloved's simultaneous presence and absence into a sensual site of illumination and seduction. It is through Lacis and the places she 'haunts'[27] that the city is disclosed and comprehended,[28] while at the same time, the secretive city becomes a metaphor for her alluring, enigmatic otherness.[29] As the intellect penetrates the mysteries of the cityscape, so the imagination imbues it with new life. The dead and decaying spaces and objects of the modern, bourgeois city are revitalized and eroticized. The metropolis is both disenchanted and re-enchanted. This is the key to understanding Benjamin's attempt to 'feel' his way through the urban environment: he seeks to rediscover and reactivate it through proximity and tactility, to develop new modes of receptivity and representation, to interweave a metropolitan aesthetic sensibility with an urban erotic sensuality.

There is a second model for this transformation of the city in *One-Way Street*: not the erotic imagination of the adult, but the ludic practices of the child. In an extended series of reflections, which were later to be rewritten and incorporated in his 1932 Berlin studies, Benjamin sees in children's play an imaginative, magical engagement with the world of objects, which is antithetical to the insatiable avariciousness, calculating instrumentalism and cold estrangement of bourgeois adulthood.[30] Mimesis, reciprocity, creativity – these are the hallmarks of the child's spontaneous, playful activity and the prerequisites for 'dexterity' and 'warmth'. Far from complicity with 'the degeneration of things' (*OWS*, p. 58), the child salvages and redeems despised and discarded objects. The child does not scorn such wretched things – perhaps this is why they do not 'insistently repel' him or her with their icy sharpness. Rather, childhood is a time when one is 'closely mingled with people and things' (*OWS*, p. 191). In 'Construction Site', Benjamin contends:

> the world is full of the most unrivalled objects for childish attention and use. . . . They [Children] are irresistibly drawn by the detritus generated by building, gardening, housework, tailoring or carpentry. In waste products they recognise the face that the world of things turns directly and solely to them. In using these things they do not so much imitate the works of adults as bring together, in the artefact produced in play, materials of widely differing kinds in a new, intuitive relationship. Children thus produce their own small world of things within the greater one. (*OWS*, pp. 52–3)

This 'small world of things' is a collection of chance finds, obsolete artefacts and discarded fragments. In combining such material into new configurations, new constellations, the child as *bricoleur* magically transforms the mundane into the precious and exotic. Under the gaze of the playing child, things acquire unforeseen, multiple meanings, become allegorical objects imbued with secret significance.[31] The child playfully composes an enchanted realm of objects, a 'charmed circle of fragments', wherein he 'hunts the spirits whose trace he scents in things' with an intensity and passion 'which lingers on, but with a dimmed and manic glow, in antiquarians, researchers, bibliomaniacs' (*OWS*, p. 73).

On his or her various 'hunts', the child transforms not only the object world, but also the moribund spaces of the city – not least the nightmarish bourgeois interior, a setting where 'luxury' ensures impoverishment. In 'Hiding Child', Benjamin notes how the dead domestic environment is enlivened through mimetic play:

> Standing behind the doorway curtain, the child becomes himself something floating and white, a ghost. The dining table under which he is crouching turns him into the wooden idol in a temple whose four pillars are the carved legs. And behind a door he is himself a door, wears it as his heavy mask and as a shaman will bewitch all those who unsuspectingly enter. (*OWS*, p. 74)

In the eyes of the child, the interior becomes a site of exoticism and magical discovery: 'once each year, in mysterious places, in their empty-eye sockets, their fixed mouths, presents lie. As its engineer the child disenchants the gloomy parental apartment and looks for Easter eggs' (*OWS*, p. 74).

The reference to 'engineer' here is both intriguing and unmistakable: it links the child as the source of the imaginative transformation of the private domicile with the figure of Lacis, the 'engineer' of the public spaces of the city, and indeed of *One-Way Street* itself. Just as Benjamin's erotic quest for Lacis in Riga electrifies the cityscape, so the child imbues another hunting ground, the bourgeois interior, with expectation. To be such an engineer, one must have a good nose for the 'spirits' one 'scents in things', and a sharp eye for the 'hidden spindles and joints' of the 'vast apparatus of social existence' (*OWS*, p. 45). It is in the guise of such an expert engineer that the contemporary critic must energize the world of objects, set it in motion, in perpetual revolution. 'Genius' is to be found, not in philosophical contemplation, but in technical, tactical 'application'.

This critic-as-engineer is an exponent of a new technology, constructs a new relationship between human beings and nature, one based upon neither the ecstatic excesses of irrationalism nor the calculating instrumentalism of Enlightenment science. Instead, he or she privileges the erotic, the mimetic and the ludic, experiences and activities which point to an intimacy between human beings and their environment based upon reconciliation, reciprocity and harmonious intercourse. Benjamin's fragmentary argument in *One-Way Street* is intricate and complex in this regard. Alternative, earlier experiential forms are both a promise and a threat. 'Imperial Panorama' concludes with a positive vision of ancient modes of interaction with nature, in contrast to degenerate modern practices:

> An Athenian custom forbade the picking up of crumbs at the table, since they belonged to the heroes. If society has so degenerated through necessity and greed that it can now receive the gifts of nature only rapaciously, that it snatches the fruit unripe from the trees in order to sell it most profitably, and is compelled to empty each dish in its determination to have enough, the earth will be impoverished and the land yield bad harvests. (*OWS*, p. 60)

In 'To the Planetarium', the final section of *One-Way Street*, there is greater ambiguity, however. Although Benjamin appears to write appreciatively of the long-lost, communal 'ecstatic contact with the cosmos' (*OWS*, p. 103) enjoyed by the ancients, the mythic and the daemonic perpetually threaten to reassert themselves in the modern context as a violent, catastrophic return of repressed drives. For Benjamin, the recent Great War constitutes precisely such an instance where the frenzied forces of chaos and destruction were unleashed with the able assistance and terrifying destructive capabilities of contemporary military technology.[32]

We moderns have disenchanted the cosmos and nature, but only under the auspices and imperatives of capitalism and imperialism, the frenzied 'lust for profit' (*OWS*, p. 104) and the ruthless, remorseless pursuit of power. Benjamin comments: 'The mastery of nature, so the imperialists teach, is the purpose of all technology. But who would trust a cane-wielder who proclaimed the mastery of children by adults to be the purpose of education? And likewise technology is not the mastery of nature but of the relation between nature and man' (*OWS*, p. 104). The expertise of the critic is important here. Neither magic nor science, astrology nor astronomy, neither the 'ecstatic trance' of the shaman nor the brutal indifference of the 'cane-wielder' enable such insight. Rather, Benjamin advocates the sober scrutiny, the aesthetic sensibility, the erotic sensitivity of the urban engineer, the master of technology, who knows how and when to 'feel', how and when to 'cut', her way through the city and the author.

Surrealism and profane illumination

Benjamin's collection of urban aphorisms and his fragmentary *Passagenarbeit* are indebted not only to a Latvian engineer, but also to a Parisian peasant (Louis Aragon's *Le Paysan de Paris*, 1926) and an urban apparition (André Breton's *Nadja*, 1928). Of all the avant-garde movements of the time, it was Surrealism which most excited and influenced Benjamin, though this enthusiasm did not blind him to its limitations, as his 1925–6 fragment 'Dreamkitsch' (*Traumkitsch*)[33] and the 1929 essay 'Surrealism: The Last Snapshot of the European Intelligentsia' make clear. *Einbahnstrasse* is shot through with Surrealist techniques and motifs: the poetic envisaging of an imaginatively, erotically energized cityscape as a site of intoxication and seduction; the reconfiguration of the seemingly banal object world into a source of revolutionary illumination and explosive critique; the development of new modes of writing which foreground dream-images and jokes; the emphasis upon imagistic modes of representation like montage. In conceiving modernity as a 'dreamworld' of phantasmagoria and mythic forms, Surrealism articulated an, albeit nebulous, vision of contemporary commodity culture which would prove central to Benjamin's *Passagenarbeit*. Moreover,

the Surrealists' emphasis upon 'profane illumination' and a 'dialectics of intoxication' would mesh with and serve to refocus some of
Benjamin's key critical principles (the monadological fragment, the
afterlife of the artwork/object, mosaic and constellation) so as to
form some of the methodological foundations for the 'Arcades'
study.

In the writings of Aragon and Breton, contemporary Paris
becomes the privileged site of new forms of aesthetic experience
and practice, forms which lead to a radical recognition of the 'marvellous suffusing everyday existence' (Aragon, 1987, p. 24). The
mundane becomes a source of inspiration, illumination and intoxication. The city becomes a dreamscape.[34] Taking the derelict Passage
de l'Opéra as his point of departure, Aragon presents a series of
extravagant imaginings in which the metropolitan environment
is transformed into the setting for distinctively modern forms of
euphoria and hallucination. In the contemporary city, the proliferation of objects, the profusion of signs, and the dizzying tempo
of movement lead to a 'vertigo of the modern' (Aragon, 1987, p.
129), an ecstatic sensibility which enables the writer to behold the
secret enchantments of the urban setting.[35] Forsaking the tedious
(and treacherous) guide provided by conventional reason, Aragon
searches for a new sensory (and, especially, tactile) appreciation of
the metropolis, to 'feel' his way through the city:

> I no longer wish to refrain from the error of my fingers, the error of
> my eyes. I know now that these errors are not just booby traps but
> curious paths leading towards a destination that they alone can
> reveal to me. . . . New myths spring up beneath each step we take.
> Legend begins where man has lived, where he lives. . . . A mythol-
> ogy ravels and unravels. It is a knowledge, a science of life open only
> to those who have no training in it. (Aragon, 1987, p. 24)

These intuitive and imaginative perambulations uncover the
city's hidden, fantastical features, its real 'unreal' character. Paris
has a surreal visage,[36] a mythic quality. Aragon writes: 'I set about
forming the idea of a mythology in motion. It was more accurate to
call it a mythology of the modern. And it was under that name that
I conceived it' (1987, p. 130). This notion of a 'modern mythology'
identifies not the ancient worship of the daemonic forces and creaturely compulsions of nature,[37] but rather the contemporary subservience to the powerful machines, the alluring commodities and
suggestive brand-names and logos of modern capitalism.[38] While
seemingly the 'overheated fantasies' (*OWS*, p. 232) of a fevered

artistic imagination, Aragon's *mythologie moderne* nevertheless represents for Benjamin a technique of estrangement which disturbs our complacent, habitual gaze, and thereby re-sensitizes us to the quotidian cityscape. In 'the dialectics of intoxication' (*OWS*, p. 229),[39] Surrealism affirms the distinction between what appears to be and what is, attends to the beguiling and duplicitous character of surface manifestations. In making the cityscape bizarre, monstrous and outlandish, Aragon intimates its profane secrets, brings us closer to the hidden truth of things.[40] Proximity creates a new sense of estrangement, estrangement a new intimacy. Surrealism disenchants the city though enchantment – this is the power and the promise of Surrealist 'profane illumination' (*OWS*, p. 227).

In Breton's *Nadja*, this heightened appreciation of the cityscape[41] coincides with the erotic sensibility engendered by the author's encounters with his haunting, elusive eponymous muse.[42] In Breton's seductive adventures, Paris takes on a combustible character, just as Riga did for Benjamin. Benjamin writes:

> Breton and Nadja are the lovers who convert everything that we have experienced on mournful railway journeys . . . on God-forsaken Sunday afternoons in the proletarian quarters of the great cities, in the first glance through the rain-blurred window of a new apartment, into revolutionary experience, if not action. They bring the immense forces of 'atmosphere' concealed in these things to the point of explosion. (*OWS*, p. 229)

Surrealism charges the banal and monotonous with incendiary power. Under such hazardous conditions, one must handle things with care. A new proximity to the realm of objects emerges: Breton is 'closer to the things that Nadja is close to than to her. What are these things? Nothing could reveal more about Surrealism than their canon' (*OWS*, p. 229). 'These things' are *objets trouvés*, obsolete and unfashionable artefacts from the recent past, remnants unearthed in the ruinous arcades and the Parisian flea markets,[43] the 'bazaar of the bizarre' (Aragon, 1987, p. 114). Liberated from their original context and use, these eccentric, expiring objects have a particular 're-use' value for the Surrealists as images and sources of illumination.[44] Obsolescence reveals the secrets of modernity. This insight is Breton's most 'extraordinary discovery' (*OWS*, p. 229). In a key passage Benjamin writes:

> He was the first to perceive the revolutionary energies that were to appear in the 'outmoded', in the first iron constructions, the first

factory buildings, the earliest photos, the objects that have begun to be extinct, grand pianos, the dresses of five years ago, fashionable restaurants when the vogue has begun to ebb from them. The relation of these things to revolution – no one can have a more exact concept of it than these authors. No one before these visionaries and augurs perceived how destitution – not only social but architectonic, the poverty of interiors, enslaved and enslaving objects – can be suddenly transformed into revolutionary nihilism. (*OWS*, p. 229)

Benjamin discovers in Surrealism a radical appreciation of the afterlife of the object which mirrors his own understanding of the afterlife of the text. In the posthumous existence of architecture, commodities and technological innovations, original intentions and meanings are superseded and negated. The hidden truth content of these things manifests itself only through a process of ruination. The moment of extinction is that of a final profane illumination. Here, too, Surrealism comes to annihilate the tastes, prejudices and sensibilities of bourgeois art and culture through relentless ridicule. Surrealism is, Benjamin observes, nothing other than 'the death of the nineteenth century in comedy' (N5a,2, *ARC*, p. 56).

Abolishing the reverential distance between spectator and traditional artwork,[45] Surrealism inaugurates new aesthetic practices based on immediacy in time and space. Aragon offers 'entrance to the realms of the instantaneous, the world of the snapshot' (1987, p. 78), where the powers of intoxication and imagination (understood here as the formation of images) are unleashed. He writes:

The vice named *Surrealism* is the immoderate and impassioned use of the stupefacient *image*, or rather of the uncontrolled provocation of the image for its own sake and for the element of unpredictable perturbation and of metamorphosis which it introduces into the domain of representation: for each image on each occasion forces you to revise the entire Universe. (Aragon, 1987, pp. 78–9)

The image is not simply the pre-eminent mode of representation; it is also the only point of access or insight into the profane world, 'the path of all knowledge' (Aragon, 1987 p. 214).[46] It is in Aragon that the sphere of images, the possibilities of genuine thought, and the capturing of the concrete come together, and that Benjamin's thought-images, his miniature and fragmentary *Denkbilder*, find their inspiration and necessity.[47]

For Aragon, the image is 'a secret stairway' to the 'fantastic or marvellous' (1987, p. 213), the realm of the unconscious, of dreams

and visions. The everyday as a dreamworld awaiting interpretation[48] – this was one of Surrealism's profoundest insights for Benjamin. Surrealism directs our attention to those startling perceptual
transformations brought about by accidental occurrences, lucky
finds, half-remembered dream fragments, felicitous misunderstandings,[49] jokes,[50] puns and wordplays.[51] Coincidences and contingencies provide entry into, and intervention within, the sphere
of images. Above all, it is in the incongruous juxtaposition of fragmentary elements, in the technique of montage, that Surrealism
maximized the shock-value of the trivial utterance, the inconsequential expression, the arcane object.[52] In montage, images,
sounds, words, even individual letters,[53] are recomposed in startling
configurations. The distinctions and boundaries between things
are sometimes accentuated, sometimes erased. This is the price and
the pleasure of the dialectics of intoxication. Benjamin writes of
Surrealism:

> Everything with which it came into contact was integrated. Life only
> seemed worth living where the threshold between waking and sleep-
> ing was worn away in everyone as by the steps of multitudinous
> images flooding back and forth, language only seemed itself where
> sound and image, image and sound interpenetrated with auto-
> matic precision and such felicity that no chink was left for the penny
> in the slot called 'meaning'. Image and language take precedence.
> (*OWS*, p. 226)

And thus a new mode of writing is imperative: 'the writings of this
circle are not literature but something else – demonstrations, watch-
words, documents, bluffs, forgeries if you will, but at any rate not
literature' (*OWS*, p. 227). Could there be a more fitting description
of *One-Way Street* than this?

Caution is needed here, however. Notwithstanding its numerous
surrealistic elements and techniques, it would be a mistake to
regard Benjamin's *Einbahnstrasse* as an experiment in Surrealist
writing. It also reflects his strong reservations regarding the writings of Aragon and Breton. Margaret Cohen states that 'while multiple features of *One-Way Street* recall Surrealism, a polemic against
the movement runs through the text', one which is most acute 'in
what might seem like its most obvious nod to the movement's practices, the use of dreamlike juxtapositions to produce arresting
descriptions' (1993, p. 174). Benjamin's dream imagery, Cohen
argues, is of a different order from that of the Surrealists. Her

example is a fragment from Benjamin's 'Travel Souvenirs' section, in which he draws a series of parallels between the newly built Marseilles cathedral and the railway station.[54] While the playful juxtaposing of these edifices suggests Surrealist influences, Benjamin offers 'a striking but thoroughly intelligible synthesis more resembling Eisensteinian montage than the transformations of the surrealist image' (Cohen, 1993, p. 178). The meaning of Benjamin's metaphor is clear, contained and available – whereas the Surrealist image is extraordinary, excessive and elusive. For all its dream imagery, *Einbahnstrasse* is an exercise in literary sobriety, not poetic abandon.[55] Indeed, for Benjamin, dream-images have critical value only for those who are fully awake and in possession of themselves. The distinction between sleep and wakefulness must not be 'worn away', since, Benjamin warns, 'only from the far bank, from broad daylight, may dream be recalled with impunity' (*OWS*, p. 46). The error of 'Recounting dreams on an empty stomach' (*OWS*, p. 45) when one is 'still half in league with the dream-world' (*OWS*, p. 46) is one to which the Surrealists were all too prone. For Benjamin, there must be a 'rupture between the nocturnal and day-time worlds' and a 'combustion of dream in a concentrated morning's work' (*OWS*, p. 46). The genuine critical theorist does not languish drowsily in the realm of dreams, but rather perceives the pressing need to bring about awakening. The shock of recognition is intended not as an intoxicant, but rather as a call to action, as an alarm clock.

Benjamin's essay on Surrealism is not a paean to its 'heroic phase' (*OWS*, p. 226), but rather a critical intervention in its brief afterlife so as to tease out and redeem its own revolutionary truth content. To do this, Benjamin points out in an extended analogy, one must stand a little downstream from the source, away from the first babbling torrents, to see whether such 'intellectual currents can generate a sufficient head of water for the critic to install his power station on them' (*OWS*, p. 225). Down 'in the valley', one is less likely to dismiss it as a 'paltry stream' (*OWS*, p. 225) or to be swept away in gushing enthusiasm. Here one can calmly 'gauge the energies of the movement' (*OWS*, p. 225), test the clarity, purity and power of its ideas. And for Benjamin, Surrealism is all too often found wanting.

The 'dubious books of the surrealists' (*COR*, p. 277)[56] tend to be 'enmeshed in a number of pernicious romantic prejudices' (*OWS*, p. 237). While Benjamin praises their uncompromising, 'radical concept of freedom', one purged of bourgeois 'sentiment' and 'sclerotic liberal-moral-humanistic' pieties, the 'ecstatic component' of their politics remains problematic (*OWS*, p. 236). Benjamin comments: 'To win the energies of intoxication for the revolution – this is the project about which Surrealism circles in all its books and enterprises' (*OWS*, p. 236). But it is an undertaking which is only ever circled. In tarrying too long among dreams and visions, the Surrealists suffer from 'an inadequate and undialectical conception of the nature of intoxication' (*OWS*, p. 236). It is only in the active *interrogation* of the phantasmagorical and mythic that insight is acquired. Benjamin writes that 'histrionic or fanatical stress on the mysterious side of the mysterious takes us no further; we penetrate the mystery only to the degree that we recognise it in the everyday world, by virtue of a dialectical optic that perceives the everyday as impenetrable, the impenetrable as everyday' (*OWS*, p. 237). Hence, his verdict is pointed: 'profane illumination did not always find the Surrealists equal to it, or to themselves' (*OWS*, p. 227). Aragon is enthralled by the marvellous modern mythology he discerns; Breton is bewitched by mysterious hauntings and the occult.[57] But freedom is compromised by superstition. If one possesses 'character', one has no need to enquire as to one's 'fate'.[58]

Surrealism's significance can be gauged only by its political efficacy. Its 'poetic politics' (*OWS*, p. 237) intervene in the sphere of images to break with bourgeois aesthetic and cultural hegemony, and move beyond mere 'contemplation' (*OWS*, p. 238), but its esoteric inclinations limit any appeal to the revolutionary proletariat.[59] The transformation of everyday material life (of technologies and bodies) is prefigured by, and must come to accord with, 'that image sphere to which profane illumination initiates us' (*OWS*, p. 239), that realm of the free play of the imagination. For Benjamin, the Surrealists are the only ones to recognize this imperative, and flow in its direction, albeit via some distinctly eccentric meanders and murky courses. Surrealism's radical currents, its revolutionary energies, its electrifying potential, are to be rechannelled and reutilized in the mobilization of discontent.[60] To rouse the dreaming collectivity from its complacent slumbers – this becomes the key to Benjamin's abiding fascination with Paris, and the point of departure for his fragmentary exploration of the city's recent past: the 'Arcades Project'. The Critical Theorist must learn to be both hydraulic and urban engineer.

Conclusion

Benjamin's writings from the mid-1920s onwards start to develop a vital, virulent critique of modern culture. Although he was to remain a prolific literary critic and reviewer, his *Einbahnstrasse* 'production cycle' recognizes that the task of recreating criticism is not simply a literary endeavour, but rather a political undertaking encompassing domains such as commodity culture, the new mass media, and metropolitan architecture and experience. Influenced by historical materialism, and encouraged by the Surrealist integration of aesthetics, politics and the everyday, Benjamin increasingly recognized the obsolescence of 'literary criticism' as a distinct genre or activity divorced from wider cultural, social, economic and political concerns. The genuine contemporary critic is not the follower of a narrow vocation, but rather a cultural 'jack-of-all-trades', a *bricoleur*. He or she must be transformed through a polytechnical apprenticeship from a reader and writer of weighty tomes into an explosives expert, an engineer demolishing the dreamworld of modernity itself.

This widening of critical horizons does not mean abandoning the principles of immanent criticism developed by Benjamin in his German 'production cycle'. On the contrary, these are to be transposed from the textual realm to that of material analysis, and given a contemporary inflection: the commodity form rather than the artwork as monadological fragment, architectural ruins rather than mortified texts, thought-image rather than treatise, cinematic montage rather than mosaic, the dialectical image rather than the origin of the constellation. Benjamin's conceptual vocabulary may have changed, but the principles remained the same: destruction, fragmentation, (re)construction, representation. Notwithstanding his perception of production 'cycles', closure and *caesura*, Benjamin himself was fully aware of the continuities of his approach. If the neglected, despised form of the *Trauerspiel* gave expression to, and could disclose, the *Weltanschauung* of the baroque, then perhaps modernity too could be deciphered by the critical recovery, interrogation and depiction of its marginalia, its waste products, its outcasts and cast-offs. This was to be the goal of the 'Arcades Project', his 'prehistory' of the present, or 'origins' of modern culture. The 'origins' of the *Passagenarbeit* are to be found not only in Italy in 1924, but also in Switzerland in 1919. Indeed, one could write of it with some justification: 'Conceived 1916. Unwritten 1940.'

4

Paris and the Arcades

Introduction

If *Einbahnstrasse* constitutes Benjamin's 'first attempt to come to terms with' Paris (*COR*, p. 325), his second, a 'book called *Paris Arcades*' (*COR*, p. 325) was to prove far more sustained and extensive, though equally fragmented and enigmatic. Arising from the most humble of intentions, the 'Arcades Project' was to grow in ambition, scope and complexity to become an unending intellectual preoccupation for Benjamin, the 'theater of all my conflicts and all my ideas' (*COR*, p. 359), as he once described it.[1] Originally conceived during a visit to Paris in March 1926, as a collaborative essay with Franz Hessel, 'Arcades' (*Passagen*), a brief description of a dilapidated contemporary Parisian shopping arcade, was composed during 1927 for the journal *Querschnitt*. By the end of the year, Benjamin was working alone on a second, 'highly remarkable and precarious essay "Paris Arcades: A Dialectical Fairy Play" [*Pariser Passagen: Eine Dialektische Feerie*]' (*COR*, p. 322).[2] This text, he estimates, 'will take a few weeks' (*COR*, p. 322) and was supposed to complete, as we have seen, a distinctive Parisian 'cycle' of literary miniatures.[3] A few weeks later, however, Benjamin revised this timescale, as the essay 'might turn out to bemore extensive than I had thought' (*COR*, p. 327).[4] The spring of 1928 saw Benjamin working 'almost exclusively on the *Paris Arcades*' (*COR*, p. 334).[5] The widening scope of the project started to become apparent as its historical and methodological contours emerged more clearly. From a brief stroll in the arcade, the *Passagenarbeit* was becoming an all-encompassing, ever-expanding critical-historical exploration of nineteenth-century Paris, an urban archaeology of the recent past. Benjamin's study was becoming ever more intriguing, ever more demanding.[6]

Benjamin considered his essay on Surrealism written in the first few months of 1929 to stand in the closest relation to the ongoing *Passagenarbeit*:

> This work is, in fact, a screen [*Paravent*] placed in front of the *Paris Arcades* . . . [T]he issue here is precisely what you once touched on after reading *One-Way Street*: to attain the most extreme concreteness for an era, as it manifested itself in children's games, a building, or a real-life situation. A perilous, breathtaking enterprise. (*COR*, p. 348)[7]

In the 'Arcades Project' the 'concreteness' of the *Denkbild*, the topicality of mundane phenomena so decisive for *One-Way Street*, and the techniques of Surrealist profane illumination were to be combined and intensified. The everyday objects, edifices and experiences of nineteenth-century Paris were to be unveiled as phantasmagoria and chimeras, as modern mythological forms, as elements of a dreamworld. The explosive juxtaposition of artefacts and images culled from this fabulous realm was to transform contemporary consciousness, and bring an abrupt awakening from the recent past. Benjamin expressed his complete preoccupation with this project in typically Surrealist fashion: 'I am at the Arcades – "to me, it is as though in a dream, as though it were a part of me"' (*GS* V, p. 1091).[8]

Financial insecurities, difficult personal circumstances and the worsening political situation in Germany conspired to hamper progress on the *Passagenarbeit* during the early 1930s.[9] Notwithstanding these distractions and problems, particularly his final departure from Berlin in March 1933, Benjamin retained a clear sense of the significance of the 'Arcades Project', 'in which . . . for me, the most important directives lie' (*GS* V, p. 1095).[10] These 'directives' suggested a number of tangential studies in this period: an unwritten 'major essay on *art nouveau* (*Jugendstil*)' (*GS* V, p. 1095),[11] and the 1931 text 'A Small History of Photography' which developed materials collected in Convolute Y ('Photography'). But these peripheral writings were a source of exasperation, rather than satisfaction: 'you recognize that my essay on photography developed from prolegomena; but what more can there ever be than prolegomena and paralipomena; I could conceive of bringing the project to fruition only if I were guaranteed two years of uninterrupted work' (*COR*, p. 385).[12] In 1932 Benjamin's attention turned ironically, if understandably, to Berlin, the city he was so soon to leave. 'Berlin Chronicle' and 'A Berlin Childhood around 1900' were explorations in urban memory which constituted historiographic experiments for the *Passagenarbeit*.[13] Yet, more 'prologomena and paralipomena', these texts provided further proof of his resigned, but perceptive comment: 'though many . . . of my works have been small-scale victories, they are offset by large-scale defeats' (*GER*, p. 14).

The 'Arcades Project' gained fresh impetus in the period 1934–5, with Benjamin working intensively in the Bibliothèque nationale. After a summer of sustained activity, he confidently informed Horkheimer in late autumn 1934 that 'the clear structure of the book stands before my eyes' (*GS* V, p. 1105).[14] Horkheimer's response was encouraging: the Institute for Social Research, then temporarily based in Geneva, invited Benjamin to submit an *exposé* or sketch of the *Passagenarbeit*. As a result, 'the work', Benjamin notes, 'has entered a new phase, in which for the first time it bears more resemblance – even if from afar – to a book' (*GER*, p. 158). This 'new phase' also involved a new nomenclature: 'the title "Paris Arcades" has been discarded and the draft is entitled "Paris Capital of the Nineteenth Century"; privately I call it "Paris capitale du XIXe siécle"' (*GER*, p. 159).[15]

The *exposé* got a mixed reception. Horkheimer's enthusiasm was undiminished,[16] but Adorno's letter of 2 August 1935 expressed numerous, serious misgivings. He was unimpressed by Benjamin's characterization of nineteenth-century Paris as a dreamworld, and by his use of categories such as commodity fetishism, phantasmagoria and dreaming collectivities. For Adorno, such notions – precisely those most influenced by Surrealist motifs – possessed insufficient clarity, lacked discrimination, and seemed naively to transpose individual psychological states and psychoanalytical categories to complex, material social processes.[17] In particular, Adorno regarded Benjamin's conception of the commodity as a 'wish image', as an expression in distorted form of genuine utopian impulses emanating from some kind of 'dreaming collectivity', as a most unhappy formulation. It failed to attend, for example, to different historical class positions, and also to the dialectical character of commodity fetishism.[18] Indeed, it bore far too many resemblances to the notions of ahistorical archetypes, archaic/primal images, and the collective unconscious posited by Carl Jung and Ludwig Klages. Adorno's criticisms hit home, with some justification, though the notion of the commodity as 'wish image' is, as I hope to show, thoroughly dialectical. In any event, at Adorno's suggestion, Benjamin began to prepare a critical *excursus* which, in clearly distinguishing his own concept of the dialectical image from Jung's notion of the 'archaic image', would serve 'to safeguard certain foundations of the "Paris Arcades" methodologically' (*GER*, p. 197).[19] This, like the *Passagenarbeit* itself, was destined to remain unwritten.

Benjamin was soon to discover that he was not the only one undertaking research into Parisian life and culture in the Second Empire. His fellow exile Siegfried Kracauer was also working on this theme, tracing the fantastical illusions and self-deceptions of the era by unfolding the life and work of the composer Jacques Offenbach. *Jacques Offenbach and the Paris of his Time* interspersed details of Offenbach's character and career with a pointed socio-historical critique so as to form a 'social biography', a portrait not just of a musician, but also of a city and an epoch. Written with a lightness of touch and delicacy of wit which completely escaped Adorno and Benjamin, the book was published in 1937 to widespread critical acclaim. Predictably, Adorno denounced it: first, for adopting the individualizing, subjectivizing bourgeois biographical form; and second, and more significantly, for its apparent inattention to the specific details of Offenbach's music. 'The few passages which touch on music are crassly erroneous,' Adorno complained in a letter of 4 May 1937 (*ABC*, p. 184). Benjamin had more cause and less reason to be sour: the book set in merry dance before his eyes so many of the categories on which he had been labouring so painstakingly for the 'Arcades Project' – nineteenth-century Paris as a dreamworld; the precarious economics of imperial adventure, stockmarket speculation and gambling; the niceties of the salons and the *demi-monde* of the boulevards; the pretensions of the flâneur, the journalist and the bohemian; novelty and frivolity as antidotes to unendurable boredom; the superficial 'joy and glamour' of the World Exhibitions and, not least, of the arcades themselves. To read and represent the political, social and culture sensibility of an 'enchanted' epoch through the experiences and artworks of a particular individual, to turn them into monadological fragments – this was Kracauer's purpose. Adorno castigated the 'shameless and idiotic' notion of a '"biography of society"' (*ABC*, p. 184), and Benjamin rejected Kracauer's attempted '"salvation" of Offenbach's operetta' (*ABC*, p. 186) as a pathetic 'apologia' (*ABC*, p. 186). From

1937 onwards, Benjamin was to work on a project which might be seen as a thoroughgoing 'corrective' to the supposed exemplary failings of Kracauer's book, one which would provide a genuinely critical illumination of Paris in the Second Empire and the dazzling commodity culture of the recent past – a study of the poet Charles Baudelaire. Emerging directly out of material collected for Convolute J, this was intended to serve, first and foremost, as a miniature model of the 'Arcades Project', presenting in revised form some of its key 'philosophical contents' (*GS* V, p. 1167).[20] Conceived as a tripartite structure, this too was never finished. Indeed, the central section which Benjamin eventually did complete was received so unfavourably by Adorno that he was compelled to redraft the text before publication in the Institute's *Zeitschrift für Sozialforschung* in January 1940.

Benjamin's last text, the enigmatic and programmatic 'Theses on the Concept of History', was also intimately connected with the 'Arcades Project'. Drawing upon and elaborating the fragmentary historiographic principles sketched in Convolute N ('Re The Theory of Knowledge, Theory of Progress'), the 'Theses' were to be developed into an epistemological preface to the *Passagenarbeit* which would have paralleled the 'Epistemo-Critical Prologue' to the *Trauerspiel* study. From 1935 until his untimely death in 1940, Benjamin's writings would remain 'small-scale victories', but 'large-scale defeats'.

Benjamin fled Paris in 1940 as Nazi troops advanced on the city. Before leaving, he passed his various papers comprising the *Passagenarbeit* to his friend Georges Bataille, who placed the texts in the Bibliothèque nationale for safe keeping. This material was first published in 1982 as the fifth volume of the *Gesammelte Schriften*, under the rather controversial title *Das Passagen-Werk*. Now finally available in a single-volume English-language translation, *The Arcades Project* contains a plethora of Benjamin's Paris texts: the original 1927 essay 'Arcades' (*ARC*, pp. 871–2), a series of early notes and sketches from the late 1920s[21], some 800 pages of notes and quotations collected and numbered in folders (or *Convolutes*) and designated by letter (A–Z and a–r) and subject heading ('H. The Collector', 'Y. Photography', 'k. The Commune', etc.); and different versions of Benjamin's ill-fated 1935 *exposé*.

The *Passagenarbeit* became much more than an essay on the shopping arcades. It was to be a kaleidoscopic, critical presentation of nineteenth-century Paris as the pre-eminent site of consumer culture, of pioneering forms of engineering, architecture and

design, of the transformation of artistic and literary practices and
sensibilities, as home to radical political ideas and revolutionary
struggles. The 'Arcades Project' became nothing less than an unfinished, and unfinishable, analysis of the 'origins' of contemporary
capitalism – indeed, of modernity itself. Moreover, this was to be
no ordinary, scholastic, historical overview. Benjamin sought not
only to present a critical vision of the previous century, but also to
reconfigure and reorient the practice of historical writing itself, so
as to make an explosive intervention in the cultural and political
conditions of his own time. To win the energies of the recent past
for the revolution – this was the task about which Benjamin circles
in his 'Arcades Project'.

To highlight and clarify some of the continuities between Benjamin's German and Parisian 'production cycles' or constellations,
this chapter examines some of the perhaps surprising parallels
between Benjamin's *Trauerspiel* study and the *Passagenarbeit*. Monad
and image, the principle of construction and the notion of contemporary actuality – the importance of these for both projects is
underlined. Then, taking one particularly puzzling fragment from
Convolute K as a point of departure, the remainder of the chapter
explores some of the main themes and concepts of the 'Arcades
Project': the prehistory of modernity, fashion and commodity
fetishism, novelty and repetition, and the architecture of dreaming.
It is suggested that the phantasmagoria of the object world, of time
and of space, each find a corollary and/or exponent in a particular
figure borrowed from Baudelaire's gallery of urban types, his
'heroes' of modern life: the prostitute, the gambler and the flâneur.
The chapter concludes by demonstrating how the tensions and contradictions inherent in the material forms of this urban dreamworld
are manifested in their afterlife and mobilized by Benjamin to
critical effect. The enchantments of modernity contain within them
the seeds of their own disenchantment – this insight into the dialectical nature of the mythological forms of modernity is the key
to understanding Benjamin's Parisian 'fairy-play'.

Construction and ruination

Although the 'Arcades Project' emerges principally from Benjamin's engagement with Surrealist motifs and Marxist categories,
the temptation to regard the 'Parisian cycle' of writings as a decisive break from his earlier theological and literary concerns should

be resisted.[22] In the epistemological and methodological reflections of Convolute N one finds a particularly fortuitous, suggestive counterpoising of ideas, one which might suggest the provocative combination of extreme elements characteristic of Surrealist montage techniques. In N1a,1 Benjamin writes, quoting Siegfried Giedeon:

> 'In the windswept stairways of the Eiffel Tower . . . one meets with the fundamental aesthetic experience of present-day architecture: through the thin net of iron that hangs suspended in the air, things stream – ships, ocean, houses, masts, landscape, harbor. They lose their distinctive shape, swirl into one another as we climb downward, merge simultaneously.' . . . In the same way, the historian today has only to erect a slender but sturdy scaffolding – a philosophic structure – in order to draw the most vital aspects of the past into his net. But just as the magnificent vistas of the city provided by the new construction in iron . . . for a long time were reserved exclusively for the workers and the engineers, so too the philosopher who wishes to garner fresh perspectives must be someone immune to vertigo – an independent, and if need be, solitary worker. (*ARC*, p. 459)

The next entry reads: 'The book on the Baroque exposed the seventeenth century to the light of the present day. Here, something analogous must be done for the nineteenth century but with greater distinctness' (N1a,2, *ARC*, p. 459).

Benjamin presents us here with two seemingly incongruous versions of the task of the historian and the character of the *Passagenarbeit*. In the first fragment, the urban engineer of *One-Way Street* has become a structural engineer erecting the most modern of edifices, one which, even long before completion, offers a breathtaking panoramic view of an entire metropolis at a given historical moment. Perched precariously, the engineer and the worker with a good head for heights are the sure-footed pioneers and privileged spectators of views which, once the project is completed, will be available to all those who relish the vertiginous delights of the modern.

In the second fragment, Benjamin notes the exemplary character of his *Ursprung des deutschen Trauerspiels* for the illumination of a particular dramatic idea and, through it, of a specific historical sensibility. Here it is not the panoramic 'vistas' provided by a lofty elevation, but immersion in the depths of the monadological fragment which is decisive. These scraps are hieroglyphs, or runes, which demand the deciphering of arcane correspondences and innumerable allegorical meanings. The critic must patiently sift through these fragments so as unfold their multiple meanings, represent their secret affinities by means of the mosaic, and finally recognize their configuration as a constellation, as an Idea, within the realm of art. The task of the critic is not so much the construction of modern monuments as the redemption of the purpose-built ruins of the past.

In juxtaposing these two methodological reflections, Benjamin might be seen as setting up a dialectical tension between the architectonic practices of *Einbahnstrasse* and the critical principles and concerns of the *Trauerspiel* book. Buck-Morss writes:

> the *Passagen-Werk* emerged in the eddy between two antithetical moments, the disappearing, 'outmoded form' of the *Trauerspiel* study and the bourgeois intellectual world it represented on the one hand, and Benjamin's new avant-garde literary attitude and political commitment to Marxism that determined the 'process of becoming' on the other. (Buck-Morss, 1989, p. 20)

But this both underestimates the *Trauerspiel* text and overstates any supposed subsequent rupture with its approach. One may discern in the image of structural engineering not so much a counterpoint to, but a fresh articulation of, notions developed in the baroque study. Although 'between the *Trauerspiel* study and *One-Way Street*, the author's understanding of his trade had changed from esoteric treatise writer to mechanical engineer' (Buck-Morss, 1989, p. 17), the practices themselves exhibit some striking correspondences and continuities.[23]

First, the imperative of construction is foregrounded in each case. Iron construction involves the painstaking piecing together of the most precisely fashioned miniature components into an integrated totality. The success of the entire structure depends on each minute, individual element. Benjamin writes, quoting A. G. Meyer:

> Never before was the criterion of the 'minimal' so important. And that includes the minimal element of quantity: the 'little,' the 'few.' These are dimensions that were well established in technological and architectural constructions long before literature made bold to adapt them. Fundamentally, it is a question of the earliest manifestation of the principle of montage. On building the Eiffel Tower: '. . . Each of the twelve thousand metal fittings, each of the two and a half million rivets, is machined to the millimeter. (F4a,2, *ARC*, pp. 160–1)

As an image of montage, Benjamin discovers in iron construction a principle of fragmentary composition which unmistakably parallels that of the mosaic.

Second, the contrast between the panoramic experience of the urban historian and the downcast gaze of the baroque critic should not be overplayed. The term 'panorama' does not refer solely to an outdoor view. The nineteenth-century panorama was a visual entertainment in which a picture (or series of pictures) of a city or landscape was revealed to the spectator in successive stages, so as to give the illusion of a continuous scene. The panoramic in this sense is, paradoxically, the experience of an interior, inner-directed gaze. Benjamin writes:

> The interest of the panorama is in seeing the true city – the city indoors. What stands within the windowless house is the true. Moreover, the arcade, too, is a windowless house. The windows that look down on it are like loges from which one gazes into its interior, but one cannot see out these windows to anything outside. (What is true has no windows; nowhere does the true look out to the universe.) (Q2a,7, *ARC*, p. 532)

This passage calls to mind that other windowless structure which permits the observer to peer into the truth of things: the monad. Indeed, for Benjamin, the arcade as a windowless glass construction,[24] a human aquarium, becomes the definitive monadological fragment within which one may read the totality of nineteenth-century Parisian life. The structural engineer of the *Passagenarbeit* neither craves nor enjoys the luxury of a spectacular overview of the city, but rather engages in a metropolitan monadology.

Third, the notion of an 'intentionless' approach to truth is highlighted. In the *Trauerspiel* book, the critic is to allow things to unfold themselves from within, to speak for themselves in critical reflection. One does not pursue the truth, but relies instead on the efficacy of detours. Benjamin's image of the Eiffel Tower suggests a similar patience in the treatment of phenomena. The struts of the edifice form an iron 'net', a giant metallic spider's web, into which vital images and impressions are drawn. The past is lured into, and entrapped by, the present. The historian, like the critic, is receptive to what fortuitously ensnares itself in the contemporary. Construction is also a mode of digression, of patient expectation. Nevertheless, certain preparations are necessary. Such '"Construction" presupposes "destruction"' (N7,6, *ARC*, p. 470). Under the relent-less gaze of the critic, the deceptive surfaces of the object crum-ble to disclose the truth content beneath. The text is subject to a process of mortification. Engineering presupposes a similar ruinous moment. The engineer who cuts his or her way through the city must be familiar with the use of explosives, and be prepared in the first instance to reduce the past to rubble.

Finally, the historian captures 'the most vital aspects of the past' in this net. This notion of the 'vital', the actual, is significant. The engineer and the critic are concerned with how the past is con-structed by, and read through, the present. Benjamin's *Trauerspiel* study is an exemplary instance of this – the concept of origin refers precisely to that moment of historical becoming and recognition in which a constellation is formed by what was and what is. In dusting off these dismal dramas, Benjamin discovered in them a *Weltan-schauung* with a special resonance for a modern world traumatized by war, revolution and economic ruin. In the *Passagenarbeit*, Benjamin similarly insists upon the interplay of past and present moments, in order to capture the *Urgeschichte* ('prehistory') of modernity. He writes:

> We can speak of two directions in this work: one which goes from the past into the present and shows the arcades, and all the rest, as precursors, and one which goes from the present into the past so as to have the revolutionary potential of these 'precursors' explode in the present. (O°56, *ARC*, p. 862)

Like the literary critic, the historian-as-engineer intervenes in the afterlife of objects so that past events and their actuality are recog-nized, and their critical power is realized.

Fragmentary configuration and composition, monadological inspection and introspection, intentionlessness insight, ruination, actualization of the past, redemption of the forgotten – these are the common principles of the *Trauerspiel* study, of *Einbahnstrasse*, of the 'Arcades Project', and indeed of Benjamin's work as a whole. If there is any disjunction between Benjamin's 'German cycle' of writ-ings and his later Parisian texts, it is only that which occurs when elements forming one constellation are suddenly recognized as those of another, the fleeting moment of origin.

Construction, ruination and redemption are not only historio-graphic principles of the *Passagenarbeit*, but also indicative of pos-sible interpretations of Benjamin's fascinating, fragmentary study.

For, as it exists today, the *Passagen-Werk* might be thought of as both building site and purpose-built ruin, as locus of both construction and disintegration. On the one hand, its repeatedly redrawn plans and piles of textual elements invite the reader to search for an inner logic of construction, so that he or she too might come to savour the dizzying panoramic views of the structural engineer. On the other, the improbability – and perhaps inappropriateness – of such an undertaking reduces the reader to a state of *acedia*, in which one fiddles forlornly with the pieces of an impossible puzzle. The 'Arcades Project', like the arcade itself, is part iron construction, part ruin, a setting for surreal fantasies and baroque sorrows, an edifice located at the crossroads of dream and despondency, *Traum* and *Trauer*. It is not my intention to provide a blueprint for the 'Arcades Project'. Such lofty ambitions and feats of engineering I leave to those with a better head for heights. In what follows, my aim is far more modest: to trace and introduce some of the central principles, themes and categories of this intriguing, labyrinthine textual sprawl.

The dreamworld of modernity

In Convolute K Benjamin writes: 'The imminent awakening is poised, like the wooden horse of the Greeks, in the Troy of dreams' (K2,4, *ARC*, p. 392). While recognizing the changing intentions and conceptions of the 'Arcades Project', I think this puzzling trope succinctly captures much of the work's purpose and promise. To explain and substantiate this claim requires an aptly circuitous route through Benjamin's labyrinthine study, one which touches upon a number of his key concerns: the phantasmagorical forms of the metropolis, the architecture and afterlife of the arcade, and finally, the methodological and historiographic principles which underpin the *Passagenarbeit*.

The 'Arcades Project' had two highly paradoxical goals. First, the city of Paris, the definitive modern metropolis, the 'capital of the nineteenth century', was to be revealed as the principal locus of the reconfiguration of myth, of archaic forces and creaturely compulsions. The *Passagenarbeit* was to be a critical investigation of the 'prehistory' (*Urgeschichte*) of modernity:

> 'primal history of the nineteenth century' – this would be of no interest, if it were understood to mean that forms of primal history are to

be recovered among the inventory of the nineteenth century. Only where the nineteenth century would be presented as the originary form of primal history – in a form, that is to say, in which the whole of primal history groups itself anew in images appropriate to that century – only there does the concept of a primal history of the nineteenth century have meaning. (N3a,2, *ARC*, p. 463)[25]

In the contemporary city, human beings are subject not to the daemonic powers of nature, but to the domination and delusions of 'second nature', the human-made environment of commodities, machines and edifices. Nineteenth-century Paris is home to the deceptive allure of fetishized industrial products and consumer goods, to the mystifications promulgated by bourgeois ideology, to the illusions of enlightenment and 'progress'. In the 'era of high capitalism' the critical faculties are lulled into stupefied slumber. Benjamin writes: 'Capitalism was a natural phenomenon with which a new dream-filled sleep came over Europe, and through it, a reactivation of mythic forces' (K1a,8, *ARC*, p. 391). The 'Arcades Project' was to develop this insight, and envision the Paris of the Second Empire as a '*Zeitraum*' (a 'time-space') and a '*Zeit-traum*' (a 'dream-time') in which 'the collective consciousness sinks into ever deeper sleep' (K1,4, *ARC*, p. 389). This prehistory of the recent past was intended to excavate, identify and explode the manifold manifestations of this dreaming collectivity, so as to bring modernity to its sober senses.[26]

Secondly, as the principal locus of such modern mythic forms, Paris was to be disenchanted, paradoxically, through enchantment itself. Benjamin boldly asserts:

> Forge ahead with the whetted axe of reason, looking neither right nor left so as not to succumb to the horror that beckons from deep in the primeval forest. Every ground must have at some point been made arable by reason, must have been cleared of the undergrowth of delusion and myth. This is to be accomplished here for the terrain of the nineteenth century. (N1,4, *ARC*, pp. 456–7)[27]

This invocation of the liberating tendencies of rationality is misleading. For Benjamin, the Enlightenment concept of reason, and its naive alignment with human emancipation, had itself become enmeshed in the very illusion of 'progress' which the 'Arcades Project' sought to expose. To confront and contest the myths of the modern metropolis, one must look beyond calculating reason, and instead adopt the cunning[28] and trickery of a 'dialectical fairy-play' (*GS* V, p. 1083).[29] The 'Arcades Project' was to liberate and redeem genuine utopian moments buried in mythic forms. Such a complex operation goes far beyond the capabilities of an axe-wielder, a figure all too reminiscent of the callous 'cane-wielder' in 'To the Planetarium'. Myth is not to be cut down from without, but rather demolished from within, through the ignition of combustible elements secretly hidden in the cityscape itself. Whereas in Riga, it was Benjamin himself who was ready at any moment to go up 'like a magazine', in Paris the entire urban dreamworld is set to explode. Such pyrotechnics require the skill and dexterity of an urban engineer, not the brute strength of the backwoodsman. Critical historiography requires that one blast, rather than cut, one's way through. To this end, the *Passagenarbeit* would have to be, as Adorno insisted, 'laden with dynamite'.[30]

Following the completion of the 1935 *exposé*, Benjamin reflected on the staccato process of the 'Arcades Project' and recalled its inception: 'There stands Aragon at the very beginning – Le Paysan de Paris, of which I could never read more than two or three pages in bed at night before my heart started to beat so strongly that I had to lay the book aside' (*ABC*, p. 88).[31] Despite Benjamin's critical reception of Surrealism, Aragon's *mythologie moderne* was inspirational in its vision of Paris as a dreamscape, as the chimerical site of the proliferation of phantasmagorical forms and deities. For Benjamin, myth appears in the modern metropolis in a plethora of new guises: artefactual (the commodity form), temporal (fashion, repetition and 'progress'), and spatial (the arcade as dream-house). Each has its own representative figure: the prostitute, the gambler and the flâneur.

Commodity fetishism

Benjamin's explosive critique of the mythology of modernity was to have the commodity and, in particular, commodity fetishism at its centre.[32] Benjamin had a shifting, differentiated understanding of commodity fetishism, which combined Marxist, Freudian and Surrealist elements[33] in typically idiosyncratic manner. Commodity fetishism involves a complex, contradictory set of mystifications and misrecognitions: the deification of the industrial product, the eroticization of the inanimate object, and the projection of genuine aspirations and longings on to artefacts. Moreover, as a form of disjuncture between the actual usefulness of an object (its use-value) and its monetary value (its exchange-value within a system of commodities), commodity fetishism is not only part of the phantasmagoria of the city, but also suggests processes leading to the de-fetishization (ruination) of the artefact.

In the first volume of *Capital* Marx famously writes of commodity fetishism thus:

> It is nothing but the definitive social relation between men themselves which assumes here, for them, the fantastic form of a relation between things. In order, therefore, to find an analogy we must take flight into the misty realm of religion. There the products of the human brain appear as autonomous figures endowed with a life of their own, which enter into relations both with each other and with the human race. So it is in the world of commodities with the products of men's hands. I call this the fetishism which attaches itself to the products of labour as soon as they are produced as commodities, and is therefore inseparable from the production of commodities. (Marx, 1976, p. 165)[34]

For Benjamin, too, commodity fetishism refers in the first instance to the misperception of the manufactured object under the conditions of capitalist domination. The commodity appears in the marketplace not as the product of an exploitative labour process, as the embodiment and expression of systems of alienation and dehumanization, but rather in the deceptive guise of an independent entity, one with a 'life' of its own. Mass production promises the magical creation and proliferation of an endless array of commodities, objects whose pristine, lustrous surfaces bear no trace of their laborious origin. Housed in luxurious arcades, boutiques and department stores, the commodity assumes its place as an object of cultic worship. Paris, capital of capitalism, witnessed and celebrated the 'enthronement of the commodity and the glitter of distraction' (*CB*, p. 165), the adoration of the object for the prestige and promise of novelty, for the seductiveness and sex appeal of fashion.

Here the Freudian elements of Benjamin's understanding of commodity fetishism come into play. Commodity fetishism is not only a misrecognition of human social relations, but also a particular distortion of human sexual relations. Fetishism involves the direction of erotic desires and impulses away from their legitimate object, the vital body of the other, and their projection instead onto inanimate objects. For Benjamin, unlike Freud, such fetishism is to be understood not as the peculiarity of pathological individuals, but as a generalized cultural condition in consumer capitalism. Through modes of design, display and advertising, modern commodities are sexualized. Commodity fetishism is an eroticization of the lifeless artefact, a necrophilial desire to possess dead things.[35] Moreover, such an elevation of the world of things is directly proportional to the devaluation of human life. Commodity fetishism finds its counterpart in the transformation of actual living bodies into objects for purchase and sale. Hence, the figure of the prostitute comes to serve as an allegory for – indeed, the very embodiment of[36] – the commodity form. The proliferation of commodities in the nineteenth-century metropolis was matched by the burgeoning numbers of prostitutes,[37] as the industrial labour process itself reduced work[38] and workers to prostitution.[39]

The transformation of the object into a sexual fetish is only one aspect of Benjamin's use of psychoanalytic categories in the *Passagenarbeit*. Commodities are not to be understood solely as the source and concrete manifestation of 'false consciousness', but are also indicative of a 'dream consciousness'. Just as, according to Freud, the frustrated impulses and repressed desires of the individual reappear in disguised, symbolic form in dreams, so for Benjamin the edifices and the objects of the metropolis are fantastical emanations of the so-called dreaming collectivity.[40] Commodities and edifices are nothing other than 'wishimages', disguised representations of genuine wants and aspirations that remain thwarted under capitalism. This radically recasts Marx's formulation of commodity fetishism. As a wish image, the commodity points beyond the suffering of human labour in the production process to a realm which encompasses the free play of human faculties. Material abundance, freedom from want and necessity, liberation from the drudgery of labour, human progress and self-determination – these are not so much fetishistic illusions as unfulfilled utopian impulses and promises which lie embedded in the architecture, fashions and commodities of the recent past. The phantasmagoria of modernity are mythic entities which secretly suggest the overcoming of mythic compulsion and fate. In Benjamin's *Urgeschichte* of modernity, this dream element is to be disclosed and redeemed as the hidden truth content of the fetishized commodity.

This notion of the commodity as a wish image is important. The fetishized commodity is not rejected as a mere product of ideological mystification attending economic exploitation. Rather, it is seen as a complex, contradictory entity possessing both negative

and positive moments – capitalist deceptions, but also utopian aspirations. Immanent criticism consists not so much in patiently
unfolding the object as in exacerbating and intensifying this inherent tension beyond the breaking point. Benjamin seeks to *implode*,
rather than explode, the phantasmagoria of capitalism. And this is,
contra Adorno, a thoroughly dialectical undertaking. Indeed, it is
one which acknowledges and utilizes the dialectical character of the
commodity form itself. The concept of the wish image suggests a
highly differentiated understanding of the dreamworld of modernity in which, as in Surrealism, the radical potential of apparently
regressive and/or obsolete forms is rediscovered. In rethinking
commodity fetishism in such terms, Benjamin begins to sketch a
rather subtle, nuanced appreciation of the potential of mass cultural
phenomena, an appreciation which would later extend to the new
mass media as well, and one which, above all, exists in stark contrast to the tirade later unleashed against the abominations of the
'culture industry' by Adorno and Horkheimer. Benjamin ruins
and redeems the objects, images and edifices of commodity culture.
Such intricate, implosive engineering hardly stands in need of
'more dialectics', and compares most favourably with Adorno's
indiscriminate, unilluminating critique.

Novelty, repetition and boredom

Marx writes of the fetishized commodity: 'It not only stands with
its feet on the ground but, in relation to all other commodities, it
stands on its head, and evolves out of its [wooden] brain grotesque
ideas, far more wonderful than if it were to begin dancing of its own
free will' (1976, pp. 163–4). Dance it does, though, and the rhythm
and tempo of the commodity's merry jig are set by another key
element of the phantasmagoria of modernity: fashion. The home of
the foppishly attired, narcissistic dandy, nineteenth-century Paris
smugly regarded itself as home to the very latest trends, the most
original styles, and the most discerning and daring tastes. For Benjamin, following Simmel,[41] fashion appears initially as the embodiment of the modern, of the fleeting and ephemeral. In fashion, the
commodity world seems subject to perpetual change and constant
innovation. However, it is not so much transience which characterizes fashion, but rather the infernal cycle of repetition.[42] As Simmel
observes, fashion 'repeatedly returns to old forms . . . and the
course of fashion has been likened to a circle. As soon as an earlier

fashion has partially been forgotten, there is no reason why it should not be allowed to return to favour' (1971, p. 320). Fashion is the always-the-same disguised as the endlessly new – it is this which defines its phantasmagorical character. Fashion thus appeals to, and appeases, two childish desires: the desire for superficial novelty and frivolous difference and the wish for repetition, for the same-again, the just 'once more'. This 'infinite sameness' (*CB*, p. 172) of fashion, this tedium of the nothing-new, is a source of *ennui*, of a weary boredom which measures the slumbers of the dormant, dreaming collectivity.[43]

Further, fashion as the representative of repetition is deeply implicated with another temporal mystification: the doctrine of 'progress'. With the profusion of commodities and their ever more spectacular display in the city's arcades, department stores and World Exhibitions, Paris saw itself as the centre of technological advance, capital accumulation and modern, civilized bourgeois life. For Benjamin, such developments are suggestive not of enlightenment and genuine human liberation, but rather serve as evidence of a new epoch of deception and domination. Developing his biting critique in *One-Way Street* of technological instrumentalism and exploitation, 'progress' for Benjamin involves the avaricious pillaging of nature, the plundering of colonized peoples in pursuit of 'exotic' luxuries, and the excesses of financial wealth amid the persistence of poverty and human degradation.[44] The remorseless, rapacious expansion of capitalism is sufficient to disabuse the critic of any belief in 'progress'. Indeed, the smug, complacent affirmation of 'progress' itself becomes the quintessential modern myth – both the key instance of erroneous thought and the ground of tyrannical domination. In his notes for his 'Theses on the Concept of History', the historiographical prologue to the 'Arcades Project', Benjamin writes emphatically that 'the catastrophe is progress, progress is the catastrophe' (*GS* I, p. 1244). 'Progress' is the great impostor, the perpetual nothing-new of barbaric history, class oppression and human misery.

Just as the prostitute becomes the human embodiment of the fetishized commodity, so another of Baudelaire's figures – the gambler – exemplifies the temporal phantasmagoria of fashion.[45] With each throw of the dice, each turn of the cards, each spin of the wheel, gambling promises the thrill of novelty. Yet, for Benjamin, gambling is only the semblance of the something-new, for, as an endless series of utterly disconnected, exactly repeated actions, it offers no possibility of development, no opportunity for change, no progress.[46] It is the gambler who desperately insists upon playing just 'one more time' in the forlorn hope of an upturn in fortune. He is the one who, trapped in the tedious nothing-new of the game, numbed by traumatic events, abandons himself to the daemonic forces of chance, and is finally left, like the fashionable commodity, broken and ruined.[47]

Arcade and dream-house

Neither the commodity nor fashion was to serve as Benjamin's principal monadological form, but rather, their principal location in the city: the arcade. The arcades have a double significance for him: first, in their opulent heyday during the 1830s and 1840s,[48] these 'dream houses of the collective' (L1,3, *ARC*, p. 403) were home to,[49] and examples of, the phantasmagoria of modernity;[50] secondly, in their dilapidated contemporary condition, they provide an image of his own critical historiographical practice. The arcade as fashionable fantasy turned derelict ruin encapsulates Benjamin's attempt to articulate the afterlife of dreaming, to disenchant modernity through enchantment.

Benjamin finds the '*locus classicus* for the representation of the arcades' in a Parisian journal from 1852:

> These arcades, a recent invention of industrial luxury, are glass-roofed, marble-panelled corridors extending through whole blocks of buildings, whose proprietors have joined together for such enterprises. Lining both sides of these corridors, which get their light from above, are the most elegant shops, so that the arcade is a city, a world in miniature. (A1,1, *ARC*, p. 31)[51]

This extract suggests a number of the arcade's fantastical features: it was a monument to progress, the ultimate myth of modernity; it acted as home to the fetishized commodity and fashion; and it involved a series of spatial deceptions and reversals.

In terms of its form, design and decor, the arcade, as a glass and iron construction, was one of a number of innovative, extravagant edifices which utilized the latest architectural and engineering techniques and materials to spectacular effect. For Benjamin, the museums, railway stations, World Exhibitions and the arcades of the nineteenth-century metropolis formed a complex of ostentatious constructions which celebrated, on the one hand, imperial prestige and power, and, on the other, the accomplishments of science and technological development. The World Exhibitions,[52] in particular, provided lavish (and sometimes ludicrous) settings devoted to the marvels spawned by the industrial age, with modern machinery and fetishized commodities[53] housed in fabulous fairy-tale environments[54] and staged in exotic simulations.[55] While the World Exhibitions 'erected the universe of commodities' (*CB*, p. 166), the rather more modest arcades served 'as temples of com-modity capital' (A2,2, *ARC*, p. 37). Magically lit by flickering oil (and later gas) lamps, with their numerous boutiques and shops crammed with the latest, most luxurious merchandise, the arcades were 'fairy palaces' (D°,6, *ARC*, p. 834), enchanted 'grottoes' (a°,2, *ARC*, p. 874) for the phantasmagoria of commodity fetishism and the pretensions of fashion. Kracauer writes:

> Anyone who lost his way in these passages might well have been pardoned for supposing he had entered a fairy grotto. . . . The city's magic seemed concentrated here. Remote from earth and sky, it seemed a realm exempt from natural laws, preserving marvellous illusions, like the stage. (Kracauer, 1937, p. 22)

These 'marvellous illusions' involved, in particular, the use of glass to produce, through transparency and reflection, forms of perspec-tival play and optical phantasmagoria, the *'fata morgana'* (R1,6, *ARC*, p. 538) of the modern metropolis. Although Benjamin was enthusi-astic about the radical promise of glass architecture in overcoming the dismal seclusion of the bourgeois interior,[56] the new visibility provided by the glass of the arcade was of a fundamentally differ-ent order. The arcade was an example of, not an antidote to, private space, a locus of the exclusive and of exclusion. Fully enclosed and illuminated from above, permitting no outward gaze, the arcade's only windows were inside, the 'blind' (a°,2, *ARC*, p. 874) display windows of the shops which lined the passages. These presented commodities not as objects for use, but as pure spectacle. The glass screen ensured visibility, suggested proximity, yet denied tactility. Enthroned in such crystal casings, luxury goods remained distant no matter how close they appeared: 'auratic'.[57] Within the arcade, commodities became objects of unrequited desire.[58]

If the transparency of the display window transformed the arcade into the phantasmagorical setting for fetishized commod-ities, the devilish trickery of its mirror-walls seemed to endlessly duplicate its interior spaces,[59] objects[60] and customers.[61] Benjamin observes: 'Let two mirrors reflect each other; then Satan plays his favorite trick and opens here in his way (as his partner does in lovers' gazes) the perspective on infinity. Be it now divine, now satanic: Paris has a passion for mirror-like perspectives' (R1,6, *ARC*, p. 538).[62] The arcade involved an infernal, 'infinite sameness' which mirrored that of the fashions it housed and the crowds it attracted. As a glass labyrinth, the Parisian arcade formed nothing less than a mirror-city,[63] a mirror-world, in miniature.[64]

For Benjamin, it was not only the black magic of the mirror which made the arcade a setting of optical illusion and spatial ambiguity,[65] but also the practice of architectural reversal upon which the edifice was based: the street is turned into an interior.[66] Benjamin writes of the arcade thus: 'The street itself is thereby manifest as [x] well-worn interior: as living space of the collective, for true collectives as such inhabit the street' (A°9, *ARC*, p. 828).[67] If the city street was home to the collective, the dream-street was dream-house only to the dormant collectivity, or rather to that figure whose slothful, somnambulist wanderings set its tempo and rhythm,[68] the flâneur.[69]

Although the arcade was a favourite haunt of the flâneur,[70] this figure is an unlikely representative of the dream-street. As Benjamin points out, the arcade was designed to maximize commodity consumption, not to encourage through-traffic, let alone loitering.[71] While the flâneur-as-dandy did frequent the fashionable boutiques of the interior street, admiring himself in its mirrors, the flâneur-as-idler was drawn there more as blasé browser than customer. The flâneur went to the arcade to see and to be seen. The arcade was to form the theatre of his fantastical display of snobbish superiority and affected indolence. In one particularly memorable example of this, Benjamin observes: 'Around 1840 it was briefly fashionable to take turtles for a walk in the arcades. The flâneurs liked to have the turtles set the pace for them' (*CB*, p. 54). The flâneur luxuriated in conspicuous crawling.

In the arcade, the flâneur was part of, and came to view, the spectacle of the city, the phantasmagoria of panoramic urban vistas in an interior setting. Just as there was a Passage du Désir, so there was also a Passage des Panoramas. The flâneur was at home in the arcade precisely because he was addicted to its optical illusions, 'to the phantasmagoria of space' (*CB*, p. 174). Benjamin writes:

> the interest of the panorama is in seeing the true city. 'The city in the bottle' – the city indoors. What is found in the *windowless* house is the true.[72] . . . Those passing through arcades are, in a certain sense,

inhabitants of a panorama. The windows of this house open out on them. They can be seen out these windows but cannot themselves look in. (F°24, *ARC*, p. 840)

It is the flâneur who regards the arcade as a panorama, a vantage-point from which to observe the 'real' city miraculously encased in glass, 'in a bottle'. It is under his casual gaze that the dream-street becomes a city in miniature, a microcosm of the metropolis.

The arcade was the 'most important architecture of the nineteenth century' because it was home to the fetishized commodity, the seductive prostitute, the whirl of fashion, the theatricality of the dandified flâneur, home to the phantasmagoria of time and space, to the *Zeitraum* and *Zeit-traum* of high capitalism. The arcade was the phantasmagorical home to the phantasmagoria of the recent past, the dream-house of the dream-sleep of an epoch. It is this that makes it the ultimate mythical and monadological form for Benjamin's prehistory of modernity. The arcade as 'fairy palace' was to be the perfect setting for his 'dialectical fairy-tale'.

The dialectics of dreaming

Benjamin's 'Arcades Project' constitutes 'an experiment in the technique of awakening' (K1,1, *ARC*, p. 388) from the dream-sleep of capitalism. The need to move beyond Surrealism is apparent here: 'whereas Aragon persists in the realm of dream,[73] here the concern is to find the constellation of awakening. While in Aragon there remains an impressionistic element, namely the "mythology" . . . here it is a question of the dissolution of "mythology" into the space of history' (N1,9, *ARC*, p. 458).[74] Drawing nevertheless on Surrealist motifs, myth was to be 'dissolved' into history in three ways: through the exploration of the afterlife of the object, in the notion of 'natural history' (*Naturgeschichte*), and in the shock engendered by historical materialist montage. Benjamin's prehistory of the nineteenth century sought not merely to recognize the proliferation of phantasmagoria in the modern metropolis, but also to engineer their destruction by setting in play their inherently contradictory impulses. Modern mythic forms contain the seeds of their own demise, the promise of their own transcendence. *Urgeschichte* disenchants through enchantment.

In this respect, fashion provides 'A canon of the dialectic' (*GS* V, p. 1213). The cycle of fashion and the illusion of novelty were to be understood not only as modes of fetishization, but also, ironically, as de-fetishizing forces. Fashion produces the fashionable, the modish, and in the same moment creates the *old*-fashioned, the obsolete. Fashion generates its antithesis and, in so doing, points to the ultimate fate of the fashionable object. Obsolescence is the critical counterpoint to, and ruinous afterlife of, the thing. Just as the truth content of the work of art emerges in the course of its critical mortification, so the posthumous existence of the once-fashionable artefact comes to negate its original meaning and evaluation. Hence, Benjamin observes: 'Historical "understanding" is to be grasped, in principle, as an after-life [*Nachleben*] of that which is understood; and what has been recognized in the analysis of the "afterlife of works," in the analysis of "fame," is therefore to be considered the foundation of history in general' (N2,3, *ARC*, p. 460). It is not 'fame' which awaits the fetishized commodity, however, but ridicule. The new becomes the archaic, the anachronistic and the absurd. Distaste quickly displaces desire as the sexualized commodity becomes 'the most radical antiaphrodisiac imaginable' (B9,1, *ARC*, p. 79).

The connection between afterlife and allegory so central to the *Trauerspiel* study is significant here too. In his writings on Baudelaire's allegorical poetics,[75] Benjamin discerns an 'elective affinity' between the commodity form and allegory. Whereas in allegory the ever more obscure, contrived associations begin to hollow out meaning and create a multitude of possible referents and references, the constantly changing price of the commodity and, in particular, the suddenly diminishing price of the unfashionable artefact reveal the arbitrary, illusory character of exchange-value. The discrepancy between use- and exchange-value is not only an element of the commodity's fetishistic character, but, in its correspondence with the disjuncture of signifier and signified, is suggestive of allegory. The link may seem tenuous, but it is none the less a decisive one for Benjamin, since allegory is the very antithesis of the mythic.[76] If 'The commodity form emerges in Baudelaire as the social content of the allegorical form of perception' (J59,10, *ARC*, p. 335), then it does so under a gaze which recognizes things subject to the ruinous forces of time. The allegorist perceives the transience of the material world as part of a natural history, witnesses the disintegration of the world of things, and confronts 'the *facies hippocratica* of history as a petrified, primordial landscape [*Urlandschaft*]' (*OGTD*, p. 166). The task of *Passagenarbeit* was precisely to recognize the dreamworld of nineteenth-century Paris as such a

'Primordial landscape [*Urlandschaft*] of consumption' (A°5, *ARC*, p. 827). It was to trace, moreover, the ruination of its objects and structures as a natural history of 'second nature', and come thereby to stare at the *facies hippocritica* of the recent past.

The commodities and edifices of the era of high capitalism appear as the ancestors of the present-day world of things, and as the lingering remnants of forms of life, species of objects, which have now vanished.[77] Hence, for Benjamin, it is as a scientific specialist in the realm of extinct things, as a palaeontologist, that the dreamworld of the nineteenth century is to be explored. He charts a natural history of the commodity, its inevitable and unenviable transformation from fetish to fossil. The commodity becomes an after-image of itself, a 'trace' left behind.[78] And it is as trace that the inscrutable fetish and stupefying spectacle of the recent past is demystified and rendered legible for the contemporary critical theorist as archaeologist, as prehistorian.

The principal setting for this excavation of fossilized forms is the arcade: 'As the rocks of the Miocene or the Eocene in places bear the imprint of monstrous creatures from those ages, so today arcades dot the metropolitan landscape like caves containing the fossil remains of a vanished monster: the consumer of the pre-imperial era of capitalism, the last dinosaur of Europe' (R2,3, *ARC*, p. 540). Benjamin's fascination with the Parisian shopping arcades stems from their obsolescence in the present. The very height of fashion in the 1830s, the interior street rapidly lost its appeal and fell into disrepair and relative neglect.[79] The fashionable, fetishized goods of luxury boutiques were replaced by, or themselves turned into, the miserable mouldering merchandise of the bric-a-brac shop.[80] Such curios and oddities attracted their own motley customers: outsiders, eccentrics, collectors with a penchant for the perverse and *outré*.[81] The first decades of the twentieth century saw the demolition of many of the increasingly derelict arcades. Indeed, it was precisely the imminent destruction of the Passage de l'Opéra which inspired Aragon's book. He wrote of the arcades:

> although the life that originally quickened them has drained away, they deserve, nevertheless, to be regarded as the secret repositories of several modern myths: it is only today, when the pick-axe menaces them, that they have at last become the true sanctuaries of a cult of the ephemeral, the ghostly landscape of damnable pleasures and professions. Places that were incomprehensible yesterday, and that tomorrow will never know. (Aragon, 1987, pp. 28–9)

Known today yet gone tomorrow, known today *because* gone tomorrow, the truth of this former dreamworld can be apprehended only
at the instant of its extinction, 'at last sight'. Benjamin observes that
'Being past, being no more, is passionately at work in things. To this
end the historian trusts for his subject matter. He depends on this
force, and knows things as they are at the moment of their ceasing
to be. Arcades are such monuments of being-no-more' (D°,4, *ARC*,
p. 833). The *Passagenarbeit* explores the 'residues of a dream-world'
(*CB*, p. 176) and articulates a distinctively urban archaeology of
dreaming – perilous, hasty, at the last and only opportunity.

In the chaotic windows of the bric-a-brac shops of the disinte-
grating arcade, the random juxtaposition of expiring commodities
creates

> the most irregular combinations. A world of secret affinities opens up
> within: palm tree and feather duster, hairdryer and Venus de Milo,
> prostheses and letter-writing manuals. The odalisque lies in wait next
> to the inkwell, and priestesses raise high the vessels into which we
> drop cigarette butts as incense offerings. These items on display are
> a rebus: how ought one to read here the birdseed in the fixative pan,
> the flower seeds beside the binoculars, the broken screw atop the
> musical score, and the revolver above the goldfish bowl – is right on
> the tip of one's tongue. (R2,3, *ARC*, p. 540)

The fabulous, fossilized objects of the recent past compose a bizarre
still life, a *commodité mort*. In the right hands, such material could
be explosive. Like the Surrealists, Benjamin sought to mimic such
incongruity, to combine diverse elements in original, provocative
configurations. The trivial, the despised and the ridiculous are precious things to be salvaged, deciphered and assembled in new constellations to produce 'profane illumination'. Benjamin writes:

> Method of this project: literary montage. I needn't *say* anything.
> Merely show. I shall purloin no valuables, appropriate no ingenious
> formulations. But the rags, the refuse – these I will not inventory but
> allow, in the only way possible, to come into their own: by making
> use of them. (N1a,8, *ARC*, p. 460)

Ruinous objects housed in ruinous buildings – these provide a
model of, and material for, montage. Adorno notes that Benjamin's
intention was ' "to abandon all apparent construction and to leave
its significance to emerge out of the shock-like montage of the ma-

terial. Philosophy was not merely to have recourse to Surrealism but was itself to become Surrealistic"' (Adorno, quoted in Frisby, 1988, p. 188). Or rather, urban, for it is precisely the fundamental experiences of the modern metropolis identified by Benjamin (fragmentation and incongruity, the fleeting and visual, the principle of 'shock') which inform and inspire the methodological innovations and historiographical practices of the *Passagenarbeit*. Benjamin's text becomes 'city-like'.[82]

Moreover, as Buck-Morss (1989) notes, the architecture of the city is also suggestive. Benjamin writes:

> In what way is it possible to conjoin a heightened graphicness [*Anschaulichkeit*] to the realization of the Marxist method? The first stage in this undertaking will be to carry over the principle of montage into history. That is, to assemble large-scale constructions out of the smallest and most precisely cut components. Indeed, to discover in the analysis of the small individual moment the crystal of the total event. (N2,6, *ARC*, p. 461)

Here, the architecture of the arcade, like that of the Eiffel Tower, becomes a metaphor for the construction of a critical, redemptive historiography, a metaphor for the 'Arcades Project' itself: an iron skeleton scrupulously composed of innumerable miniature elements; a transparent structure of brilliant illumination, spectacular exhibition and panoramic perspective; an untimely ruin filled with the fragmentary remainders and reminders of the recent past; a final, forlorn haven for the castaways and exiles of the object and social worlds. For Benjamin, the arcade serves as a model for textual practices and modes of representation that will bring about awakening. The historian thus recognizes that the dreamworld of the metropolis contains the moment of awakening itself, hidden in structures which are hollowed out, scorned, seemingly bereft of life and abandoned without hope. Benjamin notes that 'we seek a teleological moment in the context of dreams. Which is the moment of waiting. The dream waits secretly for the awakening' (K1a,2, *ARC*, p. 390). Awakening, the afterlife of dreaming, is cunningly lodged in the dream as a clandestine, implosive force.[83] Benjamin appropriately articulates this with respect to a figure which combines myth and metropolis: 'The imminent awakening is poised, like the wooden horse of the Greeks, in the Troy of dreams' (K2,4, *ARC*, p. 392).

Conclusion

Benjamin's unwritten 'Arcades Project' is a profound and fascinating study of the origin and evolution of modern capitalist culture. In it, he extends and expands his reconfiguration of contemporary criticism by elaborating a thoroughly unorthodox, but highly suggestive, historical materialist critique of nineteenth-century Paris. To this end, many of the critical principles he developed earlier with regard to textual analysis are transformed into techniques for reading the material culture of the recent past. Like its German predecessor, the Parisian 'production cycle' foregrounds the immanent unfolding of truth content, mortification and afterlife, and the monad and fragmentary representation. At the same time, the *Passagenarbeit* constitutes Benjamin's most explicit, sustained engagement with the Marxist tradition and comes to form, thematically and conceptually, an important counterpoint and corrective to conventional materialist analysis.

Drawing upon the pioneering work of Veblen and Simmel, Benjamin's emphasis upon consumption, culture and leisure constitutes a significant, timely departure from the usual Marxist focus on production. His prehistory of modernity recognized the mythic forms and mystifications attending the incipient development of 'consumer capitalism' – commodity fetishism, fashion cycles, advertising and display, extravagant architecture, technological marvels – as the forerunners, the ancestors, of contemporary cultural phenomena, an undertaking which clearly has a particular relevance for us today, ensconced in the latest shopping complexes and megamalls, the architectural heirs of the arcades. His destructive critique of capitalist phantasmagoria characteristically eschews the language of 'enlightenment', 'rationality' and 'progress', however; such notions are themselves deeply embedded aspects of the mythology of modernity. Benjamin argues that 'disenchantment' takes place only through a process of 'enchantment', which is why he draws upon, and deploys, the conceptual vocabulary of Surrealism and, in particular, the motifs of sleeping, dreaming and awakening. Benjamin's 'dialectical fairy-tale' was to understand the material culture of the nineteenth century as wish images, or as elements of a dreamworld, as the expression in disguised form of genuine human aspirations and desires. This utopian moment of the commodity form is its hidden truth content, which manifests itself only in the artefact's afterlife, in obsolescence, when the object's use- and exchange-value have vanished. Here the 'Arcades Project' provides an intricate, sophisticated analysis of mass consumer culture which combines a dialectical appreciation and a critical combustion of its ruinous remains. The dreamworld of the Second Empire was to be imploded from within by the representation and intensification of its inherent contradictions, a blast engineered to awaken Benjamin's contemporaries to revolutionary political action in the present, and to redeem the forgotten hopes of the recent past.

5

Culture and Critique in Crisis

Introduction

Like the work undertaken for the *Trauerspiel* study, Benjamin understood his historical and historiographical research for the *Passagenarbeit* as a key part of, not as a diversion from, his abiding concern with the transformation of contemporary culture and critical practice. Indeed, his activities and writings in the early 1930s demonstrate an ever more urgent and intense engagement with three key issues in this regard, issues which form the foci of this chapter and the next. Benjamin sought to:

1 determine the political character and consequences of particular aesthetic forms and artworks and, in particular, specify the hallmarks of progressive/revolutionary art and criticism;
2 delineate the place and task of the radical intellectual as artist, writer and critic within prevailing capitalist relations of production and reproduction;
3 conceptualize and evaluate the potentialities and applications of new mass media technologies and forms (photography and photojournalism, radio and film) for the radical reconfiguration and politicization of the cultural sphere.

Benjamin's thinking was spurred on by his increasing interest in the embroiled cultural politics of Marxism. While his enthusiasm for the works of Bertolt Brecht was unequivocal, other aspects of Marxism elicited a far more ambiguous response. The demise of the experimental artistic avant-garde in the Soviet Union, and its replacement by the doctrine of 'socialist realism' and the Stalinist propaganda machine, completed the process of cultural impoverishment whose incipient traces Benjamin had noticed during his visit in 1926–7. Further, the often simple-minded, self-destructive factional arguments of the so-called popular front and the numerous cultural, literary and other associations, like the International Institute for the Study of Fascism (INFA),[1] formed to combat the growing threat of Fascism and National Socialism, were hardly inspiring. Nevertheless, Benjamin sought to intervene – or, perhaps more accurately, dabble – in these debates of the literary Left in the vain hope that it might act effectively and decisively in response to the ever more acute cultural and political 'state of emergency'. The *Passagenarbeit* was intended to illuminate the essential prehistory of this crisis of bourgeois society.

Benjamin's hopes for a secure platform from which to undertake such an intervention were briefly boosted in late 1930 when the opportunity arose to become co-editor with Brecht of a new bimonthly journal tellingly entitled *Krise und Kritik* (*Crisis and Critique'*) (*COR*, p. 369). But, like *Angelus Novus* before it, this was to prove a disappointment for Benjamin, and a few months later in February 1931 he wrote to Brecht confirming his resignation.[2] Benjamin recognized the not inconsiderable problem of finding and engaging 'people who have something to say' (*COR*, p. 368) and the first three pieces scheduled to appear in the inaugural issue confirmed his fears.[3] His disappointment and 'critical reservations' (*COR*, p. 370) concerning the quality and pertinence of these initial contributions were such that, although he remained 'entirely willing to work on the journal' (*COR*, p. 371), he considered its fundamental aims thoroughly compromised and his position as co-editor untenable.

Benjamin made clear his understanding of the significance of *Krise und Kritik* in his letter of resignation:

> The journal was planned as an organ from which experts from the bourgeois camp were to undertake a description of the crisis in science and art. This was meant to demonstrate to the bourgeois intelligentsia that the methods of dialectical materialism are dictated to them by the necessities most characteristic of them – necessities of intellectual production and research, and the necessities of existence. (*COR*, p. 370)

The journal was to have both negative and positive moments. Immanent critique of the pretensions of bourgeois aesthetics was to implode the enduring mystifications of critical discourse: 'genius', 'creativity', the 'independent' writer.[4] For Benjamin, the new media of radio and film and the ever greater proliferation of newspapers, magazines, paperback books, advertising and photographs were transforming the cultural domain and generating what he later referred to as a 'meltdown' of traditional aesthetic forms and categories. Such a recognition was a prelude to, and precondition for, new modes of aesthetic engagement and expression, new critical vocabularies, which were to foreground the political character, significance and potentialities of cultural/intellectual production and innovation.

Although Benjamin's expectations of *Krise und Kritik* seem radically different from his hopes for *Angelus Novus*, there are some striking and illuminating parallels. Like the earlier journal, *Krise und Kritik* was to recognize and intervene in the prevailing conditions of intellectual and cultural life so as to determine and implement a transformed critical practice. In the early 1920s, this was still couched in terms of a linguistic and critical renewal in the spirit of a restored Romantic sobriety and mystical purity. By 1930, however, Benjamin's perception of prevailing circumstances and the possibilities of change had undergone a fundamental reorientation, and had adopted a politically charged vocabulary and radical tone. Hence, whereas for *Angelus Novus*, Benjamin notes, 'The vocation of a journal is to proclaim the spirit of its age' (*SW1*, p. 292), *Krise und Kritik* sought to capture the material conditions and necessities which informed and compelled contemporary cultural practice.[5] Nevertheless, its target, *the conceptual vocabulary to be liquidated*, had changed little, and the overriding imperative remained clear: 'you must recreate criticism as a genre' (*COR*, p. 359).

Moreover, 'the propaganda of dialectical materialism' (*COR*, p. 370) which the journal was to advance should not be understood as the advocacy of crude didacticism or the simplistic dissemination of Marxist orthodoxy. In a letter to Max Rychner of 7 March 1931, Benjamin writes:

> the strongest imaginable propaganda for a materialistic approach came to me, not in the form of Communist brochures, but in the form of 'representative' works that emanated from the bourgeois side over the last twenty years in my field of expertise, literary history and

criticism. I have just as little to do with what academics have accomplished here as I do with the monuments erected by a Gundolf or a Bertram. (*COR*, p. 371)

The reference here to Gundolf is not insignificant. It indicates Benjamin's understanding of his engagement with Marxism as a continuation of, rather than a radical break from, his earlier aesthetic writings. Indeed, as discussed in chapter 7, the *Elective Affinities* essay, exemplary in its dialectical structure, was to provide a model for Benjamin's projected writings on Baudelaire in the late 1930s. Additionally, it is a reminder of the context in which the *Angelus Novus* appeared. And just as this journal emerged from a particular constellation of interests and writings (his reflections upon language and translation, his early *Trauerspiel* fragments, the imperatives of immanent critique, and the *Wahlverwandschaften* study), so the new one appeared as a particular point of intersection and conjunction of Benjamin's then current projects and preoccupations (the critical insights of *Einbahnstrasse*, his fascination with Surrealism and the continuing 'Arcades' study, his experience of revolutionary Moscow and his encounter with Brecht). But, despite its initial promise, *Krise und Kritik* was not to be the forum wherein such interests could be adequately addressed. Instead, Benjamin's key arguments were to be sketched in programmatic form in 'one of the most outspoken Marxist texts WB ever wrote' (*COR*, p. 441) the 1934 study 'The Author as Producer' (*Der Autor als Produzent*).[6]

This chapter outlines the main themes of this important essay: the centrality of literary technique, the notion of the aesthetic 'polytechnician', and the 'refunctioning' of the cultural sphere. Benjamin esteemed Brecht's 'epic theatre' as an exemplary case of such ideas, and valued a number of his dramatic innovations and techniques: the eradication of distance, interruption and the 'gestural', and the 'relaxed' or 'distracted' audience. The texts discussed in this chapter develop the essential conceptual repertoire for Benjamin's key studies of the mass media during the 1930s (his reflections on, and for, radio and his fascinating, now celebrated texts on photography and film – see chapter 6) and, indeed, feed back in various (especially methodological and historiographical) ways into the 'Arcades Project' (see chapter 7). These three chapters thereby explore some of the most important of the 'prologomena and paralipomena' for the *Passagenwerk*.

The literary engineer

'The Author as Producer' is a succinct treatise 'on current questions of literary politics' (*COR*, p. 440)[7] which seeks to move beyond the facile, 'unfruitful' (*UB*, p. 86) debates on the Left regarding the political character and aesthetic merits of particular artworks/texts. Benjamin accepts that some progress has been made in the sphere of 'political literary criticism' (*UB*, p. 86): the sham of the 'autonomous' author has been exposed as bourgeois mystification, and the obligation that the 'progressive' writer 'places himself on the side of the proletariat' (*UB*, p. 85) has been accepted. Benjamin argues, however, that the prevailing, wholly 'perfunctory' (*UB*, p. 86) understanding of the notion of political 'commitment' is inadequate and, worse, has created a spurious distinction between the political 'tendency' and the aesthetic quality of the artwork. Benjamin insists upon the convergence of the political and the aesthetic. The radical artist does not choose between fulfilling his artistic aspirations and carrying out his political duties: they are one and the same. Progressive art is not a matter of compromise or of reconciling competing imperatives. This is not to say, however, that the artist's 'commitment', his or her self-conscious alignment with, and espousal of, the supposed interests of the proletariat, in and of itself guarantees 'artistic' merit. Given Benjamin's consistent rejection of the recovery of authorial intentions, it is clear that the worthy political inclinations of the writer are irrelevant. Rather, Benjamin claims:

> the tendency of a work of literature can be politically correct only if it is also correct in the literary sense. That means that a tendency which is politically correct includes a literary tendency . . . [T]his literary tendency, which is implicitly or explicitly included in every correct political tendency, this and nothing else makes up the quality of a work. It is because of this that the correct political tendency of a work extends also to its literary quality: because a political tendency which is correct comprises a literary tendency which is correct. (*UB*, p. 86)

In short, *only* works or texts with a particular aesthetic quality can be politically progressive. Poor works of art make for poor politics, irrespective of the commitment of the artist, and aesthetically valuable, reactionary 'art' is a contradiction in terms.

The 'political tendency' versus 'aesthetic quality' dichotomy is based on a series of errors: a misunderstanding of the true character and location of contemporary artistic production, a misrecognition of the transformation of the aesthetic sphere brought about by new forms of mediation and reproduction, and a misperception and misuse of these potentially critical and progressive new media. The debate between commitment and quality is, Benjamin notes, 'a textbook example of an attempt to deal with literary relationships undialectically' in which 'the rigid, isolated object (work, novel, book)' is considered independently of 'the context of living, social relations' (*UB*, p. 87). The 'dialectical treatment of this problem' correctly 'inserts' (*UB*, p. 87) back into this socio-economic complex not only the artwork, but also its producer, the author. The bourgeois fiction of the solitary, literary genius is not to be superseded by the equally deceptive vision of the progressive writer as a sentimental (bourgeois) sympathizer with the worker, as one who consciously *chooses* a side in accordance with his or her conscience and sense of commitment.[8] For Benjamin, the genuinely progressive writer perceives no such choice. He or she does not seek to establish his or her *relationship with* the working class, but rather, is compelled to recognize his or her *location within* the proletariat.[9] The progressive writer is neither autonomous with respect to, nor allied with, the worker: he or she *is* a (literary) worker who values and voices the experience of 'solidarity with the proletariat' (*UB*, p. 95). Hence, the genuine work of art is to be understood neither as an independent creation nor as a token of a tendency, but rather as a *technical product* within the dominant capitalist relations of production.

This recognition of writing as a practical technique, and of the work of art as a technical accomplishment, is essential for Benjamin. This is what makes materialist analysis of artworks both possible and necessary.[10] Further, the development and pursuit of a correct *literary technique* is the very guarantor of aesthetic quality and, in turn, of political tendency.[11] Benjamin's caustic critique in *Einbahnstrasse* of the prevailing German literary scene as a sphere of fatuous 'fat books' lauded by the snobbish, myopic academy now takes on an even more radical tone. In 1934, Benjamin presents a vision of the utter obsolescence of bourgeois literature. In a key passage, he insists:

> we must rethink the notions of literary forms or genres if we are to find forms appropriate to the literary energy of our time. Novels did not always exist in the past, nor must they necessarily always exist in the future; nor, always, tragedies; nor great epics . . . [W]e are in the midst of a vast process in which literary forms are being melted

down, a process in which many of the contrasts in terms of which we have been accustomed to think may lose their relevance. (*UB*, p. 89)

The progressive writer, as pioneer and exponent of 'technical innovation' (*UB*, p. 93), understands that modern conditions require the demise both of established aesthetic forms (the novel, poem, novella, play, etc.) and of traditional distinctions between genres, writers and readers, performers and audience.[12] This is why, for Benjamin, the debate regarding political tendency and aesthetic quality is futile. Predicated on the misperception of the aesthetic sphere as a transcendent domain of immutable forms and timeless values, it is nothing other than the attempt to reconcile radical art with bourgeois aesthetic tastes, principles and conventions.

By contrast, the author as producer understands the true historical and political character of all aesthetic matters, and discerns that these are in a fundamental process of implosion, of meltdown. Bourgeois art, like bourgeois society, is in crisis. While reactionaries lament modern 'decadence', and call for 'spiritual renewal' (*UB*, p. 93) and 'cultural reawakening',[13] the progressive writer/artist perceives the interconnected character of, and applies him or herself within, the newly emerging domains of communication: radio, journalism, photography, sound recording, film. He or she must become a polytechnician:[14]

> intellectual production cannot become politically useful until the separate spheres of competence to which, according to the bourgeois view, the process of intellectual production owes its order, have been surmounted; . . . the barriers of competence must be broken down by each of the productive forces they were created to separate acting in concert. By experiencing his solidarity with the proletariat, the author as producer experiences, directly and simultaneously, his solidarity with certain other producers who, until then, meant little to him. (*UB*, p. 95)

The meltdown of bourgeois forms is a precondition for new aesthetic practices foregrounding collaboration and collective action, and abolishing once and for all the pervasive myth of the artist as lone, creative genius.

For Benjamin, the new media contribute to the ' "functional transformation" [*Umfunktionierung*]' (*UB*, p. 93), or 'refunctioning', of the aesthetic domain, and require innovative forms and practices if their technological capacities and potentialities are to be fully realized. He is careful here to avoid any reductive technological determinacy or naive celebration of the advent of new modes of communication, representation and reproduction. The dialectical – indeed, duplicitous – character of such media must be understood. Just as political commitment alone is no insurance of artistic production, so the artist's use of new technologies is no guarantee of political orientation and efficacy. Indeed, Benjamin stresses how new media can come to serve reactionary, rather than progressive, interests in a number of ways.

First, the new media may simply be used to imitate obsolete forms. In his 'Small History of Photography', for example, Benjamin observes how some photographers in the mid to late nineteenth century sought, through the use of artifice, staging and accessories, to recapture the 'aura' of the painting, the very sense of uniqueness and distance which the camera was actually eradicating.[15] Similarly, in the 'Work of Art' essay, Benjamin points out how the demise of 'aura' occasioned by film has been reversed by the Hollywood studio system such that a spurious, new 'aura' is generated in the form of the cultish adoration of movie stars and ' "the spell of the personality" ' (*ILL*, p. 233).

Secondly, even supposedly critical applications of new media may be co-opted for other purposes. Benjamin here provides a damning critique of the radical pretensions of the photoreportage of the 'New Objectivity' (*Neue Sachlichkeit*) movement. In photoreportage, the viewer is presented with supposedly frank, unadulterated images of the real conditions of the world. Stark pictures of urban poverty and destitution, for example, purport to be incisive, incontrovertible indictments of the ills of modern society. Yet Benjamin rejects this pseudo-naturalism as naive and misplaced. These pictures do not speak for themselves; rather, the very absence of comment transforms them into sentimental images evoking bourgeois pathos. In photoreportage the everyday is aestheticized,[16] and provides for 'entertainment and amusement' (*UB*, p. 96), rather than any critical consciousness. For Benjamin, the development of progressive techniques should not be confused with an unequivocal advocacy of new technical developments within the aesthetic domain. The 'modishness' of stylistic innovations, 'tasteful' touches and polished processing only 'renovate the world as it is from the inside' (*UB*, p. 95). By contrast, techniques of construction, captioning and refunctioning are transformative and transgressive.

Benjamin's example here is not *photoreportage* but *photomontage*, a practice wherein mundane images and textual elements are juxtaposed with explosive (often bitingly satirical) effect. In such works, 'the smallest authentic fragment of everyday life says more than painting. . . . You only need think of the works of John Heartfield, whose technique made the book jacket into a political instrument' (*UB*, p. 94).

Captioning – calling things by their correct name – is important, because it is the context and title of the image which determine its political significance. In the meltdown of forms, picture and text, photographer and writer, are inseparable: 'What we must demand from the photographer is the ability to put such a caption beneath his picture as will rescue it from the ravages of modishness and confer upon it a revolutionary use value' (*UB*, p. 95). Captioning as the *authority of naming* points, moreover, to the central issue within the aesthetic domain: the ownership and control of the means of cultural (re)production. The power to contextualize and frame images and texts and, therefore, to (re)construct their meanings remains firmly in the hands of the capitalist class. Hence, the author as technician recognizes 'that the bourgeois apparatus of production and publication is capable of assimilating, indeed of propagating, an astonishing amount of revolutionary themes without ever seriously putting into question its own continued existence or that of the class which owns it' (*UB*, p. 94).

Journalist, photographer, broadcaster, film-maker, writer – just as each of these must work to break down the barriers which have separated them from one another within the sphere of cultural production, so each must also critically turn their particular medium back upon the very apparatus which isolates and controls them. The author as producer perceives his or her strategic position in the social relations of production, and reorganizes and refunctions the means of cultural (re)production at his or her disposal.[17] 'Commitment alone will not do' (*UB*, p. 98). The writer must become a strategic saboteur. Benjamin quotes Aragon: ' "The revolutionary intellectual appears . . . as a traitor to his class of origin." In a writer this betrayal consists in an attitude which transforms him, from a supplier of the production apparatus, into an engineer who sees his task in adapting that apparatus to the ends of the proletarian revolution,' (*UB*, p. 102). For Benjamin, the exemplary exponent of this polytechnic aesthetic engineering was the poet, playwright and potential co-editor Bertolt Brecht.

Brecht and 'crude thinking'

In a letter to Scholem of 6 June 1929, Benjamin reports: 'I have made some noteworthy acquaintances. To name one, a close acquaintance with Brecht' (*COR*, p. 350). By the spring of the following year Brecht's work was attracting Benjamin's critical attention,[18] and by autumn 1930 collaboration on the joint editing of *Krise und Kritik* was planned. Although the journal eventually involved more crisis than critique for Benjamin, his friendship with Brecht and advocacy of his work intensified during the 1930s. He wrote extensively on Brecht's *oeuvre*,[19] and, with both writers in exile, forsook his beloved Paris on a number of occasions for lengthy stays with Brecht in Denmark.[20]

Horkheimer, Adorno and Scholem viewed Benjamin's friendship with Brecht with a mixture of anxiety and antipathy. Benjamin valued his intellectual encounter with Brecht, whereas *they* suspected undue influence. Benjamin relished the vital challenge of the playwright's 'crude thinking' (*plumpes Denken*),[21] whereas *they* reviled it as naive immediacy. Benjamin praised Brecht's theatre for its techniques of interruption, distraction and estrangement, whereas *they* lamented Benjamin's acquaintance with Brecht as an unfortunate interruption, as an unnecessary distraction and an estrangement from his own genuine intellectual concerns. Adorno's comments regarding Benjamin's 'extraordinary' (*AP*, p. 126) 'Work of Art' essay (1935–6) are indicative in this respect (see also chapter 6). In a letter of 18 March 1936, Adorno criticizes what he regards as Benjamin's overestimation of the radical potential of film as a medium for the political 'schooling' of the proletariat and his simultaneous undervaluing of the negativity inherent in 'autonomous art'. For Adorno, genuine, progressive artworks do not serve some immediate didactic or propagandistic function, such as disseminating revolutionary ideas to the proletariat. 'Autonomous art' certainly gives expression to socio-economic conditions and class positions and antagonisms – how could it not? – but only obliquely, through manifold, complex levels of mediation and abstraction. Indeed, a fully dialectical understanding of the contradictory impulses at play within such artworks – and Adorno is thinking here above all of the 'difficult' works of 'high' modernism and the avant-garde, such as the plays of Samuel Beckett and the music of his own mentor, Arnold Schoenberg – would lead to a greater recognition and appreciation of their critical significance as forms of negation. These works seldom make any claim to revolutionary pedagogy, and usually have precious little appeal for the masses, accustomed to the banalities of the 'culture industry' as they are. Rather, such works rely upon technical innovation and experimentation to produce forms of dissonance and disturbance which lay bare the plight of an alienated humanity under modern capitalist domination.

It was precisely the absence of such complexity, dialectics and mediation[22] in Brecht's dramas, and his insistence instead upon 'the didactic play as an artistic principle' (*AP*, p. 185), that Adorno found so detestable. For Adorno, Brecht's political polemics and sloganeering were 'merely infantile' (*AP*, p. 183), and his plays nothing but childish pantomimes filled with spurious equations between, for example, gangsters and politicians (*Arturo Ui*)[23] and the Thirty Years War and modern warfare (*Mother Courage*).[24] Trite correspondences made for trivial dramas. 'Bad politics becomes bad art and vice-versa', and Brecht's art was, Adorno insists, thoroughly 'poisoned by the untruth of his politics' and 'infected by the deceptions of his commitment' (*AP*, p. 187). Adorno detected signs of such contamination in Benjamin's 'Work of Art' essay, and argued that a process of conceptual cleansing was necessary, one which 'would involve nothing less than the complete liquidation of the Brechtian motifs which have already undergone an extensive transformation in your study' (*AP*, p. 124). '*More* dialectics' (*AP*, p. 124) meant an end to the residues of 'crude thinking'.

For Horkheimer and Adorno, Brecht's influence resulted in an impoverishment of Benjamin's work through the diminution of dialectical complexity and subtlety. For Scholem, who was similarly not averse to expressing his aversion for Brecht, it was a dangerous diversion leading to the most damaging 'self-deception' (*COR*, p. 373).[25] The 'crude' Communist thinking of Brecht's 'dialectical materialism' was leading Benjamin away from his real interests: the promise and profundities of Judaic thought and the mystical tradition. If he were to follow his 'true' mode of thinking, Benjamin could, Scholem informed him, 'be a highly significant figure in the history of critical thought, the legitimate heir of the most productive and most genuine traditions of Hamann and Humboldt' (*COR*, p. 374). Instead, 'in the last few years you have been trying . . . to present your insights, which are in part far-reaching, in phraseology that is conceptually close to Communist phraseology' (*COR*, p. 374). Benjamin had unwisely forsaken his genuine language, that of theology, and lapsed into Brechtian 'prattle'. Moreover, the adoption of this 'alien form' (*COR*, p. 374) was to no avail, since his work was far too original and idiosyncratic for acceptance by the Communist Party, with its narrow orthodoxies and blinkered dogmatism. The issue, Scholem insisted, was 'not that you are fighting but that you are fighting under a disguise' (*COR*, p. 379),[26] and that this was inevitably self-defeating. 'I can only suggest', Scholem counselled, 'that you acknowledge your genius, which you are so hopelessly attempting to deny' (*COR*, p. 379). In short, Benjamin should abandon his Communist charade and join Scholem in Palestine, where he would be able to pursue his true vocation.

Benjamin remained unmoved by Scholem's arguments. He had not 'the slightest illusions concerning the fate of my writing within the party, or concerning how long a possible membership in the party would last' (*COR*, p. 377).[27] He understood his own Communist leanings not as a 'credo', but as a practical response to the exigencies attending his own writing.[28] Indeed, this was precisely one of his reasons for 'championing' Brecht.[29] For Benjamin, Brecht offered the most astute insight into the prevailing circumstances of European culture and, in particular, the trials and tribulations besetting the critical intellectual in Germany.[30] Nevertheless, Benjamin was loath to leave his native city, and certainly not for Jerusalem. Ironically, he saw the eminently bourgeois location ('Berlin W.W.')[31] of his 'small writing factory' (*COR*, p. 378) as facilitating, rather than forbidding, radical provocations: 'do you want to prevent me from hanging the red flag from my window . . . ?', he asked Scholem (*COR*, p. 378). Here, Benjamin anticipated his theme in 'The Author as Producer' of the radical intellectual as, first and foremost, a traitor to his class. And it is wise for traitors to disguise themselves. Scholem's complaint that Benjamin was sailing under false colours was insightful, yet missed the point. Such duplicity is the very cunning which the engineer must perfect. It is the stealth of the Greek wooden horse which brings about awakening. It is the deceit and trickery of the chess-playing automaton secretly worked by the little hunchback described in the first of Benjamin's 1940 'Theses on the Concept of History' (see chapter 7). Such may be the relationship between Benjamin's own avowed dialectical materialism and his Judaic, Messianic concerns in the 1930s: 'crude thinking' – whether conceived as political pragmatism or as a strategy of deception – was as necessary as 'more dialectics' and mystical illumination for the critical implosion of bourgeois culture.

To regard Benjamin's advocacy of 'crude thinking' – and there is an important difference between being an advocate and being a practitioner – as conceptual camouflage is neither to downplay its significance nor to deny the sincerity of his friendship with Brecht. It is merely to recognize that it was propelled by a perceived necessity, that same necessity which Benjamin saw as cementing the radical writer's solidarity with the proletariat. Whereas Adorno saw in Brecht only the failures of Communistic commitment, Benjamin found a co-conspirator for acts of sabotage and re-engineering. Indeed, in 'The Author as Producer', Brecht figures as the exemplary aesthetic engineer, the very individual who promises a radical departure from the futility of the commitment debate. This evaluation is not altogether surprising, given that the 'lecture' was conceived by Benjamin as a 'companion piece' (*COR*, p. 443) to his writings on epic theatre.[32] Brecht was the model 'author as producer', his epic theatre a 'model' of the refunctioning of aesthetic forms for proletarian purposes.[33] Brecht's epic theatre had five important features for Benjamin: the creation of a new proximity, the foregrounding of artifice, the use of interruption, gesture and estrangement; the elevation of the audience, and the connection with new media. The remainder of this chapter focuses upon these aspects.

The origins of German epic theatre

In 'What is Epic Theatre?' Benjamin points out that the traditional relationship 'between stage and public, text and performance, producer and actors' (*UB*, p. 2) has been irrevocably changed in contemporary culture. The essay opens with:

> The point at issue in the theatre today can be more accurately defined in relation to the stage than to the play. It concerns the filling-in of the orchestra pit. The abyss which separates the actors from the audience like the dead from the living, the abyss whose silence heightens the sublime in drama, whose resonance heightens the intoxication in opera, this abyss . . . has lost its function. (*UB*, p. 1)

Whereas bourgeois writers remain oblivious of this new condition,[34] Brecht's so-called epic theatre is concerned with developing a new sense of audience participation and involvement. In epic theatre there is a reduction of distance between performer and audience, and an interchangeability of roles such that 'Every one of the spectators can become one of the actors' (*UB*, p. 20). This is not to foster a cosy intimacy between actor and audience, but rather to facilitate direct engagement with political content. Spectators become 'collaborators' (*UB*, p. 98) in the unfolding drama. For Brecht, the stage 'has become a public platform. Upon this platform the theatre now has to install itself' (*UB*, p. 1).

The collaboration of actors and audience recalls the leitmotif of the 'Moscow' *Denkbild*: the experience of being 'closely mingled with people and things' (*OWS*, p. 191). In the museums, theatres and cinemas of Moscow, the proletariat were seen to 'take possession of bourgeois culture' (*OWS*, p. 183), and radically refunction artistic and intellectual life. Moreover, this principle of proximity anticipates the key aesthetic category of Benjamin's dialectical materialist writings of the 1930s: 'aura'. As elaborated in his writings on photography and film, 'aura' refers to the awe and wonder experienced by the onlooker in the presence of the authentic artwork. Dependent upon an *insuperable distance* between viewer and viewed, subject and object, aura is the basis of the cultic adoration of art and the bourgeois aesthetics of solitary contemplation. For Benjamin, the task of the genuine revolutionary artist, and the promise of new modes of artistic production and reproduction, are the disintegration of aura and the politicization of art. The 'filling-in of the orchestra pit' in epic theatre is the overcoming of those 'two metres' which separate 'art' from the spectator.[35]

The eradication of distance is not so as to permit a facile identification with the dramatic characters. Indeed, epic theatre makes no attempt at naturalism or realism. It neither portrays the everyday world just as it is, nor requires its audience to suspend disbelief. Instead, the privileged, politicized proximity developed by epic theatre highlights the artificiality of the artwork, the very theatricality of theatre.[36] Rather than erasing the traces of its own production, Brecht's dramas foreground their own 'construction'. Acting is presented self-consciously as acting,[37] illusion unambiguously as illusion. Epic theatre thus becomes educative, not mystifying; the stage is no longer a 'magic circle', but rather a 'convenient public exhibition area' (*UB*, p. 2).

This 'disillusionment' is achieved through the use of interruption.[38] The continual punctuation of dramatic action through the sudden introduction of music and song,[39] or through some other form of disturbance (a startling sound off-stage, the unexpected opening or closing of a door or window, etc.) is decisive for Brecht.

Continual discontinuity means that 'Epic theatre is gestural' (*UB*, p. 3) in character. Interruption produces gesture.[40] The sudden break in the flow of events paralyses the bodies of the actors in particular poses and positions, like the freeze-frame effect of a paused film. Benjamin writes of epic theatre:

> often its main function is not to illustrate or advance the action but, on the contrary, to interrupt it: not only the action of others, but also the actions of one's own. It is the retarding quality of these interruptions and the episodic quality of this framing of action which allows gestural theatre to become epic theatre. (*UB*, pp. 3–4)

Benjamin's example here is of a stranger who enters upon the calamitous scene of an ongoing family row. The moment this unexpected figure appears, the family members are momentarily arrested in their arguments and actions such that they are seemingly transformed into statues in a theatrical tableau. 'The stranger', Benjamin notes, 'is suddenly confronted by certain conditions: rumpled bedclothes, open window, a devastated interior' (*UB*, p. 5), a set of circumstances which he or she must, like a detective, decipher as clues to the course of events. Epic theatre not only presents sequences of dramatic action on stage, but also prompts their careful scrutiny by the spectator. Interruptions are pauses for critical reflection. In this manner, the audience becomes a witness not to the mere reproduction of circumstances as they appear to be, but to the dramatic 'uncovering of conditions' (*UB*, pp. 4–5) as they really are: the self-disclosure of their truth content.

Realism, naturalism, the 'New Objectivity' of photoreportage – these all simply reproduce the banal appearance of things without discovering, let alone denouncing, their underlying causes. The representation of the mundane simply remains mundane. Truth eludes such superficial approaches. The staccato rhythm of epic theatre entails disturbances in the events unfolding on stage, breaks which cause shock and consternation. It is in these fractures that truth appears.[41] Through proximity, the emphasis upon artifice, repeated interruptions and the adoption of the gestural, there is a process of estrangement and re-cognition. Epic theatre presents a sequence of fragmentary moments of rethinking, of thinking 'other': a series perhaps of thought-images, of dramatic *Denkbilder*.

Indeed, just as the notion of the diminution of distance echoes Benjamin's ideas from the mid-1920s and prefigures key categories of his subsequent writings, so too does the concept of interruption.

The significance of discontinuity is found in Benjamin's reflections on the practice of writing in his earlier *Trauerspiel* study and *One-Way Street* and, above all, in his insistence upon the broken form of the treatise as the proper technique for philosophical disquisition. In the treatise there is a recognition of the Sisyphean task of both author and reader, who must begin again with each fresh sentence. The pause which accompanies every full stop is that in which thought fleetingly renews and falteringly advances itself.[42] 'Genius is application' (*OWS*, p. 48), not inspiration, and it is this painful, incremental technical process which is the mark of profound writing, genuine reading and true theatre. The treatise, as an episodic, discontinuous form in which truth reveals itself, serves as a model for his understanding and advocacy of epic theatre. Both treatise and epic theatre are 'finely stitched together with punctuation' (*OWS*, p. 89).

Benjamin links interruption and the gestural not only with the technique of writing, but also with the 'origin of quotation' (*UB*, p. 19). In suspending action and striking a gestural pose, a particular moment is distinguished from the train of events. Similarly, the act of quotation identifies a particular passage in a text as an exemplary instance, and removes it from its original context.[43] Relocated to a new (con)text, the quotation becomes an alien, disturbing presence. For Benjamin, quotation involves an unexpected, arresting moment for the reader: 'Quotations in my work are wayside robbers who leap out armed and relieve the stroller of his conviction' (*OWS*, p. 95). In this audacious ambush, the quotation, like the gesture, becomes startling and memorable. Here the affinity between the gesture and the quotation is extended by Benjamin. Just as the reader remembers the quotation and is able to cite it, so, ' "Making gestures quotable" is one of the essential achievements of epic theatre. The actor must be able to space his gestures as the compositor produces spaced type' (*UB*, p. 19).

This juxtaposing of the theatrical techniques of interruption and gesture with the practices of writing, quotation and composition leads to an important insight for Benjamin. In its fleeting crystallization of distinct moments which can be extracted from their original location and reconceptualized in new configurations, its use of shock as a sudden stimulus to thought, and its concern with the fragmentary revelation of truth, 'epic theatre adopts a technique which has become familiar to you in recent years through film and radio, photography and the press. I speak of the technique of montage, for montage interrupts the context into which it is inserted.... this technique enjoys special, and perhaps supreme, rights' (*UB*, p. 99). Like montage, epic theatre provides for the critical illumination of phenomena, rather than their mere presentation. Juxtaposition and construction are decisive here. Epic theatre does not lapse into the 'wide-eyed presentation' of things as they are, but rather 'lets the conditions speak for themselves, so that they confront each other dialectically. Their various elements are played off logically against one another' (*UB*, p. 8).

Temporality is important in this interplay. Interruption corresponds precisely to the fleeting moment in which elements come together in a distinctive, legible pattern, the instant in which a constellation comes into being. For what does epic theatre present to the spectator in the tableau of gestures if not a transient constellation to be recognized and read? And if this is the case, then the moment of interruption in which the constellation both constitutes itself, and discloses its truth, is nothing other than that disturbance in the flow of transformations, that 'eddy in the stream of becoming' which Benjamin understood in his *Habilitationsschrift* as origin. Indeed, if the concepts of 'origin' and 'constellation' pioneered in the *Trauerspiel* study find clear echoes in those of interruption and gesture in his work on Brecht, this is apt, because Benjamin sees in Brecht an – albeit unwitting – heir of baroque drama.[44] Moreover, Benjamin begins to translate elements of his critical vocabulary of the *Trauerspiel* study into a conceptual repertoire appropriate to the study of epic theatre. It is in this context that one begins to discern the complex ground and full force of Scholem's dismay regarding Benjamin's new 'materialist phraseology'. And what could be a more fitting, profane counterpart to the hymns of the evanescent *Angelus Novus* than the songs of the misfits, miscreants and molls which puncture the action of Brecht's plays?

Adorno's demand for '*more* dialectics' is also pertinent here. In his notion of interruption, Benjamin perceives, and begins to articulate, an idea which becomes central to his understanding of history and historiography: the fleeting cessation of the dialectical process itself, such that, in the tension created, an image or representation of truth constitutes itself. Epic theatre is not undialectical, Benjamin claims; rather, it is in Brecht's drama that dialectics, like the actors themselves, appears momentarily at a standstill, as if illuminated by a flash of lightning:

> The thing that is revealed as though by lightning in the 'condition'
> represented on the stage – as a copy of human gestures, actions and

words – is an immanently dialectical attitude. The conditions which epic theatre reveals is the dialectic at a standstill. For just as, in Hegel, the sequence of time is not the mother of the dialectic but only the medium in which the dialectic manifests itself, so in epic theatre the dialectic is not born of the contradiction between successive statements or ways of behaving, but of the gesture itself. (*UB*, p. 12)

This elaborates an insight already present in *One-Way Street*. In 'Costume Wardrobe', Benjamin interweaves history, theatre, interruption and gesture thus:

> Again and again, in Shakespeare and Calderon, battles fill the last act, and kings, princes, attendants and followers "enter fleeing". The moment in which they become visible to spectators brings them to a standstill. The flight of the *dramatis personae* is arrested by the stage. Their entry into the visual field of non-participating and truly impartial persons allows the harassed to draw breath, bathes them in new air. The appearance of those who enter "fleeing" takes from this its hidden meaning. Our reading of this formula is imbued with expectation of a place, a light, a footlight glare, in which our flight through life may be likewise sheltered in the presence of onlooking strangers. (*OWS*, p. 100)

The task of the critical historian for Benjamin becomes precisely that of apprehending and redeeming moments, events and objects which 'enter fleeing' by transfixing them in the ephemeral light of profane illumination (see chapter 7).

In Benjamin's writings on Brecht and epic theatre, the notion of 'dialectics at a standstill' figures as a didactic device to startle the spectator into recognition. In a passage reminiscent of his earlier discussion of origin, he notes: 'The damming of the stream of real life, the moment when its flow comes to a standstill, makes itself felt as a reflux: this reflux is astonishment. The dialectic at a standstill is its real object' (*UB*, p. 13). The metaphor here is suggestive: an expert in 'damming', a technician who harnesses the energy generated by the disturbance of flow, the epic dramatist is an exemplary hydraulic engineer.

Interruption and gesture radically alter the attitude and attention of the audience. Intense concentration and individualistic contemplation – the hallmarks of bourgeois aesthetic experience – are replaced by an altogether different mode of receptivity: 'relaxation'.[45] Prefiguring the notion of 'distraction' (see chapter 6), 'relaxation' does not mean disinterest or disengagement. The relaxed audience is attentive, but never suspends disbelief, never loses itself in the unfolding drama. Importantly, the individual spectator cannot identify with any specific character, but instead discerns the conditions in which the figures operate. It is this lack of individual 'empathy'[46] which distinguishes the relaxed audience and epic theatre as a collective experience, and which creates 'astonishment' at the circumstances disclosed. For Benjamin this has two corollaries: expertise and laughter.

The 'educative' role of epic theatre consists neither in the initiation of the audience into the 'enlightened' realm of bourgeoisie *Kultur*, nor in the peddling of revolutionary proletarian propaganda. Rather, it involves the elevation of the audience to the position of 'expert' – not only of the drama, but, more significantly, of the conditions revealed in it. The relaxed audience measures what it sees on stage 'against its own experience' (*UB*, pp. 15–16). The success and efficacy of the play depend upon the vital resonance of its scenes and insights for the spectators. They recognize and reassess both the circumstances laid bare and themselves. Hence, Benjamin observes, 'the supreme dialectic' of epic theatre is that 'between recognition and education. All the recognitions achieved by epic theatre have a directly educative effect; at the same time, the educative effect of epic theatre is immediately translated into recognitions' (*UB*, p. 25). This means that epic drama must appeal to, and bring into focus, the everyday understandings and experiences brought by the audience to the theatre. Benjamin's model is the crowd at a sporting event. Here the proletariat needs no instruction from the bourgeoisie to appreciate the finer points of the game. They are there to witness and applaud the technical skills and commitment of the players – abilities and attitudes with which they are long familiar.[47]

As 'technical experts' (*UB*, p. 4), the audience becomes both critical and reflexive. The role of the theatrical critic is usurped by the audience.[48] And as their sense of critical expertise develops, there arises a collective self-consciousness and confidence. The audience becomes aware of itself and its interests; it reconstitutes itself into factions and blocs: workers, intellectuals, the avant-garde. The spectators do not identify with the characters on stage, but come to identify themselves in the auditorium. In this process the pretensions of the critic are exposed and overcome.[49] The expertise of the spectators of epic theatre does not consist in the demonstration of bourgeois refinement and aesthetic 'good' taste, but rather manifests itself in uproarious laughter. Epic theatre

sets out not so much to fill the audience with feelings – albeit pos-
sibly feelings of revolt – as to alienate the audience in a lasting
manner, through thought, from the conditions in which it lives. . . .
[T]here is no better starting point for thought than laughter; . . .
spasms of the diaphragm generally offer better chances for thought
than spasms of the soul. Epic theatre is lavish only in the occasions
it offers for laughter. (*UB*, p. 101)

Such mirth has nothing to do with the 'entertainment' of the culture
industry. It is the bitter, withering laughter of romantic irony which
liquidates mediocrity; it is the scornful, ruinous ridicule of Surrealism which humiliates the obsolete and absurd. Brecht's plays
resound to a loud, liberating laughter.

Brecht is an exemplary aesthetic engineer, because epic theatre
both recognizes the meltdown of traditional artistic forms occasioned by the development of 'new technical forms' (*UB*, p. 6) and
pioneers innovative practices and principles which correspond to
them.[50] Central to Brecht's polytechnical expertise is his insight into
the applicability of features of these media, and his skill in refunctioning them into dramatic devices. Benjamin sees in this 'a theatre
which, instead of competing against the newer means of communication, tries to apply them and to learn from them – in short, to
enter into a dialogue with them. This dialogue the epic theatre has
adopted as its cause. Matching the present development of film and
radio, it is the theatre for our time' (*UB*, p. 99). The use of interruption, for example, clearly parallels photographic and cinematic
techniques. Action and movement are broken down into discrete
moments and gestures. The photographic snapshot arrests the flow
of life to capture a fleeting gesture, while film is, of course, nothing
other than the illusion of living movement created by the sequencing of manifold gestures.[51] Similarly, montage as a method of representation is an established part of the photographic and cinematic
repertoire. In his 1932 fragment 'Theatre and Radio'[52] Benjamin
explicitly connected the interruption and montage of 'the progressive stage' (*SW2*, p. 584) with that of the new media, and film in
particular. Epic theatre's

discovery and construction of *gestus* is nothing but a retranslation of
the methods of montage – so crucial in radio and film – from a technological process to a human one. It is enough to point out that the
principle of Epic Theater, like that of montage, is based on interruption. The only difference is that here interruption has a pedagogic
function and not just the character of a stimulus. It brings the action

to a halt, and hence compels the listener to take up an attitude toward the events on the stage and forces the actor to adopt a critical view of his role. (*SW2*, pp. 584–5)

Film viewers and radio listeners are also, like the sports spectators, a model for the 'relaxed' audience of epic theatre. Benjamin writes:

> In film, the theory has become more and more accepted that the audience should be able to 'come in' at any point, that complicated plot developments should be avoided and that each part, besides the value it has for the whole, should also possess its own episodic value. For radio, with its public which can freely switch on or off at any moment, this becomes a strict necessity. Epic theatre introduces the same practices on stage. For epic theatre, as a matter of principle, there is no such thing as a latecomer. (*UB*, p. 6)

The experience of the spectator of epic theatre is more akin to that of the cinema-goer than the traditional theatre public.

If Brecht's accomplishment is, in part, to recognize the new technical possibilities and necessities of a 'theatre for our time', then it is for the polytechnicians of other media to adapt and adopt the principles of epic theatre as a model within their own spheres of expertise. The photographer, the film-maker, the musician, the broadcaster, the author – these producers must learn from epic theatre as Brecht has learnt from them. This is the basis for the meltdown of bourgeois aesthetic forms, the precondition for radical artistic practices, the promise of a new solidarity between artists, critics and audiences as cultural conspirators and pioneers.

Conclusion

Benjamin's championing of Brecht in the early 1930s endured despite the most bitter opposition from his closest friends and colleagues, which says much about its importance for him. For Benjamin, Brecht as exemplary polytechnical aesthetic engineer expressed the decisive experiences and articulated the essential responses to the increasingly unstable, threatening political conditions of the time and the 'implosion' of traditional bourgeois culture. Amid such crises, political necessities, not philosophical niceties, were the main imperatives behind Brecht's and Benjamin's writings and the ground of their perhaps unlikely, but nevertheless unyielding, friendship. At the same time, it is important to recognize that Benjamin's fascination with the techniques of epic drama also involves an important continuation, elaboration and reconfiguration of his enduring attempt to 'recreate criticism' – criticism, that is, no longer understood as a distinctly (or even principally) literary endeavour, but rather conceived as a wider cultural undertaking and, above all, an urgent political intervention. In this respect, the politicized vocabulary now adopted by Benjamin is clearly recognizable as an extension and radicalization of many of the earlier concepts and insights pioneered in *Einbahnstrasse*: the critique of the mediocrity of conventional bourgeois scholarship, the search for more immediate forms of cultural production, the emphasis upon literary technique and, above all, the figure of the engineer as a new kind of aesthetic producer and critic. Moreover, and more surprisingly, there are, as I have suggested in this chapter, a number of subtle, intriguing correspondences between some of the dramatic principles of Brecht's epic theatre and critical ideas found in the *Trauerspiel* study: for example, Benjamin's advocacy of the discontinuous treatise form as a cognitive, philosophical practice finds a clear echo in the interruption of action as a pedagogic imperative, and the notion of origin as the instant in which a constellation manifests itself prefigures the gestural moment in epic drama in which recognition occurs. Benjamin's engagement with Brecht was not a diversion from his true intellectual vocation, as Adorno and Scholem so presumptuously complained, but a deliberate re-channelling of his concepts to maximize their energy and efficacy in the present. It was an act of reflexive hydraulic engineering as actualization.

At the same time, Benjamin's writings on Brecht contain the initial formulation of a number of concepts which were to prove crucial in his later writings on the mass media (see chapter 6) and on historiography (see chapter 7). In his writings for radio of the early 1930s, Benjamin sought to transpose some of the principles of epic theatre into experimental pedagogic practices for the new medium: the foregrounding of artifice and construction, the diminution of distance, the use of interruption and digression, and the direct appeal to the audience's own circumstances and knowledge. He thereby came to articulate an important distinction between bourgeois 'education' (*Bildung*) and proletarian 'schooling' (*Schulung*). In his writings on photography and film, Benjamin was to develop the importance of proximity as a prerequisite for the disenchantment of the work of art, the eradication of its aura. Further, the notion of the gestural as the fragmentation and interruption of action was significant for understanding the distinctive relationship between the film camera and the actor and, in particular, the shift from the complete dramatic performance expected by the traditional theatregoer to the discontinuous series of miniature performances demanded by the film director. The notion of the 'relaxed' spectator as expert was also to be elaborated in Benjamin's later reflections on film in terms of a privileging of 'distraction' and 'habit'. Most significant, though, is Benjamin's idea of dramatic interruption as the formation of a tableau of gestures. This cessation of movement so as to compose a legible figure or image corresponds to the photographic snapshot, and becomes, in the concepts of 'dialectics at a standstill' and the 'dialectical image', the very basis of Benjamin's redemptive historiographical practice in the 'Arcades Project'. The studies of Brecht are more 'small-scale victories' for the *Passagenarbeit*, vital points of critical illumination in its ever more complex constellation.

6

Benjamin On-Air, Benjamin on Aura

Introduction

Now seen as among his most suggestive works, and widely recognized by contemporary cultural, media and film theorists as essential points of departure, Benjamin's writings during the 1930s on photography and the (relatively new, though already extensively debated)[1] media of radio and film do not constitute, and were never intended as, a coherent or systematic theory of mass media as such. Rather, these texts, whose varied forms – radio scripts of the most diverse kind, 'conversations', reviews, essays and historical fragments – and numerous versions are indicative of their author's changing circumstances and intentions, present a highly ambiguous and contradictory set of concepts, principles and evaluations. For example, in his writings *on* radio, Benjamin is at pains to emphasize the vital correspondences between this medium and Brecht's epic theatre. He expounds upon the merits of the mutual invisibility of broadcaster and audience, and the potential of radio for technical experimentation and proletarian pedagogy. At the same time, Benjamin's comments in letters to Scholem and others are scornful of his own numerous writings *for* radio, dismissing them as simple economic necessities with little or no thematic or technical merit whatsoever.

There are many more discrepancies. The 1931 'Small History of Photography' offers, despite its title, precious little in the way of a reliable 'history' of the medium. Instead, it introduces one of the most intriguing and debated of all his concepts: 'aura'. Benjamin's use and evaluation of aura both here and in the later, now much-celebrated study 'The Work of Art in the Age of Mechanical Reproduction' (1935–6)[2] are fascinating and provocative, but (or perhaps because) infuriatingly imprecise and inconsistent. So, too, is Benjamin's understanding of the notion of 'habit', a disposition or sensibility lauded as a form of mastery and expertise in the 'Work of Art' essay, yet lamented in the 'Berlin Chronicle' as a source of boredom and forgetfulness. And all these ambiguities and equivocations are themselves in stark contrast to the frequently strident, uncompromising political tone of these texts. What is one to make of Benjamin's bold, though enigmatic, closing declaration in the 'Work of Art' essay – that Fascism involves 'the aestheticization of politics', whereas Communism demands the 'politicization of aesthetics'?

Such contradictions inevitably satisfied no one. For Adorno, Benjamin's writings were tainted by Brechtian 'crude thinking': on the one hand, they failed to do justice to the intricacies and negativity of his own preferred 'autonomous art', and, on the other, in their advocacy of radio and film, they opened up the disquieting possibility that modern mass media might inherently possess some radical political potential, a view which sits uneasily with Adorno's critique of mass culture in the 1930s and, of course, his later 'culture industry' thesis. For his part, Brecht, in an exemplary instance of the very 'crude thinking' which Adorno so despised, dismissed Benjamin's central category of aura as mystification and 'mysticism',[3] though Scholem would doubtless have taken little comfort in this. 'Mysticism' or dialectical materialism, or both, one disguised as the other? The complex paradoxes and plays which characterize Benjamin's *oeuvre* find full expression in these writings on media forms.

This chapter examines the most important of these texts, and seeks to unfold their key themes and concepts. It starts out by presenting some contrasting interpretations and assessments of Benjamin's radio scripts in the context of his more general reflections on the radio as a medium – Sabine Schiller-Lerg's understanding of these programmes as forms of materialist pedagogy and Jeffrey Mehlman's ingenious, though perhaps over-elaborate, allegorical interpretation. The remainder of the chapter explores Benjamin's two studies of visual culture and reproduction: his 1931 photographic 'history' and the 'Work of Art' essay. In examining their conceptual repertoire, my aim is certainly not to propose any resolution to Benjamin's dispute with Adorno, a dispute which in so many ways still frames debates about the vices and virtues of the mass media; but rather, to show the significance of these ideas and motifs for the *Passagenarbeit*, the greater intellectual project of which they were a part. Film and photography were not only thematically relevant for the 'Arcades Project' – the fate of art in modernity was to be a significant theme – but are of the utmost methodological importance. These media suggested to Benjamin practices for the imagistic presentation of the recent past, techniques for the critical and redemptive historian, the ultimate exponent of polytechnical engineering.

Enlightenment for children

'Like an engineer starting to drill for oil in the desert', Benjamin notes, Brecht 'takes up his activity at precisely calculated places in the desert of contemporary life. Here these points are situated in the theatre, the anecdote, and radio' (*UB*, p. 27). Benjamin, too, was to become an exponent of the radio, and in the least likely of guises.[4] Between March 1927 and his departure from Germany in early 1933,[5] he planned, wrote and presented around ninety radio broadcasts of various kinds: book reviews and literary discussions, interviews and conversations, plays and dialogues. Extraordinarily for this most esoteric and elusive of thinkers,[6] principal among these radio writings are some thirty scripts for two radio programmes for children,[7] texts which present the most diverse and diverting tales: of witch trials and train crashes, fires and floods, toys and tricksters, brigands and bootleggers.

These radio scripts for children not only recounted turbulent histories; they themselves experienced the most chequered literary afterlife imaginable. Benjamin took these texts with him into exile in France in 1933, but was compelled to abandon them when he fled Paris in 1940. Seized from Benjamin's Paris apartment by the Gestapo, and then filed away by Nazi officials, the scripts miraculously survived the war. They were eventually placed in the Potsdam Central Archives in former East Berlin around 1960, and were then moved to the archives of the Akademie der Kunst in April 1972.[8] First published under the unlikely title of 'Enlightenment for

Children' (1985),[9] Benjamin's radio broadcasts for children were finally republished in the seventh and final volume of his *Gesammelte Schriften* (1989). Sadly, there appear to be no surviving recordings of Benjamin's actual broadcasts.

Benjamin exhibited considerable interest in radio as a medium,[10] and valued his friendship with Ernst Schoen, artistic director of Südwestdeutscher Rundfunk and the key figure in facilitating Benjamin's brief broadcasting career. Nevertheless, with one or two exceptions, the radio writings were held in low regard by their author. Scholem's request for copies of the scripts met with little enthusiasm. Benjamin's letter of 23 February 1933 reports that his 'countless talks' are 'of no interest except in financial terms', and that only one of the radio plays is 'Notable from a technical point of view' (*COR*, pp. 403–4).[11] Benjamin saw the radio scripts as a mere economic expediency, a view which should be neither accepted uncritically, nor taken as reason to neglect them.[12] After all, as he himself insists in his own critical practice, the author's own intentions and judgements regarding his or her texts should never be treated as the final word on them. Accordingly, a number of recent commentators have sought to rehabilitate these radio scripts and suggest their complex connections with Benjamin's other writings. Schiller-Lerg's 1984 study *Walter Benjamin und der Rundfunk* was the first, and certainly remains the most comprehensive, reappraisal. Benjamin's radio scripts have, she argues, a threefold significance: first, in their connection with his other writings; second, as forms of pedagogic practice; and finally, as experiments in the possibilities of a new medium.

The first of these is most clearly apparent in the dozen or so children's broadcasts for Berlin radio which took the capital city itself – its inhabitants, buildings, vernacular, literature and history – as their theme.[13] These Berlin anecdotes and stories clearly prefigure Benjamin's own fragmentary reflections on his native city – the 'Berlin Chronicle' and 'Berlin Childhood around 1900'.[14] He is concerned throughout with, on the one hand, the manner in which the apparently banal features of the cityscape are imbued with, and set in train, histories, associations and memories, and, on the other, how particular narratives and narrators, especially those intended for and attentive to children, illuminate the urban setting.

The radio broadcasts were also clearly linked with Benjamin's materialist writings on epic theatre and on the contemporary 'author as producer'. Indeed, for Schiller-Lerg, 'they can be considered as practical examples of Benjamin's own pedagogic work'

(1984, p. 9), exploring the didactic possibilities of the medium. While Adorno and Horkheimer came to view the radio as an instrument of propaganda[15] and soporific 'entertainment', Benjamin retained a positive view of its potential. In 'Theatre and Radio' he writes:

> In comparison to the theater, radio represents not only a more advanced technical stage, but also one in which technology is more evident. . . . The masses it grips are much larger; above all, the material elements on which its apparatus is based are closely intertwined in the interests of its audience. Confronted with this, what can the theater offer? The use of live people – and apart from this, nothing. (*SW2*, p. 584)

More importantly, what the theatre does have to offer is, of course, the model of epic drama, and it is precisely the confluence of the communicative potential of radio and the techniques of Brecht which guides the form and content of Benjamin's broadcasts.

In Benjamin's 'Conversation with Schoen' it is stressed that radio should serve neither as an instrument for the wider dissemination of outmoded bourgeois culture, nor as a vehicle for the presentation of bland amusement. Schoen accordingly rejects the content of radio programmes hitherto: ' "That was, in short, Culture with a capital C. It was thought that radio could serve as the instrument of a gigantic drive towards educating the people. Lecture series, courses of instruction, pompous didactic events were instigated and ended in fiasco . . . The listener wants entertainment [*Unterhaltung*]" ' (*GS* IV, p. 548). The double meaning of *Unterhaltung* in this context is illuminating. First, it means 'entertainment'. What Schoen has in mind here is not simply replacing 'the dryness and limited subject matter' (*GS* IV, p. 549) of worthy, learned broadcasts with frivolous trivia, but rather the development of genuinely popular cultural forms possessing a critical edge. This involves more than just a change of programming content. It requires, Benjamin observes, 'a politicization' (*GS* IV, p. 549) of the radio. The second sense of *Unterhaltung* is significant here, for the word can also be translated as 'conversation' or 'chat'. And it is precisely the possibility of 'conversation', of a dialogue between an invisible voice and an unseen audience, which interests Benjamin, and for which epic theatre provides a kind of mirror-image. For just as Brecht's plays utilize the co-presence of actors and audience to particular effect – proximity, estrangement, expertise – so the radio must play with the mutual absence of speaker and listener so as to involve and inter-pellate the audience as collectivities.

Here Benjamin introduces the notion of 'training', or 'schooling' (*Schulung*) as opposed to 'culture', or 'education' (*Bildung*).[16] The lis-tener is not to be instructed in, and improved by, the accomplish-ments, virtues and tastes of the bourgeois, but given insight into his or her own daily circumstances. *Schulung* strives for the same moment of audience (self-)recognition to which epic theatre is directed.[17] Indeed, as Schiller-Lerg emphasizes,[18] many of the tech-niques of Brechtian drama are employed in Benjamin's radio broad-casts for children: the narrator directly addresses, and locates himself on the side of, the particular audience for whom the stories are intended; the tales are told in an open, easy manner, free of pious moralizing; there is no attempt at 'realism' or 'naturalism', and the artifice of the mediated form is continually stressed; the stories are interrupted by the narrator through asides and anecdotes, or are even unexpectedly transformed into another tale altogether; such interruptions are often used to comic effect, disturbing the flow of the story through laughter; and the listener is encouraged to reflect upon the narrative and the new light that it may shed upon every-day events and experiences.

Benjamin's radio broadcasts were not simply 'enlightenment for children' (and adults); they were also technical experiments for broadcasters. While epic theatre provides an invaluable model for his broadcasting practice, he is also attentive to the distinctive fea-tures of the new medium. Radio, like every other medium, must be developed in accordance with its own specific technical logic. Benjamin's attempts at experimentation in this regard are perhaps best illustrated by his one-hour 'radio play for children' (*Hörspiel für Kinder*), *Radau um Kasperl*. First broadcast on Südwestdeutsche-Rundfunk on 10 March 1932, and then in a twenty-minute shorter version on 9 September 1932 by the Cologne-based Westdeutscher Rundfunk,[19] this is the piece identified by Benjamin as 'Notable from a technical point of view' in his February 1933 letter to Scholem.[20]

The action proceeds as follows: while at the market, the radio pre-senter Herr Maulschmidt[21] fortuitously spots Kasperl (Mr Punch), who has been sent out to buy some fish. He is cordially invited to the radio station to address the audience, but, while Maulschmidt is explaining the workings of the various pieces of equipment, takes the opportunity to launch into an abusive tirade. Pursued by the radio presenter, Kasperl flees from the studio to a hotel, where he hopes to find employment as a waiter. Mayhem ensues in the hotel's kitchens and dining rooms before Kasperl beats another hasty retreat, first to the railway station, then to the zoo. Kasperl takes a taxi, which predictably crashes, and he eventually winds up in a hospital bed, where he finally receives compensatory payment from the radio station.

Uwe Lothar Müller stresses the Brechtian features and techniques of this play: its contemporary characterization,[22] the foregrounding of artifice through the tour of the studio, and the use of comic asides to interrupt action.[23] He and Schiller-Lerg both focus on how sound effects are utilized. Each of the various scenes (market, studio, hotel, railway station, zoo, taxi) is suggested, and made readily identifiable, by the use of appropriate acoustic elements: the hubbub of street traffic and passers-by, the clinking of glasses and crockery amid the murmurings of diners, the noise of trains arriving and departing punctuated by passenger announcements over the tannoy, the sounds of exotic animals and the laughter of visiting schoolchildren, etc.[24] The city is made strangely familiar as it is reconceptualized and recognized as a series of 'Hörbilder',[25] or urban soundscapes.[26]

As *Radau um Kasperl* illustrates, the separation of radio broadcasters and listeners is not an insurmountable obstacle to interaction and participation, but rather the spur to new programme forms and formats.[27] In 'Reflections on Radio', Benjamin writes:

> The crucial failing of this institution has been to perpetuate the fundamental separation between practitioners and the public, a separation that is at odds with its technological basis. A child can see that it is in the spirit of radio to put as many people as possible in front of a microphone on every possible occasion; the public has to be turned into the witnesses of interviews and conversations in which now this person and now that one has the opportunity to make himself heard. (*SW2*, p. 543)

Moreover, Benjamin views the 'privatized' situation of the radio listener as a positive feature, because it means that the radio enters the listener's life as an everyday experience. The audience engages with the radio on home ground, rather than in such intimidating cultural venues as the museum, theatre or concert hall. The radio broadcast, like the photograph and the sound recording, meets the 'beholder halfway' (*ILL*, p. 222), such that 'the choral production, performed in an auditorium or in the open air, resounds in the drawing room' (*ILL*, p. 223). This domestication of the radio broad-cast has important consequences: it diminishes its authority over the listener, who is not compelled to sit in rapt contemplation, but chooses to listen sometimes attentively, sometimes in a state of distraction. The radio plays to a relaxed audience, and, as with the spectators of epic theatre, this is a precondition for their engage-ment. Here schooling, technique and experimentation combine. The goal of experimental productions like *Radau um Kasperl* is precisely to familiarize the listener with the techniques of the radio broad-cast, to foster expertise and facilitate criticism.[28] It is not only the contemporary radical artist who must become an aesthetic, poly-technical engineer, but also the audience as critic. And this is the essential promise of radio, photography and film.

Allegories for adults

Jeffrey Mehlman (1993) is also keen to correct Benjamin's downbeat assessment of his radio programmes for children. He does so in two ways. First, these scripts take on a special significance for Mehlman because of their method of composition. Benjamin informed Scholem (25 January 1930) that 'I no longer write out most of the things that must be considered as work done simply to earn a living, whether for periodicals or the radio. Instead, I simply dictate things like that' (*COR*, p. 361). As stories born from his stream of con-sciousness, the scripts for children offer privileged insight into Benjamin's thinking. Indeed, Mehlman claims, the radio scripts as artless artefacts are 'as close to the transcript of a psychoanalysis of Walter Benjamin as we are likely to see' (1993, p. 3), though this sug-gestive idea is not developed further.

Secondly, Mehlman contends that the broadcasts should be understood as 'toy-texts' (1993, p. 5), as exercises in technical skill and dexterity and experiments in ideas and design.[29] Rejecting 'Schiller-Lerg's pat formulation' (1993, p. 37) of such scripts as instances of materialist pedagogy, Mehlman treats them instead as '"theoretical" toys' (1993, p. 4), miniature models for, and playful treatments of, Benjamin's most important philosophical, theologi-cal and historical themes and motifs: mystical conceptions of language and translation, Messianic notions of destruction and redemption, the work of allegory, and the character of memory and critical historiography.[30]

Mehlman begins by dividing the scripts for children into three main thematic sets: first, a series of tales relating instances of deception and fraud ('Caspar Hauser', 'Cagliostro', 'Briefmarken-schwindel', 'Die Bootleggers'); secondly, stories recounting catastrophes and disasters ('Untergang von Herculaneum und Pompeji', 'Erdbeben von Lissabon', 'Theaterbrand von Kanton', Die Eisenbahnkatastrophe vom Firth of Tay', 'Die Mississippi-Ueberschwemmung 1927'); and thirdly, scripts concerned with Berlin. He then takes Benjamin's story of bootlegging during the Prohibition period in the United States as a point of departure. An African-American boy proceeds along a train waiting at a station selling what he claims is 'iced tea' to the passengers. With a knowing smile, they readily purchase it at exorbitant prices in the belief that this so-called tea is really alcohol. To their disappointment, however, the 'tea' actually proves to be tea. The passengers are swindled by not being swindled; they are cheated not by the boy, but by themselves. They are deceived when things are what they seem – that is, by the truth – by the surprising coincidence of name and thing.[31] Here notice is duly given that in the radio broadcasts things are, and are not, what they seem.

Mehlman's reading of the disaster stories throws up some equally intriguing ideas. The story of the Roman cities of Herculaneum and Pompeii is most significant here. In the sudden eruption of Mount Vesuvius in AD 79, the two towns and their unfortunate inhabitants were completely engulfed by volcanic rock, ash and debris. They were utterly destroyed and yet, paradoxically, in the very same moment, perfectly preserved. Catastrophic destruction and instantaneous preservation – what better image could be found of Benjamin's understanding of the Messianic end of profane human history and divine redemption? The tales of hoaxers and fraudsters are also pertinent in this respect. The arch swindler, the charlatan *par excellence*, is the false Messiah, the seventeenth-century Jewish 'apostate Messiah' (Mehlman, 1993, p. 42) Sabbatai Zevi.[32] Threatened with execution, Zevi preferred conversion to Islam to martyrdom. This ultimate act of betrayal, far from disillusioning his followers, convinced them of his status as redeemer. Who else but the true Messiah, they reasoned, would acquiesce to such humiliation and scorn? Sabbatianism perfected manifold modes of duplicity and disguise. And what could be more appropriate for Benjamin's radio scripts, since, preoccupied with things masquerading as something else, they are swindles themselves, ideas sailing under false colours, even if called by their proper name. Saying one thing, meaning another: this is, of course, as Mehlman (1993, p. 46) points out, what allegories are, and it is in allegory that the most extreme reversals of meaning occur, that signs of damnation are miraculously transformed into signs of redemption. It is as disquisitions upon, and experiments in, allegorical writing that the radio broadcasts for children are to be understood.

Rhetorical ruses and allegory combine in the third series identified by Mehlman, the Berlin texts. Mehlman focuses on two key texts here: 'Berliner Spielzeugwanderungen I' and 'II'. In these 'theoretical toys' about toys, Benjamin recounts the fairy story of Schwester Tinchen. Four little brothers are set against one another by an evil magician who ensnares them with enticing presents and kidnaps them. Only their sister Tinchen remains untempted, and escapes the sorcerer's clutches. Under the protection of the good fairy Concordia, she sets off to find her brothers in the enchanted land of the magician and to free them from his wicked spell. The magician places the most wondrous toys, sweets and other distractions along the route she must take. Tinchen knows, and is continually reminded by a small bluebird who sits on her shoulder, that if she forgets her purpose and lingers even for a moment among these alluring attractions, her brothers will be lost for ever. As Mehlman points out, Benjamin abruptly abandons the telling of this story at this point, and compares the 'Zauberland' which Tinchen must cross to the wonders and marvels of the toy departments in Berlin department stores. This sudden change in the narrative highlights the key significance of this tale. Mehlman notes: 'It is difficult to read of the "enchanted land" of the evil magician and its counterpart, the "enchanted" galleries of Berlin department stores without being reminded of Benjamin's comments on the fetishization of merchandise in the Arcades Exposés' (1993, p. 69). As Benjamin makes clear in his early notes for the *Passagenarbeit*, the 'enchanted land' crossed by Tinchen provides a potent image of the fascinating phantasmagoria of commodities, arcades and World Exhibitions, the devilish dreamworld of capitalist industry and colonial adventure.[33] Like Tinchen, one must resolutely resist the seductive sirens of the commodity world in the quest for liberation. Moreover, the bluebird who prompts one forward on the errand of rescue is perhaps none other than the Critical Theorist. The tale of Tinchen is not only 'at some level an allegorization of the Arcades' (Mehlman, 1993, p. 69); it is also an allegory of the duties of the historian. The story of Tinchen is precisely that 'dialectical fairy-tale' which, breaking the enthralling power of commodity culture, Benjamin once envisaged as the title for his Paris study. The radio broadcasts are not 'enlightenment for children', but rather 'fairy-tales for dialecticians' (*ILL*, p. 117). For what could be more delight-fully dialectical than to present the ideas of the paradisiacal identity of name and thing, of the momentary revelation of truth, of Mes-sianic history-as-catastrophe, of remembrance and redemption – in short, to present theological motifs and political imperatives disguised as children's stories? Only, perhaps, to proffer them as *'plump'* pedagogy, or 'crude thinking'.

Photography, art and aura

Benjamin's 'A Small History of Photography' (1931) was composed in the midst of his engagement with the radio broadcasts, and 'developed from prolegomena' (*COR*, p. 385)[34] for the 'Arcades Project'. Benjamin's essay is very different from the material found in Convolute Y ('Photography'),[35] however, and its title is certainly misleading. As Mary Price (1994, pp. 38–9) points out, it fails to provide an accurate chronology of the photographers and pho-tographs discussed, and offers only the most meagre consideration of photography's technical transformations. Benjamin's 'small history' is not an abridged biography of the medium. Instead, it is an extended series of critical reflections occasioned by a number of 'fine recent publications' (*OWS*, p. 241)[36] on early photography and exemplary photographers, reflections which constitute a philo-sophical disquisition upon the changing character of perception, visual representation and the aesthetic sphere.

In extending his analysis of the 'meltdown' of bourgeois culture, Benjamin's concern in both his 'Small History' and his later 'Work of Art' essay is to examine the manner in which the advent and development of photography and film irrevocably change the char-acter and role of art. It is time, he argues, to abandon the 'devious and confused' debate of the nineteenth century concerning the 'artistic value of painting versus photography' and the pointless 'question of whether photography is an art' (*ILL*, pp. 228–9). While the 'theoreticians of photography' typically sought 'to legitimise the photographer before the very tribunal he was in the process of over-turning' (*OWS*, p. 241), the real question of 'whether the very inven-tion of photography had not transformed the entire nature of art' (*ILL*, p. 229) remained unaddressed. For Benjamin, photography and film are qualitatively new media which can be neither understood nor evaluated with respect to traditional aesthetic categories and criteria. Only the most muddled or mischievous of contemporary commentators could persist in the thoroughly 'dubious project of authenticating photography in terms of painting' (*OWS*, pp. 241–2) or film according to the conventions of theatre.

Benjamin's critique of Franz Werfel is particularly illuminating. For Werfel, film was an impoverished artistic form because of its seeming preference for aesthetically displeasing subject matter: 'it was the sterile copying of the exterior world with its streets, interiors, railroad stations, restaurants, motorcars, and beaches which until now had obstructed the elevation of the film to the realm of art' (*ILL*, p. 230). Film would assume its proper place among the arts only when it attended to genuinely 'artistic' themes: ' "all that is fairylike, marvellous, supernatural" ' (*ILL*, p. 230).[37] Benjamin's comments on the power of cinematic techniques such as close-up and slow motion offer the most decisive rebuttal of this view:

> Our taverns and metropolitan streets, our offices and furnished rooms, our railroad stations and our factories appeared to have us locked up hopelessly. Then came the film and burst this prison-world asunder by the dynamite of the tenth of a second, so that now, in the midst of far-flung ruins and debris, we calmly and adventurously go travelling. (*ILL*, p. 238)

The true task of film and photography is not to offer up facile, 'fairylike' phantasmagoria, nor to present the everyday in all its banality just as it is (the failing of reportage). Rather, these new media promise to penetrate and explode the quotidian realm. Questions of good 'taste' or 'elevated' subject matter are utterly irrelevant, for the role of film and photography is conditioned by the most radical realization of their inherent technical capacities and possibilities. Indeed, it is not only the mundane world that is to be detonated; the very categories of art itself – above all, the ineffable power or aura of the unique, authentic artwork – are to be imploded. Herein lies the goal of film and photography: the ruination of traditional art and aesthetics and their revolutionary reconfiguration within political practice.

Benjamin begins his photography essay by tracing the successive phases through which photography distances itself from painting and other forms of depiction: initially, as an instrument of science and art; subsequently, in its displacement of portrait and landscape painting; and finally, as a technique enabling the precise representation of the physical environment (Atget's deserted Parisian streets), the social sphere (Sander's physiognomical portraits) and the aesthetic form itself (photographs of artworks).

One of the key transformations brought about by photography is the discovery of what Benjamin terms the 'optical unconscious' (*OWS*, p. 243): that is, the revelation of what the eye must have seen but the conscious brain cannot discern or grasp, due to size or motion.[38] Photography is able to detect and register elements that the human optical system cannot distinguish or abstract from its surroundings or the flow of movement. The camera records and permits us to see the previously invisible, renders 'analysable things which had heretofore floated along unnoticed in the broad stream of perception', and brings a fundamental 'deepening of apperception' (*ILL*, p. 237). It captures, for example, 'what happens during the fraction of a second when a person *steps out*' (*OWS*, p. 243). This capacity to arrest the flow of action corresponds closely to the technique of interruption in Brecht's epic theatre. Photography fragments motion and produces gestures.[39] Whereas painters and sculptors seek to give the illusion of fluidity and life, the photographer faithfully and directly records each minute frozen gesture of the subject so that movement itself, be it that of a galloping horse or of water dripping from a tap, can be examined and eventually replayed.[40] Photography, Benjamin notes, 'reveals the secret' (*OWS*, p. 243) of motion through staccato representation.[41]

The optical unconscious is captured not simply because of the speed of the photographic process, but also because of its capacity to record exactly and exhaustively. The camera registers everything in front of it. Foreground and background, the important and the trivial, formal pose and figure in flight – the photograph presents each minute detail without discrimination.[42] Moreover, through the technique of enlargement, that which is undetected by the ordinary gaze may be perceived and explored, so as to reveal 'visual worlds which dwell in the smallest things' (*OWS*, p. 243).[43] The photograph is not only immediate, but also meticulous and complete. It is characterized by a fleeting plenitude.[44]

For Benjamin, the skill of the photographer consists in capturing and attesting to a momentary presence, full yet ephemeral. Indeed, the task of the photographer is to coax the subject to give up something of his or her own life to the photographic image. Benjamin writes of David Octavius Hill's photographic portrait of Mrs Elizabeth Hall, the 'Newhaven fishwife':

> there remains something that goes beyond testimony to the photographer's art, something that fills you with an unruly desire to know what her name was, the woman who was alive there, who even now is still real and will never consent wholly to be absorbed in art... The most precise technology can give its products a magical value, such as a painted picture can never again have for us. (*OWS*, pp. 242–3)

This 'magical value' of the photograph resides less in the intentions of the photographer than in the subject herself, who 'even now is still real'. Indeed, the viewer of the photograph is attracted to precisely those contingencies which elude the photographer's purpose:

> No matter how artful the photographer, no matter how carefully posed his subject, the beholder feels an irresistible urge to search such a picture for the tiny spark of contingency, of the Here and Now, with which reality has so to speak seared the subject, to find the inconspicuous spot where in the immediacy of that long-forgotten moment the future subsists so eloquently that we looking back may rediscover it. (*OWS*, p. 243)

The 'spark of contingency' is that moment of reciprocity in which the 'Here and Now' recognizes itself in the 'then and there', in which the figures in the photograph appear to look at us in return.[45]

Early photography retained the unique, authentic presence of the subject and possessed a 'magical value'. Here Benjamin introduces the key term in his discussion of photography and film: 'aura'. He writes of the first people to stand before the camera's lens: 'There was an aura about them, an atmospheric medium that lent fullness and security to their gaze even as it penetrated that medium' (*OWS*, p. 247). It is the subject who gives to the earliest photographs their 'auratic' quality, perhaps on account of the investment of time required on the part of the sitter,[46] perhaps because of the sense of permanence of the bourgeois subject depicted, their posture, their fashions and accessories, the paradoxical 'permanence' of those who are no more, but whose traces remain.[47] Aura attaches itself, above all, to the human face, and to the face of the now dead in particular. In the 'Work of Art' essay he notes:

It is no accident that the portrait was the focal point of early photography. The cult of remembrance of loved ones, absent or dead,
offers a last refuge for the cult value of the picture. For the last time
aura emanates from the early photographs in the fleeting expression
of a human face. This is what constitutes their melancholy, incomparable beauty. (*ILL*, p. 228)

'Aura' is an elusive term for that which *is* elusive. Benjamin's
response to the aura of early photographs is, consequently, equivocal.[48] 'Aura' refers to the mysterious gloom enshrouding the
earliest photographs, wherein 'light struggles out of darkness'
(*OWS*, p. 248). 'Aura' is 'A strange weave of space and time: the
unique appearance or semblance of distance no matter how close
the object may be' (*OWS*, p. 250): that is, the specific conjunction of
time and place (the long-forgotten and long-lost) to which photography attests. 'Aura' is the individual quality of the sitter which
emanates from his or her eyes[49] and which meets the gaze cast upon
it.[50] 'Aura' is unfathomable darkness, unbridgeable distance, unexpected reciprocity. As such, it combines both negative and positive
moments. On the one hand, it is a form of obscurity and inscrutability, a murky residue of the cultic origins of the work of art; on the
other, it is a source of 'melancholy, incomparable beauty' (*ILL*, p.
228), a moment of mutual recognition, a mnemonic device for the
remembrance of the dead. It is little wonder that Brecht was so mys-
tified by the concept. What *is* clear in Benjamin's puzzling essay,
however, is that the subsequent development of photography
brings with it the demise of aura – in an absurd, reactionary manner
through commercialization; in a profound, revolutionary way in the
images of the avant-garde.

Pumping aura out

Benjamin describes how, in the second phase of photography, 'busi-
nessmen invaded . . . from every side' (*OWS*, p. 246), precipitating
'a sharp decline in taste' (*OWS*, p. 246). The profundity of the earlier
photographs was replaced by the mediocrity of the market: sentimental portraits commissioned for the family album and absurdly
posed and composed 'artistic' pictures, photographs conceived in
the image of paintings. Dressed in humiliating costumes before
'scenic' painted backdrops – 'a parlour Tyrolean, yodelling, waving
our hat against a painted snowscape' (*OWS*, p. 246) – the sitter was

now crowded out by all manner of accessories: pillars, pedestals and drapery. Such theatricality evokes not awe but laughter in the present-day beholder, and aura cannot survive ridicule. Once lost, the subject's haunting presence cannot be restored. Attempts to create an 'artificial aura' through new techniques of lighting, retouching and tinting were bound to fail because an 'artificial aura' – a fabricated authenticity – is itself a contradiction in terms.

For other photographers, the rapidly increasing technical capacities of photography were to be utilized for an altogether different purpose: instead of plunging the subject back into sombre shadows and misty obscurity, social and material reality was to be laid bare. In putting 'darkness entirely to flight' (*OWS*, p. 248), such photography brought into sharp focus and close-up that which previously remained distant despite its proximity. Benjamin's exemplary figure here was the French photographer Eugène August Atget (1856–1927). In his concern with what was 'unremarked, forgotten, cast adrift' (*OWS*, p. 250), Atget 'was the first to disinfect the stifling atmosphere generated by conventional portrait photography in the age of decline. He cleanses this atmosphere, indeed he dispels it altogether: he initiates the emancipation of object from aura which is the signal achievement of the latest school of photography' (*OWS*, pp. 249–50). In a memorable though puzzling trope, Benjamin notes that the photographs of Atget 'pump the aura out of reality like water out of a sinking ship' (*OWS*, p. 250). Once a mark of an authentic presence, aura has become the murky waters into which the real might disappear without trace.

In capturing a quotidian reality which everyday perception overlooks, Atget's photographs capture the image of Paris of the recent past. For Benjamin, Atget's images are, above all, those of repetition and reproducibility, of objects and settings left by humans as traces of their existence: 'a long row of bootlasts . . . hand-carts . . . in serried ranks . . . tables after people have finished eating and left, the dishes not yet cleared away – as they exist in their hundreds of thousands at the same hour' (*OWS*, pp. 250–1). In these photographs of the metropolitan environment, 'The stripping bare of the object, the destruction of the aura, is the mark of a perception whose sense of the sameness of things has grown to the point where even the singular, the unique, is divested of uniqueness – by means of reproduction' (*OWS*, p. 250). This is important, because photography itself involves exactly this movement from 'the singular, the unique' work of art to the multiple copy, the 'copy' without an 'original'. In the 'Work of Art' essay, Benjamin writes: 'To an ever greater degree the work of art reproduced becomes the work of art designed for reproducibility. From a photographic negative, for example, one can make any number of prints; to ask for the "authentic" print makes no sense' (*ILL*, p. 226). In presenting eminently reproducible images of endlessly reproduced artefacts, Atget's photography not only pumps aura out of reality; it also points directly to the demise of the authentic, auratic work of art.

It is not only aura that is expelled from Atget's images: the human subject, too, vanishes. The photographer's attention to detail is combined with the most rigorous, unsentimental depopulating of the Parisian cityscape.[51] In this respect, Benjamin contends, Atget's 'Paris photos are the forerunners of surrealist photography' (*OWS*, p. 249). Benjamin observes:

> the city in these pictures looks cleared out, like a lodging that has not yet found a new tenant. It is in these achievements that surrealist photography sets the scene for a salutary estrangement between man and his surroundings. It gives free play to the politically educated eye, under whose gaze all intimacies are sacrificed to the illumination of detail. (*OWS*, p. 251)

Atget's photography does not so much disclose what the eye cannot see, as reveal what goes unnoticed or remains obscure. By 'removing the make-up from reality' (*OWS*, p. 241), he ensures that the viewer directly confronts the unembellished countenance of the object world and becomes its physiognomer.[52]

In this disenchantment of the modern city, Atget's photography combines scientific and aesthetic dimensions in a manner that Benjamin sees as the hallmark of radical, politicized representation. Atget's photographs of empty Parisian streets have a forensic quality and value: 'he photographed them like scenes of a crime. The scene of a crime, too, is deserted; it is photographed for the purpose of establishing evidence. With Atget, photographs become standard evidence for historical occurrences, and acquire a hidden political significance. . . . For the first time, captions have become obligatory' (*ILL*, p. 228). Images do not speak for themselves. The caption turns the picture into a vehicle for comment. The 'illumination of detail' allows political judgement: 'Is not the task of the photographer . . . to reveal guilt and to point out the guilty in his photographs?' (*OWS*, p. 256). Herein lies the pedagogical potential of mass-(re)produced photographs. The techniques of close-up and enlargement offer the possibility of a new critical proximity and physiognomic expertise. Multiple reproduction permits proliferation and possession of such images.[53] The caption prompts recognition, and is a key aspect of proletarian schooling. The vital question for photography is not whether it is an art form, but how, with the demise of aura, a new form of political practice can be constituted. To answer this question, and to meet the political imperatives of the present moment, the task of the polytechnic aesthetic engineer is clear: 'start taking photographs' (*UB*, p. 95).

Reproduction and the afterlife of aura

Written in two versions (autumn 1935 and spring 1936), Benjamin's essay 'The Work of Art in the Age of its Technological Reproducibility' is probably the most famous and widely discussed of his writings. It was not his only, or even his first, study of film and cinema – he also wrote studies of, for example, Soviet film and Charlie Chaplin – but, taken together, Benjamin's writings on the moving image and cinema are surprisingly few and disparate, certainly in comparison to those of Kracauer, who was to become without doubt the pre-eminent film theorist associated with the Frankfurt Institut für Sozialforschung. By contrast with Kracauer's ever greater preoccupation with the character and experience of the cinematic medium, with its 'psychology' and aesthetics, an intense concern which culminated in his *From Caligari to Hitler* (1947) and *Theory of Film* (1997 [1960]), Benjamin's studies of film are fragmentary forays. Yet, while Kracauer's film studies have been unjustly neglected by present-day scholars, Benjamin's 'Work of Art' has become an essential text for contemporary film and media theorists.[54] Nevertheless, and albeit from rather different vantage-points, Kracauer and Benjamin shared two key themes in their film writings: first, the essential connection between film and photography, and second, the intimate relationship between these media and memory, history and historiography. Accordingly, Benjamin's 'Work of Art' essay not only elaborates and reconfigures many of the themes and concepts from his own earlier photography essay, but is also closely connected with the ongoing *Passagenarbeit* in the context of developing its fundamental methodological principles.[55]

There are at least two dimensions to the essay's methodological significance: historiographic and cinematic. Writing to Horkheimer on 16 October 1935, Benjamin mentions some 'constructive reflections' which 'advance the direction of a materialist theory of art' (*COR*, p. 509). He continues:

> The issue this time is to indicate the precise moment in the present to which any historical construction will orient itself, as to its vanishing point. If the pretext for the book is the fate of art in the nineteenth century, this fate has something to say to us only because it is contained in the ticking of a clock whose striking of the hour has only just reached *our* ears. What I mean by this is that art's fateful hour has struck for us and I have captured its signature in a series of preliminary reflections entitled 'The Work of Art in the Age of Mechanical Reproduction.' These reflections attempt to give the questions raised by art theory a truly contemporary form. (*COR*, p. 509)

In this intriguing passage Benjamin emphasizes that historical change and transformation are always viewed from the perspective of a particular present instant and interest. This is far more than a simple acknowledgement of the inevitably retrospective character of historical enquiry and the role of hindsight. The 'Work of Art' essay articulates the current condition of the aesthetic object and domain against which 'the fate of art in the nineteenth century' can be measured.[56] The history unfolded is that of the demise of the unique, authentic work of art, the disintegration of its accompanying aura, and the transposition of art from the sphere of ritual and tradition to that of political practice. It is a history of the vanishing of aura which *can only be told from the 'vanishing point' itself*. Like the *Angelus Novus*, like the Parisian arcades on the brink of demolition, the aura of the artwork is fleetingly recognizable only at the moment of its extinction, at last sight.[57]

Moreover, this should not be understood as a history of the life of aura, its 'biography' so to speak. It is, rather, a 'small history' of the *afterlife* of aura, its existence after the death-knell has sounded. The 'fateful hour' for the traditional work of art – that is, the invention and development of photography – struck in the mid-nineteenth century, yet this sound 'has only just reached *our* ears' now. If, for Benjamin, the *Passagenarbeit* was to concern itself with tracing the afterlife of the arcade, the striking of *its* 'fateful hour', and the process of its gradual ruination during the course of the nineteenth century, then the 'Work of Art' essay was intended to sketch the afterlife of aura and the mortification of the work of art during the same period.

The methodological significance of the 'Work of Art' essay for the 'Arcades Project' extends beyond this shared concern with writing the afterlife of a cultural form. Although downplayed by Benjamin, the substantive content of the study, photography and film, is also crucial. First, as he makes clear in his methodological reflections for the *Passagenarbeit*, the critical exploration of the recent past must adopt a visual form as 'history decays into images, not into stories' (N11,4, *ARC*, p. 476). If the task of the historian as technician is to collect, scrutinize and assemble these fragmentary images and insights into a powerful, illuminating mosaic or montage, then understanding the attributes and techniques of photographic and cinematic representation is essential. Secondly, as Benjamin observes on a number of occasions, cinema and the city have a special connection, an 'elective affinity'. This was nothing new. The correspondence between the rhythms and tempi of modern metropolitan life and those of moving images was one of the earliest insights of film commentators[58] and film-makers themselves – from the pioneering documentary 'street films' in the 1900s, to the mingling of factual and fictional footage in films immediately prior to the Great War, to, of course, those masterpieces of silent cinema, Fritz Lang's *Metropolis* (1925–6), Walter Ruttmann's *Berlin, Symphony of a Great City* (1927), and Dziga Vertov's *Man with a Movie Camera* (1929).[59]

Appropriately, it is in his 'Moscow' *Denkbild*[60] and the later 'Berlin Chronicle'[61] that Benjamin emphasizes the cinematic character of urban experience and space. He notes how film offers both a privileged proximity to the urban labyrinth and an incomparable insight into its secrets. Film not only unmasks the cityscape, but also explodes it with the 'dynamite of the tenth of a second' (*ILL*, p. 238) so that we may calmly survey its ruinous remains. Close-up, enlargement, slow motion, montage – such cinematic techniques were not only to be the subject matter of the 'Work of Art' essay; they were also to serve as the methodological arsenal for the historian-as-engineer, the Critical Theorist of the modern metropolis who seeks to booby-trap each sentence, each image, with explosives.

At the heart of Benjamin's 'Work of Art' essay is the attempt to develop the exploration of aura begun in such ambiguous fashion in 'A Small History of Photography'. Aura is the particular power which an image or object has by virtue of its singularity, authenticity, and 'embeddedness in the fabric of tradition' (*ILL*, p. 225) to stimulate in the spectator or listener a sense of reverence and wonder. As 'the unique phenomenon of distance however close it may be' (*ILL*, p. 224), as 'unapproachability' (*ILL*, p. 245), aura stands in opposition to 'the desire of the contemporary masses to bring things closer spatially and humanly' (*ILL*, p. 225), and the imperative for progressive cultural forms 'to meet the beholder half-way' (*ILL*, p. 222).

In Convolute M, Benjamin articulates this in terms of a particular antithesis: 'Trace and aura. The trace is the appearance of a nearness, however far removed the thing that left it behind may be. Aura is the appearance of a distance, however close the thing that calls it forth. In the trace, we gain possession of the thing; in the aura it takes possession of us' (M16a, *ARC*, p. 447). As a residue of what is now absent, the 'trace' paradoxically offers proximity, tactility and decipherment; aura, by contrast, involves a permanent presence which ironically rests on invisibility,[62] inscrutability and illegibility. In certain respects, the opposition between trace and aura here corresponds to that between allegory and symbol informing the *Trauerspiel* study. The trace which bears witness to the dissolution of the object is intimately connected to the transient, ruinous realm of allegorical expression. Aura, by contrast, shares the immediate and intensive totality, the instantaneous yet enduring potency, of the symbol.[63] Aura involves the concentration and projection of the power of tradition through the object, not the work of art's subjection to the withering forces of history. Hence, whereas the trace can only dwindle with the passage of time, aura may grow in magnitude. However, despite Adorno's insistence on '*more* dialectics', Benjamin does not elaborate this dichotomy of trace and aura in the 'Work of Art' essay. His purpose is more intricate and illuminating. He develops the notion of aura *as* trace, as the momentarily readable remnant of that which is about to disappear once and for all. Aura as trace, the trace of aura – this fleeting legibility of the 'signature' of the illegible discerned at the 'vanishing point' is what preoccupies Benjamin here. We are now privileged to apprehend the last vestiges of what has hitherto only 'possessed' us. The profane illumination of what has imbued and eluded us as magical intoxication, the disempowering and 'disenchantment of art' (Adorno, in *AP*, p. 120) through explosive engineering – these are the goals of Benjamin's 'preliminary reflections'.

The unique, original painting, sculpture or performance 'possesses' the beholder. Benjamin connects this sense of 'possession' with what he sees as the cultic origins of art itself. Music, dance, painting and statuary have their beginnings in magical ceremonies, as modes through which to commune with ancestors, appease spirits and control nature.[64] Images, objects and bodily performances were employed for ritualistic purposes; that is, they possessed a particular 'magical' (*OWS*, p. 243) or 'cult value' (*ILL*, p. 226). This cult value of the work of art continued in the later production of religious imagery (icons, altar paintings, frescoes) and the composition of sacred song (chants, motets, masses). Since the Renaissance, this ritualistic cult value has waned as the 'secular cult of beauty' has increasingly displaced religious devotion as the basis for the production and appreciation of the artwork. The aura possessed by the work of art today is the last vestige of this original cult value.[65]

Here Benjamin's earlier equivocation regarding the evaluation of aura gives way to an unambiguous critique of it as 'distance' and as ritualistic remnant. It is this thoroughly negative view of the 'counter-revolutionary function' (*AP*, p. 121) of the original work of art which Adorno disputes in his letter to Benjamin of 18 March 1936.[66] Some of the letter's contents have already been sketched, but they bear repeating and clarifying. Adorno insists upon what he considers a more differentiated understanding of the 'autonomous' work of art, one which acknowledges the dialectical tensions within it. The artwork may be enchanted in its origins and enthralling in its effects, as Benjamin's notion of aura suggests, but it also contains utopian elements and/or moments of negativity which must be recognized and critically mobilized. For example, religious paintings of the Renaissance might, in their contrasting images of the joys of heavenly life and the miseries of profane existence, offer a powerful indictment of prevailing human circumstances and a provocative vision of an earthly paradise. Beauty and perfection as dream- or wish images might have an important critical role in a world seen as hideously disfigured.[67] In demanding a more complex understanding of such contradictory tendencies, Adorno advocates the 'dialectical penetration of the "autonomous" work of art' (*AP*, p. 124), so as to reveal how it 'juxtaposes the magical and the mark of freedom' (*AP*, p. 121). He takes issue with two principal themes of the 'Work of Art' essay: first, that the demise of aura in the present is a consequence of the inherent technical character and potential of film and photography; and second, that these new media engender particular forms of performance and reception which are politically progressive. In short, Adorno demands 'the complete liquidation of ... Brechtian motifs' (*AP*, p. 124).

Benjamin asserts: 'that which withers in the age of mechanical reproduction is the aura of the work of art' (*ILL*, p. 223). Film and photography inevitably play a decisive role in this. First, they undermine the notions of originality and uniqueness. While, 'In principle a work of art has always been reproducible', the advent of the 'Mechanical reproduction of a work of art' in film, photography and sound recording 'represents something new' and radically transforms the aesthetic domain (*ILL*, p. 220). This is because these new media are *inherently concerned with reproducibility*. It no longer makes sense to speak of an 'original' or 'authentic' work of art as opposed to a 'fake' or 'copy'. For the first time, one is confronted by a series of identical, wholly interchangeable images and objects, none of which can claim primacy. The singularity, uniqueness and exclusiveness of the auratic painting give way to the multiplicity, ubiquity and availability of the photographic print. Benjamin writes:

> By making many reproductions it substitutes a plurality of copies for a unique existence. And in permitting the reproduction to meet the beholder or listener in his own particular situation, it reactivates the object reproduced. These two processes lead to a tremendous shattering of tradition which is the obverse of the contemporary crisis and renewal of mankind. (*ILL*, p. 223)

Reproducibility leads to the demise of the artwork's cult value. It is no longer hidden away in those hallowed spaces of bourgeois culture frequented by the privileged few. After all, while it may make sense to visit the Louvre, for example, in order to gaze upon the original *Mona Lisa*, it is less clear why one should visit an exhibition of photographs when, for the price of admission, one could be sent copies of all the photographs on display. Film and photography facilitate, and ensure, a new visibility. They possess not a 'cult value', but rather an 'exhibition value', a readiness and 'fitness' to be seen and heard, a 'public presentability' (*ILL*, p. 227).[68] In displacing the notion of authenticity, the inherent reproducibility of film reconfigures and reorients the aesthetic sphere: 'the instant the criterion of authenticity ceases to be applicable to artistic production, the total function of art is reversed. Instead of being based on ritual, it begins to be based on another practice – politics' (*ILL*, p. 226). Reproduction disenchants the work of art through the displacement of cult value by exhibition value, and through the liquidation of ritual and tradition by politics.

Moreover, film disenchants reality. Just as photography promises to expel aura from the modern cityscape, so film penetrates and demystifies the world. In a suggestive analogy, Benjamin writes:

> The surgeon represents the polar opposite of the magician. The magician heals a sick person by the laying on of hands; the surgeon cuts into the patient's body. The magician maintains the natural distance between the patient and himself; though he reduces it very slightly by the laying on of hands, he greatly increases it by virtue of his authority. The surgeon does exactly the reverse; he greatly diminishes the distance between himself and the patient by penetrating into the patient's body, and increases it but little by the caution with which his hand moves among the organs. . . . Magician and surgeon compare to painter and cameraman. The painter maintains in his work a natural distance from reality, the cameraman penetrates deeply into its web. (*ILL*, p. 235)

This important passage reiterates the key dichotomies of the 'Work of Art' essay: tradition and the archaic versus the most modern, residual magic versus technical expertise, auratic distance versus critical proximity, the superficiality and duplicity of appearance versus the profound penetration of depth. Further, one is reminded of another moment of incision: Benjamin's dedication to Lacis in *One-Way Street*. The 'cameraman' slices into the 'web' of the modern cityscape just as she, as exemplary urban engineer, 'cut' through Benjamin.

This opposition between the magical basis of auratic art and the technical character of the new media dismays Adorno. For him, such a view involves two interconnected errors.[69] First, Adorno contends, Benjamin underplays the technical component of the contemporary (and indeed, traditional) autonomous artwork. The work of the modernist avant-garde, for example, was precisely concerned with pushing the formal and technical possibilities of painting, music, theatre and literature to the very limit and beyond, a point Benjamin himself emphasized in his writings on Surrealism and Brecht. Adorno reminds Benjamin that the aura of the traditional work of art was being imploded from within by modernist practices and experiments:

> Dialectical though your essay may be, it is not so in the case of autonomous art itself; it disregards an elementary experience which becomes more evident to me every day in my own musical experi-

ence – that precisely the uttermost consistency in the pursuit of the technical laws of autonomous art changes this art and instead of rendering it into a taboo or fetish, brings it close to the state of freedom. (*AP*, pp. 121–2)

Film and photography might provide insights and imperatives for these processes, but these new media should not be seen as providing the sole technical template for progressive aesthetic practices.

Secondly, such an opposition overstates the actual experimental applications and accomplishments of film. Adorno suggests that film and photography have only rarely been used to 'penetrate' the 'web' of the everyday through the deployment of their full technical repertoire. Instead, these media are routinely engaged in the most simplistic portrayal and spurious restaging of 'reality'. Adorno recalls a visit to the German film industry (Ufa)[70] studios at Neubabelsberg near Berlin: 'what impressed me most was how *little* montage and all the advanced techniques that you emphasize are actually used; rather, reality is everywhere *constructed* with an infantile mimetism and then "photographed"' (*AP*, p. 124). Benjamin was not unaware of such a discrepancy between the inherent potential and the actual utilization of the new media – as we have already seen, he was highly critical of photoreportage precisely because of its facile recording of superficial phenomena. Similarly, in the 'Work of Art' essay, while stressing the positive political potential of the cinematic medium as realized, for example, in the work of the Soviet film-maker Dziga Vertov,[71] Benjamin also acknowledged that 'the film industry is trying hard to spur the interest of the masses through illusion-promoting spectacles and dubious speculations' (*ILL*, p. 234). Indeed, instead of exploding the workaday world with 'the dynamite of the tenth of a second', film production under capitalism resurrects cultic distance and creates an 'artifical' aura. Benjamin writes of the Hollywood 'star' system: 'film responds to the shrivelling of aura with the artificial build-up of the "personality" outside the studio. . . . So long as moviemakers' capital sets the fashion, as a rule no other revolutionary merit can be accredited to today's film than the promotion of a revolutionary criticism of traditional concepts of art' (*ILL*, p. 233). The creation of so-called idols of the silver screen by the Hollywood film industry is the very antithesis of Benjamin's view of the progressive relationship between actor and movie-goer, an understanding which, indebted to Brecht and contested by Adorno, forms the second main theme of the 'Work of Art' essay.

Film and the politics of distraction

Benjamin's advocacy of film stems not only from its technical penetration of reality and political disenchantment of art, but also from his vision of the new kinds of performance and audience it engenders. Film brings with it a form of proximity based on a mutual absence mediated by the camera. This involves new demands and challenges. On the one hand, the actor plays before the camera to an invisible, unknown spectator; on the other, the viewer has to adopt the perspective of the lens. Both these unprecedented situations are significant and consequential.

In theatre, the performance of the actor is an 'integral whole' (*ILL*, p. 230). The process of filming, by contrast, involves a series of disconnected, discrete elements of action, often shot out of sequence. While action on screen may appear to flow seamlessly from one scene to the next, these scenes may have been filmed not only weeks apart, but also in a completely different order. The film actor is thus beset by problems of discontinuity, interruption and fragmentation, which preclude the empathetic characterization of theatrical method acting.[72] The film actor can neither identify with the figure he plays, nor 'adjust to the audience during his performance' (*ILL*, p. 230). He or she is confronted by the probing lens of the mobile camera. Unlike a seated theatrical audience, the camera continually changes position and angle, moves in for close-ups, and pursues the actor so that he or she is 'subjected to a series of optical tests' (*ILL*, p. 230).

The camera 'tests' the actor just as it 'penetrates' reality. And the result is the same: disenchantment. In the act of mediation, the camera fragments and then eradicates the presence of the actor. In so doing, the power, the aura, of the theatrical performance and the individual performer is dispelled. Benjamin writes:

> for the first time – and this is the effect of the film – man has to operate with his whole living person, yet forgoing its aura. For aura is tied to presence; there can be no replica of it. The aura which on stage emanates from Macbeth, cannot be separated for the spectators from that of the actor. However, the singularity of the shot in the studio is that the camera is substituted for the public. Consequently, the aura

that envelopes the actor vanishes, and with it the aura of the figure he portrays. (*ILL*, p. 231)

As with the invisible voice of radio, the image of film involves a mediated presence in which aura cannot endure.

If the camera tests the actor, then the spectator, who is only able to observe actions and events through the camera, becomes an examiner of the performance. In adopting its viewpoint, the audience identifies with the camera rather than the actor.[73] This affords a certain degree of detachment, Benjamin claims, and 'permits the audience to take the position of a critic, without experiencing any personal contact with the actor' (*ILL*, p. 230). In film, the actor cannot empathize with his or her character, and the audience empathizes with neither.

This notion of the spectator as critic clearly echoes Benjamin's earlier writings on epic theatre. Indeed, just as the 'expertise' of the Brechtian audience derives from a state of mirthful relaxation, so the testing perception of the cinema-goer is also a consequence of a certain nonchalance. Here Benjamin introduces a key term to describe the mode of perception and appreciation of the film audience: 'distraction' (*Zerstreuung*).[74] Film ushers in not only a new form of artistic reproduction, but also a distinctive mode of aesthetic reception. The auratic work of art demands veneration, contemplation and concentration from the viewer. The solitary, undisturbed immersion in the individual artwork has been the basis of bourgeois aesthetic experience.[75] Indeed, the singularity of the artwork finds its exact counterpart in the solitary, 'asocial' (*ILL*, p. 240) act of reception.

The radically debunking, transgressive anti-art of the Dadaist movement was the first to puncture the wistful musings of the bourgeois subject.[76] The principal aim of Dada was 'to outrage the public', to make art 'the centre of a scandal', to generate a 'shock effect' (*ILL*, p. 240), and it is this notion of film reception as 'shock' which is decisive for Benjamin. Violent impact, tactility, shock – these experiences, distinctly metropolitan in character, are the hallmarks of film.[77] And it is that most definitive of urban demeanours, Simmel's disinterested, dispassionate metropolitan, the blasé personality,[78] who most closely corresponds to the distracted film-goer. Benjamin here reverses the conventional privileging of concentration vis-à-vis distraction:

Distraction and concentration form polar opposites which may be stated as follows: A man who concentrates before a work of art is absorbed by it. . . . In contrast, the distracted mass absorbs the work of art. This is most obvious with regard to buildings. Architecture has always represented the prototype of a work of art the reception of which is consummated by a collectivity in a state of distraction. (*ILL*, p. 241)

This emphasizes and rearticulates the distinction between aura and trace, between the traditional artwork which entrances the onlooker, and the products of the new media which are grasped by the sober spectator. It is distraction which facilitates this 'tactile appropriation' (*ILL*, p. 242) of the work of art.

Architecture makes a sudden, unexpected appearance at this point in the essay as Benjamin's model. Architecture is

appropriated in a two-fold manner: by use and by perception – or rather, by touch and sight. Such appropriation cannot be understood in terms of the attentive concentration of a tourist before a famous building. On the tactile side there is no counterpart to contemplation on the optical side. Tactile appropriation is accomplished not so much by attention as by habit. (*ILL*, p. 242)

Architecture is the art form *par excellence* which is apprehended in a state of distraction by the collective. Encountered daily at close quarters, the streets, structures and signs[79] which compose the cityscape seldom excite our undivided attention. It is only the tourist, the newcomer, who is captivated by the unfamiliar environment. Distraction is not an extraordinary experience. For the native of the city, architecture forms a backdrop to the daily routine of urban life. Habit, forgetfulness born of long acquaintance, has done its work. In the 'Berlin Chronicle' Benjamin writes:

it is true that countless façades of the city stand exactly as they stood in my childhood. Yet I do not encounter my childhood in their contemplation. My gaze has brushed them too often since, too often have they been the *décor* and theatre of my walks and concerns. (*OWS*, p. 315)

In the 'Work of Art' essay, however, habit emerges as a complex term in an intricate interplay with distraction. First, Benjamin contends, most of our skills and aptitudes are 'mastered gradually by habit' (*ILL*, p. 242) through repetition, and often in the process of doing something else. Distraction, then, is a common condition of learning, of habit formation. Moreover, complete mastery of a practical activity is indicated precisely when one can perform tasks competently without thinking about them – that is, while distracted. Habit is not forgetfulness as such, but rather a form of accomplishment amidst amnesia. Second, distraction is not to be understood as simple inattention. Distraction involves *paying attention elsewhere*. Distraction is a mode and measure of technical skill, and also a response to alterations within the familiar. Distracted, one acquires and demonstrates habits; yet one is also distracted when these habits are disturbed and interrupted. One is distracted by something which fleetingly catches the eye, something perhaps readily recognizable but out of place or glimpsed in a new light. Indeed, distraction, observing that which is apparently insignificant or overlooked, attending to that which is customarily marginalized and neglected, appears here as the very hallmark of Benjamin's own enduring preoccupation with artefacts and ideas which fall outside the conventional parameters of philosophical contemplation. Distraction as a collective experience and political imperative suggests a fundamental reorientation towards, and re-evaluation of, the excluded and despised. Distraction is a mode of recognition and remembrance.

For Benjamin, it is film which combines these different moments of habit and distraction. Film captures the strangely familiar environment of the modern city, and makes it available to collective 'mastery', to 'tactile appropriation', to explosive engineering. Film detonates the city so that we can peruse the rubble 'calmly', unperturbed. Film involves shock and estrangement, but it does not lead to the kind of hostile incomprehension with which the proletariat greeted the experimental efforts of the modernist avant-garde. This is because distraction also involves amusement and pleasure:

> Mechanical reproduction of art changes the reaction of the masses towards art. The reactionary attitude toward a Picasso painting changes into the progressive attitude toward a Chaplin movie. The progressive reaction is characterised by the direct, intimate fusion of visual and emotional enjoyment with the orientation of the expert. (*ILL*, p. 236)

Distraction also entails diversion and entertainment. Film may be an explosive medium, but it also engages with the proletariat in and on their own terms:

> Reception in a state of distraction, which is increasing noticeably in all fields of art and is symptomatic of profound changes in apperception, finds in the film its true means of exercise. The film with its shock effect meets this mode of reception halfway. The film makes the cult value recede into the background not only by putting the public in the position of the critic, but also by the fact that at the movies this position requires no attention. The public is an examiner, but an absent-minded one. (*ILL*, pp. 242–3)

In providing an enjoyable expertise, cinematic distraction imbues the spectator with the 'cunning and high spirits' needed to conquer the mystifications and melancholy of the modern metropolis. Distraction is not only the distinctive form of cinematic reception, it is also the hallmark of urban experience, a form of accomplishment, an interplay of forgetfulness and amnesia, a sensitivity to what occurs on the margins of the customary field of perception, and, above all, the basis of a new collective political practice.

Adorno's response to Benjamin's thesis was predictable and unequivocal: 'I do not find your theory of distraction convincing' (*AP*, p. 123). For Adorno, distraction involves no technical expertise, but is simply an index of capitalist domination; it is not linked with genuine enjoyment and pleasure, but signifies only the demise of the subject's capacity for real happiness; it is devoid of critical potential. For him, distraction is a symptom of, not a solution to, prevailing conditions. Far from exhibiting a subtle mastery of tasks or engaging in the 'tactile appropriation' of artworks, the distracted audience is a consequence of the monotonous, mind-numbing routine of mechanized labour under capitalism.[80] Distraction in the cinema is merely the corollary of alienation and exploitation in the factory and the boredom, apathy and atrophied sensibilities of the modern city.

For Adorno, distraction as 'deconcentration' is to be understood as the inability or disinclination to perceive and appreciate complex and critical works of art. Distraction is indicative of the diminishment of modern humanity's reception of cultural and aesthetic forms. In his 1938 essay 'On the Fetish Character in Music and the Regression of Listening',[81] Adorno argues that listening to 'Tin Pan Alley' jazz involves a process of inattention and infantilization whereby 'the capacity for conscious perception of music' (1991, p. 41) is enfeebled. The audience 'cannot stand the strain of concentrated listening and surrender themselves resignedly to what befalls them, with which they come to terms if they do not listen to it too closely' (Adorno, 1991, p. 43). Such music places few demands on its audience, and these listeners ask little of it in return. Hence, for Adorno, distraction offers precious little in the way of, or cause for, 'high spirits' – quite the opposite. Distraction involves only a weary satisfaction with the banalities of the 'culture industry'. Unlike the withering irony of the Romantics or the raucous scorn of the Surrealists, 'The laughter of the audience at a cinema . . . is anything but good and revolutionary; instead, it is full of the worst sadism' (*AP*, p. 123). In this connection, Adorno singles out the 'Chaplin movie' in a direct riposte to Benjamin's optimistic affirmation: 'the idea that a reactionary is turned into a member of the avant-garde by expert knowledge of Chaplin films strikes me as out-and-out romanticisation' (*AP*, p. 123). The envisioning of polytechnic proletarians as an expert audience is a naive overestimation both of the meltdown of bourgeois cultural forms and of the extent of revolutionary class consciousness.

For Adorno, Benjamin has 'magnificently inaugurated a debate' but 'a true accounting of the relationship of the intellectuals to the working class' (*AP*, p. 125) remains elusive. However, Adorno's own views are not immune to criticism. If in the 'Work of Art' essay Benjamin offers a one-dimensional analysis of the autonomous artwork and a romantic advocacy of film and distraction, Adorno's writings on jazz and the culture industry present an even less sophisticated understanding of popular media as an undifferentiated 'mass' culture catering to the abysmal tastes of an indiscriminate, infantilized audience. If Benjamin began a debate – and it is clearly one that continues to this day within cultural analysis – then it is because the positions he and Adorno adopted themselves constitute 'torn halves of an integral freedom to which, however, they do not add up' (*AP*, p. 123).

For Benjamin, the 'Work of Art' essay was intended precisely as a 'true accounting', not only of the relationship between the intellectual and the proletariat, but also of the cultural conditions, aesthetic imperatives and political exigencies of the moment. Reproduction, interruption, appropriation, detonation, distraction, examination – these are the new categories and principles of aesthetic production, reception and criticism, which 'differ from the more familiar terms in that they are completely useless for the purposes of Fascism. They are, on the other hand, useful for the formulation of revolutionary demands in the politics of art' (*ILL*, p. 220). This theme of the character and role of art and aesthetics within contemporary political movements is addressed by Benjamin in his

Epilogue. Here, in one of his most provocative formulations, he articulates what he regards as the decisive tendencies of contemporary culture and technological change: Fascism as the aestheticization of politics, and Communism as the politicization of aesthetics.

Of these, the second conceptualization is the more readily comprehensible, reiterating as it does both the principal theme of the essay, and indeed his long-standing preoccupation with the politicized transformation of aesthetics and criticism, a concern that can be traced back to the first appearance of the aesthetic engineer in *Einbahnstrasse*. For Benjamin, Communism involves the progressive and humane unfolding of the productive and reproductive possibilities of technological innovation. Within the cultural sphere, in film, photography and the new media, collective proximity, accessibility and tactility replace 'distance', 'invisibility' and 'unapproachability' as exhibition value displaces cult value. In this manner, 'for the first time in world history, mechanical reproduction emancipates the work of art from its parasitical dependence on ritual', so that, 'instead of being based on ritual, it begins to be based on another practice – politics' (*ILL*, p. 226). The new media provide for cultural forms which not only penetrate prevailing social and political conditions, but also engage with an expert, collective spectatorship on its own terms. Shorn of the last remnants of cultic irrationalism, the aesthetic domain is able to take its proper place within the progressive political sphere of proletarian debate, contestation and revolutionary action.

By contrast, Benjamin notes, 'the logical result of Fascism is the introduction of aesthetics into political life' (*ILL*, p. 243). In its most obvious manifestations, this can be understood in terms of how the Fascist and Nazi regimes sought to transform political events into spectacles, parades and staged mass rallies.[82] Politics is reduced to the third-rate theatricality and pantomime posturing of the dictator. Moreover, power and domination, embodied in the figure of the Führer, become aesthetic objects themselves. Benjamin here broadens the scope and complexity of his critique, first, to launch a bitter attack upon that most reactionary of avant-garde movements, Italian Futurism, and then, in passages echoing 'To the Planetarium', upon the catastrophic consequences of technological transformation under the domination of capitalist and imperialist interests.

In Futurism, human conflagration and extermination come to 'supply the artistic gratification of a sense perception that has been changed by technology' so that humanity 'can experience its own destruction as an aesthetic pleasure of the first order' (*ILL*, p. 244). Intoxicated by the immense powers and remorseless energies of modern technology, the Futurists came to celebrate the monstrous, mechanized forces of violence and destruction which hapless humanity unleashes upon itself. War becomes the 'apotheosis' (*ILL*, p. 243) of this mobilization of machinery. Citing Marinetti's frenzied refrain ' "War is beautiful" ' (*ILL*, p. 243) as exemplary, the Futurist demand for ' "an aesthetics of war" ' (*ILL*, p. 244) encapsulates the aestheticization of politics as ecstatic violence and the victory of mythic domination. Benjamin's 'Work of Art' essay concludes with a stark political choice: the explosive engineering of the radical critic who rightfully presses technology into the service of humankind, or the violence of a technology fettered and frustrated by the regressive interests of capitalism: revolution or world war. Such an apocalyptic conclusion may seem out of keeping with the prior discussion of aura, but as Fascism reigned triumphant across Europe and the prospect of war steadily increased, the stakes were high, and the need pressing. In such circumstances, the artificial preservation or recreation of aura is symptomatic of a betrayal of progressive technological innovation and the return of the daemonic forces of irrationalism. The cultural critic must be mobilized in the urgent, desperate struggle against the descent into modern barbarism. In the final instance, this is the actuality, the necessity, of Benjamin's small history of the work of art told from the vantage-point of the present; this is why 'art's fateful hour has struck for us' – indeed, this is why the fateful hour of materialist criticism and, even of history itself, unambiguously approaches.

Conclusion

Benjamin's various writings on radio, photography and film during the 1930s are significant in a number of respects. They are an important part of his continuing project of reconfiguring and redefining the task of contemporary criticism and fuelling the meltdown of traditional boundaries between different media and genres. The transformed cultural conditions of modernity have rendered the narrowly focused literary specialist obsolete. The bourgeois accomplishments of *Bildung* and *Kultur* are anachronisms. Instead, the new mass media require the acquisition and utilization of a polytechnical, political expertise. This notion of the progressive writer as an aesthetic engineer is central, because it points directly to Benjamin's preoccupation with the concept of literary technique and with the technical possibilities of new media. Eschewing the commitment debate, he insists that it is the duty of the radical writer/artist to pioneer and develop the *technical innovations and potentialities* of the medium in which he or she is working. Certain techniques may be adaptable or translatable (elements of epic theatre, for instance), but each medium has its own inherent logic, which must be pursued to its furthest point. *This* is what determines the artwork's political orientation, actuality and efficacy. The imitation of traditional forms is, at best, nostalgic nonsense. The radio broadcaster is no storyteller, the photographer no painter, the cinematographer no theatre director, and the film actor no stage player. And the positing of 'eternal' aesthetic values to which these new media forms and practices must conform is utter idiocy. New technologies do not accord with old principles. After all, one would not hitch a carthorse to a car, still less expect the vehicle to gallop. The very bases of the traditional artwork – ritual and cult value, aura, distance – and the aesthetic discourse and practices which it engendered – beauty, genius, concentration and contemplation – are irrevocably transformed by the new mass media.

Although supposedly among his most outspokenly materialist writings, Benjamin's reflections on radio, photograph and film combine to articulate a highly idiosyncratic Marxist vision of the radical potential of new media and popular cultural forms. Taken together with the equally unorthodox works of Kracauer and, later, Leo Löwenthal and Herbert Marcuse, they offer an appreciation of mass/popular culture which avoids the conventional conceptual Scylla and Charybdis of crude Marxist analysis: the naive celebration of popular culture as the authentic expression and revolutionary art of the proletariat, or its cynical denunciation as the ideological tool of the dominant capitalist class. Indeed, a serious examination of these writings would lead to a rather different understanding of Critical Theory and popular culture to that conventionally derived from the culture industry thesis. Benjamin's writings on the mass media, however fragmentary and contradictory, are an important reminder that Adorno and Horkheimer's critique of mass culture should not be conflated, as it so often is, with the Frankfurt School *per se*.

Lastly, it should not be forgotten that the studies of mass media were important contributions to Benjamin's work for the *Passagenarbeit*. The studies of film and photography are particularly important in this respect, because of Benjamin's insistence upon the imagistic character of historical representation. As we will see in the next chapter, photographic and cinematic techniques and practices became important metaphors for conceptualizing memory and the task of the redemptive historian. The notions of 'dialectics at a standstill' and 'gesture' formulated in his writings on epic theatre are mapped on to the instantaneous interruption of movement of the photographic snapshot and the cinematic freeze-frame. It is in this moment of tension, Benjamin argues, that the dialectical image is formed, a precious and precarious instant of historical recognition in which the 'then and there' is fleetingly legible in the 'here and now'. The critical historian, the ultimate polytechnical engineer, is dedicated to capturing, developing and preserving such images, images in which the incidental, the marginal and the neglected are disclosed and remembered, images which are to nourish the struggles of the present, images about to vanish.

7

Love at Last Sight

Introduction

This final chapter explores some of the most important texts in the constellation of Benjamin's prehistory of modernity: his renowned studies of Charles Baudelaire from the late 1930s, his 1929 essay on Marcel Proust composed as a companion piece to the Surrealism text, his 1932 reflections on his childhood and native city of Berlin, and finally, the enigmatic, now celebrated 'Theses on the Concept of History' of 1940. In different ways, each of these studies was envisaged as a vital contribution – be it thematic, be it historiographical – to the *Passagenarbeit*. As such, they contain many of its key figures and concepts: the highly suggestive motifs of the flâneur and the labyrinthine crowd, the relationship between allegory and the commodity, the pre-eminence of new and distinctive forms of experience and memory in the urban environment, and the formulation of history as a simultaneously critical and redemptive undertaking.

Taking one of Baudelaire's sonnets from the *Tableaux parisiens* – 'To a Passer-by' (*À une passante*) – as both a point of departure and a fundamental leitmotif for Benjamin's late writings, this chapter starts out by examining the changing context of, and intention behind, Benjamin's study of the Parisian poet. This is followed by a consideration of Benjamin's complex, compelling reading of Baudelaire's poetry and prose. In another exemplary instance of immanent criticism, he interprets Baudelaire as a modern urban allegorist, and thereby identifies an unlikely correspondence between Baudelaire's allegorical poetics and the commodity form. For Benjamin, Baudelaire's writings give expression to the fragmentation of experience in the nineteenth-century metropolis occasioned by the advent of the anonymous crowd and the commodification of the cultural domain under the remorseless logic of capitalist exchange relations. For Baudelaire, the task of the modern artist and poet is to give aesthetic form to the ephemeral sensations and abrupt encounters of the cityscape, to wrest meaning and painful pleasures from the intoxicating yet impoverished modern condition. *À une passante* is an exemplary instance, the *locus classicus*, for this arduous and amorous undertaking.

Drawing on the writings of his former professor in Berlin, Georg Simmel, Benjamin identifies the experience of 'shock' as the hallmark of metropolitan life. This in turn has particular consequences for the character and work of memory in the modern epoch. Benjamin seeks to articulate the intricate relationship between the contemporary urban setting and the remembering subject with reference to Proust's intriguing notion of the *mémoire involontaire*. Benjamin was fascinated by Proust's masterpiece *À la recherche du temps perdu* (*The Remembrance of Things Past*), and worked on a German translation of various sections of it with his early 'Arcades' collaborator, Franz Hessel. It is appropriately in Hessel's numerous writings on Paris and Berlin of the 1920s and 1930s that the Baudelairean flâneur is reconceptualized as a figure of remembrance. The Hesselian flâneur loses himself not only in the spatial maze of the city, but also, as a native of the metropolis, in the temporal labyrinth of his own memories. Hessel's metropolitan reflections become the principal inspiration for Benjamin's reminiscences regarding his own childhood and youth in Imperial Berlin. As we will see, these at times poetic studies were conceived as important, if ultimately unsuccessful, experiments in writing a critical 'counter-history' of the present moment, one which would brush not only the recent past, but also the cityscape itself, 'against the grain' to disclose its secrets.

It is with Benjamin's envisioning of the historian that this chapter concludes. His 'Theses on the Concept of History', fragments sketched for an epistemological-methodological prologue to the 'Arcades Project', constitute a biting critique of what Benjamin terms 'historicism', and an uncompromising rejection of the quintessential modern myths of historical progress and enlightenment. Perhaps the most powerful and evocative of all his writings, these miniatures combine Marxist and Messianic motifs in a desperate appeal to remember and redeem the 'hidden', broken tradition of the oppressed – the victims of past injustice and of present barbarism. This discontinuity cannot find representation in the conventional linear narratives of the historicist, but can be conceptualized only as an ephemeral moment of recognition when a fleeting constellation between past and present is formed. It is here, I contend, that the true significance of Baudelaire's 'To a Passer-by' becomes clear: it is an image of remembrance and redemption as the supreme tasks of the genuine historian of modernity.

An overwhelming sense of urgency and despair permeate the 'Theses'. This is not unique to these fragments. Benjamin's writings during the 1930s were composed against a background of turmoil and crisis, both political and personal. The rise of Nazism in Germany, the ultimate form of modern barbarism, confirmed all Benjamin's fears regarding the real character of supposed 'enlightenment' and 'progress'. His exile in Paris was characterized by impoverishment and a sense of isolation, exacerbated by strained relations with friends and colleagues.[1] Fear occasioned by the military expansion of the Third Reich was compounded by a sense of utter betrayal following the signing of the Hitler–Stalin non-aggression pact, an event which threw the political Left in Europe into chaos. The eventual outbreak of war in 1939 brought with it the miseries and uncertainties of internment in a French camp for German refugees. Upon release, Benjamin, his health failing fast, found his escape route from Marseilles into Spain blocked by petty bureaucratic formalities as transit visa regulations changed daily. It is no exaggeration to say that Benjamin's texts of this period are overshadowed by the prospect of death. His 'autobiographical' reflections on Berlin, for example, are in no sense whimsical or nostalgic musings. Scornful of the dull suffocation of bourgeois life in Wilhelminian Germany, they are, like the earlier 'Imperial Panorama', 'nothing but bitter, bitter herbs' (*COR*, p. 298). Benjamin's recollections, as I have argued elsewhere,[2] are haunted by the suicide in 1914 of his close friend Fritz Heinle and the appalling self-sacrifice of his generation that was to follow, by the imminent prospect of exile and abiding thoughts of his own suicide, and by the spectre of National Socialist dictatorship.

Benjamin's writings on Baudelaire, too, are indelibly marked by a sense of bitterness and forlorn longing. In disclosing the truth content of Baudelaire's poetry, immanent criticism was to reveal him as an untimely, incomparable 'brooder', as a melancholy figure who detested the bourgeois pretensions and mediocrity of his own era. Baudelaire fought to salvage, and give voice to, the transformation of experience in the modern epoch – modernity understood, that is, as the ruination of experience itself. In his concern with Baudelaire, Benjamin sought to rescue from the wreckage a lyricist writing amidst the most hostile of circumstances and to an uncomprehending and ill-disposed readership, a poet who understood only too well the despised roles of ragpicker, prostitute and outcast.

Suicide, betrayal, tyranny, exile, war, deportations, the threat of extermination – these catastrophic experiences are the sombre background to, and inevitably colour, Benjamin's writings in the 1930s. Amid such darkness, the genuine writer as redemptive historian must preserve in memory and for future generations each fleeting moment of hope, hope like a sad but beautiful face once glimpsed among a crowd of shadows.

The Image of Baudelaire

Amid the deafening traffic of the town
Tall, slender, in deep mourning, with majesty,
A woman passed, raising, with dignity
In her poised hand, the flounces of her gown;

Graceful, noble, with a statue's form.
And I drank, trembling as a madman thrills,
From her eyes, ashen sky where brooded storm,
The softness that fascinates, the pleasure that kills.

A flash . . . then night! – O lovely fugitive,
I am suddenly reborn from your swift glance;
Shall I never see you till eternity?

Somewhere far off! too late! *never*, perchance!
Neither knows where the other goes or lives;
We might have loved, and you knew this might be![3]

This sonnet, 'To a Passer-by', from the *Tableaux parisiens* section of *Les Fleurs du mal*, stands at the very centre, both literally and figuratively, of Benjamin's work on Baudelaire in the late 1930s. Benjamin had translated the poem as *Einer Dame*[4] during his work on Baudelaire's cycle of poems between 1914 and 1924, work which was to have 'The Task of the Translator' as its preface and which he vainly hoped to publish in *Angelus Novus*. In the course of his labours on the equally ill-fated 'Arcades Project', Benjamin came to focus once more on the poet. Convolute J, the longest of the folders of the *Passagenarbeit*, bore his name as its title and principal theme, and several of the other Convolutes explored his motifs.[5] Moreover, 'Baudelaire or the Streets of Paris' formed the fifth section of Benjamin's 1935 *exposé*, 'Paris Capital of the Nineteenth Century', and it was Horkheimer's positive reaction to this text which provided the catalyst for renewed study.

Writing to Benjamin on 14 March 1937, Horkheimer enthuses: 'A materialist article on Baudelaire has . . . long been desirable. If you could in fact decide to write this chapter of your book first I would be extremely grateful to you' (*GS* I, p. 1067).[6] In response to the *exposé*, Adorno initially advised Benjamin to clarify the notions of dream-image and dreaming collectivity through a sustained critique of the writings of Klages and Jung. He nevertheless recognized that the completion of the Baudelaire chapter of the 'Arcades Project' was a far more attractive prospect, and, persuaded by Benjamin that this would provide an invaluable initial opportunity 'to promote the crucial methodological interests of the Arcades' (*ABC*, p. 192),[7] he, too, endorsed the undertaking.[8] On 9 August 1937, Benjamin informed Fritz Lieb: 'I am turning now to a study of Baudelaire' (*GS* I, p. 1070).

Although Benjamin reports working exclusively and intensively on materials for this study during the autumn and winter of 1937,[9] Adorno's hopes that the proposed chapter would materialize 'in effective form soon [*bald, und schlagend*]' were not to be fulfilled. In a letter of 14 April 1938, Benjamin informed Scholem of both his progress and purpose:

> Not a word of it has yet been written, but I have been schematising the whole thing for a week now. The organisation is, as goes without saying, decisive. I want[10] to show how Baudelaire is embedded in the nineteenth century, and the vision of this must be seen as fresh as that of a stone that has been lodged in the soil of a forest for decades, and whose imprint – after we have laboriously rolled it away from its place – lies before us with pristine clarity. (*COR*, 554)[11]

Here Benjamin stresses the actuality, the current possibility and necessity of his reading of Baudelaire. Although he is concerned with how Baudelaire is embedded within the nineteenth century, it is only now as the stone is rolled away that this is disclosed. The significance of the poet and his verse is legible only as an imprint, as a trace, in the present. In his later methodological fragments for the Baudelaire studies,[12] this sylvan metaphor is interestingly reconfigured in terms of photography.[13]

Benjamin writes: 'An image of Baudelaire is presented. It is comparable to the image in a camera' (*GS* I, p. 1164). The 'dialectical materialist' as photographer

> may seek a larger or smaller aperture, select a more glaring political or a more muted historical exposure – in the end he releases the shutter and presses. Once he has removed the plate – the image of the thing as it entered the social tradition – the concept takes its rightful place and he develops it. For the plate can only offer a negative. It comes from an apparatus which substitutes shadow for light and light for shadow. (*GS* I, p. 1165)

The imprint of the embedded stone in the forest floor has here become the negative image on the photographic plate. The surface in which this reverse image is perceptible has also changed: instead of Baudelaire's mark in the nineteenth century, the concern has shifted to his appearance in the 'social tradition'. The current legibility of Baudelaire, his actuality, is not immediately available, but must be recognized in terms of, and mediated through, a continuing literary afterlife. The critic's task is to intervene in this tradition so as both to read the image of the past afresh and to develop it anew. But whether the imprint of a stone or a photographic negative, the importance accorded in each case to the visual is decisive. The afterlife of the object has been transposed into an optical register – Benjamin examines the *afterimage* of the poet.

Two days after writing to Scholem, Benjamin included a detailed plan of the Baudelaire text in a letter to Horkheimer.[14] Taking the *Elective Affinities* essay of fifteen years earlier as his model,[15] the 'essay' (as it was now termed) was to have a dialectical, tripartite structure. The first part, provisionally entitled 'Idea and Image',[16] was to provide a methodological introduction, 'demonstrate the importance of allegory for the *Flowers of Evil*' and examine 'how the allegorical vision in Baudelaire is constructed' (*COR*, p. 556). The second, 'Antiquity and Modernity', was to explore the representation of the metropolitan crowd as 'the latest and most unfathomable labyrinth in the labyrinth of the city' (*COR*, p. 557).[17] The third part of the study, 'The New and the Immutable',[18] was to examine the fetishized commodity form, focusing on the figure of the prostitute as 'the commodity that most perfectly realises the allegorical vision' (*COR*, p. 557). The Baudelaire study was thus to juxtapose the ruinous, melancholic gaze of the allegorist with the phantasmagoria of the commodity and the spectacle of the urban crowd. Further, it was to synthesize these moments in one of Baudelaire's most common motifs: the prostitute as elusive, alluring figure in the crowd, as the embodiment of the fetishized commodity, and as an allegory of ruination. In this way, 'some of the fundamental categories of the Arcades project are developed' such that 'motifs that had appeared to me only as spheres of thought, more or less isolated from one another, are brought into conjunction for the first time' (*COR*, p. 570).[19] The overall significance of the text was clear: 'I can say that a very precise model of the *Arcades* project would be furnished if the "Baudelaire" were to succeed' (*COR*, p. 567).[20]

At the end of May 1938, Benjamin informed Horkheimer, 'I have completed the schematization of the "Baudelaire"' (*GS* I, p. 1076). However, like the 'Arcades Project', the Baudelaire study had outgrown its original conception. From around July 1938, a year after the initial plan to work up the Baudelaire material 'in effective form soon', Benjamin began to envisage a separate *book*[21] on Baudelaire, distinct from, but intimately related to, the *Passagenarbeit*. On 28 August 1938, Benjamin told Pollock: 'This book is not the same as the "Paris Arcades." But it contains not only a considerable part of the material collected in its name but also a number of its philosophical contents' (*GS* I, p. 1086). Indeed, the book form was necessary to do justice to this conceptual repertoire[22] and its proper relation to the wider 'Arcades Project'.[23] The book was to retain the tripartite structure, but a new nomenclature appeared: it was to bear the title *Charles Baudelaire – a Lyric Poet in the Era of High Capitalism*, and the second of the three parts was now to be called ' "Das second empire in der Dichtung von Baudelaire"' (*GS* I, p. 1086). Benjamin focused his attention on writing this central part, which, further subdivided into three sections ('The *Bohème*', 'The Flâneur' and 'Modernism'), was eventually finished and dispatched to Horkheimer at the end of September 1938.

Benjamin's 'Paris of the Second Empire in Baudelaire' did not meet with a warm reception. Adorno's letter of 10 November 1938 expressed his disappointment and a number of serious misgivings. He claimed that the material assembled by Benjamin lacked the necessary theoretical armature and adequate interpretation.[24] This theoretical 'asceticism' resulted in a failure to ground the key concepts of the 'Arcades Project'.[25] Moreover, Adorno detected a worrying tendency to equate prevailing 'concrete' material conditions *immediately* with cultural practices and literary forms. This encompassed two elements: on the one hand, a conception of metropolitan experience in terms of crude, mechanical reflexes;[26] on the other, an understanding of Baudelaire's poetry as a simplistic reflection of determining social processes and 'economic characteristics' (*COR*, p. 581), rather than a complex expression of them.[27] Devoid of such mediation, Benjamin's vain attempt to let the material speak for itself 'reverts tendentially to a wide-eyed presentation of bare facts. . . . [Y]our work settled the crossroads of magic and positivism. This location is bewitched. Only theory could break the spell: your own, ruthless, quite speculative theory. It is only its claims I level against you' (*COR*, p. 582). In Adorno's eyes, Benjamin had sacrificed the precious insights of 'profane illumination' for the crudest, most banal of Marxist approaches. In terms reminiscent of Scholem, he complains: 'you have done violence to yourself in it, . . . in order to pay tribute to a Marxism that does justice neither to you nor to Marxism . . . [Y]ou have denied yourself your boldest and most productive thoughts in a kind of precensorship . . . based on materialist categories' (*COR*, p. 583). These criticisms are familiar ones: what are needed are *more* dialectics, *more* mediation and the elimination of Brechtian motifs. In order to 'save' Benjamin from the consequences of these deficiencies, Horkheimer and Adorno shelved the long-standing plan to publish the essay in the *Zeitschrift für Sozialforschung*.[28]

In his reply of 9 December 1938, Benjamin defended his text: it was, after all, only one-third of the full study whose unwritten first part was to contain the theoretical principles. Further, 'Paris of the Second Empire in Baudelaire' was intended as a 'philological' (*COR*, p. 587) exercise, one whose validity consisted precisely in the quotation of historical and other sources, in the 'wide-eyed presentation' of textual material without intrusive interpretation. Benjamin's plea for the publication of a modified central section of the text ('The Flâneur') as a way of inaugurating debate[29] was accepted by Adorno, whose letter of 1 February 1939 conspicuously fails to engage with Benjamin's arguments and confines itself instead to a reiteration of criticisms and a detailing of necessary corrections.

With 'the "physiology of idleness"' as its new focus, Benjamin's 'fundamentally new sketch of the flâneur chapter' (*GS* I, p. 1118) proved a dispiriting undertaking.[30] Nevertheless, despite 'unspeakably unfavorable' (*COR*, p. 608) circumstances, and with his 'thoughts fixed on this text day and night' (*COR*, p. 609),[31] the accumulation of material proceeded apace, so much so that, contrary to one of Adorno's explicit conditions for publication,[32] it would 'go far beyond the size of last year's flâneur' (*COR*, p. 610). 'On Some Motifs in Baudelaire', as the text was now entitled, was completed by the beginning of August 1939. Benjamin's letter to Adorno of 6 August 1939 emphasizes both its transformed aspect and its revised context:

> The motifs of arcade, noctambulism, the *feuilleton*, as well as a theoretical introduction of the concept of the phantasmagoria, are reserved for the first section of the second part. The motifs of the trace, the type, and empathy for the commodity soul are earmarked for the third section. The present middle section of the second part will set forth the complete figure of the flâneur but only in conjunction with its first and third sections. (*COR*, p. 611)

Given the importance which Benjamin accords in this letter to Adorno's critical input, it is perhaps not surprising that the new text met with a response as enthusiastic as the previous one had been hostile. Gretel Adorno admired the 'marvellous construction' (*GS* I, p. 1125) of the piece;[33] Horkheimer stated his (and Adorno's) 'profound admiration for this penetrating work', with particular reference to 'the elucidation of the philosophical thought which is all yours' (*COR*, p. 1126).[34] Adorno's own response was especially positive, celebrating the text as one of Benjamin's finest literary accomplishments[35] – indeed, acclaiming it as nothing less than ' "one of the greatest historical-philosophical testimonies of the epoch" ' (*GS* I, p. 1135).

Benjamin's intention to write a tripartite study of Baudelaire, initially as a chapter of the *Passagenarbeit*, then as an accompanying essay, and finally as a book, was never to be realized. Instead, it resulted only in the draft of one part, a rewrite of the central section of this draft, and a plethora of various notes and fragments, both methodological and substantive, the most developed of which Benjamin collected under the perplexing title of 'Central Park'. As Benjamin's focus became ever narrower, from Paris as capital of the nineteenth century to Baudelaire, from Baudelaire to the flâneur, the material itself grew so much that the form of the intended whole became confused.[36] The more Benjamin worked on the project, the more remote its completion became. The Baudelaire study was to prove an all too precise model of the *Passagenarbeit*: it was nothing other than an inexorably expanding mess in miniature.

In the very middle of this textual muddle stands 'To a Passer-by.' In this chapter I suggest that this sonnet not only occupied a central position in the projected book on Baudelaire, but also proved significant for Benjamin's late writings more generally. Given the ambiguous, ever-changing complexion of the Baudelaire studies, this is necessarily a tentative claim. Clearly, there are many potentially fruitful levels of interpretation both of the Baudelaire studies and of this poem in particular. Nevertheless, the sonnet may be seen to have a threefold importance. First, it presents the quintessential experiences of the modern city – the fascination and shock which attend the flâneur's encounter with the metropolitan crowd. The poem hence serves as an exemplary instance of a new urban aesthetic, *modernité*, the artistic imperative for Baudelaire's famous 'painter of modern life'. Second, it provides an image of the transformed condition of memory. The forms of remembrance in the metropolis are subject to the same processes of diminution and disintegration which afflict modern experience. 'To a Passer-by' serves as an allegory of the fleeting, fortuitous Proustian *mémoire involontaire*. This connection with memory points to a third crucial significance: the momentary encounter and mutual recognition of which the poem speaks may be seen as an image of Benjamin's key redemptive, historiographical category: the dialectical image. Hence, 'To a Passer-by' is an allegorical representation of the historiographical basis of the entire *Passagenarbeit*.

Allegory, melancholy and the commodity

The poet Charles Baudelaire is not the most obvious starting point for a critical, historical materialist analysis of nineteenth-century Paris. After all, he is more conventionally seen as an impoverished, bourgeois bohemian, an aesthete who, though outraging prevailing public morals, scorned political movements. Moreover, Baudelaire's concern with mystical natural 'correspondences', with the 'forest of symbols',[37] is often seen to anticipate the Symbolist movement and the doctrine of *l'art pour l'art*.[38] Hence his poetry was esteemed by the Georgekreis, with Stefan George himself translating *Les Fleurs du mal*. In writing against such interpetations, Benjamin saw his analysis of Baudelaire as a timely, necessary intervention in the afterlife of his texts. His purpose was twofold. First, in order to rescue Baudelaire from the attentions and appropriations of the Georgekreis and others, Benjamin intended the opening part of the book to show how his poetry must be understood as the modern reconfiguration of the allegorical intention, the very negation of the symbol.[39] Secondly, the book was to demonstrate how, irrespective of his intentions, Baudelaire comes to register and voice the experiences afforded (and denied) by contact with the metropolitan crowd. Baudelaire's allegorical poetics capture the utter impoverishment of human life subject to the commodity form.[40] In his concern with the individual's shock encounter with the urban multitude, he articulates the fragmentation of coherent experience (*Erfahrung*) and its replacement by a plethora of disparate, discontinuous impressions (*Erlebnis*). Baudelaire thus presents modern experience subject to processes which are of decisive importance for Benjamin: ruination and mortification, intoxication and interruption, boredom and melancholy.[41] Read against the grain of prevailing criticism and authorial intention, Baudelaire's work would offer the most precise, profane illuminations of nineteenth-century Parisian social life.[42]

If the *Passagenarbeit* was to explore the nineteenth century as the *Trauerspiel* study had illuminated the seventeenth century, then Baudelaire as allegorist provided a key point of contiguity between the two projects, a sun in each constellation.[43] Whereas baroque allegory gave sorrowful expression to, and mirrored, a profane world bereft of meaning, Baudelaire's allegorical poetics articulated and corresponded to the commodity's proliferation and pre-eminence. Indeed, for Benjamin there was a special affinity between the commodity form and allegory which was central both to his understanding of Baudelaire and to the critical redemptive work of the 'Arcades Project'. This has three main aspects: the ruination of the object world, the connection with the human body, and the evocation and experience of melancholy.

As Benjamin makes clear in his *Trauerspiel* study, one of the hallmarks of allegory is the profusion of ever more obscure referents such that one witnesses the hollowing-out of meaning. The surfeit of signs, emblems and hieroglyphs spawned by the baroque allegorist exemplified the senseless babble of fallen human language. For Benjamin, the commodity form under capitalist exchange relations exhibits a similar tendency. The use-value of the object, its meaning, is subsumed under the arbitrariness of the commodity's exchange-value – that is, a monetary value dependent upon the contingencies of fashion and taste. Benjamin highlights this point of correspondence: 'The modes of meaning fluctuate almost as rapidly as the price of the commodity. In fact, the meaning of the commodity *is* its price; it has, as a commodity, no other. Hence the allegorist is in its element with commercial wares' (J80,2; J80a,1; *ARC*, p. 369).

Indeed, if 'allegories are, in the realm of thoughts, what ruins are in the realm of things' (*OGTD*, p. 178), then allegory is certainly 'in its element' with the commodity. After all, the eventual fate of the commodity is disintegration, obsolescence and ridicule. The afterlife of the object is exactly that process of decay and decomposition in which the spell of the fetishized commodity, resplendent in the fashionable arcades, is broken. The commodity is destined to ruination. In this despised form, the commodity, like allegory, gestures towards the catastrophic truth of the unredeemed world. Just as allegory hollows out language and tumbles into the abyss of meaninglessness, so the commodity empties out use-value and circulates within the dizzying vertigo of the market. In so doing, both allegory and the commodity reverse direction, and point towards forms of salvation: of the mortified flesh in the resurrection, and of the obsolete object by the Critical Theorist as collector.

Secondly, allegory and the commodity correspond to the decaying human *physis*, the natural history of the body. In the *Trauerspiel*, the body of the sovereign as martyr is torn apart in torture and execution. As the body is dismembered, so its constituent parts are imbued with, and lend themselves to, allegorical interest. Allegory is at home with the grinning skull and the corpse. The commodity, too, is bound up with the ruination of the human body. The key figure here, and one of Baudelaire's most important motifs, is the prostitute.[44] In transforming her own body into an item for sale, the prostitute becomes the exemplary embodiment of the commodity. The prevalence of prostitution in the nineteenth-century city comes to mirror the profusion of commodities, such that 'the woman herself becomes an article that is mass produced' (*CB*, p. 40). Indeed, one of the attractions of the Parisian arcades was that they were frequented by prostitutes. In the fairy palaces of consumption, under the fetishizing gaze of the customer, the prostitute was framed by the other commodities produced by the alienating labour processes of capitalist industry and the exploitative workings of colonial markets.[45] Above all, like the commodities in the arcades, the prostitute is, over time, subject to declining favour, physical disintegration and eventual ruinous impoverishment. In his notes for the Baudelaire study, Benjamin makes clear this connection between allegory, the commodity and the prostitute: 'The specific devaluation of the object world, as found in the commodity, is the foundation of the allegorical intention in Baudelaire. The prostitute, as the embodiment of the commodity, has a central place in Baudelaire's poetry. The prostitute is, on the other hand, allegory made human' (*GS* I, p. 1151). Hence one might say, playing on Benjamin's formulation, that the prostitute is, in the realm of human beings, what the obsolete commodity is in the realm of things, and what allegory is in the domain of language. Indeed, the prostitute as a figure of ruination comes to serve as an allegory of the commodity and thereby as an allegory of allegory itself. As the living human incarnation of both commodity and allegory, the prostitute was to take on a special significance in the final part of the proposed Baudelaire book, 'The Commodity as Poetic Object', since, as Benjamin notes, 'The commodity form emerges in Baudelaire as the allegorical form of perception. Form and content are united in the prostitute, as in their synthesis' (J59,10, *ARC*, p. 335).

Thirdly, in laying bare the world of decaying bodies and expiring things, allegory comes to evoke a sense of melancholy. This is important because it is his bitter, brooding perception of the Parisian cityscape as ruinous and petrified, as the *'facies hippocratica* of history' (*OGTD*, p. 137), which elevates Baudelaire's work. Benjamin writes: 'Baudelaire was a bad philosopher, a better theorist in matters of art; but only as a brooder was he incomparable. ... The brooder is at home among allegories' (J55a,1, *ARC*, p. 328). In the profusion of referents characteristic of allegory, it is the allegorist as brooder who is absorbed by the intricate relationship between, and articulation of, image and meaning. For the allegorist, the image is a complex form, a hieroglyph, whose exact meaning eludes decipherment. The world never appears unified as a legible totality, but always instead as an irresolvable puzzle which reduces the thinker to endlessly accumulating and fruitlessly contemplating fragments. This is what defines the brooder. Benjamin writes:

> The case of the brooder is that of the man who has arrived at the solution of a great problem but then has forgotten it. And now he broods – not so much over the matter itself as over his past reflections on it. The brooder's thinking, therefore, bears the imprint of memory. Brooder and allegorist are cut from the same cloth. (J79a,1, *ARC*, p. 367).

Benjamin elaborates upon this and links it back to the arbitrariness of the commodity:

Through the disorderly fund which his knowledge places at his disposal, the allegorist rummages here and there for a particular piece,
holds it next to some other piece and tests to see if they fit together
– that meaning with this image or this image with that meaning. The
result can never been known before hand, for there is no natural
mediation between the two. But this is just how matters stand
between commodity and price. (J80,2; 80a,1; *ARC*, p. 368)

Baudelaire as poet-turned-ragpicker is engaged in this protracted,
painful piecing together of imagistic shards salvaged from the
tumult of the metropolis, an activity which provides a provocative
model for Benjamin's own work on the 'Arcades Project'.[46]

Baudelaire's writings are testimonies to the ruination of modern
urban experience. In his saturnine contemplation and splenetic representation of metropolitan existence, Baudelaire 'lays himself open
to the deepest possible experience of modern life, and to everything
in modern life which is antagonistic to the capacity for experience
itself' (CP, p. 68). This takes a number of forms. First, it involves a
profound sense of estrangement from the physical world and the
prevailing social milieu, and of untimeliness.[47] An environment
inimical to intimacy[48] and reciprocity, Paris was both necessary for
Baudelaire's aesthetic activity and a site of permanent alienation.[49]
Secondly, there is a sense of pessimistic resignation before the unrelenting, calamitous course of events. The experience of the crowd is
exemplary here: ' "lost in this mean world, jostled by the crowd, I
am like a weary man whose eye, looking backwards into the depths
of the years, sees nothing but disillusion and bitterness, and before
him, nothing but a tempest which contains nothing new, neither
instruction nor pain" ' (CB, pp. 153–4). The individual is caught in
the maelstrom of the modern, and must suffer its rude blows
without hope. The great 'nothing new' of continuing historical
catastrophe produces a characteristic response in the allegorist:
'spleen'.[50] The futility and monotony of things leads to that *ennui*
which Baudelaire dreaded most of all.[51] Thirdly – and this is the
heroic element in Baudelaire – notwithstanding the listlessness
occasioned by the always-the-same, one encounters in his writings
an unrelenting hostility towards the modern world and a vainglorious impulse to defy it,[52] to halt it in its tracks, to bring it to a standstill.[53] It is this ambition to bring about a cessation of occurrences,
'Joshua's gesture' as Pierre Missac puts it,[54] which defines Baudelaire's 'heroic melancholy' (CP, p. 54) as modern hubris. Moreover,
it suggests his relevance for the critical representation of modernity,
for such interruption is also to be found, of course, in the gestural

in epic theatre and the cinematic freeze-frame. In his concern with a poetics of radical discontinuity and remorseless antagonism, Baudelaire brushes modernity against the grain, and becomes an unlikely, unwitting precursor of the polytechnical aesthetic engineer advocated by Benjamin.

Modernité, flânerie and the crowd

For Benjamin, Baudelaire is a key contemporary thinker in two respects: first, his embeddedness in, and imprint on, the nineteenth century are legible only in the present moment; second, Baudelaire is preoccupied with capturing and articulating the contemporary itself. To suspend the flow of events in midstream is not simply a wish born of melancholic spite; it is also a fundamental aesthetic imperative for Baudelaire, because therein lies the possibility of giving form to the modern. This is the distinctive task of the modern artist and the key to his heroic constitution. Baudelaire insists that the principal duty of the genuine modern artist is to depict the ephemeral beauty of the passing moment. The 'painter of modern life'[55] abandons the studio, and, taking to the metropolitan streets,

> goes and watches the river of life flow past him in all its majesty and splendour. He marvels at the eternal beauty and amazing harmony of life in the capital cities, a harmony so providentially maintained amid the turmoil of human freedom. He gazes upon the landscapes of the great city – landscapes of stone, caressed by the mist or buffeted by the sun. (Baudelaire, 1986, p. 11)

In so doing, this figure becomes the astute observer and attentive recorder of 'Beauty in its most minute manifestations' (Baudelaire, 1986, p. 34) and most modern form – the 'pageant of fashionable life' (Baudelaire, 1965, p. 118).

Hence, for Baudelaire, the hastily composed and executed pen-and-ink sketches and watercolours of the little-known artist Constantin Guys are infinitely more valuable than the grand canvases and formal subjects of the academicians. Guys' images give genuine form and expression to the myriad sights of the urban kaleidoscope. In so doing, they exemplify new modes of perception and representation, and, in particular, a sensitivity to, and appreciation of, the aesthetics of the fleeting and transient: *modernité*. Baudelaire explains: 'by *modernité* I mean the ephemeral, the fugitive, the contingent, the half of art whose other half is the eternal, the immutable' (1986, p. 13). *Modernité*, inevitably and confusingly translated as 'modernity', refers not to a specific historical epoch, but rather to a concern with the beauty of the moment and the momentary. Each era, Baudelaire claims, has its own *modernité*, its own beauty, which the authentic contemporary artist must endeavour to capture. This is the achievement of the great works of art of the past: they have succeeded in rendering the beauty of their time, their own *modernité*, with such originality and intensity that they endure in subsequent ages as exemplary instances of beauty *per se*.

The genuine painter of modern life may learn from the techniques of earlier masters,[56] but must not imitate the styles and subjects of the past.[57] Rather, he must endeavour 'to distil the eternal from the transitory' (Baudelaire, 1986, p. 12) – that is to say, to give form to the subjects of his own time, in the hope that his works will survive and eventually be counted among the masterpieces. The genuine artist takes the fashionable as his subject matter with the aim that, in so doing, his depiction of it will transcend the fate of fashion, and be deemed 'worthy of one day taking its place as "antiquity"' (Baudelaire, 1986, p. 13).[58]

Baudelaire emphasizes the distinctive character of the painter of *modernité* thus: 'Observer, philosopher, *flâneur* – call him what you will; . . . Sometimes he is a poet; more often than not he comes closer to the novelist or the moralist; he is the painter of the passing moment and of all the suggestions of eternity that it contains' (1986, pp. 4–5). Although he later opposes the 'loftier aim' of the artist to the mere 'fugitive pleasure of circumstance' (Baudelaire, 1986, p. 12) characteristic of flânerie, the reference here to the flâneur is significant. This figure is one of a gallery of social types who, as allegories or incarnations of the poet, come to embody Baudelaire's 'heroism of modern life'. Gambler, idler, dandy, ragpicker, prostitute, lesbian, detective and collector – these figures undergo and exemplify the most telling experiences of the modern. They are marked and ruined by it. At the same time, they signal implacable yet futile opposition to contemporary tendencies and tastes: commodification and ruination, massification and rationalization, sobriety and propriety. The flâneur, like the prostitute and the gambler, serves as a figure of the intensification and disintegration of experience in the modern city. Moreover, the flâneur provides Benjamin with a heuristic device for exploring the experiences and memories of the cityscape, with a model and method for his own reading of the contemporary metropolitan environment. In the writings of his friend Franz Hessel, the flâneur returns in the twentieth century as the privileged physiognomist of the urban setting, transforming the city into a locus of reading and remembering. The flâneur, then, is heroic in exemplifying contradictory moments in the city: on the one hand, the ruination of experience and the fragmentation of memory; on the other, the decipherment of meaning and the recollection of lost moments.

In origin a specifically Parisian character,[59] and one closely tied to the fortunes of the arcades,[60] the flâneur is the dawdling, dandified, disdainful bourgeois male[61] who meanders through the streets of the city and negotiates its teeming crowds for the purposes of distraction and stimulation. Baudelaire writes of the 'painter of modern life' as flâneur:

> the crowd is his element, as the air is that of birds and water of fishes. His passion and profession are to become one flesh with the crowd. For the perfect *flâneur*, for the passionate spectator, it is an immense joy to set up house in the middle of the multitude, amid the ebb and flow of movement, in the midst of the fugitive and the infinite. (1986, p. 9).

For the flâneur, ambling and observing are forms of intoxication in their own right.[62] To see and to be seen, and, especially, to be seen doing nothing – these are the joys of the flâneur as ostentatious idler and frivolous fop. One step ahead of fashion, one step behind on the boulevard, the flâneur is a self-consciously untimely figure. The most extraordinary and memorable image of this is the tortoise-walker in the arcades.[63] Such eccentricities indicate the idiosyncratic style and essential 'incognito' (Baudelaire, 1986, p. 9) of the haughty flâneur, and come thereby to distinguish him from the anonymous, ignoble crowd through which he moves. The flâneur is *in* the crowd but not *of* it. Indeed, as Benjamin stresses, the flâneur is precisely the aloof individual who regards the crowd with aristocratic contempt, refusing to become 'one flesh' with it. The flâneur is no casual stroller: he is, rather, a 'heroic' pedestrian, a self-styled 'prince' (Baudelaire, 1986, p. 9) of the pavement. As such, his reign was brief. The burgeoning urban crowd, that living labyrinth contained within the greater labyrinth of the cityscape, was both necessary to him and his eventual undoing. The requisite 'elbow room' (*CB*, p. 54) for the sauntering snob was in ever shorter supply. He eventually became 'one flesh' with the crowd, and vanished from the scene. Indeed, the ruinous experience of the crowd and that of the commodity combine in the 'last incarnation' of the forlorn flâneur, in his afterlife as the pathetic 'sandwich-man', the walking advertisement.[64]

Baudelaire writes that 'the lover of universal life enters into the crowd as though it were an immense reservoir of electrical energy' (1986, p. 9). This is an apt analogy, because the experience of shock is the hallmark of metropolitan experience and the definitive signature of modernity itself.[65] To the dismay of Adorno, Benjamin here draws on the work of Georg Simmel.[66] For both Benjamin and Simmel, the modern urbanite is subject to a surfeit of stimuli and sensations which threaten to overload and overwhelm the human consciousness. Walking in the city 'involves the individual in a series of shocks and collisions' (*CB*, p. 132) which are only partially registered by the conscious mind. Integrated, intelligible experience (*Erfahrung*) is replaced by a plethora of discontinuous, disparate, disorderly particles of experience (*Erlebnis*). *Erlebnis* refers less to experience itself than to its residues left in the unconscious. Benjamin observes that 'the greater the share of the shock factor in particular impressions, the more constantly consciousness has to be alert as a screen against stimuli; the more efficiently it is so, the less do these impressions enter experience (*Erfahrung*), tending to remain in the sphere of a certain hour of one's life *(Erlebnis)*' (*CB*, p. 117). The flâneur both revels in this transformation, and ultimately falls victim to it. The superabundance of images and impressions is what makes flânerie so inviting and intoxicating. The heroic poet and painter vainly seek to capture and give form to this flood of phenomena, to reconstitute and reconfigure experience in the face of this disintegration. This ambition has its price: escalating eccentricity, absurd obsolescence and neurasthenia. Flânerie leads inexorably to spleen and melancholy.

The poet of modern life as flâneur is open to, and registers, the '"heartaches and thousand natural shocks" which a pedestrian suffers in the bustle of a city' (*CB*, p. 61). As a passionate, princely spectator of the modern scene, he is attuned to the 'special beauty' of the city and its seductive secrets. Indeed, the possibilities of amorous flirtation and sexual intrigue are so central to Baudelaire that one might describe him as the prototypical 'erotic engineer' of the cityscape. Here the meaning and significance of *À une passante* emerges. The sonnet tells of a momentary encounter between the poet and a beautiful, unknown woman, spied suddenly and fortuitously amid the urban crowd. The eyes of the poet and of this apparition meet fleetingly and longingly, before she vanishes once more into the sea of faces, never to be seen by again by the lovelorn poet. Benjamin comments: 'what this sonnet communicates is simply this: far from experiencing the crowd as an opposed, antagonistic element, this very crowd brings to the city-dweller the figure that fascinates. The delight of the urban poet is love – not at first sight, but at last' (*CB*, p. 125).

The ambiguous relationship between flâneur and crowd is encapsulated in this poem. On the one hand, it is an exemplary instance of that intense excitement and intoxication which are unique to the cityscape[67] and the very *raison d'être* for flânerie. Indeed, the unexpected shock encounter and its reverberations, 'love at last sight', mirror Benjamin's incendiary anticipation of seeing Lacis in Riga, of 'love before first sight', so to speak. Baudelaire's unknown muse cuts through him just as Lacis cut through Benjamin in *One-Way Street*. On the other hand, such erotic incisions are deeply wounding. Benjamin notes that 'the inner form of these verses is revealed in the fact that in them love itself is recognised as being stigmatised by the big-city' (*CB*, p. 46). The crowd may bring the poet's object of desire into view,[68] but it is the anonymous multitude into which she also vanishes. Like the *Angelus Novus*, the 'figure that fascinates' is enchanting, but ephemeral. The look of 'love at last sight', even though requited, always remains unfulfilled: 'there is always something inaccessible about the woman one wants to love. The *passant* and the *passante*, the male and the female passer-by, can meet only "for the length of a flash of lightning": the two senses of the word "passion" are reunited in unhappiness' (Missac, 1995, pp. 5–6). Yet it is precisely the appreciation of this elusiveness and evanescence which is decisive. *À une passante* gives form to the modern in that it poetically and posthumously captures the shock-like character of urban experience and melancholy. The sonnet records transient beauty for posterity. 'Love at last sight' becomes a definitive instance of Baudelaire's aesthetic of *modernité*.

Proust and the remembrance of places past

The demise of *Erfahrung* and pre-eminence of *Erlebnis* lead to a profound transformation in the character of memory. On the one hand, the city is home to an amnesia born of sensory overstimulation and fatigue, a forgetfulness which leads to a misrecognition of the always-the-same as the ever-new, and thereby dooms the individual to fateful repetition.[69] On the other, the abrasive encounters and surfeit of stimuli to which the modern urbanite is subjected produce deep, enduring scars upon the unconscious mind.[70] These traces may be lasting, but they are inaccessible to the conscious work of remembering. In this way, *Erlebnis* is the corollary not so much of simple forgetfulness, but rather of a particular form of memory which resembles forgetting: Marcel Proust's notion of the *mémoire involontaire*.[71]

Benjamin considered Proust's *À la recherche du temps perdu* (*Remembrance of Things Past*) to be the 'outstanding literary achievement of our time' (*ILL*, p. 203). During the mid-1920s Benjamin worked with Hessel on translations of the second (*À l'ombre des jeunes filles en fleurs*), fourth (*Sodome et Gomorrhe*) and fifth (*La Prisonnière*) volumes of Proust's masterpiece.[72] Although their translations met with critical acclaim, their work on *La Prisonnière* was never completed, and the whole project ended in acrimonious disputes with the publishers.[73] Benjamin subsequently brought together his own critical reflections in 'The Image of Proust', an essay published in the *Literarische Welt* in 1929.[74]

Benjamin understood his Proust essay as a 'companion piece' (*COR*, p. 352) to his Surrealism study published in the same year. A number of connections are evident. First, Benjamin sees in Proust and the Surrealists a shared concern with the unconscious mind – with spontaneous memories and associations, and with dreams and automatic writing. McCole (1993, pp. 266–7) highlights a number of similarities between Proustian remembrance and Surrealist dreaming: their unintended appearance and inaccessibility to conscious thought, their nocturnal character,[75] their intoxicating, erotic and imagistic quality,[76] and their manifestation as 'intricate, entangled arabesques' (McCole, 1993, p. 268). Memories and dreams are immaterial, ineffable and inscrutable. They are characterized by complexity and convolution,[77] rather than linearity and clarity; they present multiple layers of meaning and significance, and thereby provide for 'endless interpolations into what has been' (*OWS*, p. 305). Benjamin himself interweaves memories and dreams when he describes his own childhood recollections as being as 'evanescent and as alluringly tormenting as half-forgotten dreams' (*OWS*, p. 316).

The second connection is the use of comedy and irony to critical effect. Proust, too, contributes to the 'death of the nineteenth century in comedy' (*ARC*, p. 467) by ridiculing his own pseudo-aristocratic social circles, a milieu preoccupied with gossip and petty snobbery. Benjamin notes that 'it was Proust's aim to design the entire inner structure of society as a physiology of chatter. In the treasury of its prejudices and maxims there is not one that is not annihilated by a dangerous comic element' (*ILL*, p. 208). The minutiae of the everyday serve both as the ammunition for this critique and as its target. Benjamin appreciates 'the explosive power of Proust's critique of society. His style is comedy, not humor; his laughter does not toss the world up but flings it down – at the risk that it will be smashed to pieces, which will then make him burst into tears. . . . The pretensions of the bourgeoisie are shattered by laughter' (*ILL*, p. 209). In this way Proust, like Baudelaire, gives the most precise expression to the social world of the nineteenth century, albeit unintentionally.[78]

Thirdly, the Proust and Surrealism essays were both written as 'prolegomena' to the 'Arcades Project', and as such derive their ultimate significance from it. For Benjamin, Proust offers the key element so crucially lacking in Aragon: the constellation of awakening. Benjamin notes: 'Just as Proust begins the story of his life with an awakening, so must every presentation of history begin with awakening; in fact, it should treat of nothing else. This one, accordingly, deals with awakening from the nineteenth century' (N4,3 *ARC*, p. 464). Moreover, just as the Surrealist principle of profane illumination through montage underpins the early methodological reflections for the *Passagenarbeit*, so the notion of *mémoire involontaire* comes to prefigure Benjamin's later category of the dialectical image. Indeed, in the late 1930s Benjamin largely abandons the Surrealist-inspired vocabulary of dreaming and awakening, reformulating it in terms of remembrance and amnesia.

The *mémoire involontaire* is an attempt to conceptualize an intimate, intriguing experience: the power of the most trivial and ephemeral sensations – Proust's examples include the smell and taste of madeleines dipped in tea and the scents of various shrubs and flowers[79] – to awaken unexpectedly and inexplicably long-dormant memories of childhood experiences. Such memories return and flow effusively and effortlessly from a fortuitous, fleeting coincidence and correspondence[80] of past and present, from a momentary constellation akin to that 'eddy in the stream of becoming' which Benjamin terms origin. Like the *Angelus Novus*, they appear unannounced and vanish irrevocably – though, unlike Benjamin's 'new angel', their passing may not go unmourned. This elusiveness of the *mémoire involontaire* is emphasized by Proust in 'Swann in

Love' with respect to a suggestive analogy. M. Swann tries to recall the haunting little phrase of Vinteuil's piano sonata which so delighted him;

> but when he returned home he felt the need of it: he was like a man into whose life a woman he has seen for a moment passing by has brought the image of a new beauty which deepens his own sensibility, although he does not even know her name or whether he will ever see her again. (Proust, 1983, p. 229)

When Swann hears the sonata again at the home of the Verdurins, Proust reiterates the trope and observes that 'it had so individual, so incomprehensible a charm, that Swann felt as though he had met, in a friend's drawing room, a woman whom he had seen and admired in the street and had despaired of ever seeing again' (1983, p. 231). The characteristics of the *mémoire involontaire*[81] – memories come unbidden, there is surprise engendered by momentary recognition, such memories are enigmatic and elusive, they disappear as suddenly as they come and are never to be seen again – are thus perfectly encapsulated in 'To a Passer-by'. For Benjamin, Baudelaire's sonnet not only constitutes a definitive moment of *modernité*, of the experience of the flâneur; it may also be seen as an image or allegory of the *mémoire involontaire*, of modern metropolitan memory.

At this point one may discern the outline of a particular constellation formed by the conjunction of time (the correspondence of the recent past and the present), space (the city, proximity and distance) and the subject (native, stranger, flâneur). Central to this for Benjamin is the work of Hessel, a writer whose acute metropolitan sensibility and expressivity made him an erotic urban engineer *par excellence*. Benjamin enthusiastically reviewed Hessel's work – in particular, the 1927 novel *Heimliches Berlin* (*Secret Berlin*)[82] and, most notably, the 1929 urban odyssey *Spazieren in Berlin* (*Walking in Berlin*).[83] For Benjamin, Hessel not only provides the definitive contemporary instance of the flâneur as a predatory, privileged reader of the metropolitan environment,[84] but also reconstrues him as a figure of remembrance – indeed, as the subject/object of memory. For the flâneur, the city is not simply a semiological universe to be deciphered, but also a mnemonic setting which is both imbued with, and evocative of, memories.[85] The cityscape bears the lingering imprint of the past and of those who are no more,[86] traces which serve as a series of prompts to the present-day pedestrian. Indeed, the shock experience characteristic of the flâneur results not only from the jostling crowd, but also from the jolts of memory.[87] The flâneur is, in his idleness and absent-mindedness, open to such contingencies as moments of 'anamnestic intoxication' (McCole, 1993, p. 255). His receptivity to recollections derives from his observation of the cityscape in a state of distraction, that same lack of concentration which distinguishes and elevates the film-goer.

Benjamin's review of *Spazieren in Berlin* bears the suggestive title 'The Return of the Flâneur' ('Die Wiederkehr des Flâneurs'). This 'return' takes both temporal and spatial form. On the one hand, the flânerie 'that we thought had been finally relegated to the past' makes a surprise reappearance 'in Berlin of all places, where it never really flourished' (*SW2*, p. 263). The flâneur who was inelegantly elbowed off the Parisian boulevards and/or degenerated into the abject sandwich-man is miraculously reincarnated in contemporary Berlin. On the other hand, the traveller/exile returns to the city of his or her birth with the perceptiveness and purpose which only a true native possesses. Walking in Berlin, the adult returns to his or her childhood:

> The superficial pretext – the exotic and the picturesque – appeals only to the outsider. To depict a city as a native would calls for other, deeper motives – the motives of the person who journeys into the past, rather than to foreign parts. The account of the city given by a native will always have something in common with memoirs; it is no accident that the writer has spent his childhood there. (*SW2*, p. 262)

Hessel's reflections provide the decisive inspiration for Benjamin's own Berlin recollections: the 'Berlin Chronicle' and 'A Berlin Childhood around 1900'. These clearly 'have something in common with memoirs', but Benjamin also stresses that they should not be understood simply as autobiographical:

> Reminiscences, even extensive ones, do not always amount to an autobiography. And these quite certainly do not, even for the Berlin years that I am exclusively concerned with here. For autobiography has to do with time, with sequence and what makes up the continuous flow of life. Here, I am talking of space, of moments and discontinuities. (*OWS*, p. 316)

Indeed, there is a whole complex series of dialectical plays within the Berlin studies which point beyond the parameters of autobiography: between space and time, memory and flânerie, distance and proximity, voluntary and involuntary memory, adult and child, the 'at first' and the 'at last sight'.

The Berlin writings articulate a complex relationship between the city and individual memory. They present the metropolitan environment as it appears in memory, as a plethora of disparate edifices, images and associations – the modern city remembered. At the same time, this act of recollection takes a particular form – that of the *mémoire involontaire* – which is conditioned by the 'most ruthless demands' (*OWS*, p. 318) of urban existence. Benjamin articulates the distinctive qualities of *urban* memory. The Berlin writings set in play memories both in and of the city.

In the 'Berlin Chronicle', Benjamin reflects upon the possibility of giving memory a spatial form. He notes an enduring concern: 'I have long, indeed for years, played with the idea of setting out the sphere of life – *bios* – graphically on a map. First I envisaged an ordinary map, but now I would incline to a general staff's map of the city centre, if such a thing existed' (*OWS*, p. 295).[88] Attempting, then losing, such a mapping, Benjamin later adds: 'Now, however, reconstructing its outline in thought without directly reproducing it, I should, rather, speak of a labyrinth' (*OWS*, p. 319). The figure of the labyrinth captures not only the perplexing, disorienting urban environment, but also the convolutions and complexities of memory.[89] To lose oneself in memory as one does in the city takes practice. Here the meanderings of the *mémoire involontaire* may themselves be understood as forms of flânerie in time which correspond to the perambulations of the urban stroller. Dreaming, remembering and flânerie share a concern with the intentionless, the imagistic and the intoxicating. These three experiential modes combine in an illuminating passage:

> The flâneur is the creation of Paris. The wonder is that it was not Rome. But perhaps in Rome even dreaming is forced to move along streets that are too well-paved. And isn't the city too full of temples, enclosed squares, and national shrines to be able to enter undivided into the dreams of the passer-by, along with every paving stone, every shop sign, every flight of steps, and every gateway? The great reminiscences, the historical *frissons* – these are all so much junk to the flâneur, who is happy to leave them to the tourist. And he would be happy to trade all his knowledge of artists' quarters, birthplaces, and princely palaces for the scent of a single weathered threshold or the touch of a single tile – that which any old dog carries away. (*SW2*, p. 263)

Two points emerge here: First, one is reminded of Benjamin's description of Atget, though the passage actually pre-dates the photography essay. The connection with photography is significant, though. For Benjamin, Hessel's *Heimliches Berlin* 'is technically close to photomontage' (*SW2*, p. 70). Indeed, if the task of the radical writer is to 'start taking photographs', then Hessel is a pioneer in this regard, a prototypical polytechnical aesthetic engineer of the cityscape. Secondly, the flâneur appears as a figure who is sensitive to, and appreciative of, a secret counter-history of the city, one concealed by its monumental façades and deceptive surfaces. The flâneur not only rubs shoulders with the crowd, he also 'brushes history against the grain'. The city is thereby transformed, not into a text to be read, but into a plethora of overlapping texts, a palimpsest to be deciphered.

The flâneur 'excavates and remembers'. Indeed, the analogy of archaeological exploration becomes a central trope in Benjamin's articulation of the relationship between city and memory, and between different forms of memory:

> He who seeks to approach his own buried past must conduct himself like a man digging. . . . True, for successful excavations a plan is needed. Yet no less indispensable is the cautious probing of the spade in the dark loam, and it is to cheat oneself of the richest prize to preserve as a record merely the inventory of one's discoveries, and not this dark joy of the place of the finding itself. Fruitless searching is as much a part of this as succeeding, and consequently remembrance must not proceed in the manner of a narrative or still less that of a report, but must, in the strictest epic and rhapsodic manner, assay its spade in ever-new places, and in the old ones delve to ever-deeper layers. (*OWS*, p. 314)

Here the work of voluntary and involuntary memory appears as complementary rather than antithetical moments. Both the formal archaeological 'plan' and the serendipity of 'fruitless searching' must play their part if remembrance is to be rewarding. Nevertheless, Benjamin clearly privileges the 'epic and rhapsodic', the discontinuous rhythm of Brechtian theatre and the cunning playfulness of the 'dialectical fairy-tale'.

These temporal and spatial themes are bound up with notions of proximity and distance, intimacy and estrangement, child and adult. On the one hand, the native flâneur is doubly at home: he is not only in his definitive element, the metropolitan environment, but also in that most familiar to him, the city of his birth. On the other, he remains a stranger: he continues to be subject to the alienating tendencies of urban existence, and is remote from his own childhood experiences. Travel into the distance has been replaced by the journey into the past.[90] In Berlin, as in Moscow, 'The instant one arrives, the childhood stage begins' (*OWS*, p. 179). The child, of course, is the ultimate figure of tactile appropriation and appreciation in the realm of objects. In becoming a child once more and/or in remembering one's childhood, one returns to a time when one is 'closely mingled with people and things'. In remembrance, the modern cityscape is subject to a process of 'enlargement'.[91] An intriguing play of perspectives is at work here. The remembering adult, who as a native has long mastered the cityscape in a state of distraction, recalls the impressions and experiences of the child for whom the city was still unfamiliar and unexplored. This gaze of the newcomer is not counterpoised to that of the native, so as to appear naive or credulous. Rather, these ways of seeing are juxtaposed so that they may be recognized as, borrowing Adorno's phrase, the 'torn halves of an integral freedom' (*AP*, p. 123).

Indeed, the 'at first sight' of the child has a special significance for Benjamin. Composed in the early 1930s, the Berlin studies were written just as the Nazi terror began to make life in the German capital impossible for him. They are composed from the precarious position of the prospective refugee rather than the comfortable vantage-point of the native. Benjamin's texts recover his childhood experiences of Berlin at precisely the moment when he is compelled to bid the city a forlorn, final farewell. Berlin becomes legible only in the last throws of departure.[92] 'Berlin Chronicle' and 'A Berlin Childhood around 1900' are thus far more than mere autobiographical exercises. They are fragile constellations constituted at a specific historical moment: when the 'at first sight' of the child intersects with the 'at last sight' of the imminent exile. They are Benjamin's *Tableaux berlinoises*, precious pictures of places past and places passed, written by the leave-taker with the urgency and intensity, the heartache and hopelessness, of 'love at last sight'.

The angel of history and the image of the past

In capturing the cityscape of the recent past, Benjamin's Berlin studies constituted experiments in the writing of a secret, critical history, and thus had an important bearing on the 'Arcades Project'.

Benjamin had long recognized that the *Passagenarbeit* would require its own distinctive epistemological-methodological preface like the earlier *Trauerspiel* study.[93] Although he eventually came to see the Berlin studies as providing an inadequate historiographical model for the prehistory of modernity,[94] Benjamin's fragmentary notes for this prologue, Convolute N ('On the Theory of Knowledge. Theory of Progress'), the now justly celebrated 'Theses on the Concept of History' of 1940, and some of the 'Central Park' entries are unmistakably prefigured by the themes of the 'Chronicle' and 'Childhood': amnesia and remembrance, depiction and discontinuity, the constellation and contestation of past and present. Most significantly, the Proustian notion of the *mémoire involontaire* comes to inspire and inform Benjamin's notion of the 'dialectical image'.

Benjamin's historiographical reflections possess both a destructive and constructive moment. First, they sought to engage critically with conventional historical practices and, in particular, to unmask the falsifications and phantasmagoria of what he termed 'historicism', exemplified by the principles of Gottfried Keller and Leopold von Ranke.[95] Secondly, they were concerned with the elaboration of a radically new set of imperatives and techniques which provide for the genuine, materialist comprehension and representation of the past. These historiographical principles thus bring together in a powerful conjunction two of his most important and long-standing motifs: the continual ruination and reconfiguration of the past in the present – in other words, the concept of afterlife – and the techniques of imagistic construction and composition undertaken by the polytechnical engineer.

In his notes for the 'Theses', Benjamin explicitly identifies what he regards as the three erroneous axioms upon which the historicist vision is based: first, the claim of a 'universal history [*Universalgeschichte*]' (*GS* I, p. 1240); secondly, the privileging of historical narration – that is, history as 'something which permits itself to be recounted' (*GS* I, p. 1240); and thirdly, the insistence upon historical 'empathy'. For the historicist, the past is readily identifiable, comprehensive and unambiguously given. In this sense, its premise is the absence of theory and mediation as such, resulting in that undialectical 'wide-eyed presentation of mere facts' of which Benjamin himself was once accused.[96] For historicism, the duty of the historian is to describe the past in a way that is supposedly uncontaminated by present interests, to 'tell it like it was'. The historian establishes a 'causal connection' (*ILL*, p. 264) between events, and, sequencing them according to a linear logic,[97] relates them as a simple narrative.[98] History is understood as a teleological process, as a continuum characterized by accumulation, development and advance, as benign human progress. For historicism, the past appears 'perfect' – it is finished, complete and free of contemporary impurities; it is readily and impartially open to narration; and it consists in uninterrupted improvement culminating in the enlightened present.

Benjamin presents a vehement critique of such naivety and banality. For him, the past is not fixed and finalized; instead, it is endlessly (re)constructed in its afterlife.[99] The image of the past becomes a source of, and focus for, contemporary struggle and conflict. What has been is always open to (mis)appropriation and erasure. The past is always vulnerable and endangered, and this in turn brings 'the present into a critical state' (N7a,5, *ARC*, p. 471). The genuine historian, the historical materialist, recognizes the need to act decisively under the ominous conditions of today for the sake of this imperilled past. Both past and present are to be understood as part of a 'state of emergency'.[100] Benjamin writes:

> To articulate the past historically does not mean to recognise it 'the way it really was' (Ranke).[101] It means to seize hold of a memory as it flashes up at a moment of danger. . . . The danger affects both the content of the tradition and its receivers. The same threat hangs over both: that of becoming a tool of the ruling classes. . . . Only that historian will have the gift of fanning the spark of hope in the past who is firmly convinced that *even the dead* will not be safe from the enemy if he wins. And this enemy has not ceased to be victorious. (*ILL*, p. 257)

It is the unknown, unremembered, unmourned dead who must be redeemed. The critical historian bears witness to the struggles and sufferings of the nameless dead, those multitudes who have been consigned by conventional historians to the oblivion of forgetting.

For Benjamin, such amnesia is the real consequence of the historical 'empathy' advocated by historicism:

> one asks with whom the adherents of historicism actually empathise. The answer is inevitable: with the victor. And all rulers are heirs of those who conquered before them. Hence, empathy with the victor invariably benefits the ruler. Whoever has emerged victorious participates to this day in the triumphal procession in which the present rulers step over those who are lying prostrate. (*ILL*, p. 258)

But what of the unsuccessful, the downtrodden, those 'lying prostrate'? What of their distinctive history, their rather different tradition? The historical materialist is concerned precisely with this reverse side of history, this silenced, potentially subversive past. Benjamin famously insists that the historian must 'brush history against the grain' (*ILL*, p. 289) to expose its unspoken pact with the powerful.

'The task of history', Benjamin argues, 'is to grasp the tradition of the oppressed' (*GS* I, p. 1236),[102] for within it lies the inspiration for the revolutionary struggles of the present.[103] It is a broken history, a discontinuous history punctuated by catastrophe.[104] From the viewpoint of the oppressed, 'progress' is only the refinement of technical means for the ever more intensified exploitation and domination of nature and humankind. Here Benjamin consciously breaks not only with historicist thought, but also with orthodox Marxism. In envisaging human history as a teleological process based on the logic of technological change and class conflict, a process leading inexorably to proletarian revolution and the creation of a classless society, Marxism unwittingly colludes in the notion of progress.[105] Benjamin notes, in a trope appealing to the hydraulic engineer, that 'Nothing has corrupted the German working class so much as the notion that it was moving with the current. It regarded technological developments as the fall of the stream with which it thought it was moving' (*ILL*, p. 260). For Benjamin, revolution is not so much the re-channelling of this flow as its damming. Revolutionary transformation is an interruption of history, rather than its culmination. In his notes for the 'Theses' he captures this using a rather different metaphor: 'Marx said revolutions are the locomotives of world history. But perhaps it is quite different. Perhaps revolutions are the grab for the emergency brakes by the generations of humanity travelling in this train' (*GS* I, p. 1232).

Whether an emergency stop or a derailment engineered by a saboteur, the moment of historical rupture is essential.[106] Benjamin, like Baudelaire, harbours the wish of Joshua: to bring the world to a standstill. Here, the influence at work is not so much Marxism as the Messianism characteristic of Benjamin's early writings. The 'Theses' explicitly bring together Judaic and Marxist motifs to form a series of 'theologico-political' fragments. Benjamin begins with the memorable image of a chess-playing 'puppet in Turkish attire', an automaton whose hands are secretly guided by a 'little hunchback', an 'expert chess player' who hides within. Benjamin comments: 'One can imagine a philosophical counterpart to this device. The puppet called 'historical materialism' is to win all the time. It can easily be a match for anyone if it enlists the services of theology, which today, as we know, is wizened and has to keep out of sight' (*ILL*, p. 255). Messianism and historical materialism are strangely complicit in a clandestine conspiracy. This goes beyond theological and political motifs serving as necessary correctives to each other. Benjamin's reflections involve an interpenetration, rather than a juxtaposition, of the language of revolution and that of redemption.[107] In this way, Benjamin aligns – if not equates – the revolutionary punctuation of history by the proletariat with the Messianic cessation of happening occasioned by the advent of the Messiah.[108] Indeed, as Horkheimer points out, Benjamin's vision of the openness of the past, and the concomitant need to 'excavate and remember' the tradition of the oppressed, is shot through with 'theological concepts', and is fundamentally premised upon the notion of a final calling to account, or Day of Judgement.[109]

Furthermore, in the 'Theses', earlier theological figures and motifs are given a new, critical inflection, most notably the *Angelus Novus*. Benjamin presents a revised reading of Klee's inspirational painting. Instead of the 'new angel' as a figure of the fleeting and ephemeral, the image is now that of 'the angel of history' (*ILL*, p. 259), a forlorn witness to the catastrophic course of human history:

> His faced is turned toward the past. Where we perceive a chain of events, he sees one single catastrophe which keeps piling wreckage upon wreckage and hurls it in front of his feet. The angel would like to stay, awaken the dead, and make whole what has been smashed. But a storm is blowing from Paradise; it has got caught in his wings with such violence that the angels can no longer close them. This storm irresistibly propels him into the future to which his back is turned, while the pile of debris before him grows skyward. The storm is what we call progress. (*ILL*, pp. 259–60)

The angel, like the baroque allegorist, is confronted by the *facies hippocratica* of history, the past as a death's head, as a corpse.[110]

Neither this ruinous state of things nor the fractured tradition of the oppressed finds adequate expression as a coherent narrative. Such things can be represented only in fragments, debris and detritus. Accordingly, the materialist historian must pioneer practices appropriate to the disparate and the discontinuous. He or she does not ransack the past for trophies and booty, but rather, salvages its refuse in the sorrowful guise of the ragpicker. Such historical debris is destined for actualization[111] in the struggles of the oppressed of today.[112] The historian explodes the spurious continuum of history,[113] liberates its manifold images, and recomposes them as critical constellations in the present. Surrealist montage accords with the necessity of fragmentary construction, facilitates and foregrounds visual representation, and brings about a revaluation of 'the trivia, the trash' of history which it juxtaposes. Benjamin muses:

> In what ways is it possible to conjoin a heightened graphicness [*Anschaulichkeit*] to the realization of the Marxist method? The first stage in this undertaking will be to carry over the principle of montage into history. That is, to assemble large-scale constructions out of the smallest and most precisely cut components. Indeed, to discover in the analysis of the small individual moment the crystal of the total event. . . . To grasp the construction of history as such. (N2,6, *ARC*, p. 461)

This is an important passage. First, it reiterates the task of historical construction as an exercise in architectural engineering – in particular, as the constitution of significant structures through the patient piecing together of tiny individual components. Secondly, each of the structural fragments contains within it an intimation or image of the totality. The historical ruins and remnants appropriated and actualized by the genuine historian are monads. Historical materialism here becomes an undertaking in redemptive monadology.[114] Thirdly, the origins and true character of the montage principle are clearly disclosed. Benjamin's understanding of montage as a pattern of finely worked monadological fragments is nothing other than a radicalized – perhaps cinematic – version of his own earlier concept of the constellation as mosaic. Hence, the historiographical preface required for the *Passagenarbeit* was to involve not so much a break with the 'Epistemo-Critical Prologue' of the *Trauerspiel* text as a reworking of some of its key methodological elements, their translation into a new political register.

The historical materialist brings together elements of the past and present which, though perhaps inert and harmless in isolation, prove highly unstable and combustible in combination. Surrealist montage served as a model of construction, but Surrealism's intoxication with dream imagery made it an unreliable accomplice for the handling of historical dynamite. Hence, the Proustian inter-weaving of remembrance and forgetfulness comes to displace the language of dreaming and waking in Benjamin's historiographical reflections. The moment of awakening is reconfigured as an instant of recollection in which the present recovers an image from the past, as the 'now of recognisability'.[115] Benjamin describes this intersection of the here and now and then and there as a form of ephemeral illumination: 'It's not that what is past casts its light on what is present, or what is present its light on what is past: rather, image is that wherein what has been comes together in a flash with the now to form a constellation. In other words: image is dialectics at a standstill' (N2a,3, *ARC*, p. 462). 'Dialectics at a standstill', a notion first developed in connection with interruption and the gestural in epic theatre, is a 'caesura' (N10a,3, *ARC*, p. 475) in the historical process both then and now, which enables a constellation to come into momentary being, allows an image to form – the 'dialectical image'. The dialectical image appears at a moment of temporary disturbance and correspondence, within an eddy in the flow of history, at a point of origin. And just as the notion of constellation finds a contemporary counterpart in montage, so perhaps the mystical notion of origin discovers a profane, peculiar parallel for Benjamin in the photographic snapshot or the moment of the cine-matic freeze-frame. Photography, like origin, like the dialectical image, involves a moment of involution in time, an instance of tem-poral concentration and intensification.[116] Appropriately, it is in 'A Small History of Photography' that we find the first intimations of the dialectical image in the concept of the 'spark of contingency' (*OWS*, p. 243) connecting past and present. Indeed, while Ben-jamin's principal metaphor for the dialectical image is that of the lightning flash,[117] Konersmann, among others,[118] astutely observes:

> the metaphor of the photographic snapshot encapsulates and illus-trates several of those attributes which characterise the conditions and modes of this historiography: the transience of the chance which presents itself; the suddenness with which the motif appears; the momentariness of the truth which is said to be established; the fleet-ingness of the spatio-temporal constellation in which one must act; the visualisation of the past as an image which receives its illumina-tion from references to the present. (1991, pp. 73–4)

Moreover, it is in the dialectical image that the historical material-ist perceives and preserves that which has been rendered invisible or inconspicuous in the past, the 'optical unconscious' of history.[119] Dialectical images are small photographs of history. This is perhaps why, for Benjamin as for Roland Barthes, the most compelling and haunting photographic images, those wherein the last vestiges of aura remain, are portraits of the dead, pictures of those who, as Barthes puts it, are dead and are going to die, of those who await 'a catastrophe which has already occurred' (1993, p. 96), such that we, gazing upon their faces, become backward-looking prophets – like the angel of history.

An important distinction needs to be made here: the photograph is an enduring mnemonic device, whereas the dialectical image is an ephemeral moment of remembrance.[120] It is memory which opens up the past to 'endless interpolations', rendering it incomplete and contestable. Benjamin's reply to Horkheimer's invocation of the Last Judgement is telling:

> What science has 'determined,' remembrance can modify. Such mindfulness can make the incomplete (happiness) into something complete, and the complete (suffering) into something incomplete. That is theology: but in remembrance we have an experience that forbids us to conceive of history as fundamentally atheological, little as it may be granted us to try to write it with immediately theological concepts. (N8,1, *ARC*, p. 471)

The dialectical image equates with a particular form of remembrance, that which is sudden and spontaneous, intentionless yet intense – the *mémoire involontaire*. Benjamin writes that 'Historical knowledge is only possible in a historical moment. Knowledge in a historical moment is, however, always knowledge from a particular moment. As the past coalesces in such a moment – forms a dialectical image – it enters the *mémoire involontaire* of humanity' (*GS* I, p. 1233). The dialectical image, like the *mémoire involontaire*, is a moment of redemption,[121] one prompted by the most transient and trivial of traces: a glimpse, a scent, a taste, a phrase. The dialectical image apprehends that which is about to vanish for ever:

> the true picture of the past flits by. The past can be seized only as an image which flashes up at the instant when it can be recognised and is never seen again. 'The truth will not run away from us': in the historical outlook of historicism these words of Gottfried Keller mark the exact point where historical materialism cuts through historicism.

For every image of the past that is not recognised by the present as one of its own concerns threatens to disappear irretrievably. (*ILL*, p. 257)

It is in this fragment that the full significance and importance of Baudelaire's 'To a Passer-by' emerges. For Benjamin, the sonnet is much more than an exemplary instance of the experience and aesthetic of *modernité*, the pleasures and pangs of the passing moment. It is more, indeed, than an image of the Proustian *mémoire involontaire*, the elusive evocation of places and times past. *À une passante* is nothing less than an image of (the image of) history, an allegory of the dialectical image. A beautiful, beguiling figure is spied fleetingly among the swirling crowd by the world-weary flâneur. Glances are exchanged, love is glimpsed. And then the apparition vanishes for ever into the metropolitan multitude. It is as if the new angel were to appear not in the presence of God, but before the angel of history. And the sonnet is a testimony to this moment. The historian, like the poet, must give voice to this brief encounter, must safeguard its promise. 'To a Passer-by' is an allegory of the hope of redemption and the redemption of hope. Benjamin's historical vision is ultimately and inevitably the precious, passionate look of love at last sight.

Conclusion

Whereas Benjamin explicitly envisaged his *Trauerspiel* study as the moment of closure of his 'German cycle' of texts in the mid-1920s, the subsequent 'Parisian cycle' initiated by *Einbahnstrasse* was never completed. The motifs and themes which preoccupied Benjamin find expression in a plethora of 'prolegomena', but the project into which they were to be integrated, and from which they were to derive their full significance – his prehistory of modernity – remained unwritten. In many ways, of course, this is appropriate for a thinker who preferred the delights of digression to the relief of arrival, the 'charmed circle of fragments' to completions and conclusions. Indeed, Benjamin's own assessment of his work cannot be bettered – 'small-scale victories' offset by 'large-scale defeats' (*GER*, p. 14).[122] But we should also remember that for Benjamin the principle of construction was fundamental. Fragments were not to remain in isolation, but were to be brought together in mosaics, montages and constellations, because it is only in their composition and juxtaposition that these individual elements would form legible images, would allow for mutual profane illumination and prove explosive.

And so in this final chapter I have endeavoured to bring together a number of Benjamin's key themes of the 1930s drawn from a plethora of his 'small-scale victories': allegory, melancholy and the commodity; the transformation of art, aesthetics and experience in the modern metropolis; flânerie, shock and remembrance; catastrophe, redemption and hope. These form a constellation which has at its centre, I have argued, Baudelaire's sonnet *À une passante*. Indeed, they are the motifs which Benjamin 'finds' at the heart of Baudelaire's work once it has been 'brushed against the grain' – though they are, of course, very much his own preoccupations. Benjamin thus appropriates Baudelaire for his critique of modernity just as he had earlier claimed Goethe for immanent critique. This, for Benjamin, is Baudelaire's actuality. Moreover, the Parisian poet is not just 'actual', but also exemplary. For just as Baudelaire as 'hero' sought to hold on to the possibility of experience and beauty amid their very ruination in the 'era of high capitalism', so Benjamin as historian seeks to grasp the possibility of a radical critique of modernity amid the prevailing 'state of emergency'.

This task is, *contra* Adorno, a highly dialectical undertaking for Benjamin. Indeed, he derives his conceptual arsenal precisely from the characteristic experiences of modernity itself: flânerie and distraction, shock and the *mémoire involontaire*, fragmentation and discontinuity. These were not merely to be read against the grain; they were also to be re-engineered in the struggles of the present. For Benjamin, the flâneur is no longer an idle fop, but a figure who reads the city, appropriates its spaces and edifices through habit, and remembers its past. Distraction leads not to apathy and boredom, but to a relaxed expertise and critical recognition. Shock does not engender amnesia, but results in indelible memories, and prompts our most precious recollections. The fissures and fractures of the tradition of the oppressed permit a sure grasp which refuses to relinquish them. Fragmentation provides the detritus, the refuse of history, which is to be redeemed by the Critical Theorist as ragpicker. In the *Passagenarbeit*, Benjamin was to unfold the contradictions of the commodity form, and thereby implode the dreamworld of the recent past. In his Baudelaire studies, he starts to turn the *experiences* of the modern back upon modernity itself. Benjamin seeks to disenchant modernity through enchantment. Even – indeed, especially – as we are beset by horrors and death approaches, the dialectical fairy tale imbues us with cunning and high spirits, hope for the hopeless.

Conclusion: Towards a Contemporary Constellation

Afterlife

This Conclusion is Janus-faced. It is retrospective, in that it seeks to recapitulate some of the main ideas and concepts found in Benjamin's work that have been discussed in the preceding chapters. In so doing, I return to the six key themes identified in the Introduction: cultural fragmentation, consumption and commodification, metropolitanism, mass mediation and reproduction, technological change and historical progress, and alienation and the situation of the intellectual. It is also forward-looking, in that I am also concerned to suggest some of the links between Benjamin's concepts and motifs and those of more recent social theorists and critics of modernity. Here Benjamin's concepts of afterlife and the polytechnical engineer, the leitmotifs of this book, are indispensable. His understanding of the way in which meaning – of a text or of a historical event – is continually being reconstituted and reconfigured through textual mortification, political appropriation and individual/collective remembrance leads to the fundamental insight that the work of art is legible in specific ways only at particular historical moments – that is to say, as past and present interests intersect, as a critical constellation is formed. He thereby offers a way of understanding the ongoing (re)interpretation, (re)construction and (re)assessment of *his own texts* by subsequent commentators. In this way, of course, one might begin to sketch a plethora of potentially fruitful connections and contributions, all demanding further exploration and careful elaboration. What follows, then, is not intended as an exhaustive or definitive exercise, but rather is to be understood as an indication of some aspects of the actuality of Benjamin's work, a gesture towards a few key points in a contemporary constellation.

Although tentative, this is not such an innocuous or innocent undertaking as it might seem. On the one hand, much Benjamin scholarship appears to be conceived as an exclusively philological enterprise, one intended to recover or discover the 'true' Benjamin, the 'real meaning' of his words and texts, rather than their contemporary resonance (and this book itself is perhaps not immune to such a charge). This is rather ironic, of course, given Benjamin's own rejection of 'authorial intention' as the touchstone for interpretation and criticism, and his insistence upon the 'topicality' of cultural phenomena. On the other hand, the reception of Benjamin's work has been so filtered through the evaluative and, importantly, editorial work of Adorno, and then of his students, like Rolf Tiedemann, that for some Benjamin scholars the mere mention of his name alongside that of, say, the French sociologist and *provocateur* Jean Baudrillard, would, notwithstanding Benjamin's own Parisian predilections, be considered an unpardonable heresy. My principal purpose is not to provoke, however, but rather, in accord with Benjamin's own precepts, to encourage the processes of thinking in a 'polar climate', in extremes, of collecting and juxtaposing apparently disparate ideas and concepts for the purpose of mutual illumination. And so as an indication of a contemporary constellation, this final part of the book is written not so much in the spirit of a conclusion, but rather as a point of origin, as the incentive for further interpretations of, and engagements with, Benjamin's writings as part of a vital literary and theoretical afterlife.

The tremendous diversity of contemporary readings of Benjamin's work notwithstanding, the prevailing tendency has been, perhaps not surprisingly, to envisage Benjamin as an outlying star of, or some kind of brilliant comet orbiting within, the constellation of the Frankfurt School, at the centre of which stands Theodor Adorno. And there is clearly much to be said for such a view. Undeniably, Benjamin's and Adorno's friendship had a profound influence upon the writings of both men. Benjamin's writings clearly prefigure some of the most important concerns of subsequent Critical Theory – the elaboration of a complex historical materialist understanding of the cultural and ideological sphere, the transformation of art and the relationship between high and popular/mass culture in modernity, the envisioning of the catastrophic course of the historical process and the concomitant critique of the claims of Enlightenment and progress. But this should not blind us to the possibility that there might also be *other constellations, other readings,* which might situate Benjamin within rather different historical and theoretical configurations.[1] Read against the grain, Benjamin might be seen, for example, as an unwitting precursor of certain ideas and motifs in contemporary post-structuralist and post-modernist thinking. Could Benjamin's critique of modernity be understood by an archaeologist of *our* 'recent past' as the 'prehistory of *post-modernity*'? This much is certain: if Benjamin is indeed a star in the current academic firmament, it is because, in various ways, his work enters into a particularly fortuitous constellation with contemporary intellectual preoccupations and practices – not least, with the writings of other intellectual stars. In my view, Benjamin's themes and concepts find distinct, if distant, echoes in the writings of other major critics of modernity and modern culture: Roland Barthes (the death of authorial intention, everyday commodity culture as a significatory and mythological system, the interplay of photography, memory and history), Jean-François Lyotard (fragmentation and the end of 'grand narratives'), Jacques Derrida[2] (mortification/deconstruction of the text, notions of 'trace' and the deferral of meaning), Michel Foucault (the architecture of visibility/invisibility, the fragmentation of the body, the critique of narratives of 'progress'), and even, my emphasis here and elsewhere,[3] Jean Baudrillard (commodity culture; media, reproduction and simulation; cityscapes, seduction and fatal strategies). In short, Benjamin's writings have a particular presence today because they have a special pertinence today – he is very much a key contemporary thinker.

Ragpicking

The reader who searches the writings of Benjamin for a coherent, integrated, systematic critique of modernity will do so in vain. Indeed, his intellectual legacy may disappoint those who seek comprehensive explanatory schemes, those who, as Benjamin scornfully puts it in *Einbahnstrasse*, 'take an inimitable pleasure in conclusions, feeling themselves thereby given back to life' (*OWS*, p. 48). This is perhaps as it should be. For what fascinated him then is what remains now – tesserae, ruins, traces, building blocks, fragments of and for fragmentary times. These provide an embarrassment of riches for the theoretical ragpicker and a thematic, conceptual armoury for the radical critic of contemporary culture. Prefiguring the 'cultural turn' in social and cultural theory, Benjamin's writings break with both the sentimental bourgeois aesthetic categories – authorial intention, solitary genius, poetic inspiration and creativity – which have plagued literary criticism, and with the crudities of orthodox Marxist cultural analyses – art as reflection, as epiphenomenon, as bourgeois ideology or as proletarian class consciousness-raiser. He develops instead a complex, sophisticated understanding of the relationship between cultural products/texts and the socio-economic, ideological and historical conditions which they 'express', mediate and transform. He explores the metropolitan environment as the quintessential site of modern experience in terms of processes of intensification, disorientation, privatization and commodification. He is alert to how the commodity form and consumerist fantasies both shape and are shaped by the modern cityscape. He is relatively quick to respond to, and embrace, new media technologies, seeking both to understand their impact upon traditional art and aesthetics and to realize their inherent political potential. Repudiating the claims of technological and scientific progress, he is acutely sensitive to those neglected by conventional histories and to the profound and painful necessity of remembrance. Immanent criticism, allegorical ruination, explosive engineering, tactile appropriation, imagistic construction, historical redemption – in these imperatives and strategies Benjamin the polytechnical critic of modernity has left us what was most precious to him: not finished works, but the tools and tricks of the trade.

Cultural fragmentation

The world is splintered into fragments, is legible only in fragments, and is representable solely through fragments – these are axiomatic for Benjamin and have come to have an increasing importance in social and cultural theory. His interest in the *Trauerspiel*, in particular, was sparked by the recognition that the bleak, broken world of the baroque might have a special significance for, an 'elective affinity' with, his own time, convulsed as it was by the carnage of the Great War, the financial turmoil and inflation of the Weimar years, and a sense of cultural crisis. Ruins and remnants are all that survive such calamitous events and the shattering of ontological certainties and existential consolations.[4] They perhaps have an acute relevance, too, for the post-modern condition today, defined in terms of the obsolescence and collapse of venerable 'grand narratives' (Lyotard, 1984); a radical scepticism with respect to the grand claims of science, humanism and 'progress'; a privileging of eclecticism, alterity, irony and the sublime; and a pervasive sense of melancholy,[5] boredom,[6] and *acedia*.[7] As totalizing theoretical systems with their universal ambitions and teleological promises become ever less tenable, we are left to play ruefully with their broken pieces, to survey their grandiose foundations, now understood as vainglorious ruins.

For Benjamin, as we have seen, the shattered condition of modernity demanded particular techniques of reading and writing: the world was to be deciphered in the monad, and recomposed in the mosaic or montage. If this predilection for, and sensitivity to, the fragmentary seems to have fallen out of favour with the so-called second generation of Frankfurt School writers, like Jürgen Habermas, it is nevertheless vital to the work of cultural critics like Barthes and Baudrillard, writers who are, like Benjamin, profoundly influenced by the intellectual legacy of the Surrealists. Barthes's critical reading of capitalist culture from a plethora of its marginalia and trivia in *Mythologies* (1973) might be seen as a *locus classicus* of the technique of monadological analysis, and Baudrillard (1988) makes the so-called holographic method central to his eccentric American odyssey.[8] In each of these studies, the most precise unfolding and suggestive juxtaposing of microscopic and heterogeneous manifestations of the quotidian realm are for the purpose of their radical disenchantment and demythification. Benjamin's textual shock tactics – the apposite aphorism, the quotation out of context, montage – certainly have a special attraction for the social theorist in the era of late capitalism.

As we have seen, Benjamin's concern with the 'recreation' of criticism leads to the foregrounding of immanent criticism as an unfolding of the text, as the continual (re)constitution of its meaning in its afterlife. This concept of criticism also prefigures some important post-structuralist and post-modern principles. Immanent criticism seeks neither to (re)discover some privileged authorial purpose nor to impose the canonical aesthetic judgements of self-appointed expert arbiters of 'taste'. Rather, it recognizes that the meaning of a text is determined by the critical constellation it enters into in and with the present. This involves both a 'decentring' of the author and a privileging of reading and interpretation understood as historically specific, 'situated' practices. Textual meaning is never fixed and finalized, but always contingent, open to 'endless inter-polations', infinitely subject to Derridean deferral. As the notion of allegory suggests, textual meanings are manifold and multiple, characterized by a radical ambiguity and indeterminacy. Texts are 'daemonic'. The importance and radicalism of what Benjamin is demanding here should not be underestimated. Immanent criticism opens up the possibility – indeed, the necessity – of challenging and disturbing the dominant, established meanings attributed to liter-ary texts, artworks and all other cultural products. Culture is not a sphere of eternal values, but is here conceptualized as a domain of bitterly contested meanings. Moreover, this contestation is to be understood not as arcane aesthetic debates, but rather as a vital part of contemporary political struggles.

For the radical critic, the whole of modern culture must be 'brushed against the grain' of conventional interpretation. Tradi-tional cultural hierarchies distinguishing high and popular/mass cultural forms, hitherto neglected and disdained aesthetic ideas and genres, and distinctions between supposed canonical and banal 'lesser works' – all these categories and judgements of 'bourgeois' criticism are to be destabilized and exploded. Benjamin's texts zealously undertake this sabotage. The *Trauerspiel* study overturns the prevailing assessment, such as it was, of these obscure baroque dramas, and rehabilitates allegory as a legitimate linguistic figure. *Einbahnstrasse* castigates established German scholarship and letters, and privileges new, direct literary forms – slogans, pamphlets and manifestos. 'The Author as Producer' denounces the preten-sions of the artist as 'creative genius', reconfiguring the writer as a technical worker. The most profound theological and philosoph-ical ideas are not to be found in 'fat books', but are to be concealed within radio broadcasts for children. Read against the grain, Baude-laire's poetry and Proust's remembrances intricately express and critically articulate the experiences and tendencies of modern metropolitan existence. Such plays and reversals have a particular appeal for those who argue for textual deconstruction, for the ruth-less interrogation and debunking of aesthetic conventions, and for the liberating possibilities attending the post-modern implosion of high and popular cultural forms.

For Benjamin, the cultural crisis of his time was not a source of lamentation, but an opportunity to be grasped. The tradition of the oppressed is, after all, long acquainted with such ruptures and fis-sures, for it exists in a perpetual state of emergency. The destruc-tive moment in Benjamin's work – ruination, mortification – is concerned with exacerbating the contradictions of bourgeois culture, bringing them to the point of combustion. The critic then sifts the debris of this explosion for what is worth salvaging, if anything, for the purpose of construction according to a radically new pattern – mosaic, montage, constellation. Afterlife and polytechnical engineering – these concepts are the key to Benjamin's attempt to 'recreate criticism as a genre', and ensure that this is conceived as nothing less than a complete cultural revolution.

Consumption and commodification

Benjamin identifies two main foci for the crisis of bourgeois culture and the ruination of experience: the proliferation of the commodity form and the alienation of urban existence. These are, of course, intimately connected in Benjamin's *Passagenarbeit* and his related studies of Baudelaire, in which commodity consumption is envisaged as the very *hallmark* of metropolitan modernity. As we have seen, Benjamin is indebted to Lukács for the fundamental insight that the historical materialist critique of capitalism must have the analysis of the commodity form at its centre. With this in mind, he breaks with the orthodox Marxist preoccupation with the sphere of commodity production, pioneering instead a subtle, sophisticated critique of consumption in terms of commodity fetishism and the phantasmagoria of fashion, advertising and spectacle which attend it. Moreover, commodity fetishism is itself to be understood as a complex fusion of elements drawn not only from the Marxist tradition, but also from Freud and the Surrealists, an integration of economic and sexual motifs which prefigures the work of later Critical Theorists like Marcuse (1964). Benjamin thereby comes to offer a highly differentiated account of the industrial product as a dream object, a wish image which contains both mythic and utopian aspects. The fetishism of the commodity is not simply to be dismissed as 'false consciousness' or ideological mystification; it is to be unfolded so that its antithetical moments can be set in play. In Benjamin's 'dialectical fairy tale' the commodity is to be imploded, and its genuine aspiration redeemed.

Benjamin's analysis of fashion also involves this intricate articulation of contradictions to critical effect. Drawing heavily upon Simmel's understanding of fashion as social differentiation, Benjamin conceives fashion as the natural history of the commodity. Fashion both fetishizes and de-fetishizes the commodity. On the one hand, fashion is duplicitous; it is the illusion of novelty attending the always-the-same. On the other, fashion produces the unfashionable, the outdated and obsolete. Fashion brings ruination and ridicule. Here again, for Benjamin, it is the interplay of these contradictory moments inherent within modernity and commodity culture that is decisive. Modernity is to be subject to immanent critique, disenchanted through enchantment.

The reversal of meaning and ruination of the commodity during the course of its afterlife suggest an important parallel to Benjamin, one which becomes central to his reading of Baudelaire: the correspondence between the commodity form and allegory as a literary device. Benjamin draws upon this connection to envisage the commodity culture of the recent past as a world whose meaning and significance have been hollowed out, as a counterpart to the God-forsaken creaturely condition of the baroque. What is important here is that the elective affinity between the commodity and allegory begins to establish a relationship between the seemingly disparate spheres of economic production, on the one hand, and forms of signification, on the other. Commodities are associated with signs, *become signs* – this is a fundamental insight for Barthes in his conception of the mythological functions of objects, and also, in more radical form, for Jean Baudrillard's (1996 and 1998) envisioning of the 'system of objects' as a linguistic or semiological universe. The consumer buys commodities not just for their use-value, but also – sometimes solely – for what they represent, for what they signify. Objects have a connotative value, or, as Baudrillard puts it, a 'sign value'. Commodities stand for something else – status, prestige, taste. In this sense, we consume them as allegories. Such a view, central to our contemporary understanding of commodities and consumption practices, may go well beyond Benjamin's formulation – but is certainly indebted to it.

The commodity was to be the key category for Benjamin's prehistory of modernity. For him, consumption was the key to, and had to be located within, wider cultural contexts and patterns: fashion, advertising and display; architecture, design and lighting; notions of progress and technological change; and fantasy, fetishism and sexuality. As we have seen, however, it was not the commodity form as such that was to serve as Benjamin's monadological element for the *Passagenarbeit*, but rather the shopping arcade. The arcades are of the greatest significance for the critique of contemporary consumer culture. In their phantasmagorical construction and duplicitous inversion of space, these pioneering forms of the architecture of consumption are readily recognizable as the precursors of today's shopping malls with their sanitized street simulations and themed interiors. Displacing the downtown department stores which were the immediate heirs of the arcades, these air-conditioned dream-worlds of consumption today are increasingly the principal settings for the spectacular proliferation of the commodity form and the seductive superabundance of signs and images. As such, they are frequently subject to the same descriptive vocabulary that Benjamin used to designate their forebears: cathedrals of consumption, temples to the fetish commodity. Baudrillard's (1998, pp. 25–6) account of the Parley 2 'drug-store' (a prototypical mall) as a 'jungle' of exotic, 'proliferating vegetation' clearly echoes Benjamin's account of the arcade as an anachronistic 'aquarium' with 'deep sea fauna',[9] as a modern menagerie[10] or now-fossilized 'primeval forest'.[11] Arcades, World Exhibitions, winter gardens and panoramas – these are the ancestors of the sham utopian dream-spaces of our own dream-time: malls,[12] theme parks,[13] urban tableaux.[14] And Benjamin was their first critical physiognomist. One might speculate as to what it will be like to confront the mega-malls of today when they are ruined and abandoned, when they fascinate the Surrealists and critical theorists of fifty years hence. But this much seems certain: we are ever more surrounded by kitschy corporate fairy-tale worlds-in-miniature, worlds which the 'dialectical fairy tales' of today must cunningly undo.

Metropolitanism

Benjamin was fascinated by metropolitan space, experience and culture, and came to focus his critique of modernity upon the two cities which attracted him most: Berlin and Paris. This paradox captures his own ambiguous response to urban life. On the one hand, the city was at the forefront of intellectual life and cultural innovation and change. It was an environment of dynamism, energy and stimulation, of revolutionary possibilities. It was home to the fleeting, the fragmentary, the fortuitous. It promised electrifying encounters, seductive labyrinths and erotic adventures. Where else could the engineer operate? On the other, the metropolis was the pre-eminent locus of capitalism with all its mystifications and miseries. The city housed the mythic forms of modernity: dreamworlds, fetishes, phantasmagoria, monuments to progress. It was a site of exploitation, alienation and amnesia. The engineer must reduce it to rubble. Hence Benjamin's characterization of Baudelaire as a writer for whom metropolitan existence was absolutely indispensable, if also in the same moment utterly intolerable, is, of course, a self-portrait too.

For Benjamin, the urban *was* the modern, and the space in which it could be read. He articulates a fragmentary, critical physiognomy of the cityscape which is concerned with deciphering urban objects and structures, with making them legible as hieroglyphs, signs and rebuses. Under his gaze, the city is transformed into a 'semiotic universe', a text.[15] And this reading concentrated upon the most marginal and contemporary of phenomena as monadological fragments: Neapolitan swindlers, Muscovite tram rides, memories of the Tiergarten, derelict buildings on the verge of demolition. The *Passagenarbeit* was to be the most ambitious of such readings – an experiment intended to trace the contours and fate of an entire epoch by means of an architectural or urban archaeological monadology, an undertaking which anticipates more recent attempts to discern the cultural conditions and logic of 'late' modernity in terms of particular urban edifices.[16]

In his urban *Denkbilder*, his reflections on Berlin and his writings on Baudelaire, Benjamin introduces one of the most suggestive and frequently invoked figures in discussions of metropolitan experience and urban (and visual) culture: the flâneur.[17] The 'sandwichman' is most assuredly *not* 'the last incarnation of the flâneur' (M19,2, *ARC*, p. 565).[18] Indeed, the recent afterlife of this eccentric figure has been truly spectacular. The heroic pedestrian has been reconfigured (and regendered) as a trope to elucidate a plethora of urban (and virtual) practices, activities and experiences. The flâneur has become the prototypical sociologist,[19] the embodiment of the privileged male gaze, the focus of debate concerning the absence/presence of woman in the city,[20] and an exemplary model for streetwise radicals, subversives and Situationists.[21] The flâneur has returned in a manifold of guises: as shopper, tourist and traveller; as channel-hopper and sampler; and as internet browser and cybersurfer.[22] One reading envisages the flâneur as the quintessential post-modern pedestrian: the banal seeker of distraction within the pseudo-public spaces of the post-modern city.[23] Another conceives him or her as an intrepid expert in the knowing, nonchalant use of public space.[24] To be a flâneur is to walk without fear in the modern city – what could be more appealing to an age witnessing the militarization of urban space,[25] the 'strategic uglification' of the post-modern cityscape? The flâneur has been transformed into the utopian urbanite.[26]

The flâneur has a particular relevance for post-modern theory beyond such identifications and debates. He or she is the ultimate figure of fragmentation, limitation and motion. As a wanderer in the city, it is the flâneur who lacks an overview of the metropolitan whole, who is denied any panoramic or bird's-eye perspective. Even if the very embodiment of the male gaze, the flâneur is not a privileged spectator, because she or he is granted only an ant's-eye view. The flâneur is a limited witness of a complexity which eludes her or his vision and understanding, a melancholy, 'heroic' actor buffeted by forces but dimly perceived. Indeed, the flâneur is a part of that which she or he observes. She or he watches the crowd, and is a member (however reluctantly) of that crowd. Spectator and spectacle coincide. As part of the crowd, the flâneur is a figure in perpetual motion – there is no safe and stable perspective from which to behold events, but only a series of briefly held positions offering glimpses of a world in flux. Imploding subject and object, partial in scope, situated yet shifting, the vision of the flâneur provocatively prefigures that of the post-modern writer[27] and social theorist. The flâneur and flâneuse today are fascinating, fascinated, forlorn figures lost in cyberspace, lost in hyperspace.[28] Aren't we all?

Mass mediation and reproduction

Benjamin's positive evaluation of the radical potential of film, radio and photography provides a welcome counterpoint and much needed corrective to the seemingly indiscriminate tirade against the culture industry penned by Horkheimer and Adorno. Indeed, only Benjamin and Kracauer among the Frankfurt School writers genuinely appreciate and explore the complexities of new visual media and the consequences of the mass reproducibility of images. Benjamin's concern was twofold. First, he sought to develop a new – and still suggestive – conceptual vocabulary for the analysis of photographic and cinematic images: the 'optical unconscious', the 'spark of contingency', 'exhibition value', 'distraction', and, most importantly, the notion of 'aura'.[29] These ideas do not form a coherent theory of photography and film, but they mark an important first step – the recognition that the language of conventional aesthetics was inapplicable to these forms, indeed, was no longer valid even for traditional art. Herein lies Benjamin's most significant contribution: his prescient recognition of the fundamental transformation of the artwork occasioned by the advent of new technologies of reproducibility and the move from the dichotomy of original/ fake to an endless series of identical terms. For Baudrillard (1993 and 1994), Benjamin thereby identifies a fundamental stage in the history of representation, one which has now given way to an era distinguished by the precession of simulacra, by the primacy of the model, the 'fake'. The demise of aura and the proliferation of the copy suggested and endorsed in the 'Work of Art' essay are given a bitter, doleful inflection by Baudrillard in his vision of the end of seduction and the constitution of the more real than real, the 'hyperreal'.

The fate of the image under the conditions of modernity – nothing was more important for Benjamin than this. He is, as we are, everywhere and always preoccupied by the realm of images. And for him, importantly, visual media and phenomena are both the objects of analysis and the method of their textual reconstruction and representation – an eminently immanent approach, and one that finds a contemporary corollary in, for example, Baudrillard's concern with imagistic 'fatal strategies'.[30] Like Simmel, Benjamin identifies the preponderance of visual stimuli as one of the hallmarks of urban experience. He sought, moreover, to render the kaleidoscopic cityscape explicitly in optical terms: the thought-image, the dream-image, the mirror-image and the mosaic or montage. The photographs of Atget pumped the aura out of the abandoned cityscape; film uncovers its labyrinthine secrets and explodes its most mournful settings with the dynamite of the 'tenth of a second'. And, most importantly, the counter-history of the metropolis, the tradition of the oppressed, can be captured only as a fleeting picture, as the dialectical image, the historical snapshot. Like the cityscape, the past breaks down, Benjamin claims, into images, not stories, and it is this broken-down history that is most precious. The genuine historian must undertake an imagistic apprenticeship, must 'start taking photographs'. He or she must become an optical engineer.

Technological change and historical 'progress'

Benjamin is important not only for the history of the image, but also for the image of history. And this image of history, of the recent past, of the prehistory of modernity, is perhaps the most bitter and biting element of his critique. His historiographical 'Theses' interweave theological and historical materialist motifs to unmask progress as the ultimate myth of modernity. Scientific progress and technological innovation ensure the ever more ruthless domination and exploitation of nature for ever greater capitalist profit; social progress and improvement are thin veneers concealing the nothing-new of alienation and injustice. Rejecting both Enlightenment and orthodox Marxist understandings of historical change and teleology, Benjamin argues that human emancipation does not reside in the mere overcoming of scarcity through the instrumental utilization of nature, nature here conceived as mere material for human purposes and satisfactions, but rather only in the development of a harmonious relationship with nature. In so doing, Benjamin prefigures *the* principal theme of subsequent Critical Theory – the predominance of instrumental rationality as the 'eclipse of reason' itself, the self-negation, the 'dialectic of enlightenment'[31] – and provides a prescient warning of the ecological and environmental destruction occasioned by capitalist avarice and expansion. For Benjamin's prehistory of modernity it was axiomatic that 'catastrophe is progress, progress is the catastrophe' (*GS* I, p. 1244), and that this in turn leads to the inevitable 'definition of the present as catastrophe' (*GS* I, p. 1243). The critical historian who, like the angel of history, is witness to the piling of the horrors of the recent past upon those which preceded it, is aware that genuine human liberation is to be achieved only in the interruption, the cessation of history.

The 'Theses' point to the construction and fabrication of history. History is made in the image and interests of those who have won in the past and are powerful in the present – hence its characterization as progress. Benjamin recognizes the significance of the cultural sphere in this. Culture is no innocent bystander – the cultural tradition is deeply implicated in the course of catastrophic history. He writes:

> Whoever has emerged victorious participates to this day in the triumphal procession in which the present rulers step over those who are lying prostrate. According to traditional practice, the spoils are carried along in the procession. They are called cultural treasures, and a historical materialist views them with cautious detachment. For without exception the cultural treasures he surveys have an origin which he cannot contemplate without horror. They owe their existence not only to the efforts of the great minds and talents who have created them, but also to the anonymous toil of their contem-

poraries. There is no document of civilisation which is not at the same time a document of barbarism. And just as such a document is not free of barbarism, barbarism taints also the manner in which it was transmitted from one owner to another. A historical materialist dissociates himself from it as far as possible. (*ILL*, pp. 258–9)

This is an important passage. Here Benjamin's notion of recreating criticism as a form of cultural revaluation and revolution combines with his vision of history – culture, and especially 'high culture', *Kultur*, the great and the good, the Arnoldian best that has been said and done in the world, is to be viewed with 'horror'. It is contaminated by both the circumstances attending its original production – for every Michelangelo commissioned by the Pope, how many anonymous victims of the Inquisition? – and those of its transmission, its afterlife. Nor is this merely to be brushed against the grain. Benjamin advocates not just a a counter-history, but also a *counter-culture* of modernity. It is the duty of the critic as cultural historian, the historian as cultural critic, to reveal and redeem the past of those who are powerless in the present – the poor, the oppressed, the downtrodden and disadvantaged, women, workers, persecuted ethnic minority groups and dispossessed indigenous peoples. He or she must remember the sufferings of the forgotten dead, and redeem their traces for the sake of the living. Benjamin's 'Theses' are a final trumpet call to the awaken the dead, an alarm call to those who dream, a call to arms in the struggle to rethink the past so as to refashion the present and future. Benjamin articulates a politics, not an 'aesthetics' (Wolin, 1982), of redemption.

'Alienation' and the intellectual

Given his highly precarious position, it is not surprising that Benjamin should devote so much time to the identification and elaboration of the tasks and techniques of the radical critic and historian. For him, the notion of the 'independent writer', whether as artist or as intellectual, was a fiction. He also rejected the notion of intellectual and artistic commitment as a failure to perceive the true condition and position of the contemporary writer. Following Baudelaire, following Kracauer,[32] Benjamin's modern intellectual sets up home in the only place possible – among the 'homeless', among the other exiles, vagabonds and ragpickers,[33] among the other lowly 'heroes' of modernity. The genuine, revolutionary thinker makes common cause with the alienated, the dispossessed, the downtrodden, because he or she is one of them.[34] They are all 'companions in misfortune' (Kracauer, 1995, p. 129). The historical materialist is the heir, the voice of the 'tradition of the oppressed', its storyteller. I think this is how Benjamin finally came to envisage himself *then*; I think it is how we can begin to understand him *now*.

Benjamin's texts clearly bear the traces, the stigmata, of the barbarism of his own time, atrocities which haunt us to this day. Indeed, his world is all too recognizable in ours. Exploitation, inequality, injustice, domination, brutality, genocide – progress has brought no respite from these. We still live in a 'state of emergency' with our eyes closed. We slumber in the dream-space and dream-time of the here-and-now. In this context, Benjamin leaves us a set of urgent, enduring imperatives: to 'read what was never written', to recover and represent the fleeting and fragmentary, to remember the forgotten dead and redeem their hopes. And, of course, Benjamin's writings are themselves texts to be redeemed, reconfigured and reinterpreted as part of a vital, critical 'tradition of the oppressed'. To read, recognize and remember Benjamin as a key figure for contemporary social theory is the undertaking to which this book has sought to contribute, however modestly, however imperfectly. It is with this aim that I have attempted to provide an introduction to Benjamin's work. It is a 'leading into' his ideas, an invitation to engage with them, to enter into and form new constellations with them, to actualize them, in the social, political and economic struggles of today. One must become not just the student of his texts, but their engineer. If the present reader is encouraged and inspired to undertake such challenges, this study will have fulfilled its own immodest ambition. This is not a conclusion, but a starting point for endless further interpolations, endless future constellations.

Notes

Introduction: Benjamin as a Key Contemporary Thinker

1   An original research thesis above and beyond the doctoral dissertation and a prerequisite for an academic post within the German university system.
2   See, e.g., Caygill, 1998, p. xi.
3   Susan Sontag's famous 1979 characterization of Benjamin as melancholy outsider born 'under the sign of Saturn' is, however eloquent, a case in point. See *OWS*, pp. 7–28.
4   The translation of the title of this work is ironic, given Benjamin's concern to distinguish *Trauerspiel* from tragedy.
5   See McCole, 1993, p. 297.
6   Of course, Benjamin was not the only thinker at this time to privilege the textual fragment. He shared this with a number of other key cultural and Critical Theorists such as Georg Simmel, Siegfried Kracauer and Ernst Bloch.
7   Gilloch, 1996.
8   Kracauer, 1995, pp. 75–88.
9   Parini, 1997.
10   Markner and Weber, 1993, list more than 2,000 publications in the period 1983–92.
11   The International Walter Benjamin Association is based in Amsterdam, and held its first annual congress there in July 1997.
12   For a discussion of the diversity of the Youth Movement, see Brodersen, 1997, p. 47.
13   Benjamin later described such elitist aspirations as 'a final heroic attempt to change the attitudes of people without changing their circumstances' (*OWS*, p. 307).

14   See Elias's (1994 [1939]) discussion of how the notions of *Kultur* and *Zivilisation* were projected on to, and became identified as, national characteristics. See also Fletcher, 1997, pp. 6–10.

15   See Brodersen, 1997, pp. 71–2.

16   Ibid., p. 69.

17   See Benjamin's letter of 9 Mar. 1915 to Wyneken: *COR*, pp. 75–6.

18   Benjamin declined invitations to contribute to Buber's journal *Der Jude* in 1916 because of its pro-war rhetoric and militarist sympathies. See Biale, 1982, p. 137.

19   Zionism had developed as a political programme under Theodor Herzl (1860–1904), and took on a particular urgency after 1918, with the new possibilities of emigration to Palestine as these lands passed from Turkish to British possession. See Roberts, 1982, pp. 43–8.

20   See *OWS*, p. 49.

21   Their treatment of Kracauer, who was suffering under similar circumstances in Parisian exile, was even more shabby. Asked by the Institute to collaborate on a study of propaganda, Kracauer produced an *exposé* which was completely rewritten by Adorno without further discussion. When presented with this text, Kracauer refused to allow it to bear his name, and it was never published.

22   Adorno detected an unfriendly tone in Benjamin's apparently glowing review of Kracauer's 1929 *Die Angestellten* and his celebration of its author as 'A ragpicker at daybreak – in the dawn of the day of the revolution' (Kracauer, 1998, p. 114). See also Kracauer's critical reception of Benjamin's *Trauerspiel* study and *Einbahnstrasse* (Kracauer, 1995, pp. 259–67).

23   On occasions Kracauer also criticized Adorno for his tendency to adopt Benjamin's theological categories.

24   See Kracauer's letter to Ernst Bloch of 13 Dec. 1929 (Bloch, 1985, p. 329).

25   See Kracauer, 1995, pp. 323–8.

26   See Adorno's letter to Horkheimer of 23 Nov. 1936, in Horkheimer, 1995, p. 740. The projected collection was to be completed by an essay on contemporary architecture by Siegfried Giedion.

27   See *OWS*, pp. 318–19.

Chapter 1   Immanent Criticism and Exemplary Critique

1   Benjamin's doctoral dissertation was accepted at the University of Berne on 27 June 1919, and, following the completion of his examinations between 19 and 24 July, he was awarded his doctorate *summa cum laude*. See *GS* I, p. 802.

2   See his letter to Ernst Schoen of 7 Apr. 1919: *COR*, pp. 139–40.

3   Benjamin notes that 'the Romantic concept of criticism is itself an exemplary instance of mystical terminology' (*SW1*, p. 141).

4 And, according to Andrew Bowie (1997), ours too. Bowie traces the connections between early German Romantic thought, the themes and concepts of the Critical Theorists of the Frankfurt School, including Benjamin, and their linkages with contemporary post-structuralist and post-modern notions.

5 Benjamin also gives two other main sources for Schlegel's work: the *Lyceum* and *Characterizations and Critiques* (*Charakteristiken und Kritiken*): *SW1*, p. 120.

6 For Novalis, '"humanity does not speak alone – the universe also speaks – everything speaks – endless language"' (cited by Frank, 1989, p. 281). It is the work of Johann Wilhelm Ritter on the origins of script, rather than Novalis's vision of found natural signs that came to fascinate Benjamin, however. See his letter to Scholem of 5 Mar. 1924: *COR*, p. 239.

7 Schlegel claims that '"knowledge of Revelation is too elevated for sensuous human beings and so art enters as a means to present to humanity the objects of Revelation through sensuous representation and clarity"' (cited by Frank, 1989, p. 291).

8 Benjamin's early writings on the philosophy of language are usually viewed as among the principal texts of his engagement with Judaic mysticism and the Kabbalah. Nevertheless, despite his lifelong friendship with Scholem, who was later to become the leading scholar of Judaic mystical thought at the Hebrew University in Jerusalem, Benjamin himself had only a limited knowledge of this tradition. As Menninghaus correctly observes, Benjamin's engagement with the Judaic tradition was primarily filtered through the writings of Hamann, Schlegel and Novalis. Menninghaus (1980, p. 192) is at pains to stress that it is this 'filtered' mysticism, which he terms the 'second Kabbala', rather than any direct knowledge of the 'first Kabbala' (the sacred texts of Judaic mysticism proper) that forms the principal source of Benjamin's insights.

9 Isaiah Berlin describes Hamann (1730–88) as 'the most passionate, consistent, extreme and implacable enemy of Enlightenment and in particular, all forms of rationalism of his time' (1994, p. 1). Although Berlin sees in Hamann's rejection of reason the distant precursor of modern irrationalism in its most barbarous form, he also stresses the importance of Hamann's ideas both for the Romantics and as a necessary corrective to the naive affirmation of historical progress. In his advocacy of tradition and faith, Hamann 'spoke for ultimate human values no less than did his enlightened opponents, Voltaire and Kant, who are rightly admired as defenders of human rights' (Berlin, 1994, p. 117).

10 The significance of Benjamin's mystical understanding of language for his conception of mourning is discussed further in the next chapter.

11 Benjamin notes that this was 'explicitly developed' only in Schlegel's later Windischmann Lectures of 1804–6 (SW1, p. 120).

12 Benjamin states that 'Thinking that reflects on itself in self-consciousness is the basic fact from which Schlegel's and, in large part, Novalis' epistemological considerations take their start' (SW1, p. 120).

13 See SW1, p. 126.

14 See SW1, p. 123.

15 See SW1, p. 134.

16 Benjamin states that 'The task for the criticism of art is knowledge in the medium of reflection that is art' (SW1, p. 151).

17 See Caygill, 1998, p. 43, and Pensky, 1993, p. 58.

18 Benjamin writes that 'criticism when confronting the work of art is like observation when confronting the natural object' (SW1, p. 151).

19 This notion of a privileged proximity with respect to a work of art anticipates Benjamin's later concern with the demise of aura as the overcoming of distance. See ch. 6.

20 Benjamin notes: 'In this sense, Novalis says of the genuine experimenter that nature "reveals itself all the more completely through him, the more his constitution is in harmony with it"' (SW1, p. 148).

21 See Caygill, 1998, p. 35.

22 Novalis writes: '"A review is the complement of the book"' (SW1, p. 66).

23 Schlegel writes: '"All poems of antiquity link up to one another, until the whole is formed out of continually greater masses and members. ... And thus it is no empty metaphor to say that ancient poetry is a single, indivisible perfected poem. Why shouldn't what has already been come about once again? ... And why not in a more beautiful, greater way?"' (SW1, p. 167).

24 Benjamin notes that Schlegel 'wanted to define this concept of the idea of art in the Platonic sense ... as the real ground of all empirical works' (SW1, p. 167).

25 Benjamin writes: 'Schlegel repeatedly and emphatically designates the unity of art, the continuum of forms itself, as one work. It is this invisible work which takes up into itself the visible work' (SW1, p. 167).

26 See Benjamin's letter to Belmore: COR, p. 84.

27 See SW1, p. 178.

28 Of Hölderlin's statement regarding the 'sobriety of art', Benjamin notes: 'This principle is the essentially quite new and still incalculably influential leading idea of the Romantic philosophy of art' (SW1, p. 175).

29 In contrast to this view, and prefiguring Benjamin's own understanding of the 'author as producer', Schlegel writes: '"One often thinks to shame authors by comparisons with manufacturing. But shouldn't the true author also be a manufacturer? Shouldn't he devote his whole life to the business of working literary materials

into forms that in great manner are purposeful and useful?"' (*SW*1, p. 176).

30 Benjamin writes: 'Kircher could justly maintain: "These Romantics were aiming to fend off precisely the 'Romantic' – as it was understood then and is understood today"' (*SW*1, p. 177).

31 For Novalis, 'antiquity arises only where a creative spirit recognizes it' (*SW*1, p. 183).

32 For Novalis, '"all power appears only in passing"' (cited in Frank, 1989, p. 267).

33 Schlegel terms this moment of illumination '*Witz*' (see Frank, 1989, p. 295).

34 Novalis notes: '"The principle is in each tiny fragment of everyday life – visible in everything"' (cited in Frank, 1989, p. 272).

35 Frank notes that allegory 'is thus the necessary manifestation of the unrepresentability of the infinite' (1989, p. 293). For Schlegel, '"It goes to the gates of the highest, and satisfies itself in the indeterminate intimation of the infinite, the divine, that which does not permit itself to be designated and explained philosophically"' (cited in Frank, 1989, p. 294).

36 Schlegel writes: '"All beauty . . . is allegory. The highest can only be stated allegorically because it is inexpressible"' (cited in Frank, 1989, p. 293).

37 Schlegel writes: '"Each allegory . . . signifies God and one can only talk of God allegorically"' (cited in Frank, 1989, p. 294).

38 The name is derived from a painting by Paul Klee which Benjamin bought in Munich in the summer of 1921 and which held a particular fascination for him. In his later 'Theses on the Concept of History' Benjamin refers to Klee's figure as the 'Angel of History' (*ILL*, pp. 259–60). See ch. 7.

39 In addition to his own 'The Task of the Translator', the first issue of the journal was to publish poems by Fritz and Wolf Heinle, two stories by Agnon, and essays by Scholem and Rang.

40 Benjamin's model for these endeavours was the early Romantics' own publication, the *Athenaeum*.

41 See Brodersen, 1997, pp. 131–7, for a fuller discussion of the journal and the reasons for its ultimate failure.

42 See *SW*1, pp. 97–9, 217–25.

43 As Roberts notes, Gundolf was 'popularly regarded as the "chancellor" of George's spiritual empire' (1982, p. 122).

44 In their rejection of rationalism and systematic scientific thought, the Georgekreis may appear to be the heirs of Hamann. However, Hamann rejected pantheism (Berlin, 1993, p. 55), and, in his insistence on the revelation of God's divine order through faith, came much closer to Benjamin's theological position.

45 The First World War was seen, initially at least, as the great opportunity for such cultural crusaders. Gay (1968, p. 12) cites some of

Gundolf's postcards to Stefan George in August 1914 as exemplary instances of the pro-war euphoria of the time. It is instructive that Gay chose Gundolf (and Thomas Mann) to illustrate this zeal among intellectuals – they were ordinarily no military fanatics.

46 See Benjamin's letter to Scholem, 5 Dec. 1923: *COR*, p. 222.

47 See *GS* I, pp. 816–17.

48 They did not. See Witte, 1985, p. 48.

49 For an overview of the essay's structure, see *GS* I, pp. 835–7.

50 See Goethe, 1971, pp. 236–44.

51 Benjamin writes: 'for the most part the meaning of the concrete realities in the work will no doubt be hidden from the poet and the public of his time' (*SW1*, p. 298).

52 Benjamin claims: 'To wish to gain an understanding of *Elective Affinities* from the author's own words on the subject is wasted effort' (*SW1*, p. 313).

53 The early Romantics themselves are a case in point. In a letter to Scholem of 23 Feb. 1918, Benjamin, writing of Goethe's *Maximen und Reflexionen*, asserts that 'Detailed involvement with them reinforces me in the old opinion that ours is the first generation to [confront?] Goethe critically, and is consequently grateful to succeed him. The romantics were much too close to Goethe to grasp more than some *tendencies* of his work' (*COR*, p. 117).

54 See McCole, 1993, pp. 121–2.

55 Subjecting one of Gundolf's phrases to particularly severe scrutiny, Benjamin wittily writes: 'The whole craft of the critic here consists in nothing else but catching hold, like a second Gulliver, of a single one of these lilliputian sentencelets, despite its wriggling sophisms, and examining it in one's own time' (*SW1*, p. 326).

56 Letter to Scholem, 27 Nov. 1921.

57 See Roberts, 1982, p. 122.

58 Benjamin insists that 'the life of a man, even that of a creative artist [*des Schaffenden*], is never that of the creator' (*SW1*, p. 324).

59 Benjamin writes: 'the artist is less the primal ground or creator than the origin or form giver [*Bildner*]' (*SW1*, pp. 323–4).

60 The hero is distinguished by 'his complete symbolic transparency', whereas 'the life of the poet – like the life of any man – scarcely displays an unambiguous task, any more than it displays an unambiguous and clearly demonstrable struggle' (*SW1*, p. 324).

61 Benjamin responds: 'The most thoughtless dogma of the Goethe cult ... asserts that among all the works of Goethe the greatest is his life: Gundolf's *Goethe* took this up. Accordingly, Goethe's life is not rigorously distinguished from that of the works' (*SW1*, p. 324).

62 See *SW1*, p. 321.

63 See Witte, 1985, p. 42.

64 See *SW1*, p. 305.

65 In Benjamin's 1919 fragment 'Fate and Character' (*OWS*, pp. 124–31), this opposition is configured as the conflict between 'character', the

inner 'core' of 'an active human being' (OWS, p. 125) and the constraints and forces of the external world in which they live, 'fate'.

66 See Goethe, 1971, pp. 236–44.

67 Benjamin writes: '*Elective Affinities* itself was originally planned as a novella . . . but its growth forced it out of that orbit. The traces of its original formal conception, however, are preserved, despite everything that made the work become a novel' (SW1, pp. 329–30).

68 This notion of narratives which relate the defeat of mythic forces is elaborated in Benjamin's essays on 'The Storyteller' (1936) and 'Franz Kafka' (1934) with respect to the fairy tale. In fairy tales, benign nature and humankind join together to outwit mythic domination: 'in the shape of the animals which come to the aid of the child in the fairy tale it shows that nature not only is subservient to myth, but much prefers to be aligned with man. The wisest thing – so the fairy tale taught mankind in olden times, and teaches children to this day – is to meet the forces of the mythical world with cunning and with high spirits' (ILL, p. 102). In 'Franz Kafka', Benjamin notes that 'Fairy tales are the traditional stories about victory over these forces, and fairy tales for dialecticians are what Kafka wrote when he went to work on legends' (ILL, p. 117).

69 Benjamin writes: 'Passion and affection are the elements of all semblance-like love, which reveals itself as distinct from true love not in the failure of feeling but rather uniquely in its helplessness. And so one must emphasize that it is not true love which reigns in Ottilie and Eduard' (SW1, pp. 344–5).

70 Benjamin notes that 'The norm of law makes itself master of a vacillating love' (SW1, p. 345).

71 'Passion', Benjamin observes, 'loses all its rights and happiness when it seeks a pact with the bourgeois, affluent, secure life' (SW1, p. 343).

72 Benjamin writes of Goethe that 'in this pair he depicted the power of true love' (SW1, p. 345).

73 Hence, Goethe concludes the novella with the rhetorical question: 'who could have had the heart to refuse them one's blessing?' (Goethe, 1971, p. 244).

74 See SW1, p. 342.

75 See SW1, p. 336.

76 SW1, p. 336.

77 Benjamin writes: 'For the beautiful is neither the veil nor the veiled object but rather the object in its veil' (SW1, p. 351).

78 Benjamin writes: 'The task of art criticism is not to lift the veil but rather, through the most precise knowledge of it as veil, to raise itself for the first time to the true view of the beautiful' (SW1, p. 351).

79 Benjamin writes: 'Never yet has a true work of art been grasped other than where it ineluctably represented itself as a secret' (SW1, p. 351).

80 Benjamin notes that 'beauty makes visible not the idea but rather the latter's secret' (SW1, p. 351).

81 Accordingly, in the novella there is an instance of the unveiling of beauty. The young man, having rescued his beloved from the river, divests her of her wet clothes in the process of reviving her apparently lifeless body. Salvation and revelation intersect here. The stripping of the body is a decisive, practical moral act which precedes the discovery of the characters' mutual love and their reconciliation in God. Naked before one another and before God, there is no lust or shame, but rather the (transient) triumph of love over death amid the joyful certainty of blessing.

82 See *SW1*, p. 353.

83 'We hope', Benjamin notes, that the dead lovers, 'awaken, if ever, not to a more beautiful world but to a blessed one' (*SW1*, p. 355).

Chapter 2   Allegory and Melancholy

1 Benjamin's letter of 13 Jan. 1920: *COR*, p. 156.

2 *COR*, p. 150.

3 *COR*, p. 204.

4 Benjamin notes that 'the obscure physiognomy of the authors peering out through uncomprehended works did little to inspire historical-biographical sketches' (*OGTD*, p. 49). He adds: 'Burdened down by so many prejudices, literary scholarship necessarily failed in its attempts to arrive at an objective appreciation of baroque drama, and has moreover only intensified the confusion with which any reflection must now grapple from the outset' (*OGTD*, p. 51).

5 Steiner, *OGTD*, p. 15.

6 *SW1*, pp. 55–61.

7 Writing to Scholem on 3 Mar. 1918, Benjamin recalls: 'I was unable to reconcile myself to this', since 'in German the lament appears in its full linguistic glory only in the *Trauerspiel*' (*COR*, p. 120).

8 'This time of the tragic hero', writes Benjamin, 'describes all his deeds and his entire existence as if with a magic circle' (*SW1*, p. 56).

9 In *Trauerspiel*, 'everything depends on the ear for lament, for only the most profoundly heard lament can become music. Whereas in tragedy the eternal inflexibility of the spoken word is exalted, the mourning play concentrates in itself the infinite resonance of its sound' (*SW1*, p. 61). Its language 'describes the path from natural sound via lament to music' (*SW1*, p. 60).

10 Composed 'as a form of self-clarification', this dense study may be, as Menninghaus points out, 'the early work by Benjamin' (Menninghaus, 1980, p. 9). It was never intended for publication, though, and Benjamin only ever circulated a small number of copies among a close circle of friends, most notably Scholem, for their comments.

11 In his interpretation of Hasidism, Buber drew a distinction between two types of experience: *Erfahrung* and *Erlebnis*. *Erfahrung* consists of the communicable sense perceptions received by the human subject;

Erlebnis, to the inner, intuitive experience of mystical insight and direct communion with God (*devekut*). For Buber, this domain of *Erlebnis*, of ultimate experience, is characterized by silence on account of the inexpressible nature of its insights and truth (see Biale, 1982, p. 115). The highest domain of human experience is precisely that which eludes communication and defies expression. 'Erlebnis is utterly silent' (Biale, 1982, p. 115) and hence, for Buber, the highest sphere of human knowledge, that of divinely revealed truth, is precisely that for which language is inadequate, of which one can give no account whatsoever.

12 The notion of translation has a double significance for Benjamin. First, the perfect name language of Adam is nothing other than the translation of God's word into human language. Translation is thus the origin of human language *per se*. Second, the post-Fall manifold of human languages brings with it the task of translating them into one another. This, Benjamin argues in 'The Task of the Translator' (1921), points to the commonality of human languages, and highlights their origin in the pure language of name. Translation is both the origin of pure language and the mode of its remembrance.

13 Hence, what Saussure takes as the hallmark of language, its arbitrary character, is for Benjamin symptomatic of its fallen character. Bourgeois science mistakes 'prattle' for language, and thus becomes prattle itself.

14 Benjamin writes: 'Philosophy is meant to name the idea, as Adam named nature' (*COR*, p. 224).

15 Benjamin writes: 'Ideas are displayed, without intention, in the act of naming, and they have to be renewed in philosophical contemplation. In this renewal, the primordial mode of apprehending words is restored' (*OGTD*, p. 37).

16 Benjamin states: 'Since philosophy may not presume to speak in the tones of revelation, this can only be achieved by recalling in memory the primordial form of perception' (*OGTD*, p. 36).

17 The disjunction between the initial aspirations for the project and its inadequate realization are instructive for Benjamin, bringing him 'the following insight: every perfect work is the death mask of its intuition' (*COR*, p. 227).

18 Letter to Scholem, 16 Sept. 1924: *COR*, pp. 246–51.

19 Letter to Scholem, 12 Oct./5 Nov. 1924.

20 Letter to Scholem, 19 Feb. 1925. See Steiner's comment, *OGTD*, p. 10.

21 Letter to Scholem, 19 Feb. 1925: *COR*, pp. 260–3.

22 Letter to Scholem, *c*.20–5 May 1925: *COR*, pp. 266–70.

23 See, e.g., his letter to Hofmannsthal of 2 Aug. 1925: *COR*, p. 281.

24 See Benjamin's letter to Rang, 9 Dec. 1923 (*COR*, pp. 222–5), which anticipates many of the key concerns of the Prologue.

25 Benjamin observes that 'In the sense in which it is treated in the philosophy of art the *Trauerspiel* is an idea' (*OGTD*, p. 38).

26 Letter to Rang, 9 Dec. 1923. Benjamin reiterates this in the *Trauerspiel* study: 'philosophy is . . . a struggle for the representation of ideas' (*OGTD*, p. 37).

27 Compare his letter to Rang, 9 Dec. 1923: *COR*, p. 224.

28 *OGTD*, p. 182.

29 See Benjamin's letter of 10 Jan. 1924 regarding the composition of the *Trauerspiel* study itself: *COR*, p. 227.

30 Benjamin contends that 'The value of fragments of thought is all the greater the less direct their relationship to the underlying idea, and the brilliance of the representation depends as much on this value as the brilliance of the mosaic does on the quality of the glass paste' (*OGTD*, p. 29).

31 Hence the significance of Benjamin's own collection of some 600 quotations for the *Trauerspiel* study. See his letter to Scholem, 5 Mar. 1924: *COR*, p. 236.

32 Writing to Hofmannsthal, 11 June 1925, he comments: 'My technique of piling one quotation on top of the other may require some explanation; but here I would like merely to observe that the academic intent of the work was nothing but an occasion for me to produce something in this style' (*COR*, p. 272).

33 Benjamin writes: 'It is, moreover, precisely the more significant works inasmuch as they are not the original and, so to speak, ideal embodiment of the genre, which fall outside the limits of genre. A major work will either establish the genre or abolish it; and the perfect work will do both' (*OGTD*, p. 44).

34 Benjamin mentions Christian Gryphius and Daniel Caspers von Lohenstein, two masters of the *Trauerspiel* form, neither of whom adhere to the classical unities of time and place (*OGTD*, p. 60).

35 Benjamin notes that 'Commentators have always wanted to recognize the elements of Greek tragedy – the tragic plot, the tragic hero, the tragic death – as the essential elements of the *Trauerspiel*, however distorted they may have been at the hands of uncomprehending imitators' (*OGTD*, p. 100).

36 Benjamin cites Johannes Volkelt's *Aesthetik des Tragischen* (1917) as an example of this tendency. Benjamin writes, reiterating a point made by Nietzsche in *The Birth of Tragedy*, 'modern theatre has nothing to show which remotely resembles the tragedy of the Greeks. In denying this actual state of affairs such doctrines of the tragic betray the presumption that it must still be possible to write tragedies' (*OGTD*, p. 101).

37 See *OGTD*, p. 58.

38 The supposed 'history' of the Orient furnished many of the plots, and Byzantium the setting, for many *Trauerspiele*. See *OGTD*, p. 68.

39 Benjamin notes that, 'like the term "tragic" in present-day usage – and with greater justification – the word *Trauerspiel* was applied in the seventeenth century to dramas and to historical events alike'

(*OGTD*, p. 63). As early as the medieval period, history was ' "seen by the chroniclers as a great *Trauerspiel*" ' (*OGTD*, p. 77).

40 Benjamin notes that the figure of Herod is 'characteristic of the idea of the tyrant' (*OGTD*, p. 70).

41 Benjamin points out that the *Trauerspiele* 'are not so much concerned with the deeds of the hero as with his suffering, and frequently not so much with his spiritual torment as with the agony of the physical adversity which befalls him' (*OGTD*, p. 72).

42 See *OGTD*, p. 70.

43 Benjamin writes: 'However highly he is enthroned over subject and state, his status is confined to the world of creation; he is the lord of creatures, but he remains a creature' (*OGTD*, p. 85).

44 Benjamin writes that 'Whereas the middle ages present the futility of the world events and the transience of the creature as stations on the road to salvation, the German *Trauerspiel* is taken up entirely with the hopelessness of the earthly condition' (*OGTD*, p. 81).

45 *OGTD*, pp. 106–7.

46 *OGTD*, p. 116.

47 *OGTD*, p. 107.

48 Benjamin cheekily quotes from his own fragment 'Fate and Character': 'in tragedy pagan man realises that he is better than his gods, but this realisation strikes him dumb and it remains unarticulated' (*OGTD*, p. 110).

49 Benjamin quotes Rosenzweig: ' "The tragic hero has only one language that is completely proper to him: silence. . . . The tragic devised itself the artistic form of the drama precisely so as to be able to present silence" ' (*OGTD*, p. 108).

50 Benjamin notes that 'it is not moral transgression but the very estate of man as creature which provides the reason for catastrophe. This typical catastrophe, which is so very different from the extraordinary catastrophe of the tragic hero, is what the dramatists had in mind when . . . they described a work as a *Trauerspiel*' (*OGTD*, p. 89).

51 Benjamin writes that 'In contrast to the spasmodic chronological progression of tragedy, the *Trauerspiel* takes place in a spatial continuum, which one might describe as choreographic. The organiser of its plot, the precursor of the choreographer, is the intriguer' (*OGTD*, p. 95).

52 Benjamin writes of *Trauer-* and *Lustspiel*: 'these two forms are not only empirically connected but in terms of the law of their structure they are as closely bound to each other as classical tragedy and comedy are opposed; their affinity is such that the *Lustspiel* enters into the *Trauerspiel*' (*OGTD*, p. 127).

53 Benjamin observes that: 'The *Trauerspiel* is conceivable as pantomime; the tragedy is not' (*OGTD*, p. 118).

54 Benjamin points out that the *Trauerspiel* 'might . . . be seen as a puppet-play, with ambition and desire holding the strings' (*OGTD*, p. 83). Moreover, the *Trauerspiel* frequently made use of the device of

a play within a play, sometimes in the form of a puppet-theatre on stage (see *OGTD*, pp. 82–3).

55 Benjamin writes that 'the mourning of the prince and the mirth of his advisor are so close to each other . . . because the two provinces of the satanic realm were represented in them' (*OGTD*, p. 127).

56 Benjamin notes that 'The prince is the paradigm of the melancholy man' (*OGTD*, p. 142).

57 See Pensky, 1993, p. 23.

58 The other humours were yellow bile (associated with the choleric condition), phlegm (the phlegmatic) and blood (the sanguine). See Pensky, 1993, pp. 22–4.

59 Benjamin notes this connection: 'unfaithfulness – another feature of saturnine man – characterises the figure of the courtier' (*OGTD*, p. 156).

60 Benjamin here draws upon Erwin Panofsky's and Fritz Saxl's 'fine study' (1923) of Albrecht Dürer's engraving 'Melancholia I' (see Pensky, 1993, pp. 98–105). Melancholy as 'passionate contemplation' (*OGTD*, p. 141) finds its clearest representation here. Dürer's picture presents a solitary, central figure, seated and with downcast eyes, surveying a plethora of discarded instruments and objects strewn around him. Benjamin comments: 'the utensils of active life are lying around unused on the floor, as objects of contemplation. This engraving anticipates the baroque in many respects' (*OGTD*, p. 140).

61 Benjamin recognizes 'the melancholic's inclination for long journeys' (*OGTD*, p. 149).

62 Benjamin notes that 'The "Book of nature" and the "Book of the times" are objects of baroque meditation' (*OGTD*, p. 141).

63 The Symbolists and the Georgekreis also failed to understand the importance of allegory for Schlegel and Novalis.

64 Benjamin notes that allegory was developed by classicism 'to provide the dark background against which the bright world of the symbol might stand out' (*OGTD*, p. 161).

65 Benjamin writes: 'It is not possible to conceive of a starker opposite to the artistic symbol, the plastic symbol, the image of organic totality, than this amorphous fragment which is seen in the form of allegorical script' (*OGTD*, p. 176).

66 Benjamin writes that 'classicism was not permitted to behold the lack of freedom, the imperfection, the collapse of the physical, beautiful nature. But beneath its extravagant pomp, this is precisely what baroque allegory proclaims, with unprecedented emphasis' (*OGTD*, p. 176).

67 According to Joseph von Görres, symbol and allegory ' "stand in relation to each other as does the silent, great and mighty world of mountains and plants to the living progression of human history" ' (cited in *OGTD*, p. 165).

68 Benjamin notes that for writers of the baroque, 'nature was not seen . . . in bud and bloom, but in the over-ripeness and decay of her

creations. In nature they saw eternal transience, and here alone did the saturnine vision of this generation recognise history' (*OGTD*, pp. 179–80).

69 Benjamin notes 'the baroque cult of the ruin' (*OGTD*, p. 178).
70 Benjamin notes that 'martyrdom thus prepares the body of the living person for emblematic purposes' (*OGTD*, p. 217).
71 Benjamin writes that 'the characters of the *Trauerspiel* die, because it is only thus, as corpses, that they can enter into the homeland of allegory. It is not for the sake of immortality that they meet their end, but for the sake of the corpse' (*OGTD*, pp. 217–18).
72 Benjamin quotes Herbert Cysarz thus: ' "Every idea, however abstract, is compressed into an image, and this image, however concrete, is then stamped out in verbal form" ' (*OGTD*, p. 199).
73 In the plays of Georg Philipp Harsdörffer there is 'a veritable eruption of images, which gives rise to a chaotic mass of metaphors' (*OGTD*, p. 173).
74 Benjamin writes that 'In the anagrams, the onomatopoeic phrases, and many other examples of linguistic virtuosity, word, syllable, and sound are emancipated from any context of traditional meaning and are flaunted as objects which can be exploited for allegorical purposes' (*OGTD*, p. 207).
75 Benjamin points out that 'The phonetic tension in the language of the seventeenth century leads directly to music, the opposite of meaning-laden speech' (*OGTD*, p. 211).
76 *OGTD*, p. 233.

Chapter 3   From Cityscape to Dreamworld

1 There are relatively few specific references to Paris in *Einbahnstrasse*. Nevertheless, in a letter to Hofmannsthal of 8 Feb. 1928, Benjamin reflects: 'the book owes a lot to Paris, being my first attempt to come to terms with this city. I am continuing this effort in a second book called *Paris Arcades*' (*COR*, p. 325).
2 Publishers' Note, *OWS*, p. 35.
3 *OWS*, p. 48.
4 Buck-Morss suggests that Lacis 'was a muse who presided over the moment. Like Ariadne, she promised to lead him out of the cul-de-sac that seemed to lie before him' (1989, p. 11).
5 Benjamin writes: 'Each thought, each day, each life lies here as on a laboratory table. And as if it were a metal from which an unknown substance is by every means to be extracted, it must endure experimentation to the point of exhaustion' (*OWS*, p. 186).
6 Moscow is filled with 'topographical dummies' such that 'the city turns into a labyrinth for the newcomer' (*OWS*, p. 179).
7 *OWS*, pp. 180–1.
8 *OWS*, pp. 184–5.

9   Both effects of the snow: see *OWS*, p. 180.

10 Benjamin notes, for example, that 'In the streets of Moscow there is a curious state of affairs: the Russian village is playing hide-and-seek in them' (*OWS*, p. 202).

11 Benjamin observes that 'peasant huts alternate with *art nouveau* villas or with the sober façades of eight-storey blocks' (*OWS*, p. 203).

12 In 'Marseilles', Benjamin writes that 'childhood is the divining rod of melancholy, and to know the mourning of such radiant, glorious cities one must have been a child in them' (*OWS*, p. 211).

13 Benjamin observes: 'the complete interpenetration of technological and primitive modes of life, this world-historical experiment in the new Russia, is illustrated in miniature by a streetcar ride' (*OWS*, p. 190).

14 Benjamin writes: 'what one learns is to observe and judge Europe with the conscious knowledge of what is going on in Russia' (*OWS*, p. 177).

15 The earliest dated element of *One-Way Street*, 'Kaiserpanorama', was sent by Benjamin as a present to Scholem on the occasion of his departure for Palestine in Sept. 1923. See *GS* IV, p. 907.

16 Almost exactly two years earlier, 11 June 1925, Benjamin had sent a 'slender manuscript of aphorisms' to Hofmannsthal in the hope that he 'might want to fill an empty page of the *Beiträge* with one or another of them' (*COR*, p. 273). He did not. None of Benjamin's aphorisms were published in Hofmannsthal's journal (*GS* IV, p. 907).

17 Anxious regarding the success of such an experiment, Benjamin informed Hofmannsthal that 'it presents something heterogeneous, or rather polar. Certain lightning bolts may perhaps emerge from this tension as too harsh, and certain explosions as too blustering' (*COR*, p. 309).

18 On 8 Feb. 1928 Benjamin informed Hofmannsthal: 'Its subject matter may be expressed as follows: to grasp topicality as the reverse of the eternal in history and to make an impression of this, the side of the medallion hidden from view' (*COR*, p. 325).

19 Benjamin writes: 'if the abolition of the bourgeoisie is not completed by an almost calculable moment in economic and technical development (a moment signalled by inflation and poison-gas warfare) all is lost' (*OWS*, p. 80).

20 Benjamin writes: 'Only he who can destroy can criticise' (*OWS*, p. 67).

21 In a grotesque simile, Benjamin notes: 'Genuine polemics approach a book as lovingly as a cannibal spices a baby' (*OWS*, p. 67).

22 The advertisement 'abolishes the space where contemplation moved and all but hits us between the eyes with things as a car, growing to gigantic proportions, careers at us out of a film screen. . . . [T]he genuine advertisement hurtles things at us with the tempo of a good film' (*OWS*, p. 89).

23 It is the urbanism of advertising that fascinates Benjamin: 'What in the end makes advertisements so superior to criticism? Not what the moving red neon sign says – but the fiery red pool reflecting it in the asphalt' (*OWS*, pp. 89–90).

24 Benjamin points out that 'The critic is the strategist in the literary battle' (*OWS*, p. 66).

25 Hence Benjamin's rather inane and witless series of comparisons between 'Books and harlots': see *OWS*, pp. 67–8.

26 Implicitly juxtaposing Naples, Moscow and Berlin, Benjamin regards this urban eroticism, this sensuality of the street, as a decisive break with bourgeois privacy, prudery and corruption: 'the family is the rotten, dismal edifice in whose closets and crannies the most ignominious instincts are deposited. Mundane life proclaims the total subjugation of erotic life to privacy. . . . The shift of erotic emphasis to the public sphere is both feudal and proletarian' (*OWS*, pp. 100–1).

27 Paris as a 'haunted' city is a leitmotif in Breton's *Nadja*, 1928.

28 The presence of the beloved provides for a mapping of the city: see 'First Aid', *OWS*, p. 69.

29 Here the erotic, the political and the urban combine: see *OWS*, p. 70.

30 In 'Imperial Panorama', he notes that 'Warmth is ebbing from things. The objects of daily use gently but insistently repel us. . . . We must compensate for their coldness with our warmth if they are not to freeze us to death' (*OWS*, p. 58).

31 Benjamin observes that 'his drawers must become arsenal and zoo, crime museum and crypt. "To tidy up" would be to demolish an edifice full of prickly chestnuts that are spikey clubs, tinfoil that is hoarded silver, bricks that are coffins, cacti that are totem-poles and copper pennies that are shields' (*OWS*, p. 74).

32 *OWS*, pp. 103–4.

33 Published under the title 'Glosse zum Surrealismus' in the *Neuen Rundschau* in Jan. 1927. *GS* II, pp. 620–2, 1425–7. McCole sees this essay as decisive: 'the ideas first formulated in "Dreamkitsch" supplied the germ for Benjamin's "Arcades Project"' (1993, p. 213).

34 Benjamin notes that 'At the centre of this world of things stands the most dreamed-of of their objects, the city of Paris itself' (*OWS*, p. 230).

35 In a 1952 radio interview, Breton says of Aragon: ' "No one could have been a more astute detector of the unwonted in all its forms; no one else could have been carried away by such intoxicating reveries about a secret life of the city"' (Aragon, 1987, p. 10).

36 Benjamin notes that 'no face is surrealistic in the same way as the true face of the city' (*OWS*, p. 230).

37 Aragon states that 'nature could play no part in this mythical conception of the modern world' (1987, p. 137).

38 Aragon provides the following ironic description of one of these 'modern idols', the not-so-humble petrol pump: 'painted brightly with English or invented names, possessing just one long, supple

arm, a luminous faceless head, a single foot and a numbered wheel in the belly, the petrol pumps sometimes take on the appearance of the divinities of Egypt or of those cannibal tribes which worship war and war alone. O Texaco motor oil, Esso, Shell, great inscriptions of human potentiality, soon shall we cross ourselves before your fountains, and the youngest among us will perish from having contemplated their nymphs in naphtha' (1987, p. 132).

39 For Aragon, intoxication restores the very possibility of dialectical thinking: 'Reality is the apparent absence of contradiction. The marvellous is the eruption of contradictions within the real' (1987, p. 217).

40 Aragon offers his own urban monadology: 'The way I saw it, an object became transfigured: it took on neither the allegorical aspect nor the character of a symbol, it did not so much manifest an idea as constitute that idea. . . . I was filled with the keen hope of coming within reach of one of the locks guarding the universe: if only the bolt should suddenly slip' (1987, pp. 128–9).

41 Breton notes that Nadja 'enjoyed being nowhere but on the streets, the only region of valid experience for her' (Breton, 1960, p. 113).

42 'One need only take love seriously', Benjamin notes, 'to recognise in it, too – as Nadja also indicates – a "profane illumination"' (OWS, p. 228).

43 Breton writes of the Saint Ouen flea market: 'I go there often, searching for objects that can be found nowhere else: old fashioned, broken, useless, almost incomprehensible, even perverse' (1960, p. 52).

44 One might say that for Aragon and Breton the obsolete object has an 'image-value', an 'illumination-value'.

45 In 'Dreamkitsch' Benjamin writes: 'What we used to call art begins at a distance of two meters from the body. But now, in kitsch, the world of things advances on the human being; it yields to his uncertain grasp and ultimately fashions its figures in his interior' (SW2, pp. 4–5).

46 Aragon writes: 'the vulgar forms of knowledge are nothing more, under their guise of science or logic, than the conscious halting places past which the image scorches, the image transformed marvellously into a burning bush' (1987, p. 213).

47 Aragon asserts that 'The image is not itself the concrete, of course, but the possible consciousness, the greatest possible consciousness of the concrete . . . Basically no way of thought exists that is not an image' (1987, p. 213).

48 Benjamin notes in 'Dreamkitsch' that 'to decipher the contours of the banal as rebus . . . Picture puzzles, as schemata of the dreamwork, were long ago discovered by psychoanalysis. The Surrealists, with a similar conviction, are less on the trail of the psyche than on the track of things' (SW2, p. 4).

49 Benjamin notes that ' "Misunderstanding" is here another word for the rhythm with which the only true reality forces its way into the conversation' (SW2, p. 4).

50 Benjamin writes: 'in the joke, too, in invective, in misunderstanding, in all cases where an action puts forward its own image and exists, absorbing and consuming it, where nearness looks with its own eyes, the long-sought image sphere opened' (*OWS*, p. 238).
51 Benjamin notes that 'it is as magical experiments with words, not as artistic dabblings, that we must understand the passionate phonetic and graphical transformational games that have run through the whole literature of the avant-garde for the past fifteen years, whether it is called Futurism, Dadaism or Surrealism' (*OWS*, p. 232).
52 Breton notes 'the complete lack of peace with ourselves provoked by certain juxtapositions, certain combinations of circumstances which greatly surpass our understanding and permit us to resume rational activity only if, in most cases, we call upon our very instinct of self-preservation to enable us to do so' (1960, p. 20).
53 See, e.g., Breton, 1960, p. 56.
54 See *OWS*, pp. 81–2, and Cohen, 1993, pp. 177–8.
55 Cohen (1993, p. 178) perceptively notes that Benjamin's 'Post No Bills: The Writer's Technique in Thirteen Theses' (*OWS*, pp. 64–5) almost constitutes a point-by-point critique of Breton's 'Secrets of the Magical Surrealist Art' in his *Manifesto of Surrealism*.
56 Letter to Scholem, 21 July 1925.
57 See Benjamin's comments on Breton's visit to the clairvoyante Madame Sacco (*OWS*, p. 228). See Breton, 1960, pp. 79 and 81.
58 The visitor to the fortune-teller 'is impelled by inertia rather than curiosity, and nothing is more unlike the submissive apathy with which he hears his fate revealed than the alert dexterity with which the man of courage lays hands on the future ... Omens, presentiments, signals pass day and night through our organism like wave impulses. To interpret them or to use them, that is the question. The two are irreconcilable. Cowardice and apathy counsel the former, lucidity and freedom the latter' (*OWS*, p. 98).
59 *OWS*, p. 238.
60 Benjamin endorses Naville's call for ' "The organisation of pessimism" ' (*OWS*, p. 237).

Chapter 4 Paris and the Arcades

1 Letter to Scholem, 20 Jan. 1930.
2 Letter to Scholem, 30 Jan. 1928. This title, later abandoned, was intended to capture the 'rhapsodic character of the representation' (*GS* V, p. 1117).
3 Scholem remembers Benjamin reading him fragments from a planned 'essay of about fifty printed pages' in 1927 (Scholem, 1982, p. 135).
4 Letter to Scholem, 11 Mar. 1928.
5 Letter to Hofmannsthal, 5 May 1928.

6 Benjamin noted in a letter to Scholem of 24 May 1928 that 'the work on *Paris Arcades* is taking on an ever more mysterious and insistent mien and howls into my nights like a small beast if I have failed to water it at the most distant springs during the day' (*COR*, p. 335).

7 Letter to Scholem, 15 Mar. 1929.

8 Letter to Kracauer, 21 Mar. 1929.

9 The 'Arcades Project' took on what Frisby describes as a 'subterranean existence' at this time (1988, p. 195).

10 Letter to Scholem, May 1932.

11 Letter to Scholem, 5 Feb. 1931. See Convolute S, *ARC*, pp. 543–61.

12 Letter to Scholem, 28 Oct. 1931.

13 The ultimate inadequacy of these experiments was noted by Benjamin in a letter to Gretel Adorno, 16 Aug. 1935: 'The Ur-history of the nineteenth century reflected in the vision of a child playing on its doorstep has a totally different countenance than that in the signs that they engrave on the map of history' (*COR*, p. 507).

14 Letter to Horkheimer, Oct./Nov. 1934. See also his letter to Adorno of 1 May 1935: *GS* V, p. 1112.

15 Letter to Scholem, 20 May 1935.

16 In a letter of 18 Sept. 1935, Horkheimer states: 'your work promises to be simply excellent. Your method of rendering the epoch from small, superficial symptoms demonstrates this time its full power' (*GS* V, p. 1114).

17 For example, Adorno asks: 'who is the subject of the dream? In the nineteenth century, certainly only the individual; as unmediated replica, however, neither the fetish character nor its monuments can be extrapolated from the individual's dreams. Therefore the collective consciousness is invoked and, indeed, I fear in the present version it cannot be distinguished from the Jungian one' (*COR*, p. 497).

18 Adorno asserts that 'The fetish character of the commodity is not a fact of consciousness but it is dialectical in the preeminent sense of producing consciousness' (*COR*, p. 495).

19 Letter to Scholem, 2 July 1937.

20 Letter to Pollock, 28 Aug. 1938.

21 See 'Paris Arcades I' of 1927–30 (*ARC* 827–68), 'Paris Arcades II' from 1928/9 (*ARC*, pp. 873–84), and 'The Ring of Saturn or Some Remarks on Iron Construction' of 1928–9 (*ARC*, pp. 885–7).

22 See Benjamin's letter to Werner Kraft, 25 May 1935: *COR*, p. 486.

23 In a letter to Scholem, 20 May 1935, Benjamin notes: 'I periodically succumb to the temptations of visualizing analogies with the baroque book in the book's inner construction, although its external construction decidedly diverges from that of the former. . . . Here as well the focus will be on the unfolding of a handed-down concept. Whereas in the former it was the concept of *Trauerspiel*, here it is likely to be the fetish character of commodities. Whereas the baroque book

mobilized its own theory of knowledge, this will be the case for Arcades at least to the same extent . . . just as the baroque book dealt with the seventeenth century from the perspective of Germany, this book will unravel the nineteenth century from France's perspective' (*COR*, p. 482).

24 See Bolz and Witte, 1984, p. 13.

25 See also O°79, *ARC*, p. 864. *Urgeschichte* unmistakably calls to mind Benjamin's earlier notion of *Ursprung*, that moment of 'origin' when phenomena group themselves as a constellation.

26 Benjamin writes of the dreaming collectivity: 'We must follow in its wake so as to expound the nineteenth century – in fashion and advertising, in building and politics – as the outcome of its dream visions' (K1,4, *ARC*, p. 389).

27 See also G°,13, *ARC*, p. 842.

28 Benjamin writes: 'Only with cunning, not without it, can we work free of the realm of dream' (G1,7, *ARC*, p. 173).

29 The notion of a dialectical *Feerie* may be seen as suggestive of the fairy story, a form which Benjamin saw as antithetical to myth. Cohen (1993, p. 254) also points out that the term *Feerie* had a particular meaning in the nineteenth century. From *c*.1823 it referred to a theatrical spectacle involving fantastical characters, special effects and mechanical contrivances.

30 Letter to Benjamin, 6 Nov. 1934: *GS* V, p. 1106.

31 Letter to Adorno, 31 May 1935.

32 Tiedemann surprisingly questions the original importance of commodity fetishism for the 'Arcades Project', claiming that even as late as the 1935 *exposé*, Benjamin was still 'unfamiliar with the relevant discussion in Marx's writings' (in Smith, 1988, p. 276). But such a view underestimates the importance for Benjamin of Lukács's understanding of the commodity as the central issue in the critique of capitalism. Moreover, the theme of the human subservience to our own creations is important for Aragon.

33 For a lucid, succinct discussion of the notion of fetishism in Marx and Freud, see Dant 1999.

34 See G5,1, *ARC*, pp. 181–2.

35 The commodity 'stands in opposition to the organic. It prostitutes the living body to the inorganic world. In relation to the living it represents the rights of the corpse. Fetishization, which succumbs to the sex-appeal of the inorganic, is its vital nerve' (*CB*, p. 166; see also B9,1, *ARC*, p. 79).

36 See O°'38, *ARC*, p. 861, and J65a,6, *ARC*, p. 345.

37 Benjamin writes: 'In the form taken by prostitution in the big cities, the woman appears not only as a commodity but . . . as a mass-produced article' (J66,8, *ARC*, p. 346).

38 For Benjamin, the boundary between industrial labour and prostitution is blurred. See, e.g., J75,1, *ARC*, p. 360, and J67,5, *ARC*, p. 348.

39   See O10,1, *ARC*, p. 508.
40   Benjamin writes: 'The situation of consciousness as patterned and checkered by sleep and waking need only be transferred from the individual to the collective. Of course, much that is external to the former is internal to the latter: architecture, fashion' (K1,5, *ARC*, p. 389).
41   Benjamin explicitly draws on Simmel's 1904 essay on fashion as a mode of social identification and differentiation (see *GS* V, p. 127). A quotation from Rudolph von Jhering (1883) also contains many of Simmel's insights (see B6, B6a,1, *ARC*, pp. 74–5).
42   See S1,5, *ARC*, p. 544.
43   See D3,7, *ARC*, p. 108.
44   Benjamin insists that 'As long as there is still one beggar around, there will still be myth' (K6,4, *ARC*, p. 400).
45   Benjamin notes the 'phantasmagoria of time, to which the gambler dedicated himself' (*CB*, p. 174).
46   Benjamin writes that 'Since each operation at the machine is just as screened off from the preceding operation as a coup in a game of chance is from the one that preceded it, the drudgery of the labourer is, in its own way, a counterpart to the drudgery of the gambler' (*CB*, pp. 134–5).
47   Benjamin notes that 'The ideal of the shock-engendered experience is the catastrophe. This becomes very clear in gambling: by constantly raising the stakes, in hopes of getting back what is lost, the gambler steers toward absolute ruin' (O14,4, *ARC*, p. 515).
48   Benjamin surprisingly dates the 'height of their magic' as late as 1870 (see D°,6, *ARC*, p. 834). According to Johann Geist (1985), however, most of the main arcades were built before 1830, with the Passage de Princes of 1860 the last to be built in Paris.
49   See H°1, *ARC*, p. 844.
50   Benjamin asserts: 'Architecture is the most important testimony to latent "mythology". And the most important architecture of the nineteenth century is the arcade' (D°7, *ARC*, p. 834).
51   See also a°,1, *ARC*, p. 873.
52   The World Exhibitions were held in London (1851 and 1862) and Paris (1855 and 1867).
53   For Benjamin, 'The world exhibitions glorified the exchange value of commodities. They created a framework in which their use-value receded into the background' (*CB*, p. 165).
54   What could be more evocative of the fairy tale than the construction in London of a Crystal Palace?
55   Benjamin notes the testimonies and impressions of astonished visitors to these exhibitions: immense steam locomotives standing impassively like Assyrian bull statues and Egyptian sphinxes (see G8a,2, *ARC*, pp. 188–9), mock Egyptian temples (see G9a,6, *ARC*, p. 190); and artefacts which appear not simply foreign but, as one observer absurdly claims, wholly alien (see G9,2, *ARC*, p. 189).

56 Benjamin writes: 'To live in a glass house is a revolutionary virtue par excellence' (*OWS*, p. 228).

57 Jean Baudrillard captures this 'ambiguity' of glass: 'it is at once proximity and distance, intimacy and the refusal of intimacy, communication and non-communication. Whether as packaging, window or partition, glass is the basis of a transparency without transition: we see, but cannot touch. . . . A shop window is at once magical and frustrating – the strategy of advertising in epitome' (1996, pp. 41–2).

58 Benjamin notes that 'The arcade is a street of lascivious commerce only; it is wholly adapted to arousing desires' (A3a,7, *ARC*, p. 42). Ever mindful of the significance of names, he observes that 'There was a Passage du Désir' (A6a,4, *ARC*, p. 48).

59 See R1a,7, *ARC*, p. 539.

60 See R1,1, *ARC*, p. 537.

61 See R1a,4, *ARC*, p. 539.

62 See also c°,2, *ARC*, p. 877.

63 See R1,3, *ARC*, pp. 536–7, and c°,1, *ARC*, p. 877.

64 Compare the effects of glass and mirrors (and the notion of hyperspace) in Fredric Jameson's (1991) discussion of the Bonaventure Hotel in Los Angeles.

65 See c°3, *ARC*, p. 877.

66 Benjamin notes that 'The arcades were a cross between a street and an *intérieur*' (*CB*, p. 37). See also L1,5, *ARC*, p. 406.

67 Benjamin writes that 'Streets are the dwelling place of the collective. The collective is an eternally wakeful, eternally agitated being that – in the space between the building fronts – lives, experiences, understands and invents as much as individuals do within the privacy of their own four walls. . . . More than anywhere else, the street reveals itself in the arcade as the furnished and familiar interior of the masses' (d°,1, *ARC*, p. 879).

68 See e°,2, *ARC*, p. 881.

69 It is noteworthy that in *Paris of the Second Empire in Baudelaire*, it is no longer the collective, but the flâneur, who turns the city streets into his own domestic setting. See *CB*, p. 37, and Baudelaire, 1986, p. 9.

70 See F°,35, *GS* V, p. 1009.

71 In the arcade 'the traffic . . . is rudimentary' (A3a,7, *ARC*, p. 42).

72 There is a German pun here: the windowless arcade as panorama is home to the 'true', the 'real thing' (*das Wahre*) and the commodity (*die Ware*), an 'unreal' thing, a fetish.

73 Adorno makes a similar point: 'the surrealist experience is in essence nothing more than an unwitting record of the history of life among fetishes, rather than the explosion of this life' (cited in Pensky, 1993, p. 207).

74 See also H°17, *ARC*, p. 845.

75 See ch. 7.

76 See J22,5, *ARC*, p. 268.

77   Benjamin notes that 'In the arcades, one comes upon types of collar
      studs for which we no longer know the corresponding collars and
      shirts' (*ARC*, p. 872).
78   For the opposition of 'aura' and 'trace', see M16a, *ARC*, p. 447.
79   A number of factors led to this decline: the construction of the boule-
      vards under Haussmann, the development of electric lighting; the
      banning of prostitutes, and the rise of an open-air cult. See O°14,
      ARC, p. 858.
80   This ruinous demise finds expression in Emil Zola's novel *Thérèse
      Racquin*. See a°,4, *ARC*, pp. 875, 904.
81   Foremost among these, of course, were the Surrealists themselves.
      Benjamin notes that 'the father of Surrealism was Dada; its mother
      was an arcade. . . . At the end of 1919, Aragon and Breton . . . trans-
      ferred the site of their meetings with friends to a café in the Passage
      de l'Opéra' (h°,1, *ARC*, p. 883).
82   See Gilloch, 1996, pp. 181–4.
83   Benjamin writes of this implosive force in the arcades, 'the energy
      that works within them is dialectics. The dialectic takes its way
      through the arcades, ransacking them, revolutionizing them, turns
      them upside down and inside out, converting them, since they no
      longer remain what they are, from abodes of luxury into [x]' [ruins?]
      (D°,4, *ARC*, p. 833).

Chapter 5   Culture and Critique in Crisis

1   The INFA was founded at the beginning of 1934 by Otto Biha. For a
      discussion of the organization, see Schiller, Pech et al. 1981, p. 228.
2   See *COR*, pp. 369–70.
3   These first texts were Brentano's 'Der Generalangriff', Kurella's 'Der
      Kongress von Charkov' and Plekhanov's 'Idealismus und Material-
      ismus'. Benjamin states bluntly that 'not a single one of the three
      essays submitted can claim to have been written by an expert author-
      ity' (*COR*, p. 371).
4   These are 'concepts whose uncontrolled (and at present almost
      uncontrollable) application would lead to a processing of data in the
      Fascist sense' (*ILL*, p. 220).
5   Benjamin asserts: 'It is political in character. This means that its criti-
      cal activity is anchored in a clear awareness of the critical situation
      of contemporary society. It stands on the ground of class struggle'
      (*GS* VI, p. 619).
6   Editorial note by Scholem/Adorno.
7   Letter to Scholem, 6 May 1934. As the accompanying editorial note
      points out, the text was originally intended as a lecture for the INFA
      (see *COR*, p. 441; *UB*, p. 85; and *GS* II, p. 1462). The date given by
      Benjamin for his lecture (27 Apr. 1934) is questionable (see *GS* II, p.

1460). In any case, it seems that he did not give the lecture, and his subsequent hopes of publishing it in Klaus Mann's journal *Die Samm-lung* came to nothing (see *GS* II, p. 1461).

8 See Benjamin's criticism of Döblin regarding this, *UB*, pp. 91–3.

9 Benjamin writes that 'the place of the intellectual in the class struggle can only be determined, or better still chosen, on the basis of his position within the production process' (*UB*, p. 93).

10 See *UB*, p. 87.

11 Benjamin writes: 'If . . . the correct political tendency of a work includes its literary quality because it includes its literary tendency, we can now affirm more precisely that this literary tendency may consist in a progressive development of literary technique, or in a regressive' (*UB*, p. 88).

12 See *UB*, p. 90.

13 Not at all the same as the *political* awakening demanded by Benjamin in his critique of Surrealism and in the *Passagenarbeit*.

14 In his 1934 fragment 'The Newspaper' Benjamin notes that 'The reader is at all times ready to become a writer . . . As an expert . . . he gains access to authorship. . . . Literary competence is no longer founded on specialised training but is now based on polytechnical education, and thus becomes public property' (*SW2*, pp. 741–2).

15 See *OWS*, pp. 246–7.

16 Such photography 'is now incapable of photographing a tenement or a rubbish-heap without transfiguring it. Not to mention a river dam or an electric cable factory: in front of these, photography can now only say, "How beautiful." . . . It has succeeded in turning abject poverty itself, by handling it in a modish, technically perfect way, into an object of enjoyment' (*UB*, pp. 94–5).

17 Benjamin writes of the progressive artist: 'He will never be concerned with products alone, but always, at the same time, with the means of production. . . . [H]is products must possess an organizing function besides and before their character as finished works' (*UB*, p. 98).

18 See Benjamin's letter to Scholem, 25 Apr. 1930: *COR*, p. 365, and *SW2*, pp. 374–7.

19 'From the Brecht Commentary' (Apr. 1930) was followed by a radio broadcast entitled 'Bert Brecht' on 24 June 1930 (*SW2*, pp. 365–71). Benjamin's subsequent writings on Brecht include two versions of 'What is Epic Theatre?' (1931 and 1939), 'A Family Drama in the Epic Theatre' (Jan./Feb. 1932), 'The Land where it is Forbidden to Mention the Proletariat' (1938), 'Commentaries on Poems by Brecht' (1938–9). See *UB*, pp. 43–74, *SW2*, pp. 559–62, and *GS* II, pp. 506–72. See also 'Conversations with Brecht' (1934), in *GS* VI, pp. 523–32; 'Brecht's Threepenny Novel', in *GS* III, pp. 440–9; 'The Threepenny Opera' (1937), in *GS* VII, pp. 347–9; 'Theatre and Radio' (May 1932), *SW2*, pp. 583–6, and *GS* II, pp. 773–6; and 'Note on Brecht' (1938/9), in *GS* VI, p. 540.

20 Benjamin spent three summers in Skovsbostrand per Svendborg with Brecht: July–Oct. 1934, Aug. and Sept. 1936, and July–Oct. 1938.

21 See *UB*, p. 81. Benjamin claims that 'Crude thoughts belong to the household of dialectical thinking precisely because they represent nothing other than the *application* of theory to practice, not its *dependence* on practice. Action can, of course, be as subtle as thought. But a thought must be crude in order to come into its own in action' (*UB*, p. 81).

22 Adorno observes that 'truth involves innumerable mediations which Brecht disdains' (*AP*, p. 183).

23 See *AP*, p. 184.

24 See *AP*, p. 186.

25 Letter from Scholem to Benjamin, 30 Mar. 1931.

26 Letter from Scholem to Benjamin, 6 May 1931.

27 Letter of 17 Apr. 1931.

28 In a letter to Scholem of 6 May 1934, Benjamin notes: 'my communism is absolutely nothing other than the expression of certain experiences I have undergone in my thinking and in my life; . . . it is a drastic, not infertile expression of the fact that the present intellectual industry finds it impossible to make room for my thinking, just as the present economic order finds it impossible to accommodate my life; . . . it represents the obvious, reasoned attempt on the part of a man who is completely or almost completely deprived of any means of production to proclaim his right to them, both in his thinking and in his life' (*COR*, p. 439).

29 See Benjamin's letter of 20 Oct. 1933 to Kitty Marx-Steinschneider: *COR*, p. 430.

30 In a letter to Scholem of 20 July 1931, Benjamin writes of Brecht's *Versuche* that 'these essays are the first . . . that I champion as a critic without (public) reservation. This is because part of my development in the last few years came about in confrontation with them, and because they, more rigorously than any others, give an insight into the intellectual context in which the work of people like myself is conducted in this country' (*COR*, p. 380).

31 In a letter to Scholem of 17 Apr. 1931, Benjamin observes: 'Where is my productive base? It is – and I have not the slightest illusions about this – in Berlin W. W.W. if you like. The most advanced civilisation and the most "modern" culture not only are part of my private comforts but are in part simply the means of my production' (*COR*, p. 377).

32 Benjamin's 'lecture' was the topic of his early discussions with Brecht in the summer of 1934. See *UB*, p. 105.

33 *UB*, p. 98.

34 Benjamin notes that 'Tragedies and operas go on and on being written . . . for an apparatus which is obsolete' (*UB*, p. 1).

35 *SW2*, p. 4.

36 Benjamin comments that 'Epic theatre . . . incessantly derives a lively and productive consciousness from the fact that it is theatre' (*UB*, p. 4).

37 Benjamin notes that 'By imagining what it means to "play at acting" we come closest to understanding what epic theatre is all about' (*UB*, p. 21).

38 *UB*, p. 99.

39 *UB*, p. 99.

40 *UB*, p. 3.

41 See 'Technical Aid', *OWS*, p. 95.

42 *OGTD*, p. 29.

43 Benjamin observes that 'Quoting a text means interrupting its context' (*UB*, p. 19).

44 *UB*, p. 18.

45 *UB*, p. 15.

46 *UB*, p. 18. It is not only the audience which abstains from empathy. The actors themselves adopt a critical attitude to the characters they play. Method acting has no place in epic drama. See *UB*, p. 40.

47 Benjamin writes: 'we could very soon have a theatre full of experts, as we have sports stadiums full of experts' (*UB*, p. 4).

48 With the advent of epic theatre, 'the critic as he is constituted today is no longer ahead of that mass but actually finds himself far behind it' (*UB*, p. 10).

49 Benjamin writes that 'the critic suffers the double misfortune of seeing his nature as agent revealed, and at the same time devalued' (*UB*, p. 10).

50 Adorno's demand for a complex understanding of the technical innovations of 'autonomous art' is in marked contrast to his failure or refusal to acknowledge those of epic theatre. Perhaps '*more* dialectics' would have tempered his own critique of Brecht.

51 Benjamin notes that 'Epic theatre proceeds by fits and starts, in a manner comparable to the images on a film strip' (*UB*, p. 21).

52 *SW2*, pp. 583–6.

Chapter 6   Benjamin On-Air, Benjamin on Aura

1 Benjamin was not the first of the Frankfurt School writers to explore these popular media. Siegfried Kracauer wrote an essay on photography in 1927 (see Kracauer, 1995, pp. 47–63) and some 700 texts on film and cinema between 1920 and 1933 for the *Frankfurter Zeitung*, including numerous film reviews, genre studies, reflections on film criticism and cinema audiences, and broader considerations of the place of cinema in Weimar popular culture. See Miriam Hansen's 'Introduction' to Kracauer, 1997 [1960], p. x. See Kracauer, 1995, pp. 279–328, and also his 1974 collected writings on cinema.

2 'The Work of Art in the Age of its Technical Reproducibility' is a more accurate translation of Benjamin's title: 'Das Kunstwerk im Zeitalter seiner technischen Reproduzierbarkeit'.

3 Brecht writes of the 'Work of Art' essay, on 25 July 1938, that 'everything is mysticism while the stance is anti-mysticism. For the materialist conception of history to be adapted so! It is quite dreadful' (*GS* I, p. 1082). Benjamin's essay was rejected by *Das Wort*, a journal co-edited by Brecht. See Wolin, 1982, p. 141.

4 One should not be surprised that Benjamin worked for the radio. As Schiller-Lerg (1984, p. 48) points out, many of his colleagues, like Adorno, Hessel, Brecht and Kracauer, had done so before him, and Dora, his wife, had done a series of broadcasts for Frauenfunk in 1928.

5 For a complete listing of broadcast dates, see Schiller-Lerg, 1984, pp. 538–9.

6 See Mehlman, 1993, pp. 1–2.

7 The 'Jugendstunde' for the Funkstunde AG Berlin, and the 'Stunde der Jugend' for Südwestdeutscher Rundfunk in Frankfurt am Main.

8 See Schiller-Lerg, 1984, p. 13. The former Benjamin archive in the Akademie der Kunst also contained a twelve-page typescript of 'Questions und Theses' (dated Jan. 1938) which Adorno sent to Benjamin (folder 41, pp. 49–61). This text is referred to as an 'exposé' in Adorno's letter, 1 Feb. 1938. See also Benjamin's reply, 11 Feb. 1938: *ABC*, pp. 235–8.

9 Mehlman notes the 'odd inappropriateness of collecting them under the banner of the Enlightenment' (1993, p. 1).

10 In addition to 'Theater and Radio' (*SW2*, pp. 583–6), Benjamin wrote a plethora of fragments on the role and character of radio: the 1929 'Gespräch mit Ernst Schoen' (*GS* IV, pp. 548–51), 'Hörmodelle' of 1931 (*GS* IV, p. 628), 'Zweierlei Volkstümlichkeit' of 1932 (*GS* IV, pp. 671–3), and 'Situation im Rundfunk' (*GS* II, p. 1505) and 'Reflections on Radio' (*SW2*, pp. 543–4) both written c.1930–1.

11 See also Benjamin's letter of 18 Sept. 1929 to Scholem: *COR*, p. 356.

12 Benjamin generally had a 'negative attitude towards much of the work he did for money. Yet most of these texts also contain sediments of his decidedly original way of seeing' (*COR*, p. 404).

13 These scripts include, e.g., 'Berlin Dialect', 'Street Trade and Market in Old and New Berlin', 'Berlin Puppet Theatre', 'Daemonic Berlin', 'Berlin Toy Expeditions I' and 'II', 'Borsig' and 'Tenement Buildings'.

14 Benjamin's last radio broadcast, on 29 Jan. 1933, was a series of extracts from the then unpublished 'Berlin Childhood' (see Schiller-Lerg, 1984, pp. 302–3).

15 Adorno and Horkheimer wrote: 'the radio becomes the universal mouthpiece of the Führer . . . The National Socialists knew that the wireless gave shape to their cause just as the printing press did to the Reformation . . . The inherent tendency of radio is to make the speaker's word, the false commandment, absolute' (1986, p. 159).

16 Epic theatre 'replaces culture [*Bildung*] with training [*Schulung*], distraction [*Zestreuung*] with group formation [*Gruppierung*]' (*SW2*, p. 585).

17 Schiller-Lerg notes that 'The schooling of the listener was Benjamin's didactic concept, not in the sense of communicating knowledge which could only promote the education divide but rather as a guiding force towards the listener's own knowledge and experience. When the listener was in a position to estimate and scrutinize every representation of reality measured against his own situation, then he was also in a position to orient and organize himself in society' (in Doderer, 1988, p. 107).

18 In Doderer, 1988, p. 108.

19 For a full discussion of this play and the differences between the Frankfurt and Cologne versions, see Schiller-Lerg, 1984, pp. 252–69.

20 See Schiller-Lerg, 1984, p. 252, and Müller in Doderer, 1988, p. 119. Benjamin also drew Scholem's attention to this text in a letter dated 22 Apr. 1932: *COR*, p. 391.

21 As Müller points out, this absurd name is 'a satire on his profession: Maulschmidt – the mouthsmith' (in Doderer, 1988, p. 118).

22 Benjamin creates, Müller notes, a 'modern Kasperl' who 'struggles no longer with the devil, the sorcerer, the robber or the crocodile. Instead, Kasperl wrestles with the treachery of technology in the "modern times," which he understands as little as the human listener' (in Doderer, 1988, p. 118).

23 See Müller, in Doderer, 1988, p. 116.

24 A sketch for the play is appropriately entitled 'Kasperl und der Rundfunk, eine Geschichte mit Lärm'. See Schiller-Lerg, 1984, p. 254.

25 See Müller, in Doderer, 1988, p. 116.

26 Hence, in this play 'Benjamin makes an "acoustic virtue" out of an "optical necessity"' (Müller, in Doderer, 1988, p. 118).

27 As programme notes for *Radau um Kasperl* make clear, the active participation of the children listening was encouraged: '"Kasperl's experiences in this radio play, as the title suggests, involve rowdiness. The children are asked to guess what the ensuing noises mean and to share their opinions with Südwestfunk"' (quoted in Schiller-Lerg, 1984, p. 255).

28 See *SW2*, p. 544.

29 Mehlman here cites Benjamin's own understanding of toys: '"Originally toys were produced by artisans, on the side [*als Nebenarbeit*], in the course of their work, as mere miniature reproductions of the objects of daily life"' (1993, p. 4).

30 Accordingly, Benjamin's radio broadcasts for children 'are at times as analytically forceful as anything in what one hesitates to call his "adult" writings' (Mehlman, 1993, p. 2).

31 See Mehlman, 1993, pp. 7–12.

32 Scholem had discussed Zevi with Benjamin in 1927. See Mehlman, 1993, pp. 40–1.

33 See f°,2, *ARC*, pp. 881–2.

34 Letter to Scholem, 28 Oct. 1931.

35 See *ARC*, pp. 671–92.

36 A book on early photography by Helmuth Bossert and Heinrich Guttmann (1930); a study of David Octavius Hill by Heinrich Schwarz (1931); Karl Blossfeldt's *Urformen der Kunst. Photographische Planzenbilder* (1931); Eugène Atget's *Lichtbilder* (1931), and August Sander's *Das Antlitz der Zeit* (1930).

37 Werfel was not alone in this opinion. As Kracauer points in his 'psychological history' of German film, even the young Lukács 'wrote in 1913 that he considered the film tantamount to the fairy tale and the dream' (1947, p. 28).

38 Benjamin notes that 'The camera introduces us to unconscious optics as does psychoanalysis to unconscious impulses' (*ILL*, p. 239).

39 The sculptor August Rodin wrote: ' "People in photographs suddenly seem frozen in mid-air, despite being caught in full swing: this is because every part of their body is reproduced at exactly the same twentieth or fortieth of a second, so there is no gradual unfolding of a gesture, as there is in art" ' (quoted in Virilio, 1994, p. 1).

40 In the 'Work of Art' essay, Benjamin points out that the precision of film and its decomposing of action into analysable units serve to 'promote the mutual penetration of art and science . . . To demonstrate the identity of artistic and scientific uses of photography which heretofore were usually separated will be one of the revolutionary functions of the film' (*ILL*, p. 238).

41 Benjamin also notes how series of photographs taken at regular intervals were used to recreate the impression of movement in chronophotography. See Y7a,1, *ARC*, p. 686.

42 In his 1927 essay on photography, Kracauer makes a similar point. He contrasts the images preserved in memory – ones filled with meaning and significance since whatever is trivial has been lost – with those of photography, in which there is no distinction between the important and the merely incidental. Hence, Kracauer notes, 'from the perspective of memory, photography appears as a jumble that consists partly of garbage' (1995, p. 51). It is, of course, precisely this 'garbage' which fascinates Benjamin and, later, Roland Barthes (1993).

43 This power of enlargement is exemplified by Blossfeldt's photographs of plants (see *OWS*, p. 244). These exemplify the 'identity of artistic and scientific uses of photography' referred to in the 'Work of Art' essay (*ILL*, p. 238).

44 Kracauer notes that the photograph offers a *'general inventory'*, a 'comprehensive catalogue of all manifestations which present themselves in space' (1995, p. 61) at a given moment.

45 Benjamin cites Dauthendey: ' "We . . . believed that the little tiny faces in the picture could see *us*, so powerfully was everyone affected by

the unaccustomed clarity and the unaccustomed truth to nature of the first daguerrotypes"' (*OWS*, p. 244).

46 Benjamin notes that 'The procedure itself caused the subject to focus his life in the moment rather than hurrying on past it' (*OWS*, p. 245). However, he later insisted that aura is 'by no means the mere product of a primitive camera' (*OWS*, p. 248).

47 Benjamin notes that 'Everything about these early pictures was built to last; . . . the very creases in people's clothes have an air of permanence' (*OWS*, p. 245).

48 See Price, 1994, p. 48.

49 Describing a photograph of Kafka as a child of six, dressed up in a broad-brimmed hat and holding a spear, Benjamin suggests that the aura of the subject would have been overwhelmed by such inane accessories were it not for the boy's 'immensely sad eyes' (*OWS*, p. 247).

50 In 'On Some Motifs in Baudelaire', Benjamin writes: 'Experience of the aura thus rests on a transposition of a response common in human relationships to the relationship between the inanimate or natural object and man. The person we look at, or who feels he is being looked at, looks at us in turn. To perceive the aura of an object we look at means to invest it with the ability to look at us in return' (*CB*, p. 148).

51 'Remarkably', Benjamin observes, 'almost all these picture are empty' (*OWS*, p. 251).

52 Benjamin finds the same sensibility in the work of the German photographer August Sander, whose photographs of faces constitute not a picture book but a 'training manual' (*OWS*, p. 252).

53 Benjamin notes that 'to bring things closer to us, or rather to the masses, is just as passionate an inclination in our day as the overcoming of whatever is unique in every situation by means of its reproduction. Every day the need to possess the object in close-up in the form of a picture, or rather a copy, becomes imperative' (*OWS*, p. 250).

54 Miriam Hansen cites Norbert Bolz's evaluation of Kracauer's film writings as '"beautiful ruins in the philosophical landscape"' (Kracauer, 1997 [1960], p. viii). Hansen notes that Bolz extends this description to include Benjamin's 'film theory' too. This is surprising, given the level of current interest in the 'Work of Art' essay. Then again, some 'beautiful ruins' are simply more frequented than others perhaps.

55 In a letter to Werner Kraft of 27, Dec. 1935, Benjamin explicitly denies any thematic connection between the essay and the 'Arcades Project', and then claims: 'Methodologically, however, it is most intimately related to it, since the locus of contemporaneity in the objects whose history is to be presented must be precisely fixed before any historical work is undertaken, especially one that claims to be written from the perspective of historical materialism' (*COR*, p. 517).

56 In a letter to Scholem of 24 Oct. 1935, Benjamin notes that 'These reflections anchor the history of nineteenth-century art in the recognition of their situation as experienced by us in the present' (*COR*, p. 514).

57 In a letter to Scholem of 3 May 1936, Benjamin notes that the 'Work of Art Essay' essay 'touches on the major project only superficially, but it indicates the vanishing point for some of its investigations' (*COR*, pp. 527–8).

58 Werner Fuld cites an article by Kienzl in *Der Strom* of 1911–12: ' "the psychology of the cinematic triumph is metropolitan psychology" ' (1990, p. 250).

59 For a discussion of early cinema and the city, see Weihsmann in Penz and Thomas, 1997, pp. 8–27.

60 See *OWS*, p. 179.

61 Benjamin notes that 'Only film commands optical approaches to the essence of the city' (*OWS*, p. 298).

62 Benjamin notes that the cult value of the artwork was, and still is, frequently derived from its ability to escape the realm of mundane perception. 'Today', he writes, 'the cult value would seem to demand that the work of art remain hidden' (*ILL*, p. 227).

63 Adorno makes this identification of aura and symbol in his letter to Benjamin of 18 Mar. 1936: see *AP*, p. 121.

64 See *ILL*, pp. 225–6.

65 See *ILL*, p. 226.

66 See *AP*, pp. 120–6.

67 If Adorno is indeed advocating that the autonomous artwork be treated as a kind of wish image, this would be rather ironic, given his own criticism of this notion in Benjamin's 1935 *exposé*. There is certainly an interesting parallel between Benjamin's categories of aura and trace and those of commodity fetishism and obsolescence. With aura, as with the fetishized object, the human being is rendered subservient to the magic of the thing. In the obsolete commodity, the fetishistic spell is broken, and we directly confront the remnant, the vestigial truth content of the thing as ruin. Is aura then simply the fetish character of the artwork? This is tempting, but there is an important complication. The industrial production and reproduction of commodities under capitalism is the basis of their fetish character. Yet, these processes lead to the *demise* of aura.

68 See *ILL*, pp. 226–7.

69 See *AP*, p. 124.

70 As Kracauer notes (1947, pp. 35–9), Ufa (Universum Film AG) was set up in 1917 at the behest of the Imperial German authorities for the express purpose of producing propaganda films for the war effort. See also Kracauer, 1995, p. 382, n. 2. For Kracauer's own description of the Ufa complex, see his 1926 text 'Calico World: The UFA City in Neubabelsberg', in Kracauer, 1995, pp. 281–8.

71 Benjamin mentions Vertov's *Three Songs about Lenin* in the 'Work of Art' essay (*ILL*, p. 233), but makes no reference to Vertov's famous 1929 *Man with a Movie Camera*, a film which seems to be the very epitome of Benjamin's aesthetic and political imperatives. Kracauer (1947, pp. 182–8) makes an important distinction between the montage techniques employed by Vertov in this film and those of Walter Ruttmann's 1927 *Berlin, The Symphony of a Great City* in terms of content, context and rhythm. Kracauer's advocacy of the revolutionary enthusiasm imbuing Vertov's vision of Moscow and his rejection of Ruttmann's mere replication of the banalities and mechanical rhythms of capitalist Berlin form an interesting parallel to Benjamin's endorsement of photomontage and critique of photoreportage. Benjamin's seemingly undifferentiated understanding of cinematic montage overlooks such subtle, yet significant technical (and political) distinctions.

72 See *ILL*, p. 232.

73 See *ILL*, p. 230.

74 Kracauer also used this term in connection with the cinema. In his 1926 fragment 'Cult of Distraction: On Berlin's Picture Palaces', Kracauer offers an ambivalent response to this phenomenon. On the one hand, for Kracauer as for Benjamin, distraction represents a decisive break with outmoded traditional cultural forms, and involves a new sense of perceptual fragmentation in keeping with modern experience. On the other, it is also a form of emotional and ideological compensation for the bureaucratized, spiritually 'homeless' condition endured by the new mass of metropolitan white-collar workers. See Kracauer, 1995, pp. 23, 323–8, and Kracauer, 1998, pp. 13 and 94.

75 See *ILL*, p. 240.

76 Benjamin writes that 'the work of art of the Dadaists became an instrument of ballistics. It hit the spectator like a bullet, it happened to him, thus acquiring a tactile quality' (*ILL*, p. 240); cf. *OWS*, p. 89.

77 Benjamin observes that 'film corresponds to profound changes in the apperceptive apparatus – changes that are experienced on an individual scale by the man in the street in big-city traffic, on a historical scale by every present-day citizen' (*ILL*, p. 252).

78 See Simmel, 1971, p. 329.

79 Hessel describes the hoardings, billboards, signs and images of advertising as the 'achitecture of the instant' (*Architektur des Augenblicks*) (1994, pp. 108–9).

80 Hence, Adorno notes that 'in a communist society work will be organised in such a way that people will no longer be so tired and so stultified that they need distraction' (*AP*, p. 123).

81 As Jay Bernstein notes, Adorno's essay is 'best regarded as a polemic against Benjamin's "The Work of Art in the Age of Mechanical Reproduction"' (Adorno, 1991, p. 4).

82   Kracauer (1947, p. 301) observes, for example, how the Nazi rallies in Nuremburg were conceived as cinematic spectacles, to be recorded for posterity in Leni Riefenstahl's infamous film *Triumph of the Will*.

Chapter 7   Love at Last Sight

1   For example, with Kracauer, his fellow exile in Paris, on account of the Offenbach book, and, of course, with Scholem and Adorno over Marxism in general and Brecht in particular.
2   See Gilloch, 1996, pp. 56–7.
3   Trans. by MacIntyre, *CB*, p. 45.
4   *GS* IV, p. 41.
5   See M, 'The Flâneur'; O, 'Prostitution, Gambling'; and m, 'Idleness'.
6   Horkheimer wanted the Baudelaire study to appear in the Institute's *Zeitschrift für Sozialforschung*.
7   Letter from Benjamin to Adorno, 17 May 1937.
8   See Adorno's letter to Benjamin, 2 July 1937: *ABC*, p. 196.
9   See his letter to Adorno of 17 Nov. 1937: *ABC*, p. 226.
10   Trans. amended; cf. *GS* I, p. 1072.
11   See also J51a,5, *ARC*, p. 321.
12   See *GS* I, pp. 1161–7, partially trans. in *CB*, pp. 103–4.
13   Benjamin actually offers a third metaphor, one which echoes the fluvial opening to the Surrealism essay, and again suggests the services of the hydraulic engineer (see *CB*, pp. 103–4).
14   See *COR*, pp. 555–8. See also Benjamin's letter to Adorno of the same date: *ABC*, p. 247.
15   *COR*, p. 567. If the Baudelaire study was to provide a model in miniature of the 'Arcades Project', and the *Elective Affinities* essay was the model for the Baudelaire piece, this raises the intriguing idea that the *Wahlverwandschaften* study came to be seen as a model for the *Passagenarbeit*. See also *ABC*, p. 247.
16   Redesignated 'Baudelaire as allegorist' by Benjamin in his letter to Horkheimer, 28 Sept. 1938: *COR*, p. 574.
17   Benjamin writes that 'the function of this second part is that of antithesis. It decisively turns its back on the first part's concern with artistic theory and undertakes a sociocritical interpretation of the poet. . . . As antithesis, the second part is the one in which criticism in its narrow sense, namely Baudelaire criticism, has its place' (*COR*, p. 574).
18   This was later retitled 'The Commodity as Poetic Object' (*COR*, p. 573).
19   Letter to Gretel Adorno, 20 July 1938. See also Benjamin's letter to Horkheimer, 3 Aug. 1938: *GS* I, p. 1083.
20   Letter to Scholem, 8 July 1938. See also his letter to Horkheimer, 16 Apr. 1938: *COR*, p. 556.

21   An initial indication of this change is given in Benjamin's letter to Kitty Marx-Steinschneider of 20 July 1938; see *COR*, p. 568.
22   See Benjamin's letter to Horkheimer, 3 Aug. 1938: *GS* I, p. 1083.
23   In the letter to Horkheimer of 28 Sept. 1938 accompanying the completed text, Benjamin wrote: 'the Baudelaire was originally conceived as a chapter of the *Arcades*, specifically as the penultimate chapter . . . I came to realize as the summer went on that a Baudelaire essay more modest in length that did not repudiate its responsibility to the *Arcades* draft could be produced only as a part of a Baudelaire *book*' (*COR*, p. 573). See also Benjamin's letter to Adorno, 4 Oct. 1938: *COR*, p. 576.
24   Adorno observes that 'the work represents not so much a model for the *Arcades* as a prelude to that project. Motifs are assembled but not developed' (*COR*, p. 580).
25   For example, Adorno complained that, instead of being treated as an 'objective historicist category', the phantasmagoria of the modern metropolis appeared only as the subjective impressions of particular 'social characters' and 'literary bohemia' (*COR*, p. 580).
26   Adorno notes his 'aversion to this particular type of concreteness and its behavioristic features' (*COR*, p. 581), which stems, he observes, from the detrimental influence of Simmel.
27   By contrast, Adorno insists that 'The materialistic determination of cultural characteristics is possible only when mediated by the *total process*' (*COR*, p. 582).
28   Adorno writes with great presumption: 'I myself am unambiguously opposed [to publication]. . . . [N]ot for editorial reasons but for your own sake and that of the Baudelaire study. It does not represent you the way in which this work in particular must represent you' (*COR*, p. 583).
29   *COR*, p. 589.
30   See Benjamin's letter to Horkheimer, 18 Apr. 1939: *GS* I, p. 1119.
31   Letter to Gretel Adorno, 26 June 1939.
32   See Adorno's letter of 1 Feb. 1939: *ABC*, p. 229.
33   Letter of 1 Sept. 1939.
34   Letter of 16 Oct. 1939. This last comment is ironic, given that for some commentators, the text 'constitutes in essence a submission to the will of Adorno' (Penksy, 1993, p. 152).
35   *GS* I, pp. 1130–3.
36   In his letter to Horkheimer of 30 Nov. 1939, Benjamin unaccountably identifies 'On Some Motifs in Baudelaire' as the middle third, rather than the central section of the second part of the Baudelaire book (see *COR*, p. 619).
37   Baudelaire, 1982, p. 15.
38   For Benjamin, the creed of *l'art pour l'art* was one of the final attempts to preserve the cultic vestiges of the artwork. The belief in an autonomous, privileged artistic realm was the very antithesis of his view of the politicization of aesthetics.

39   Benjamin notes that 'The allegorical experience was primary for him' (J53a,1, *ARC*, p. 324).

40   J55,13, *ARC*, p. 328.

41   The key figures here are 'the neurasthenic, metropolitan dweller and customer' (*GS* I, p. 1169).

42   Wolin, 1982, p. 231.

43   Accordingly, Benjamin notes in a letter to Horkheimer of 3 Aug. 1938: 'The first section seeks to provide perspectives on the prehistory [*Vorgeschichte*] of Baudelaire with a comparison of the functions possessed by allegory in the seventeenth and nineteenth centuries' (*GS* I, p. 1084).

44   In 'Central Park' Benjamin notes that how 'the face of prostitution altered with the growth of the great cities' is 'one of the chief objects of his poetry' (*CP*, p. 53).

45   Benjamin develops this notion of a connection between the prostitute and the industrial worker. The factory worker also subjects his or her body to ruinous activity. Work and prostitution converge (see J75,1, *ARC* p. 360, and J67,5, *ARC*, p. 348).

46   For a discussion of Benjamin as historical ragpicker, see Wohlfahrt, 1986.

47   Baudelaire 'found nothing to like about his time' (*CB*, p. 97).

48   Benjamin observes: 'No one ever felt less at home in Paris than Baudelaire. *Every* intimacy with things is alien to the allegorical intention' (J59a,4, *ARC*, p. 336).

49   Benjamin cites Crépet's description: 'Baudelaire belonged to that family of unfortunates who desire only what they do not have and love only the place where they are not' (J31,3, *ARC*, p. 284). See also J51a,6, *ARC*, p. 322.

50   J66a,4, *ARC*, p. 346.

51   See 'To the Reader', the opening poem of *Les Fleurs du mal* (Baudelaire, 1982, p. 6).

52   Baudelaire proclaims: ' "I'd like to set the entire human race against me. That offers a pleasure that could console me for everything" ' (J46a,10, *ARC*, p. 313).

53   Benjamin observes that 'to interrupt the course of the world – this is Baudelaire's deepest wish. The wish of Joshua' (*CP*, p. 39). See also J50,2, *ARC*, p. 318.

54   Missac, 1995, p. 39.

55   The title of Baudelaire's most famous aesthetic essay written in 1859–60 and published in 1863.

56   Baudelaire, 1986, p. 13.

57   Baudelaire, 1986, pp. 12–13.

58   Baudelaire's concept of *modernité* as the latest antiquity can be seen as intimately related to Benjamin's notion of 'afterlife'.

59   M1,4, *ARC*, p. 417.

60   Benjamin notes that 'strolling could hardly have assumed the importance it did without the arcade' (*CB*, p. 36).

61 In her seminal essay on the 'invisible flâneuse', Janet Wolff argues that since women in the nineteenth century 'could not stroll alone in the city' (1990, p. 41), one must recognize that 'the experience of anonymity in the city, the fleeting, impersonal contacts described by social commentators like Georg Simmel, the possibility of unmolested strolling and observation first seen by Baudelaire, and then analysed by Walter Benjamin were entirely the experiences of men' (1990, p. 58). This has been contested by a number of writers who have offered a range of possible candidates for the flâneuse: the prostitute (Buck-Morss, 1986, p. 119; Wilson, 1991, p. 55); the West End shopper (Walkowitz, 1992, pp. 46–50; Nava, 1997, p. 72) and the East End philanthropist (Walkowitz, 1992, pp. 52–9; Nava, 1997, p. 62). For a summary of these debates, see Parsons, 1999.

62 See M1,3, *GS* V, p. 525.

63 See *CB*, p. 54.

64 See M19,2, *ARC*, p. 451.

65 Baudelaire 'placed the shock experience at the very centre of his work' (*CB*, p. 117).

66 See 'The Metropolis and Mental Life', in Simmel, 1971.

67 See J14,1, *ARC*, p. 252.

68 Despite the supposed reciprocity of glances, the unknown woman in the poem is clearly positioned as the object of the predatory male gaze (see Wolff, 1990, p. 42).

69 The gambler is thus the representative figure for this amnesia. See *CB*, p. 135.

70 Benjamin observes that 'it is to this immolation of our deepest self in shock that our memory owes its most indelible images' (*OWS*, p. 343).

71 Benjamin muses: 'Is not the involuntary recollection, Proust's *mémoire involontaire*, much nearer to forgetting than what is usually called memory?' (*ILL*, p. 204).

72 See Benjamin's letter to Scholem, 21 July 1925: *COR*, pp. 277–8.

73 See Brodersen, 1997, pp. 162–72.

74 These reflections are first mentioned in Benjamin's letter to Hofmannsthal, 23 Feb. 1926: *COR*, p. 291.

75 *ILL*, p. 204.

76 *ILL*, p. 216.

77 *ILL*, p. 213.

78 Observing that 'We do not always proclaim loudly the most important thing we have to say', Benjamin contends that 'the nineteenth century did not reveal itself to Zola or Anatole France, but to the young Proust, the insignificant snob, the playboy and socialite who snatched in passing the most astounding confidences from a declining age as from another, bone-weary Swann' (*ILL*, p. 207).

79 The *mémoire involontaire* may be imagistic, but its source is non-visual: 'Smell – that is the sense of weight of someone who casts his nets into the sea of the *temps perdu*' (*ILL*, p. 216).

80 *ILL*, p. 213.

81 McCole (1993, p. 260) helpfully identifies four distinctive features of the *mémoire involontaire*: it is spontaneous, quotidian, intuitive and non-verbal.

82 Hessel, 1982. For Benjamin's review see *SW2*, pp. 69–71.

83 Republished as Hessel, 1984. For Benjamin's review see *SW2*, pp. 262–7.

84 Hessel exemplifies 'the perfected art of the flâneur' (*SW2*, p. 264).

85 Benjamin writes: 'The city is a mnemonic for the lonely walker: it conjures up more than his childhood and youth, more than his own history' (*SW2*, p. 262).

86 Benjamin notes this ghostly quality of the city in his 'Berlin Chronicle': 'Noisy, matter-of-fact Berlin, the city of work and the metropolis of business, nevertheless has more, rather than less, than some others, of those places and moments when it bears witness to the dead, shows itself full of dead' (*OWS*, p. 316).

87 Appropriately, 'The true reader of Proust is constantly jarred by small shocks' (*ILL*, p. 210).

88 Taking Léon Daudet's *Paris vécu* (see *ILL*, p. 208) as his model, Benjamin's ambition was to capture 'Lived Berlin' (*OWS*, p. 295).

89 Szondi notes that 'the labyrinth is in space what memory . . . is in time' (Smith, 1988, p. 22).

90 Szondi, in Smith, 1988, p. 20.

91 Benjamin notes that 'in the optic of history – opposite in this to that of space – movement in the distance means enlargement' (*OWS*, p. 207). The section of *Einbahnstrasse* entitled 'Enlargements' clearly prefigures the 'Berlin Childhood' study.

92 Compare Benjamin's comments on Marseilles in 'Mixed Cargo: Carriage and Packing' (*OWS*, pp. 90–1).

93 See his letter to Scholem, 20 Jan. 1930: *COR*, p. 359.

94 See his letter to Gretel Adorno, 16 Aug. 1935: *COR*, p. 507.

95 See Konersmann, 1991, pp. 90–7, for an insightful critique of Benjamin's interpretation of Ranke.

96 Benjamin notes that 'Universal history has no theoretical armature. Its method is additive; it musters a mass of data to fill the homogenous empty time' (*ILL*, p. 264).

97 Benjamin ridicules historicism for 'telling the sequence of events like the beads of a rosary' (*ILL*, p. 265).

98 Benjamin scornfully refers to 'the whore called 'Once upon a time' in historicism's bordello' (*ILL*, p. 264).

99 N2,3, *ARC*, p. 460.

100 Benjamin notes: 'The tradition of the oppressed teaches us that the 'state of emergency' in which we live is not the exception but the rule. We must attain to a conception of history that is in keeping with this insight. Then we shall clearly realise that it is our task to bring about a real state of emergency, and this will improve our position in the struggle against Fascism' (*ILL*, p. 259). See also N10a,2, *ARC*, p. 475.

101 As Konersmann (1991, p. 90) notes, Benjamin is here quoting Ranke's *Geschichten der romanischen und germanischen Völker von 1494–1514* (1824).

102 The notion of grasping this buried history corresponds to the tactile appropriation of the work of art and the cityscape. It is a vigorous and unrelenting hold (see N9a,3, *ARC*, p. 473). Benjamin later adds that 'the task of history is not only to grasp the tradition of the oppressed but also to support it' (*GS* I, p. 1246).

103 The revolutionary working class is 'nourished by the image of enslaved ancestors rather than that of liberated grandchildren' (*ILL*, p. 262).

104 Benjamin writes: 'the continuum of history is that of the oppressor. While the notion of the continuum destroys everything, that of discontinuity is the basis of genuine tradition' (*GS* I, p. 1236).

105 In his notes for the 'Theses', Benjamin muses: 'the structure of Marx's fundamental ideas is as follows: through a series of class conflicts in the course of historical development, humanity achieves the classless society. But perhaps the classless society is not to be conceptualised as the endpoint of historical development' (*GS* I, p. 1232).

106 The broken character of the tradition of the oppressed and the *caesura* of revolution provide 'footing' and handholds for the 'seemingly brutal grasp' necessary (see N9a,5, *ARC*, p. 474).

107 N7a,7, *ARC*, p. 471.

108 Benjamin insists that 'the concept of the classless society must be given its true messianic countenance once more, for this is in the interests of proletarian revolutionary politics' (*GS* I, p. 1232).

109 Benjamin incorporated Horkheimer's letter of 16 Mar. 1937 into Convolute N. Horkheimer wrote: ' "Past injustice has occurred and is completed. The slain are really slain. . . . If one takes the lack of closure entirely seriously, one must believe in the Last Judgement" ' (N8,1, *ARC*, p. 471).

110 In 'Central Park' Benjamin notes that 'progress' involves the 'experience of the world entering rigor mortis' (*CP*, p. 50).

111 Benjamin's 'founding concept is not progress but actualization' (N2,2, *ARC*, p. 460).

112 Benjamin notes that 'the present interests of the true subject of history, "the oppressed", set the terms of historical perspective' (*GS* I, p. 1244, quoted in McCole, 1993, p. 290).

113 Benjamin writes: 'The destructive or critical momentum of materialist historiography is registered in that blasting apart of historical continuity with which the historical object first constitutes itself' (N10a,1, *ARC*, p. 475).

114 N10,3, *ARC*, p. 475.

115 N3a,3, *ARC*, p. 464.

116 Just as the dialectical image is 'saturated with tensions' (N10a,3, *ARC*, p. 475), so in early photography, 'The procedure itself caused the

subject to focus his life in the moment rather than hurrying on past it' (*OWS*, p. 245).

117 See N1,1, *ARC*, p. 456, and N9,7, *ARC*, p. 473.

118 See also Cadava, 1997, and Krauss, 1998.

119 Benjamin characterizes this with regard to another optical device for enlargement. The dialectical image involves the 'Telescoping of the past through the present' (N7a,3, *ARC*, p. 471).

120 For Benjamin, 'the image of the past flashing in the Now of its recognisability is, according to its wider definition, an image of remembrance' (*GS* I, p. 1243).

121 Benjamin states that 'the dialectical image is to be defined as the *mémoire involontaire* of a redeemed humanity' (*GS* I, p. 1233).

122 Letter to Scholem, 26 July 1932.

Conclusion: Towards a Contemporary Constellation

1 George Steiner has long claimed, for example, that the London-based Warburg Institute would have proved a more 'convivial' intellectual setting for Benjamin. See *OGTD*, p. 19.

2 See, e.g., the discussion of Benjamin and Derrida on tradition, destruction and deconstruction by Düttmann, in Benjamin and Osborne, 1994, pp. 32–57, esp. pp. 45–7.

3 See Gilloch, 1997, 2001.

4 Commenting on his own aphoristic, fragmentary style, Baudrillard wittily observes that 'Another promise of fragments is that they alone will survive the catastrophe, the destruction of meaning and language, like the flies in the plane crash which are the only survivors because they are ultra-light' (1997, p. 9).

5 For a discussion of the historical manifestations of melancholy, see Pensky's (1993) account of the writings of Julia Kristeva.

6 On the pervasive boredom and apathy of the present, see Baudrillard's (1983) notion of the inert, 'silent majorities'.

7 For Buci-Glucksmann (1994) such elements combine with others (such as an increasing emphasis on the body) to constitute what she terms 'baroque reason'. Similarly, Van Reijen claims that 'Walter Benjamin's philosophy with its logic of extremes forms the pivotal and angle point between the baroque and the postmodern' (1994, p. 15).

8 Baudrillard unmistakably captures the notion of a critical monadology: 'America is a giant hologram, in the sense that information concerning the whole is contained in each of its elements. Take the tiniest little place in the desert, any old street in a Mid-West town, a parking lot, a Californian house, a Burger King, or a Studebaker, and you have the whole of the US – South, North, East or West' (1988, p. 29). In Baudrillard's notion of the 'code', this view of the whole being

contained within the individual element is radicalized. In the 'code', the DNA code being one of his favourite metaphors, the fragment *determines* the totality.

9   See c°,4, *ARC*, p. 878.

10 See b°,2, *ARC*, p. 876.

11 See R2,3, *ARC*, pp. 540–1.

12 See Gottdiener, 1995, and Sorkin, 1992.

13 See Gottdiener, 1995, and Zukin, 1993.

14 See Boyer, in Sorkin, 1992.

15 This notion of the legibility of the cityscape is central to the work of writers like Lynch (1960) and de Certeau (1984).

16 See, e.g., Fredric Jameson's (1991) controversial reading of the 'hyper-space' of the Bonaventure Hotel in Los Angeles as a microcosm of post-modern disorientation, and Baudrillard's (1994) critique of the Pompidou Centre in 'The Beaubourg Effect'.

17 See Tester, 1994, and Gilloch, 1999.

18 Of course, given the prominence of corporate logos and brand-names on the clothes we wear and the accessories we carry, even the incon-spicuous consumer of today is nothing other than a walking collage of advertisements, a self-styled sandwich-man/woman.

19 See Frisby, 1981, and in Tester, 1994, pp. 81–110.

20 See Wolff, 1990; Wilson, 1991; Walkowitz, 1992; Nava, 1997; and Parsons, 1999.

21 See Jenks, 1995; de Certeau, 1984; Weinstein and Weinstein, 1991; and Saddler, 1998.

22 See Hartmann, 1999.

23 See Bauman, in Tester, 1994, pp. 138–57.

24 See Jenks, 1995.

25 It is both appropriate and noteworthy that Mike Davis, himself described by Ed Soja as a 'truck driving flâneur' (in Westwood and Williams, 1997, p. 21), uses a quotation from Benjamin's 'Berlin Chronicle' as the epigraph to his celebrated *City of Quartz* (1992).

26 See Morawski, in Tester, 1994, pp. 181–97.

27 Jarvis (1998, pp. 80–92) uses this notion of the post-modern flâneur to explore Paul Auster's (1985) *City of Glass*, the first part of *The New York Trilogy* (1988). Indeed, the figures in Auster's novels present themselves as a gallery of Benjaminian motifs: flâneur (*Moon Palace*, 1989), ragpicker (*In the Country of Last Things*, 1987) and gambler (*Music of Chance*, 1991). See also Kirkegaard, 1993.

28 Baudrillard's entire American odyssey may be understood as a malevolent, melancholy flânerie in the 'finished form of the future catastrophe of the social' (1988, p. 5). See Gilloch, 2001.

29 Benjamin's reflections on photography bear an unmistakable affinity with Barthes's (1993) attempt to comprehend the power of certain photographs through the notions of the *studium*, the *punctum*, and the

ça a été ('that has been'). See Krauss 1998; Price, 1994; and Cadava, 1997.

30 Baudrillard notes his own 'passion for images' (1988, p. 56). For him, 'Image alone counts' (1988, p. 109), images broken into prismatic forms (the 'fractal'), images fleetingly glimpsed *en passant*. Echoing Benjamin's metaphor of the lightning flash for the dialectical image, Baudrillard observes that 'The book must break up so as to resemble the ever increasing number of extreme situations. It must break up to resemble the flashes of the hologram' (1990, p. 116). See Gilloch, 2001.

31 See Adorno and Horkheimer, 1986; Horkheimer, 1974a,b; and Marcuse, 1964.

32 Mülder-Bach notes that Kracauer sought to adopt 'the stance of an intellectual who seeks to make the exile of transcendental homelessness, if not into a home, at least into a familiar dwelling' (Kracauer, 1998, p. 9).

33 Like Kracauer, Benjamin is also 'A ragpicker at daybreak – in the dawn of the day of the revolution' (Kracauer, 1998, p. 114).

34 It is important to note how Benjamin broadens the terrain of revolutionary contestation, from the conventional Marxist notion of the proletariat to a more inclusive, albeit more diffuse, concept of the 'oppressed', a constellation of marginalized, stigmatized groups.

Bibliography

Works by Walter Benjamin

Gesammelte Schriften, vols I–VII, ed. Rolf Tiedemann and Hermann Schweppenhäuser, with the collaboration of Theodor Adorno and Gershom Scholem. Frankfurt am Main: Suhrkamp Verlag, 1974. Taschenbuch Ausgabe, 1991.

Gesammelte Briefe, vols I–VI, ed. Theodor W. Adorno Archive. Frankfurt am Main: Suhrkamp Verlag, 1995–2000.

English language translations of Benjamin's works

Selected Writings, vols 1 and 2, ed. Marcus Bullock, Michael Jennings et al. Cambridge, MA: Harvard University Press, 1996–9.

Aesthetics and Politics: Debates between Bloch, Lukács, Brecht, Benjamin, Adorno, trans. and ed. Ronald Taylor, 'Afterword' by Frederic Jameson. London: Verso, 1980.

The Arcades Project, trans. Howard Eiland and Kevin McLaughlin. Cambridge, MA: Belknap Press of Harvard University Press, 1999.

'Central Park', trans. Lloyd Spencer, *New German Critique*, 34 (Winter 1985), pp. 28–58.

Charles Baudelaire: A Lyric Poet in the Era of High Capitalism, trans. Harry Zohn. London: Verso, 1983.

The Correspondence of Walter Benjamin, ed. and annotated by Gershom Scholem and Theodor Adorno, trans. Manfred Jacobson and Evelyn Jacobson, 'Foreword' by Gershom Scholem. Chicago and London: University of Chicago Press, 1994.

The Correspondence of Walter Benjamin and Gershom Scholem 1932–1940, ed. Gershom Scholem, trans. Gary Smith and Andre Lefevre, 'Introduction' by Anson Rabinbach. Cambridge, MA: Harvard University Press, 1992.

'Doctrine of the Similar', trans. Knut Tarnowski, 'Introduction' by Anson Rabinbach, *New German Critique*, 17 (Spring 1979).

Illuminations, ed. and with an 'Introduction' by Hannah Arendt, trans. Harry Zohn. London: Fontana, 1973.

Moscow Diary, ed. Gary Smith, trans. Richard Sieburth, 'Preface' by Gershom Scholem. Cambridge, MA, and London: Harvard University Press, 1986.

'N. (Re The Theory of Knowledge, Theory of Progress)', trans. Leigh Hafrey and Richard Sieburth, in Gary Smith (ed.), *Benjamin: Philosophy, Aesthetics, History*, Chicago: University of Chicago Press, 1989, pp. 43–83.

One-Way Street and Other Writings, trans. Edmund Jephcott and Kingsley Shorter, 'Introduction' by Susan Sontag. London: Verso, 1985.

The Origin of German Tragic Drama, trans. John Osbourne, 'Introduction' by George Steiner. London: Verso, 1985.

Reflections: Aphorisms, Essays and Autobiographical Writings, ed. Peter Demetz, trans. Edmund Jephcott. New York: Harcourt, Brace, Jovanovitch, 1978.

Theodor W. Adorno – Walter Benjamin: The Complete Correspondence 1928–1940. Cambridge, Polity, 1999.

Understanding Brecht, trans. Anna Bostock, 'Introduction' by Stanley Mitchell. London: Verso, 1983.

Selected secondary reading

Adorno, Theodor 1990: *Über Walter Benjamin*, ed. Rolf Tiedemann. Frankfurt am Main: Suhrkamp Verlag.

Benjamin, Andrew and Osborne, Peter (eds) 1994: *Walter Benjamin's Philosophy: Destruction and Experience*. London: Routledge.

Bolz, Norbert and van Reijen, Willem 1996: *Walter Benjamin*. Atlantic Heights, NJ: Humanities Press.

Bolz, Norbert and Witte, Bernd (eds) 1984: *Passagen: Walter Benjamins Urgeschichte des XIX. Jahrhunderts*. Munich: Wilhelm Fink Verlag.

Bowie, Andrew 1997: *From Romanticism to Critical Theory: The Philosophy of German Literary Theory*. London: Routledge.

Brodersen, Momme 1997: *Walter Benjamin: A Biography*. London: Verso.

Buci-Glucksmann, Christine 1994: *Baroque Reason: The Aesthetics of Modernity*. London: Sage.

Buck-Morss, Susan 1977: *The Origin of Negative Dialectics: Theodor Adorno, Walter Benjamin and the Frankfurt Institute*. Hassocks, Sussex: Harvester Press.

——1983: Benjamin's *Passagenwerk*: Redeeming Mass Culture for the Revolution. *New German Critique*, 29 (Spring/Summer), pp. 211–40.

——1986: The Flâneur, the Sandwichman and the Whore: The Politics of Loitering. *New German Critique*, 39 (Fall), pp. 99–140.

——1989: *The Dialectics of Seeing: Walter Benjamin and the Arcades Project*. Cambridge, MA: MIT Press.

Cadava, Eduardo 1997: *Words of Light: Theses on the Photography of History*. Princeton, NJ: Princeton University Press.

Caygill, Howard 1998: *Walter Benjamin: The Colour of Experience*. London: Routledge.

Cohen, Margaret 1993: *Profane Illumination: Walter Benjamin and the Paris of Surrealist Revolution*. Berkeley, Los Angeles and London: University of California Press.

Doderer, Klaus (ed.) 1988: *Walter Benjamin und die Kinderliteratur*. Weinheim and Munich: Juventa Verlag.

Eagleton, Terry 1981: *Walter Benjamin: Or Towards a Revolutionary Criticism*. London: Verso.

Ferris, David (ed.) 1996: *Walter Benjamin: Theoretical Questions*. Stanford, CA: Stanford University Press.

Fischer, Gerhard (ed.) 1996: *With the Sharpened Axe of Reason: Approaches to Walter Benjamin*. Oxford: Berg.

Frisby, David 1988: *Fragments of Modernity: Theories of Modernity in the Work of Simmel, Kracauer and Benjamin*. Cambridge, MA: MIT Press.

Fuld, Werner 1990: *Walter Benjamin: Eine Biographie*. Reinbeck bei Hamburg: Rowohlt Verlag.

Geuss, Raymond 1981: *The Idea of a Critical Theory: Habermas and the Frankfurt School*. Cambridge: Cambridge University Press.

Gilloch, Graeme 1996: *Myth and Metropolis: Walter Benjamin and the City*. Cambridge: Polity.

——1997: The Figure that Fascinates: Seductive Strangers in Benjamin and Baudrillard. *Renaissance and Modern Studies*, 40, pp. 17–29.

——1999: The Return of the Flâneur: The Afterlife of an Allegory. *New Formations*, 38, pp. 101–9.

——2001: Benjamin's Moscow, Baudrillard's America. In Neil Leach (ed.), *Hieroglyphics of Space*, London: Routledge.

Habermas, Jürgen 1983: Walter Benjamin: Consciousness-Raising or Rescuing Critique. In *Philosophical-Political Profiles*, London: Heinemann, pp. 129–64.

Handelman, Susan 1991: *Fragments of Redemption: Jewish Thought and Literary Theory in Benjamin, Scholem and Levinas*. Bloomington, IN: Indiana University Press.

Held, David 1980: *Introduction to Critical Theory*. London: Hutchinson Press.

Jäger, Lorenz and Reghely, Thomas (eds) 1992: *'Was nie geschrieben wurde, lesen'. Frankfurter Benjamin-Vortrage*. Bielefeld: Aisthesis Verlag.

Jameson, Fredric 1971: *Marxism and Form*. Princeton, NJ: Princeton University Press.

Jay, Martin 1974: *The Dialectical Imagination: A History of the Frankfurt School and the Institute of Social Research 1923–1950*. London: Heinemann.

Jennings, Michael 1987: *Dialectical Images: Walter Benjamin's Theory of Literary Criticism*. Ithaca, NY: Cornell University Press.

Kirkegaard, Peter 1993: Cities, Signs and Meaning in Walter Benjamin and Paul Auster. *Orbis Litterarium*, 48, pp. 161–79.

Konersmann, Ralf 1991: *Erstarrte Unruhe: Walter Benjamins Begriff der Geschichte*. Frankfurt am Main: Fischer Verlag.

Krauss, Rolf 1998: *Walter Benjamin und der neue Blick auf die Photographie*. Ostfildern/Stuttgart: Cantz Verlag.

Leslie, Esther 2000: *Walter Benjamin: Overwhelming Conformity*. London: Pluto Press.

Lindner, Burkhardt (ed.) 1978: *Walter Benjamin im Kontext*. Konigstein/Ts: Athenäum Verlag.

Lunn, Eugene 1985: *Marxism and Modernism: An Historical Study of Lukács, Brecht, Benjamin and Adorno*. London: Verso.

McCole, John 1993: *Walter Benjamin and the Antinomies of Tradition*. Ithaca, NY: Cornell University Press.

Marcus, Laura and Nead, Lynda (eds) 1998: *The Actuality of Walter Benjamin*. London: Lawrence and Wishart.

Markner, Reinhard and Weber, Thomas (eds) 1993: *Literatur über Walter Benjamin: Kommentierte Bibliographie 1983–92*. Hamburg: Argument Verlag.

Mehlman, Jeffrey 1993: *Walter Benjamin for Children: An Essay on his Radio Years*. Chicago and London: University of Chicago Press.

Menninghaus, Winfried 1980: *Walter Benjamins Theorie der Sprachmagie*. Frankfurt am Main: Suhrkamp Verlag.

——1986: *Schwellenkunde: Walter Benjamins Passage des Mythos*. Frankfurt am Main: Suhrkamp Verlag.

Missac, Pierre 1995: *Walter Benjamin's Passages*. Cambridge, MA: MIT Press.

Nägele, Rainer 1988: *Benjamin's Ground: New Readings of Walter Benjamin*. Detroit: Wayne State University Press.

——1991: *Theatre, Theory and Speculation: Walter Benjamin and the Scenes of Modernity*. Baltimore and London: Johns Hopkins University Press.

Parini, Jay 1997: *Benjamin's Crossing*. London: Anchor Press, Transworld Publishers.

Parsons, Deborah 1999: Flâneur or Flâneuse?: Mythologies of Modernity. *New Formations*, 38 (Summer), pp. 91–100.

Pensky, Max 1993: *Melancholy Dialectics: Walter Benjamin and the Play of Mourning*. Amherst: University of Massachusetts Press.

Price, Mary 1994: *The Photograph: A Strange Confined Space*. Stanford, CA: Stanford University Press.

Puttnies, Hans and Smith, Gary (eds) 1991: *Benjaminiana: Eine Biografische Recherche*. Giessen: Anabas Verlag.

Reijen, Willem van 1994: *Die authentische Kritik der Moderne*. Munich: Wilhelm Fink Verlag.

Roberts, Julian 1982: *Walter Benjamin*. London: Macmillan.

Rochlitz, Rainer 1996: *The Disenchantment of Art: The Philosophy of Walter Benjamin*. New York: Guilford Press.

Schiller-Lerg, Sabine 1984: *Walter Benjamin und der Rundfunk*. Munich: K. G. Verlag.

Scholem, Gershom 1982: *Walter Benjamin: The Story of a Friendship*. London: Faber & Faber.

——1983: *Walter Benjamin und Sein Engel*. Frankfurt am Main: Suhrkamp Verlag.

Smith, Gary (ed.) 1988: *On Walter Benjamin: Critical Essays and Recollections*. Cambridge, MA: MIT Press.

——(ed.) 1989: *Benjamin: Philosophy, Aesthetics, History*. Chicago: University of Chicago Press.

Steinberg, Michael (ed.) 1996: *Walter Benjamin and the Demands of History*. Ithaca, NY: Cornell University Press.

Stüssi, Anna 1977: Erinnerung an die Zukunft: Walter Benjamins *Berliner Kindheit um Neunzehnhundert*. *Paelaestra*, 266.

Tester, Keith (ed.) 1994: *The Flâneur*. London and New York: Routledge.

Tiedemann, Rolf 1973: *Studien zur Philosophie Walter Benjamins*. Frankfurt am Main: Suhrkamp Verlag.

——1983: *Dialektik im Stillstand: Versuche zum Spätwerk Walter Benjamins*. Frankfurt am Main: Suhrkamp Verlag.

Weigel, Sigrid 1996: *Body- and Image-Space: Rereading Walter Benjamin*. London: Routledge.

——1997: *Entstellte Ähnlichkeit: Walter Benjamins Schreibweise*. Frankfurt am Main: Fischer Verlag.

Wiggershaus, Rolf 1993: *The Frankfurt School*. Cambridge: Polity.
Witte, Bernd 1985: *Walter Benjamin*. Reinbeck bei Hamburg: Rowohlt Verlag.
Wohlfahrt, Irving 1986: Et cetera? The Historian as *Chiffonier*. *New German Critique*, 39 (Fall), pp. 142–68.
Wolin, Richard 1982: *Walter Benjamin: An Aesthetics of Redemption*. New York: Columbia University Press.

Special issues on Benjamin

New German Critique, 17 (Spring 1979), 39 (Fall 1986)
Philosophical Forum, 17, 3 (1986)
New Formations, 20 (1993)
Critical Enquiry, 25, 2 (Winter 1999)
See also *New Formations*, 38 (Summer 1999)

Other references

Adorno, Theodor 1991: *Notes to Literature*, vol. 1, ed. Rolf Tiedemann, trans. Shierry Weber. New York: Columbia University Press.
Adorno, Theodor and Horkheimer, Max 1986: *Dialectic of Enlightenment*. London: Verso.
Aragon, Louis 1987 [1926]: *The Paris Peasant*. London: Pan Books, Picador Publishers.
Auster, Paul 1987: *In the Country of Last Things*. London: Faber & Faber.
——1988: *The New York Trilogy*. London: Faber & Faber.
——1989: *Moon Palace*. London: Faber & Faber.
——1991: *Music of Chance*. London: Faber & Faber.
Barthes, Roland 1973: *Mythologies*. London: Paladin.
——1993: *Camera Lucida*. London: Vintage.
Baudelaire, Charles 1965: *Art in Paris 1845–62: Salons and Other Exhibitions*, ed. and trans. Jonathan Mayne. London: Phaidon.
——1975: *Selected Poems*, ed. and trans. Joanna Richardson. Harmondsworth: Penguin.
——1982: *Les Fleurs du mal*, trans. Richard Howard. London: Picador.
——1986: *The Painter of Modern Life and Other Essays*, ed. and trans. Jonathan Mayne. New York and London: Da Capo in association with Phaidon.
Baudrillard, Jean 1983: *In the Shadow of the Silent Majorities*. New York: Semiotext(e).
——1988: *America*. London: Verso.
——1990: *Seduction*. New York: St Martin's Press.

—— 1993: *Symbolic Exchange and Death*. London: Sage.

—— 1994: *Simulacra and Simulation*. Ann Arbor: University of Michigan Press.

—— 1996: *The System of Objects*. London: Verso.

—— 1997: *Fragments: Cool Memories III, 1991–5*. London: Verso.

—— 1998: *The Consumer Society: Myths and Structures*. London: Sage.

Berlin, Isaiah 1994: *The Magus of the North: J. G. Hamann and the Origins of Modern Irrationalism*. London: Fontana.

Berman, Marshall 1983: *All That Is Solid Melts Into Air: The Experience of Modernity*. London: Verso.

Biale, David 1982: *Gershom Scholem: Kabbalah and Counter-History*. Cambridge, MA: Harvard University Press.

Bloch, Ernst 1985: *Briefe*, ed. Karola Bloch et al. 2 vols. Frankfurt: Suhrkamp Verlag.

Breton, André 1960: *Nadja*, trans. Richard Howard. New York: Grove Press.

Dant, Tim 1999: *Material Culture in the Social World*. Buckingham: Open University Press.

Davis, Mike 1992: *City of Quartz*. London: Vintage.

De Certeau, Michel 1984: *The Practice of Everyday Life*. Berkeley: University of California Press.

Elias, Norbert 1994 [1939]: *The Civilizing Process*. Oxford: Blackwell.

Fletcher, Jonathan 1997: *Violence and Civilization: An Introduction to the Work of Norbert Elias*. Cambridge: Polity.

Frank, Manfred 1989: *Einführung in Die Frühromantische Ästhetik – Vorlesungen*. Frankfurt am Main: Suhrkamp Verlag.

Frisby, David 1981: *Sociological Impressionism: A Reassessment of Georg Simmel's Social Theory*. London: Heinemann.

Gay, Peter 1968: *Weimar Culture: The Insider as Outsider*. Harmondsworth: Peregrine Books, Penguin Publishers.

Geist, Johann Friedrich 1985: *Arcades: The History of a Building Type*. Cambridge, MA: MIT Press.

Goethe, Johann Wolfgang 1971: *Elective Affinities*, trans. R. J. Hollingdale. Harmondsworth: Penguin.

Gottdiener, Mark 1995: *Postmodern Semiotics: Material Culture and the Forms of Material Life*. Oxford: Blackwell.

Hartmann, Maren 1999: The Cyberflâneuse – Strolling Freely through the Virtual Worlds? In *On/Off + Across: Language, Identity and New Technologies*, London: The Cutting Edge Research Group in conjunction with I. B. Tauris.

Hessel, Franz 1982 [1927]: *Heimliches Berlin*. Frankfurt: Suhrkamp Verlag.

—— 1984 [1929]: *Ein Flâneur in Berlin*. Berlin: Das Arsena.

—— 1994: *Von den Irrtümern der Liebenden und andere Prosa*. Paderborn: Igel Verlag.

Horkheimer, Max 1974a: *Critique of Instrumental Reason*. New York: Seabury.

—— 1974b: *Eclipse of Reason*. New York: Seabury.

—— 1995: *Gesammelte Schriften*, vol. 15. Frankfurt am Main: Fischer Verlag.

Jameson, Fredric 1991: *Postmodernism, or the Cultural Logic of Late Capitalism*. London: Verso.

Jarvis, Brian 1998: *Postmodern Cartographies: The Geographical Imagination in Contemporary American Culture*. London: Pluto Press.

Jenks, Chris (ed.) 1995: *Visual Culture*. London: Routledge.

Kracauer, Siegfried 1937: *Jacques Offenbach and the Paris of his Time*. London: Constable.

—— 1947: *From Caligari to Hitler: A Psychological History of the German Film*. Princeton, NJ: Princeton University Press.

—— 1969: *History: The Last things Before the Last*. Princeton, NJ: Markus Wiener Publishers.

—— 1995: *The Mass Ornament: Weimar Essays*. Cambridge, MA, and London: Harvard University Press.

—— 1997 [1960]: *Theory of Film: The Redemption of Physical Reality*. Princeton, NJ: Princeton University Press.

—— 1998: *The Salaried Masses: Duty and Distraction in Weimar Germany*. London: Verso.

Lukács, Georg 1971 [1920]: *Theory of the Novel*. Cambridge, MA: MIT Press.

—— 1974 [1924]: *History and Class Consciousness*. London: Merlin Press.

Lynch, Kevin 1960: *The Image of the City*. Cambridge, MA: MIT Press.

Lyotard, Jean-François 1984: *The Postmodern Condition: A Report on Knowledge*. Manchester: Manchester University Press.

Marcuse, Herbert 1964: *One-Dimensional Man*. London: Routledge.

Marx, Karl 1976: *Capital*, vol. 1. Harmondsworth: Penguin.

Nava, Mica 1997: Women, the City and the Department Store. In Pasi Falk and Colin Campbell (eds), *The Shopping Experience*, London: Sage, pp. 56–91.

Penz, François and Thomas, Maureen (eds) 1997: *Cinema and Architecture*. London: British Film Institute.

Proust, Marcel 1983: *Remembrance of Things Past*, vol. 1, trans. C. K. Scott Moncrieffe and Terence Kilmartin. Harmondsworth: Penguin.

Saddler, Simon 1998: *The Situationist City*. Cambridge, MA: MIT Press.

Saussure, Ferdinand de 1966: *A Course in General Linguistics*. New York: McGraw-Hill.

Schiller, Dietrich; Pech, Karlheinz; et al. 1981: *Kunst und Literatur im Antifaschistischen Exil 1933–45*. Leipzig: Verlag Philipp Reclam.

Scholem, Gershom 1969: *On the Kabbalah and Its Symbolism*. New York: Schocken Books.

——1970: *Judaica 3*. Frankfurt am Main: Suhrkamp Verlag.

——1971: *The Messianic Idea in Judaism and Other Essays on Jewish Spirituality*. New York: Schocken Books.

Simmel, Georg 1971: *On Individuality and Social Forms*, ed. Donald Levine. Chicago: University of Chicago Press.

Sorkin, Michael (ed.) 1992: *Variations on a Theme-Park*. New York: Hill and Wang.

Spengler, Oswald 1991 [1918]: *Decline of the West*. Oxford: Oxford University Press.

Taussig, Michael 1993: *Mimesis and Alterity: A Particular History of the Senses*. London: Routledge.

Tönnies, Ferdinand 1988 [1888]: *Community and Association*. New Brunswick, NJ: Transaction Publishers.

Virilio, Paul 1994: *The Vision Machine*. London: British Film Institute.

Walkowitz, Judith 1992: *City of Dreadful Delight*. London: Virago.

Weinstein, Deena and Weinstein, Michael 1991: Georg Simmel: Sociological Flâneur Bricoleur. *Theory, Culture and Society*, 8, 3, pp. 151–68.

Westwood, Sallie and Williams, John (eds) 1997: *Imagining Cities: Scripts, Signs, Memory*. London: Routledge.

Wilson, Elizabeth 1991: *The Sphinx in the City*. London: Virago.

Wolff, Janet 1990: *Feminine Sentences: Essays on Women and Culture*. Cambridge: Polity.

Zola, Emil 1962: *Thérèse Racquin*, trans. Leonard Tancock. Harmondsworth: Penguin.

Zukin, Sharon 1993: *Landscapes of Power: From Detroit to Disney World*. Berkeley, Los Angeles and London: University of California Press.

Index

Adorno, Gretel, 206
Adorno, Theodor, 8, 19, 116, 117,
149, 161, 165, 192, 196, 205,
215, 223; and autonomy of art,
19, 149, 164, 184, 186–7; critical
of Brecht, 17, 18, 149–50, 152,
156, 184; critique of
Benjamin's work on
Baudelaire, 204–5, 206; critique
of *Passagenarbeit*, 115–16, 128,
136, 202; and 'culture
industry', 9, 244; as editor of
Benjamin, 3, 18, 235; 'On the
Fetish Character in Music . . .',
19, 192–3; and film industry,
187, 193; friendship with
Benjamin, 16, 17, 18, 235;
opinion of radio, 167
aesthetics: politicization of, 2, 4,
8, 112, 140, 144–5, 164, 194;
and new media, 187, 237,
244
'afterlife' (*Nachleben*), 2–3, 4, 21, 33,
47, 108, 134, 224, 234, 241
alienation: of the intellectual, 10,
247–8
allegory, 22, 40, 80–2, 83, 84–5, 134,
208–11, 239; and human body,

209; and symbol, 80–1, 208; *see
also under Trauerspiel*
Aragon, Louis, 17, 22, 90, 91, 109,
133, 148, 218; *Le Paysan de
Paris*, 105, 106–7, 108, 109, 125,
135
'Arcades Project' (*Passagenarbeit*), 4,
17, 22–3, 24, 88, 89, 105, 111,
113–39, 162, 173, 181, 198, 202,
204, 232, 241, 243; and
Benjamin's work on
Baudelaire, 202, 203–4, 206–7,
240; and Berlin studies, 223–4;
construction of, 123; and
Denkbilder, 93; and film, 165,
196–7; goals of, 123–4; and
historiography, 228; origins of,
17, 89, 91, 112, 113; and
photography, 165, 196–7;
prolegomena to, 218; and
Trauerspiel study, 118
architecture: of arcades, 131–2,
241–2; and distraction, 190; of
Eiffel Tower, 120–1
art: cultic origins of, 19, 183–4; and
new media, 196, 237, *see also*
media, new; and reproduction,
185; *see also* Benjamin, Walter: